D0674038

A Field Guide in
• Colour to •

PLANTS
AND
ANIMALS

A Field Guide in
· Colour to ·

PLANTS
AND
ANIMALS

Jan Toman and Jiří Felix

CHANCELLOR
PRESS

Text by Jan Toman and Jiří Felix
Illustrations by Květoslav Hísek, Libuše
Knotková, Jaromír Knotek and Jiří Polák
Translated by Olga Kuthanová
Graphic design by Josef Dvořák

Designed and produced by Aventinum
English language edition first published
in 1993 by Chancellor Press, an imprint
of Reed Consumer Books Limited
Michelin House, 81 Fulham Road,
London SW3 6RB, and Auckland,
Melbourne, Singapore and Toronto

ISBN 1 85152 175 5

A CIP catalogue record for this book is
available at the British Library

Printed in Slovakia
3/07/01/51-01

CONTENTS

Plants

Animals

Foreword

The present make-up of Europe's flora and fauna is the result of a lengthy and complex evolution in the distant past. This present-day composition of plants and animals was primarily influenced by changes that occurred from the end of the Tertiary period to the beginning of the Quaternary, in other words, approximately during the last two million years. One determining factor was extreme changes in climate that occurred: from the subtropical or nearly tropical, when palms grew in central Europe and even monkeys could be found there, to cold, sometimes near arctic, conditions. Glacial periods, with conditions similar to the present-day Siberian tundra, were interspersed at lengthy intervals with warm interglacial periods, comparable in climate to the Balkans of today. Of necessity, such climatic changes resulted in the extinction of numerous species, or even whole genera, of plants and animals, as the prevailing climate proved intolerable for their existence. There was also a great migration of species, allowing the spread of hitherto exotic animal and plant groups to biotopes that they now found congenial. The present European flora and fauna is the result of all these changes and is formed by representatives of dry, warm, cold or wet periods that prevailed thousands of years ago.

Also affecting the composition of the flora and fauna are the many differences in the make-up of the soil throughout Europe and also the topography of the land, which ranges from spreading lowlands to rolling hills, highlands and mountains including high mountain peaks. In Europe one can find the remains of sand dunes, large bodies of water, artificial ponds and dams, tumbling mountain streams and lowland winding brooks and rivers as well as the calm, unruffled waters of oxbow lakes. One may admire the gloomy, hushed environment of

Fig. 1. The Common Tern (*Sterna hirundo*) not only nests on the seacoast and on islands but also by inland lakes and ponds.

Fig. 2. The Marmot (*Marmota marmota*) feeds on seeds from the cones of the Mountain Pine (*Pinus mugo*).

deep forests, stroll across sun-dappled glades and escape the huge city conglomerates to seek green fields and meadows. Nature in Europe wears many garbs—from alder groves, pastureland and forest-steppes to mountain beech woods; from rock steppes covered with oak and pine to mountain spruce forests and alpine grasslands; from mountain tarns and glaciers to vineyards on sunny hillsides—all part of the varied landscape that is to be found on this continent rimmed by seacoast to north, south and west.

Naturally, such widely varied biotopes are home to a huge diversity of plant and animal communities. Many plants and animals have no special requirements in terms of habitat and thus may be found in several biotopes. Some, on the other hand, have very specific requirements and are closely bound to a particular environment. The scope of this book makes it impossible to examine all of Europe's many and diverse biotopes, so we shall say a few words only about the most typical biotopes and their plant and animal communities.

Broad-leaved Forest

The character of Europe's broad-leaved forest differs from lowland to mountain elevations. Near flowing waters, in regularly, or at least occasionally, water-inundated lowlands it bears the character of a flood-plain forest, with alder, willow and poplar predominating. The greater the distance from regular water courses, the greater is the number of oak, elm, ash trees, lime trees and maple trees. At median elevations oak and hornbeam predominate, lingering remnants of once-extensive oak and hornbeam forests that have, today, to a great extent, been cut down and replaced by planted conifers. At submontane elevations, beeches are found in increasing numbers among the oaks and hornbeams until, eventually, they predominate and form typical mountain beech forests with an admixture of firs and spruces.

The broad-leaved forest is arranged in distinct layers, generally divided into three: the tree layer, the shrub layer and the herbaceous layer. This arrangement allows for the growth of a greater number of plants on a small area and for the best utilization of the space above, as well as below, ground, without the plants being mutually competitive. This layering provides similar advantages for animals.

The shrub layer of flood-plain forests is often impenetrably dense. It is composed of small, young trees (such as elm and poplar, growing from the root suckers of old trees, or willow, readily spreading by vegetative means from broken-off fragments) and true shrubs. The latter include Common Elder (*Sambucus nigra*), Dogwood (*Cornus sanguinea*), Guelder Rose (*Viburnum opulus*), Alder Buckthorn (*Rhamnus frangula*), European Spindle Tree (*Euonymus europaeus*), and others. Also characteristic of the flood-plain forest are climbing plants, mainly Hop (*Humulus lupulus*), English Ivy (*Hedera helix*), and Traveller's Joy (*Clematis vitalba*).

The herbaceous layer of the flood-plain forest is also rich in flora, despite the fact that little light penetrates through the dense cover of

Fig. 3. The Slow-worm (*Anguis fragilis*) is ovoviviparous, which means that the female generally produces live offspring.

Fig. 4. *Ramaria aurea*, found mainly in broad-leaved forests in summer and autumn, is a tasty edible mushroom.

trees and shrubs. This layer is brightened by the flowers of the Yellow Wood Anemone (*Anemone ranunculoides*), Spring Snowflake (*Leucojum vernum*), Water Forget-me-not (*Myosotis palustris*), Cowslip (*Primula veris*), Common Lungwort (*Pulmonaria officinalis*), Ramsons (*Allium ursinum*), Marsh Marigold (*Caltha*), Bog Arum (*Calla palustris*), and other, often rare and protected, plants.

Despite occasional flooding, the fauna of the flood-plain forest includes a wealth of species. The same species of game are found here as in the forests of higher elevations, including red deer and roe deer. Wild boar, in particular, find the conditions of the flood-plain forest extremely congenial. Typical birds are the Blackcap (*Sylvia atricapilla*), Nightingale (*Luscinia megarhynchos*), Penduline Tit (*Remiz pendulinus*) and Golden Oriole (*Oriolus oriolus*).

Like the flood-plain forest, broad-leaved forests provide favourable conditions for the development of the shrub layer as well as the herbaceous layer. In spring the trees are without leaves and sunlight can penetrate all the way to the ground to warm the earth. Here the plants soon begin new growth. When the trees are in full leaf and their crowns shade the ground beneath them, the bright carpet of spring vegeta-

tion disappears to be replaced by shade-loving plants. Such seasonal variability is a specific characteristic of broad-leaved forests.

Early in the year spring is heralded in the oak-woods by the white flowers of the snowdrop, soon followed by the blue flowers of Noble Liverleaf (*Hepatica nobilis*), purple lungwort (*Pulmonaria*), the white, star-like flowers of the Wood Anemone (*Anemone nemorosa*), variously coloured fumeworts (*Corydalis*), asarabacca (*Asarum*), the changeably coloured Spring Votchling (*Lathyrus vernus*) and many more. In summer these are replaced by diverse hawkweeds (*Hieracium*) and grasses, such as fescues (*Festuca*) and Chalk False Brome-grass (*Brachypodium pinnatum*).

Herbaceous plants characteristic of hornbeam and oak woods include Greater Stitchwort (*Stellaria holostea*), Wood Chrysanthemum (*Chrysanthemum corymbosum*), Hairy St John's Wort (*Hypericum hirsutum*), Mountain St John's Wort (*Hypericum montanum*), brooms (*Genista*), black brooms (*Lembotropis*) and Nottingham Catchfly (*Silene nutans*).

Found in both hornbeam-oak and beech woods is Herb Paris (*Paris quadrifolia*), Coral Root (*Dentaria bulbifera*), Sweet Woodruff (*Galium odoratum*), baneberry (*Actaea*), Cuckoo-

Fig. 5. The simple, almost stark beauty of the Lily-of-the-Valley (*Convallaria majalis*).

pint (*Arum maculatum*), Solomon's Seal (*Polygonatum*) and *Lysimachia nemorum*. These and other herbaceous plants are described in greater detail in the pictorial section.

Besides the popular woodland fruits — raspberries, blackberries and whortleberries — mushrooms are also abundant, although one will not find as many in broad-leaved forests as in coniferous or mixed stands. One of the handsomest mushrooms of all is found growing at the foot of large oaks—the brown-capped *Boletus aestivalis*. Beneath aspens one will find the Orange Cap Boletus. The most poisonous European mushroom—the Death Cap (*Amanita phalloides*)—also grows at the foot of oaks and may be found in all types of broad-leaved as well as mixed forests.

The shrub layer in oak-hornbeam forests is well developed. Well represented are the Hazel (*Corylus avellana*), Spindle Tree (*Euonymus*), Red Dogwood (*Cornus sanguinea*), Viburnum,

and Common Privet (*Ligustrum vulgare*). The shrubs are thickest at the forest's edge where thorny shrubs also often grow, such as Blackthorn (*Prunus spinosa*), Midland Hawthorn (*Crataegus oxyacantha*), Common Buckthorn (*Rhamnus catharticus*) and Dog Rose.

Beechwoods have a much thinner shrub layer, with Red Elder (*Sambucus racemosa*), Black Honeysuckle (*Lonicera nigra*) and the early-spring-flowering Mezereon (*Daphne mezereum*) predominating.

Oak and hornbeam woods are inhabited by a great many insects. Most people are familiar with the cherry-like galls found on oak leaves in which the larvae of the gall wasp *Cynips quercusfolii* develop. The predaceous ground beetles *Calosoma sycophanta* and *Calosoma inquisitor* hunt the caterpillars of gipsy moths (*Lymantria*) and other Lepidoptera. Broad-leaved forests are also inhabited by many long-horned beetles (Cerambycidae), most of which are named on lists of protected species. Carrion beetles (*Necrophorus*) bury small dead animals in the ground to serve as a later food store for their larvae. The larvae of the metallic-green dung beetles (*Geotrupes*) also feed on carrion as well as on excrement and decaying fungi.

From spring until autumn the broad-leaved forests are brightened by the appearance of countless butterflies and moths. Much damage is caused by the handsome Green Oak Tortrix Moth (*Tortrix viridiana*), whose larvae are capable of stripping oak trees of their young leaves, leaving them completely bare.

The abundance of insects is welcomed by woodland birds. In old oak woods there are numerous tree cavities in which the birds can build their nests. Besides tits (*Parus*), nuthatches (*Sitta*), treecreepers (*Certhia*) and cuckoos, their number includes several species of woodpeckers (*Picidae*), with toes that are well adapted for climbing and a wedge-shaped beak for extract-

Fig. 6. The Fire Salamander (*Salamandra salamandra*) hunts earthworms, slugs, insects and spiders by clear streams. It emerges from its hiding place in the evening, and also in the daytime in rainy weather.

ing insects and insect larvae from beneath the bark of trees. Oak woods are also home to the Stock Dove (*Columba oenas*), the Jay (*Garrulus glandarius*) and the Raven (*Corvus corax*). Protected species include the Hazel Hen (*Tetrastes bonasia*), Black Grouse (*Lyrurus tetrix*), and Woodcock (*Scolopax rusticola*).

Many mammals are found in oak-hornbeam forests. Here and in beechwoods, one will find the squirrel, badger, fox, Pine Marten (*Martes martes*), European Polecat (*Putorius putorius*) and the Wild Cat (*Felis silvestris*). One common small mammal is the Common Dormouse (*Muscardinus avellanarius*).

King among the animals here is the red deer, although the roe deer is even more closely bound to the broad-leaved forest. The forest margins are often visited by hares. Small mammals inhabiting beechwoods include the Bank Vole (*Clethrionomys glareolus*), the Yellow-necked Field Mouse (*Apodemus flavicollis*), and

the Forest Dormouse (*Dryomis nitedula*) which is not often seen because of its nocturnal habits.

The bird population of beech forests is somewhat more distinctive. The Red-breasted Flycatcher (*Ficedula parva*) makes its home here, while owls, in particular the Tawny Owl (*Strix aluco*), also nest here. Submontane forests are inhabited by eagles — the Lesser Spotted Eagle (*Aquila pomarina*) and the Imperial Eagle (*Aquila heliaca*) — while mountain and submontane beechwood is where the Black Stork (*Ciconia nigra*) builds its nest.

Of all Europe's ancient forests, the original broad-leaved forests that once covered vast expanses of land were the ones most destroyed by people, particularly at lower elevations where humans settled close to the edges of open, broad-leaved woods in areas with congenial climates and good sources of food for themselves and their domestic animals.

Fig. 7. *Boletus aestivalis* is a favourite food of the Red Slug (*Arion rufus*).

Coniferous Forest

Fig. 8. A fully grown leaf and spirally furled young leaves of the Male Fern (*Dryopteris filix-mas*).

The importance of mountain coniferous forests in their effect on the water balance and their influence on the climate and in the prevention of soil erosion is inestimable. Mountain forests catch most rain and favourably affect the composition of the earth's atmosphere in vast areas; they are the sources of numerous rivers, and they prevent the washing away of humus. They are also irreplaceable as sources of quality wood. Coniferous forests are to be found at lower elevations, but, apart from the occasional exception, these are all spruce or pine monocultures artificially planted for the purpose of timber extraction. Original, natural coniferous forests are nowadays found only in the mountains.

Spruce stands often include scattered firs, larches and beeches; in pine stands one will also find oaks, birches, lime trees and poplars. The shrub layer of coniferous forests is quite sparse and that is why spruce and pine forests seem much more uniform and less diversified than broad-leaved forests. Only the Rowan (*Sorbus aucuparia*), whose young shrubs do not mind being shaded by the thick crowns of the spruce trees, is more plentiful in spruce forests, while the Juniper (*Juniperus communis*) is often found among pines. Occurring in large numbers at higher elevations is the Red-berried Elder (*Sambucus racemosa*). The bottom layer in coniferous forests is mostly composed of perennial grasses, mosses and ferns, occasionally with heather and small whortleberry and cranberry bushes.

Growing in damp, open locations are dense, spreading carpets of small-reed (*Calamagrostis villosa*); in more shaded places that are not too damp, Wavy Hair-grass (*Avenella flexuosa*) is found. As well as these two dominant plants, which are found in other types of forests as well, there are rarer species that are dependent on the specific conditions of the coniferous stands. Bound to spruce forests in this way are Hard Fern (*Blechnum spicant*), Male Fern (*Dryopteris filix-mas*) and Stag's-horn Clubmoss (*Lycopodium clavatum*). Of the herbaceous plants there is Common Wood Sorrel (*Oxalis acetosella*), One-flowered Wintergreen (*Moneses uniflora*), *Streptopis amplexifolius*, Purple Coltsfoot (*Homogyne alpina*) and Willow Gentian (*Gentiana asclepiadea*). The moss layer is likewise well developed, particularly in spruce forests where *Polytrichum commune*, *Polytrichum formosum* and *Sphagnum* grow.

Numerous medicinal herbs grow in coniferous forests, such as St John's Wort (*Hypericum*), Lungwort (*Pulmonaria obscura*) and Common or Lesser Centaury (*Centaurium minus*). Rare and protected plants include Common Helleborine (*Epipactis helleborine*) and the Lesser Butterfly Orchid (*Platanthera bifolia*). In pine stands Box-leaved Milkwort (*Chamaebuxus alpestris*) and Flesh-coloured Heath (*Erica carnea*) are found.

Fungi abound in coniferous forests. Their number includes the handsome Edible Boletus (*Boletus edulis*) and *Boletus pinicola*, plus various species of *Suillus*, *Russula* and other edible mushrooms. The Honey Fungus (*Armillaria mellea*) is a parasite of forest trees and poses a grave danger; it grows on tree stumps and roots as well as on live trunks and is capable of destroying them completely. Even more dangerous is the bracket fungus (*Fomes annosus*), which often causes the decay of spruce wood.

Pests of the coniferous forest include numerous insects. Most dreaded of all is the Spruce Bark Beetle (*Ips typographus*), which multiplies with extraordinary rapidity. Its larvae make tunnels beneath the bark of spruce trees, in which they pupate. The newborn beetles then feed on the tree's phloem, making further tunnels, on the sides of which they again lay eggs three weeks later. Spruces that are severely infested by this bark beetle will dry up and die. Luckily, the Spruce Bark Beetle has many natural enemies, among birds chiefly the Coal Tit (*Parus ater*), Crested Tit (*Parus cristatus*) and woodpeckers (*Picidae*); among insects the checkered beetle *Thanasimus formicarius*, rover beetles (*Staphylinidae*) and certain hymenopterous insects (Hymenoptera).

The caterpillars of the Pine Sawfly (*Diprion pini*) feed on pine needles and on the bark of young pine shoots. In the case of overpopulation, they may cause complete defoliation of the tree. Pine Sawfly populations are kept in check by numerous insect parasites as well as other natural enemies among the vertebrates.

Striking scaly swellings at the tips of small branches are galls caused by *Dreyfusia nordmannianae*. It is fondest of young trees and is

Fig. 9. The Yellow-necked Field Mouse (*Apodemus flavicollis*) inhabits rather damp forests with a thick shrub undergrowth.

spread from one place to another by birds or animals. The females of the horntail *Urocerus gigas* resemble large wasps. With their long ovipositors they pierce the wood of spruce trees to a depth of as much as 15 mm and lay their eggs there. The newly hatched larvae then bore tunnels in the wood. Many Lepidoptera, but mainly moths, are dreaded pests of coni-fers, particularly in monocultures. The Black Arches Moth (*Lymantria monacha*), whose larvae feed on the tree needles, may be a veritable scourge. Its natural enemies include tits, cuckoos, bats, and predacious beetles.

On the other hand the widespread Wood Ant (*Formica rufa*) is extremely beneficial. The Wood Ants' nest, a mound of pine needles and

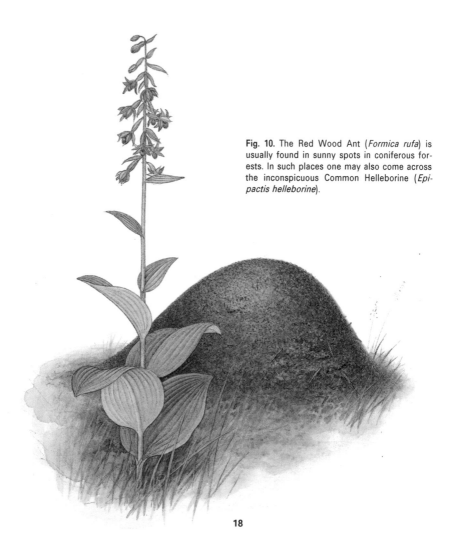

Fig. 10. The Red Wood Ant (*Formica rufa*) is usually found in sunny spots in coniferous forests. In such places one may also come across the inconspicuous Common Helleborine (*Epipactis helleborine*).

small twigs over 1 m high, is visible from afar. Ninety per cent of their diet consists of woodland pests, such as larvae, caterpillars and adult insects. It has been discovered that the ants capture all pests within 20 m of their nest, thereby effectively protecting the nearby trees from being defoliated by caterpillars. They also greatly limit the occurrence of harmful insects for a radius of a further 15 m beyond this limit.

It is mainly in coniferous forests that one will find many of the striking, long-horned beetles (*Cerambycidae*), now on the list of rare species. The larvae of *Leptura rubra* usually develop in the decaying stumps and trunks of pine and spruce trees. On newly felled trunks one will find *Rhagium inquisitor*, whose larvae live beneath the bark of dry conifers that have been attacked by bark beetles. Also frequently found on newly felled pines is *Acanthocinus aedilis*, whose males sport antennae several times longer than their bodies. The stumps of spruce, pine and fir are where the development of the larvae of *Toxotus cursor* takes place. These forests are also inhabited by other species of long-horned beetles.

Coniferous forests are the home of numerous birds. They are the nesting grounds of tits (*Parus*), woodpeckers (*Picidae*), the Bullfinch (*Pyrrhula pyrrhula*), Mistle Thrush (*Turdus viscivorus*) and Common Crossbill (*Loxia curvirostra*), which feed on the seeds of the conifers. The Common Treecreeper (*Certhia familiaris*) climbs upward and around the tree trunks in a spiral and extracts insects and insect larvae from cracks in the bark with its awl-shaped beak. Often heard in the treetops is the twittering note of the smallest European bird—the Goldcrest (*Regulus regulus*), weighing a mere 5—6 g. Open, dry coniferous forests are frequented by the European Nightjar (*Caprimulgus europaeus*), and the predacious Sparrowhawk (*Accipiter nisus*) builds its large nest in the branches of spruce trees. Coniferous forests in mountain districts are frequented by the Nutcracker (*Nucifraga caryocatactes*), a native of the northern taiga. One of the most popular game birds with hunters is the Capercaillie (*Tetrao urogallus*), the largest European grouse; the male may weigh as much as 6 kg.

Fig. 11. A Silver-washed Fritillary (*Argynnis paphia*) resting on flowering Box-leaved Milkwort (*Chamaebuxus alpestris*).

One will not find many mammals that are specifically bound to coniferous forests. Like broad-leaved forests, they are inhabited by red deer and roe deer, the Pine Marten (*Martes martes*), European Badger (*Meles meles*), fox, wild cat, and the ubiquitous squirrel. Typical inhabitants of mountain coniferous forests include the European Lynx (*Lynx lynx*), which hunts mammals as well as birds, and the now relatively rare wolf. The Northern Birch Mouse (*Sicista betulina*), which is rather like an ordinary mouse, inhabits thinner stands of spruce above the upper forest limit.

Meadows and Pasturelands

Fig. 12. The Small Tortoiseshell (*Aglais urticae*) is one of the commonest butterflies.

Not all meadows are alike. Much depends on how and to what degree they have been affected by people, and, accordingly, they may be divided into three groups. The first comprises natural meadows that formed as treeless grassy tracts located mostly in river valleys. These valleys were regularly flooded for lengthy periods and thus afforded no opportunity for the successful development of forests in the belt of land bordering the rivers. Such meadows are practically non-existent now and the few that do remain are valued as relics of natural meadows, often containing rare plant species. They are of great importance in our understanding of the evolution of the landscape.

Most of today's meadows belong to the second group, that of semi-cultivated and cultivated meadows. These came into being alongside smaller water courses through the agency of people, by felling trees, clearing land and regularly mowing the resulting vegetation. The more people affected the composition of these meadows by sowing other, economically more important grasses, and by enriching the soil with fertilizers, the more these semi-cultivated meadows became transformed into true meadow cultures.

The third group — mountain meadows — are fully dependent on the intervention of people. These meadows are relatively recent for they were formed only when humans settled in mountain districts. In order to earn a livelihood in the mountains and to be able to graze cattle, farmers had to fell trees and clear the land in places suitable for the purpose. In the mountains, however, a meadow generally cannot be tended with the aid of machines; here it can be maintained only by laborious mowing by hand or by grazing. If left ungrazed for just a few years, however, the forest will begin to encroach upon it once again. Abandoned mountain meadows are soon covered with the seedlings of woody plants and, before long, those beautiful, brightly coloured grassy tracts containing countless rare herbaceous plants are no more and the forest again reigns supreme.

In drier locations grazing gave rise to pasturelands in those places where the poor soil was not conducive to the development of rich meadow vegetation. Less-demanding grasses tolerate cropping, trampling down and natural fertilization by the manure of grazing cattle. Regular, yearly and long-term grazing thus not only has a beneficial effect on the condition of the cattle but also serves to maintain the composition of the vegetation in pasturelands and mountain meadows.

The vegetation of these areas is characterized by the absolute predominance of grasses over other herbaceous plants. Even in meadows with a brightly coloured carpet of flowers, grasses predominate. Woody plants are non-existent here. The occasional solitary trees to be seen in pasturelands were planted by farmers as points of orientation or else for ornament to break the uniformity of the meadow. Only the boundaries between meadows, fields and pastures were left to woody plants, mostly small shrubs.

Common grasses in semi-cultivated and cultivated meadows are mostly members of the Poaceae family, such as Timothy Grass (*Phleum pratense*), fox-tail grass (*Alopecurus*), Crested

Dog's-tail (*Cynosurus cristatus*), quaking grass (*Briza*), Cocksfoot (*Dactylis glomerata*), Tufted Hair-grass (*Deschampsia cespitosa*) and others. Herbaceous plants of flowering meadows include Ragged Robin (*Lychnis flos-cuculi*), buttercups (*Ranunculus*), Meadow Cranesbill (*Geranium pratense*), Lady's Mantle (*Alchemilla*) and many more.

Fig. 13. A sunny, grassy slope dotted with White Campion (*Melandrium album*) is host to the Sand Lizard (*Lacerta agilis*) which suns itself on a stone.

In pasturelands one will often find Narrow-leaved Meadow-grass (*Poa angustifolia*), Perennial Rye-grass (*Lolium perenne*), bent grass (*Agrostis*), Field Woodrush (*Luzula campestris*), Sweet Vernal-grass (*Anthoxanthum odoratum*), and other, mostly more dry-loving (xerophilous), grasses. Herbaceous plants growing here include Yarrow (*Achillea millefolium*), Dandelion

Fig. 14. On sunny summer days burnets (*Zygaena*) fly in their rather cumbersome way in meadows and on grassy slopes.

(*Taraxacum*), Ribwort (*Plantago*), Knotgrass (*Polygonum aviculare*) and the like. In hilly country and mountain districts pastureland vegetation also includes Mat-grass (*Nardus stricta*) and *Phleum alpinum*.

The fauna of meadows is extremely varied, especially in spring and summer when the meadows are carpeted with brightly coloured

flowers that attract large numbers of insects. Most conspicuous are the butterflies. Various species of blues (*Polyommatus*) and gold-coloured coppers (*Lycaena*) flutter from one flower to another. In dry meadows small burnets (*Zygaena*) are seen resting on the flowers of thistles, while flying about in the air are countless yellows (*Colias*) and browns (Satyridae) as well as brightly coloured admirals (*Vanessa*) and fritillaries (*Argynnis*). During the daytime a number of moths remain concealed beneath the broad leaves of herbaceous plants, for example tiger moths (Arctiidae). They emerge when darkness falls and fly about close above the ground in search of suitable plants on which to lay their eggs.

On warm sunny days large numbers of flies buzz about above the meadow and in the grass. In late summer, particularly, one will often find huge numbers of small grasshoppers, which make welcome food for insectivorous birds. Practically all the meadows are visited by spittle-bugs (*Cercopis*) that leap up out of the grass like huge fleas only to land and hide again a short way off. On tall herbaceous plants one may see the striking frothy secretions that contain the larvae of the spittle-bugs.

Innumerable insects hover around grazing cattle. Hundreds of small beetles lay their eggs in the pats of cow dung where the larvae will develop and feed. Flies are the troublesome and constant companions of grazing cattle, but horse-flies (Tabanidae), which mercilessly stab and suck the blood of their victims, are veritable pests, often for people as well.

Sun-warmed, grassy places are also inhabited by reptiles. The Sand Lizard (*Lacerta agilis*), adroitly capturing insects that alight in its vicinity, likes to sun itself here. When danger threatens, it disappears at lightning speed into a hole in the ground or between stones, but soon comes out again into the sunlight. In damp meadows one will also find amphibians such as frogs (*Rana*).

Of the many rodents that inhabit meadows, a typical steppe-dweller is the slender European Ground Squirrel (*Citellus citellus*), which lives on grass, fruit and insects and usually forms colonies. Once very common and widespread, it is now declining in numbers.

Forest creatures avoid meadows during the daytime but as soon as dusk falls and they are no longer conspicuous in the open, many venture forth to feed there.

Meadows are visited by many birds, particularly insectivorous species. The Yellow Wagtail (*Motacilla flava*), Whinchat (*Saxicola rubetra*) and others build their nests there, concealed by the clumps of grass. Even certain predators find the open, grassy tracts to their liking; the Hen Harrier (*Circus cyaneus*), for example, builds its nest here on the ground. Of the owls, the one most often encountered in damp meadows is the Short-eared Owl (*Asio flammeus*). The meadows are also regularly visited by the Hoopoe (*Upupa epops*), which feeds on the larvae of insects, mainly beetles. Another common sight in meadows is storks, strolling about in search of larger insects and small rodents.

Fig. 15. The Blue-headed Wagtail (*Motacilla flava*) inhabits lowland meadows, often near water.

Fields

Fig. 16. Comparison of grains (from top to bottom): wheat, oat, rye, barley.

The vast areas of forest that covered both the lowland and the hilly landscapes of Europe in the distant past were transformed by farmers into what is termed cultivated steppe. The farmers cleared the land either by felling or burning, drained the swamps, ploughed the earth and sowed seeds. A cultivated steppe or field may be defined as an area of land fully exposed to sun and wind, regularly ploughed, enriched with fertilizer, treated with chemicals and harvested every year.

Besides cultivated plants, however, fields also contain a wide variety of weeds, which form an inseparable part of even the best-cared-for land. A typical feature of field weeds is that they are capable of adapting to the growth cycle of cultivated plants as well as to many agrotechnical procedures. Some weeds readily multiply vegetatively by means of their roots or rhizomes, for example Common Couch (*Agropyron*

repens); others do so by means of underground tubers — Earth-nut Pea (*Lathyrus tuberosus*) — or bulbs — Star-of-Bethlehem (*Gagea arvensis*). The roots of some weeds extend so far down into the earth that they remain untouched even by deep ploughing. Examples are Common Horsetail (*Equisetum arvense*), Field Bindweed (*Convolvulus arvensis*) and Creeping Thistle (*Cirsium arvense*).

There are also differences between the weeds of winter and spring crops. Winter crops usually have far more weeds than spring crops, because most weeds are destroyed by the ploughing of the soil in spring. Generally to be found in spring crops are plants with a short growth cycle, such as Wild Mustard (*Sinapis arvensis*), Scarlet Pimpernel (*Anagalis arvensis*) and Field Madder (*Sherardia arvensis*). Weeds of winter crops are usually annuals that germinate in the autumn and grow and flower in the spring of the following year. These species include certain speedwells (*Veronica triphyllos, Veronica arvensis*) and Annual Knawel (*Scleranthus annuus*).

Most weeds can be classified into one of four groups. The first includes species that mature in spring, long before field crops are harvested, such as Common Whitlow Grass (*Erophila verna*), Wall Speedwell (*Veronica arvensis*) and Star-of-Bethlehem (*Gagea arvensis*). The second group includes weeds that mature at the same time as grain, their ripe seeds falling to the ground when the crop is harvested, such as Corn Cockle (*Agrostemma githago*), nowadays rapidly disappearing from the scene, and the more common Corn Crowfoot (*Ranunculus arvensis*). The plants of the third group are perennial weeds that, even though they may be damaged during harvest, immediately grow again from their undamaged roots and flower a second time that same year, for example Field Bindweed (*Convolvulus arvensis*). The fourth and last group contains species that do not mature until after the harvest. Included in this group may be those weeds that can repeat their growth cycle several times during the growing season, such as Wild Pansy (*Viola tricolor*) which often produces several generations in a single year.

In root crops the number of weed species is relatively small, often with only one predominant species, such as All-seed (*Chenopodium polyspermum*) or Redleg (*Polygonum persicaria*).

Some weeds will only occur in certain crops that suit their needs. This goes hand in hand with differences in the manner of cultivating different crops and the particular conditions under which they grow. Hop fields, vineyards, tobacco fields, fields of flax and medicinal herbs, as well as fields of nectar-secreting plants all have typical, specific associations of weeds. Examples of such specialized weeds are Branched Broomrape (*Orobanche ramosa*), a parasite mostly of tobacco only, but very occasionally of sunflowers or other plants, and *Cuscuta epilinum*, a parasite solely of flax.

Over the past decades farmers have perfected methods of protecting and influencing crops by spraying them with herbicides and pesticides, treating seeds against infection and removing the seeds of weedy plants before sowing. Perhaps one day Corn-cockle, Field Fennel (*Nigella arvensis*) and Forking Larkspur (*Consolida regalis*) will no longer be seen in fields.

The transformation of forested areas into cultivated steppe brought with it a change in the composition of the animal communities. The original animals migrated or were exterminated and were replaced by new creatures, mainly native steppe species. Many adapted rapidly to the changed conditions and the fields soon became the source of a rich supply of food. These animals sometimes multiply to such a degree that they reach plague numbers, especially in dry years which they find exceedingly favourable.

Fields provide ideal conditions for various rodents that feed on cereal grains and other field crops. The Common Hamster (*Cricetus cricetus*) consumes a large amount of grain during the summer and, in addition, stores several kilograms of seeds in its underground burrow as a reserve food supply for the winter.

Fig. 17. The caterpillar of the Convolvulus Hawk (*Herse convolvuli*) feeds on Field Bindweed (*Convolvulus arvensis*).

29

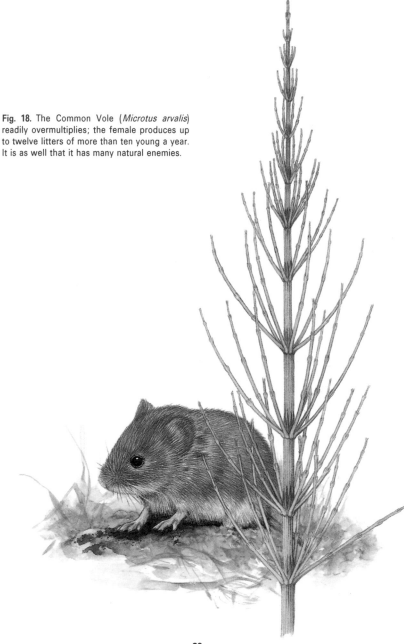

Fig. 18. The Common Vole (*Microtus arvalis*) readily overmultiplies; the female produces up to twelve litters of more than ten young a year. It is as well that it has many natural enemies.

Even more troublesome is the Common Vole (*Microtus arvalis*), whose overpopulation is reason for much concern among farmers. Luckily, the fields are visited by raptorial birds, such as the Common Buzzard (*Buteo buteo*) and Eurasian Kestrel (*Falco tinnunculus*), which can decrease the number of voles considerably. Small weasels (Mustelidae), as well as foxes, also regularly prey on harmful rodents. The most important game animal of fields is the European Hare (*Lepus europaeus*).

Insect pests are very common in extensive tracts of cultivated monocultures, both above and below ground. The larvae of the Wheat Wire-worm (*Agriotes lineatus*) nibble the roots as well as the top parts of cereal grasses and the larvae of *Zabrus gibbus* gnaw at young spring shoots, while the adult beetles feed on the ripe seeds in the spikes. Also found on cereal crops are various species of heteropterous insects (Heteroptera). The Colorado Beetle, brought to Europe from Mexico many years ago, is a troublesome pest of potatoes. Hop fields are inhabited by many species of harmful aphids (Aphidoidea), which multiply at a rapid rate and damage plants by sucking their juices and with their spittle and excrement. Their greatest natural enemy is the ladybird and its predacious larvae which feed on aphids. In spring and summer the fields of clover and alfalfa present the brightest scene, with countless fritillaries (Nymphalidae), yellows (*Colias*), blues (*Polyommatus*) and other butterflies converging there to suck the sweet nectar of the flowers.

For insectivorous birds, fields are a veritable paradise. The liquid song of the Skylark (*Alauda arvensis*) fills the air as it hovers high in the sky, and the Crested Lark (*Galerida cristata*), originally a native steppe bird of the east, frequents the edges of the fields. Among typical field birds, the Partridge (*Perdix perdix*) is one of the most popular game birds. Due to the use of chemicals in farming, however, the partridge population has decreased alarmingly in many European countries. Even worse has been the fate of the Quail (*Coturnix coturnix*), at one time

Fig. 19. The Rose Chafer (*Cetonia aurata*) visits flowering plants on sunny days.

one of the commonest birds in Europe. In the countries of southern Europe and northern Africa, where its meat is considered a great delicacy, more than twenty million quail used to be captured in nets every year during the migrating season. Nowadays this bird is on the list of protected species in most European countries and, as a result, its numbers have increased slightly in recent years.

Mountains

Environmental conditions in the mountains differ markedly from those of lowland and foothill districts. The climate here is completely different. There is lower atmospheric pressure, strong prevailing winds, a low mean annual temperature of air as well as soil, high intensity of solar radiation and high rainfall. Winter in the mountains is relatively long and harsh, thick snow often covers the ground for as long as seven months or more; on mountain glaciers it stays there permanently.

For a long time mountain plant and animal communities remained untouched by people. Farmers penetrated the mountains relatively late, long after they had transformed vast expanses in the lowlands and foothills into fields and meadows. Mountains are used primarily for grazing cattle, to a lesser degree for logging and mining relatively rare ores, and also as a place for recreation, the clean air and relatively unspoiled wilderness making them ideal for this purpose.

Above the upper forest limit one will encounter only the occasional tree, a larch or stone pine perhaps. Most woody plants here are of shrubby habit, the principal species being the Mountain Pine (*Pinus mugo*), an important plant of the alpine belt. As for herbaceous plants, low, often cushion-like, types prevail, such as Moss Campion (*Silene acaulis*), mountain saxifrages (*Saxifraga*), Least Primrose (*Primula minima*) and several others. The small, often prostrate, shrubs of Reticulate Willow (*Salix reticulata*), Least Willow (*Salix herbacea*) and *Salix serpyllifolia* trail over rocks and boulders in screes. Many mountain plants have adapted to the harsh conditions by remaining permanently green even beneath the blanket of snow. Some even flower under the snow or push their stems up through the snow cover and start to flower very early in spring, for example tassel-flowers (*Soldanella*).

Annuals are only rarely seen in the mountains for the summer there is too short for the plants to complete their life cycle within a single growing season; that is, germination of the seeds, growth of the top parts, development of the flowers and ripening of the seeds. On the other hand, plants that flower before their leaves are fully developed are common in the mountains, for example butterbur (*Petasites*).

The composition of mountain flora is readily observed as one climbs from mountain forests up to alpine grasslands and meets the fountainheads of streams beneath the steep peaks. Predominant here are robust herbaceous plants and grasses, with, here and there, the occasion-

al 'flag-form' tree, its branches pointing leeward as it braves the force of the strong winds. Mountain slopes and rocky screes are inhabited by plant communities composed primarily of low, prostrate or cushion-like species. On the highest rocky peaks one will find only lichens with corky thalli pressed to the rock substrate. Only very occasionally will one find undemanding and hardy flowering plants in rock crevices, such as *Veronica aphylla*, Small Gentian (*Gentiana nivalis*), *Androsace lactea* and *Androsace helvetica*.

Mountains also have their typical animal inhabitants, creatures that have adapted to life on rocky, often very steep, inaccessible slopes and cliffs. Some animals, such as the Chamois (*Rupicapra rupicapra*), inhabit the highest rocky regions. Here they are well protected from predators that do not possess the nimbleness of foot with which a herd of Chamois moves about over the slopes and rock ledges. In summer Chamois remain near the snow line; in winter they descend to lower elevations. They are extremely adept at climbing the steep slopes and will leap as much as 8 m across deep ravines and gorges. Even the smallest rock ledge makes a springboard for their breakneck jumps. Herds of Chamois are generally headed by an experienced female, the males living separately for the greater part of the year. The young, wobbling at first on weak legs, soon scamper fearlessly in their mothers' wake, often within a few hours of birth.

The Austrian, Italian, Swiss and French Alps are home to the Ibex (*Capra ibex*), which remains above the upper forest limit, generally at elevations of 2,300—3,200 m. It often stays there even during the cold winter months. The Ibex lives in small herds comprising females, young males and young. Older, adult males live separately in small bands, and old males live singly, except during the mating season when they visit the females. The Ibex is protected by law throughout its entire range; there are some 3,000 specimens in the national parks of the alpine region.

A typical inhabitant of mountain districts in the Alps and Carpathians is the Marmot (*Marmota marmota*), one of Europe's largest rodents. It was also introduced to the Pyrenees, the Black Forest and other places. It lives on rocky slopes at elevations of 800—3,000 m, in colonies of up to eighteen individuals, all usually related.

Mountains also have a characteristic bird population. The rocky mountain localities of the Alps, Pyrenees and Carpathians is where the beautifully coloured Wall-creeper (*Tichodroma muraria*) makes its home. Only in winter does it descend to the lowlands for more readily obtainable food. It can be identified at a glance by its red wings spotted with white.

Wheeling and gliding above mountain cliffs, one may see the Golden Eagle (*Aquila chrysaetos*), a magnificent bird with a wingspan of about 2 m. The courtship flights of eagles may be observed in spring high up above the peaks. Rocky mountain slopes and cliffs are also the nesting site of the Griffon Vulture (*Gyps fulvus*), found in Spain, northern Italy, Austria, Switzerland, south-eastern France and south-eastern Europe; it may also be seen in other European countries, where it occurs as a guest.

The Chough (*Pyrrhocorax pyrrhocorax*) lives in rocky sites in the Alps and in Spain, as well as in Britain. The Ring Ouzel (*Turdus torquatus*) is partial to mountain slopes thinly covered with dwarf pine and low spruce, where it may be spotted in the vicinity of tumbling mountain streams. It occurs in the Alps, Pyrenees and Carpathians, as well as in England and Scandinavia.

Grassy mountain slopes abound with many species of insects. In particular, butterflies add beauty and colour to the scene, for example the Apollo (*Parnassius apollo*), a large butterfly with a wingspan of up to 70 mm.

Fig. 20. The Wallcreeper (*Tichodroma muraria*) is a rare, protected bird of rocky mountain districts.

Built-up Areas

Fig. 21. Blues (*Maculinea*) flit about close above the ground on summer days, visiting one flower after another.

People live surrounded by countless cultivated plants and domestic animals. Our houses are covered with climbing plants; our neighbourhoods are made attractive by neat gardens with decorative flowers, trees and shrubs. Fruit trees hold promise of a rich harvest, in the kitchen garden we try our hand at growing the latest kinds of vegetables, and in our homes the rooms are brightened by lovely house plants.

Beside plants, our companions include animals. Dogs and cats keep us company day in and day out, our homes are brighted by aquariums filled with tropical fish, cages of exotic birds or even terrariums containing small reptiles. Our children are made happy by having a guinea pig or hamster for a pet. The range of purely utility animals we use to provide our

food, be they mammals or birds, is continually extended by breeders through the introduction of new types.

However, in spite of this great number of cultivated plants and animals our immediate neighbourhood also abounds in wild flora and fauna. Some, such as birds, are quite obvious. Others, however, are inconspicuous. Some of these plants and animals are unwelcome guests that are difficult to get rid of.

All gardeners are well acquainted with the weedy plants that invade their beautifully kept gardens, such as Canadian Fleabane (*Conyza canadensis*), Common Groundsel (*Senecio vulgaris*) and galinsogas (*Galinsoga*). The queen of weedy plants is Goatweed or Ground Elder (*Aegopodium podagraria*); it is unbelievable how tenaciously it resists all attempts to eradicate it from the garden. Some weeds are small herbaceous plants with lovely flowers, for example Common Speedwell (*Veronica persica*), *Veronica sublobata*, Common Chickweed (*Stellaria media*), Shepherd's Purse (*Capsella bursa-pastoris*) and Henbit Dead-nettle (*Lamium amplexicaule*).

The most troublesome weeds are perennials with long underground rhizomes by means of which they spread through the soil. When digging the ground we often cut up the rhizomes of Couch (*Agropyron repens*) and Goatweed, thereby actually aiding and abetting their spread.

Weedy plants growing in the garden or by waysides are generally distinguished by immense vitality, in particular those that were brought to Europe from other continents, for example Small-flowered Balsam (*Impatiens parviflora*) and Canadian Fleabane. These plants are so very invasive because Europe's native plants are unable to compete with their great reproductive powers. The ripe capsules of Impatiens, first brought here from Central Asia, burst at the slightest touch, ejecting the seeds far from the parent plant. In the case of galinsogas, brought to Europe from Central and South America, during a single growing season one plant produces thousands of light, minute achenes furnished with an ingenious apparatus called a pappus, that serves as a parachute, carrying the achenes great distances from their parent plant. A few such invasive plants are all that is needed in order for them to dominate a large area within just a few years.

Not all weedy plants are to be disdained. Many have useful characteristics. Some may be made into tasty dishes, others may contain medicinal substances of importance in the

Fig. 22. Dense thickets of Stinging Nettle (*Urtica dioica*) are where the European Hedgehog (*Erinaceus europaeus*) hides until dusk, when it emerges in search of prey.

pharmaceutical industry or are used in home remedies. The young spring leaves of Stinging Nettle (*Urtica dioica*) and Small Nettle (*Urtica urens*) are widely used in salads and stuffings and valued for their high vitamin C content. A tasty salad may also be made from Lamb's Lettuce (*Valerianella locusta*) or from the leaves of Dandelion (*Taraxacum officinale*). Delicacies with a therapeutic effect include dandelion wine or a wine or compote made from elderberries, the fruits of the Common Elder (*Sambucus nigra*). Scented Mayweed (*Chamomilla recutita*) and Coltsfoot (*Tussilago farfara*) are among the most widely used, commonly known medicinal herbs, and we could cite many more examples.

Special mention should be made of the flora of dumps, rubbish heaps and waste places. Typical are spreads of orache (*Atriplex*), chenopods (*Chenopodium*) and numerous other plants.

Fig. 23. The flea (*Pulex irritans*) is a parasite of humans. Other species of fleas parasitize domestic animals.

Most plants found growing in the neighbourhood of human dwellings, by waysides and in waste places are extremely hardy. They are able to withstand all kinds of unfavourable conditions: toxic substances in the atmosphere, high concentrations of nitrogen in the soil and even daily trampling. They are covered in detail in the pictorial section, along with plants that have spread widely as escapees from gardens. Nor should we forget the trees and shrubs planted in parks and avenues to improve the dust- and fume-polluted atmosphere of cities and built-up areas.

The development of civilization was accompanied by the disappearance of many animals from the vicinity of human dwellings and by the arrival of others to take their place. Here they found suitable hiding places and better conditions for obtaining food or for propagation. In the favourable conditions that we unwittingly prepared for them, many species have multiplied in such numbers as to reach plague proportions, and have often caused irreparable damage.

Among the small mammals it is mainly the rodents that find built-up areas to their liking, above all the House Mouse (*Mus musculus*), Black Rat (*Rattus rattus*) and Brown Rat (*Rattus norvegicus*), feeding industriously on food stores and household scraps. They are capable of causing untold damage. Attracted by the rodents, came small beasts of prey, such as the

Weasel (*Mustela nivalis*), European Marten (*Martes foina*) and European Polecat (*Putorius putorius*), which hunted and fed on the rodents. They themselves, however, also became pests after a time as polecats and martens eventually began to specialize in easier prey such as chickens, hens and ducks and their eggs.

Built-up areas also attracted numerous species of insects, chiefly flies but also butterflies, moths and beetles. Vegetable gardens are visited by countless parasites, such as whites (*Pieris brassicae*), whose females deposit hundreds of eggs on the leaves of cabbages and other cruciferous plants and whose larvae then devour the leaves right down to the leaf stalks. Decorative flowering plants in gardens and on patios and windowsills are visited by many insects, including many butterflies, that suck sweet nectar from the blossoms.

Human dwellings are visited in the autumn by numerous species of insects attempting to survive the winter in congenial conditions. These include various fritillaries (*Vanessa*), the Green Lacewing (*Chrysopa vulgaris*), ladybirds (Coccinellidae) and the ubiquitous flies. Places that are not often aired are the favourite haunts of the House Spider (*Tegenaria derhami*) which spins dense webs. Even today one will often encounter such unpleasant parasites as fleas (*Pulex irritans*) and bedbugs (*Cimex*) in warm places, as well as cockroaches. Of late, households in the large cities of Central Europe have also been invaded by the Pharaoh Ant (*Monomoria pharaonis*), introduced only recently from the south. It spreads rapidly and is very difficult to exterminate. Wardrobes and stores of flour, vegetables and other foodstuffs are visited by many storehouse pests, of which moths (Tineidae) are the most familiar, their larvae feeding on whatever they find.

In the garden slugs and snails are troublesome pests that feed on tender young vegetable plants when darkness falls. However, they may be kept in check by the frogs and toads that often visit gardens in search of a tasty morsel. Attics, steeples and other high structures are often inhabited by insectivorous bats. Nowadays some species may also be seen in large cities where they may be found in such places as the ventilation shafts of modern buildings. In many countries bats are on the list of protected species.

Last of all we come to the birds, welcome companions, whose songs brighten the built-up areas where we live. The House Sparrow (*Passer domesticus*) probably first accompanied people when they began to cultivate grain, and

Fig. 24. The Common Toad (*Bufo bufo*) is often found not only in gardens but also in cellars and sheds where it hides during the daytime. It also overwinters in damp country cellars.

was probably the first bird to settle permanently in the neighbourhood of humans. Nowadays it may be seen in the very heart of cities, on busy streets and town squares. The Blackbird (*Turdus merula*) is also our constant companion today, but this bird arrived in town at a much later date than the sparrow. As late as 1855 it was still described by ornithologists as a very shy woodland bird. Now it may be seen in town gardens and parks as well as in small courtyards where it builds its nest on windowsills and balconies.

The Swallow (*Hirundo rustica*) has almost totally abandoned its native cliffside habitat and moved to the neighbourhood of people, often settling directly inside our houses—in a hallway or even in a bathroom. Built-up areas are also inhabited by the Swift (*Apus apus*) and House Martin (*Delichon urbica*) which builds its nest on the outside walls of houses, under balconies, cornices and eaves. Worthy of particular notice is the Starling (*Sturnus vulgaris*) which will make its home wherever one hangs a nestbox, be it in a garden, park or courtyard.

Other species of birds are also moving into the neighbourhood of people in increasing numbers. They include the Black Redstart (*Phoenicurus ochruros*), Redstart (*Phoenicurus phoenicurus*), Great Tit (*Parus major*) and Blue Tit (*Parus caeruleus*). The Jackdaw (*Corvus monedula*) sites its nest in church steeples in cities. In

Fig. 25. The European Blackbird (*Turdus merula*) has become a constant companion of people. It often builds its nest directly on a windowsill, on a beam or even in a wicker basket. In the garden it nests in the forked branch of a shrub or small tree.

parks the Rook (*Corvus frugilegus*) nests. Another recent arrival in cities is the Kestrel (*Falco tinnunculus*) which is now a permanent resident. It nests in church steeples and on the cornices of tall buildings. On the other hand the Barn Owl (*Tyto alba*) builds its nest in attics, barn lofts and dovecotes. In recent years, city parks and gardens have become the nesting place of the Song Thrush (*Turdus philomelos*), while the Collared Dove (*Streptopelia decaocto*) is a permanent year-round resident of built-up areas.

In winter bird-feeders in cities are often visited by woodland birds, but even in summer one may often see typical woodland birds in a park or garden, such as the Golden Oriole (*Oriolus oriolus*) and the Green Woodpecker (*Picus viridis*). Other woodland creatures visit cities too; the squirrel, for instance, is a common sight.

Fig. 26. The Golden Oriole (*Oriolus oriolus*) suspends its hammock-shaped nest, made of long thin stalks and grasses, between the forks of branches so that the young will not fall out even in strong winds.

Flowing Waters

The vast network of blue lines drawn on a map may show all the water courses in a given region, but they can give no idea of their great diversity. Cool, clear water has its source primarily in mountain forest districts, where mountain streams force their way down through rocky troughs, rushing and tumbling over rocks and boulders that block their path. These streams converge to form larger streams and brooks and then large rivers. The rivers take on a new and different aspect in their lower reaches where their banks are often artificially strengthened. At the mouths of rivers one can see the influence of the sea — the flow of the river slows and the fresh water mingles with salt seawater.

Throughout the journey from its source to the sea, the flow of water carries with it sand, mud and soil, which it then deposits lower down in the backwaters and mouths of rivers in the form of alluvium. The amount of oxygen in the water decreases over its course from mountain region to lowland country and at the same time there is a considerable increase in the degree of the water's pollution. All of these factors — flow, the changing swiftness of the current, the removal and deposition of alluvium, amount of food, variability in the concentration of oxygen and degree of pollution — make adaptation on the part of the river's living organisms a necessity.

In clear, flowing waters at higher elevations *Fontinalis antipyretica* grows, an aquatic moss with branching stems thickly covered with keeled leaves. River Crowfoot (*Batrachium fluitans*), which has submerged stems with much-divided leaves floating on the surface, is also a common plant of slow-flowing water.

The banks of streams and rapid-flowing rivers do not have such greatly developed waterside vegetation as backwaters, ponds and boggy pools. However, even alongside flowing waters one will find interesting vegetation. Masses of *Rumex aquaticus* are often seen growing by water courses in valleys. Slow-flowing rivers are bordered by Amphibious Bistort (*Polygonum amphibium*), while on their surface the leaves of Shining Pondweed (*Potamogeton fluitans*) float. Meadowsweet (*Filipendula ulmaria*) grows in large masses by the waterside, as do other plants such as *Myricaria germanica*, found on stony, alluvial river deposits together with Sea Buckthorn (*Hippophaë rhamnoides*). Lowland rivers are bordered by typical flood-plain forests and waterside thickets composed of willows, poplars and alders. Here and there the blue-violet flowers of Bittersweet (*Solanum dulcamara*) are visible, replaced in the autumn by poisonous dark red berries. One may also find the large whitish flowers of Larger Bind-

Fig. 27. The River Crowfoot (*Batrachium fluitans*) grows in slow-flowing waters. The Blue Damselfly (*Calopteryx virgo*) lays its eggs on the plant's submerged parts.

weed (*Calystegia sepium*). Often to be seen twisting and twining through waterside thickets is wild hop (*Humulus lupulus*).

Animals that live in flowing waters, particularly in swift streams, are specifically adapted to life in this environment. They often have flattened bodies and other well-developed features that help them to hold on fast to vegetation. Fish are without doubt the most familiar denizens of this aquatic environment. The cold, clear waters of the upper reaches of rivers are visited by some marine fish that may travel many hundreds of kilometres upstream from the sea to spawn. Some fish spend their youth here, only swimming downstream in maturity.

Once vast numbers of salmon swam up Europe's rivers to spawn, but people blocked the return of these beautiful fish to their spawning ground by putting dams and high weirs in their path — obstacles that the salmon found insurmountable. In many rivers salmon 'leaps' or 'ladders' have been built to allow the fish to climb up over the weirs. Much the same happened in the case of young eels (elvers), which used to leave the sea and swim upriver where their further development took place. Nowadays fishermen transport the eels inland from river mouths by various means, even by aeroplane, to release them in the places the young eels previously reached under their own steam. Only in some rivers in western and northern Europe do eels still migrate freely without outside help.

Flowing waters are also inhabited by many species of crustaceans (Crustacea) and molluscs (Mollusca) as well as large numbers of insect larvae, such as caddis flies (Trichoptera), giant dragonflies (Anisoptera), mayflies (Ephemeroptera), water beetles and the like. Streamsides and riversides also have their typical denizens. Damselflies (Zygoptera) and giant dragonflies (Anisoptera) flit about above the vegetation. Also found here are such unpleasant insects as greenflies (*Chrysops*) and gadflies (*Tabanus*), whose females suck the blood of people. They are most obnoxious pests, particularly on warm summer days before a storm. By watersides one may also find many handsome butterflies and beetles, their larvae developing on willows, poplars, aspens, willowherbs (*Epilobium*) and spurges (*Euphorbia*).

The shores of flowing waters are brightened by numerous species of birds. Wagtails (*Motacilla*) are the most common species to be seen at, or close by, the water's edge. Dippers (*Cinclus*) are good divers, plunging underwater to gather insect larvae and crustaceans on the bottom as well as to collect material for their nests,

Fig. 28. The European Eel (*Anguilla anguilla*) grows to maturity in brooks and streams.

which they build close to the water. Riverbanks are inhabited by the Little Ringed Plover (*Charadrius dubius*) which runs rapidly over the pebbles in search of insects and worms. It nests on the stony banks, making a small scrape in washed-up gravel or amid pebbles where its brownish, speckled eggs are practically indistinguishable from their surroundings.

Flowing waters also have typical mammal populations, some of which may be found on calm bodies of water as well. The European Beaver (*Castor fiber*) is partial to slow-flowing streams where it builds its characteristic dams of twigs and small stones. The Common Otter (*Lutra lutra*) excavates simple burrows in the banks of streams and rivers, while the Muskrat (*Ondatra zibethicus*) may be seen by slow-flowing streams and larger brooks.

Still Waters

Fig. 29. The Little Bittern (*Ixobrychus minutus*) builds its nest on flattened reeds.

The range of aquatic and bog plants and animals that inhabit calm bodies of water is extremely diverse and differs in many ways from the communities of streams, brooks and rivers. There is less oxygen in pools, ponds, lakes and large dams than in flowing water; with increasing depth there is less light in the water and there are increasing deposits of nutrients from decomposed dead organisms that have not been carried away by the current.

The aquatic microcosm is extraordinarily rich. A single drop of water examined under a microscope reveals a vast number of protozoans (Protozoa), otherwise invisible to the naked eye, whirling about with the aid of typical appendages such as flagella or cilia. The plant plankton is composed of microscopic green algae, blue-green algae and bacteria; the animal plankton is chiefly composed of millions of minute crustaceans (Crustacea), and is found everywhere, in ponds and pools, as well as in small water reservoirs. These creatures are well adapted to life in water. Some move with the aid of paddling feet, others, such as water-fleas (Cladocera), leap rhythmically with the aid of enlarged forked antennae that function as oars. Small crustaceans form the main food of commercially important fish.

Still stretches of water are a congenial environment for many plants with floating leaves, such as duckweed (*Lemna*), and submerged plants, such as Canadian Waterweed (*Elodea canadensis*), Water-milfoil (*Myriophyllum*) and certain pondweeds (*Potamogeton*). On the surface of calm water float the leaves of yellow water lilies (*Nuphar*) and white water lilies (*Nymphaea*) as well as those of Water Crowfoot (*Batrachium aquatile*). Most plants root in the bottom and form typical masses by the edges of still bodies of water.

The occurrence of damp-loving plants depends on the water level. Some, such as sweet-flag (*Acorus*), reedmace (*Typha*), bur-reed (*Sparganium*), common reed (*Phragmites*) and Yellow Flag (*Iris pseudacorus*), form large masses at the water's edge only in places that remain permanently underwater even in periods of extreme drought. Damp-loving sedges (*Carex*) and club-rushes (*Scirpus*) grow on watersides that remain wet throughout spring and autumn and their occasionally flooded masses give way to meadow communities, which is why one will find numerous plants both by the waterside and in wet meadows or marshes.

The draining of bogs and marshes gives rise to new meadows or fields. This has led in the past to the irrevocable disappearance of many rare aquatic and bog plants, although nowadays these are generally protected by law, for example flowering rush (*Butomus*), *Iris sibirica*, Snake's Head (*Fritillaria meleagris*), *Orchis*, *Dactylorhiza*, Marsh Helleborine (*Epipactis palustris*), bogbean (*Menyanthes*), bladderwort (*Utricularia*), sundew (*Drosera*), butterwort (*Pinguicula*) and other damp-loving gems of the plant world.

Darting about above the surface of still stretches of water are predacious pond skaters (Gerridae). Below the surface live countless water beetles, superbly adapted to their aquatic environment, with hind legs serving as powerful oars, for example the back-swimmers (*Notonecta glauca*). Also found here are bloodthirsty leeches (Hirudinea), lying in wait for their prey.

Fig. 30. The leaf of Yellow Flag (*Iris pseudacorus*) serves as a launching, as well as landing, pad for the dragonfly *Libellula depressa*.

Calm bodies of water are inhabited by large numbers of amphibians. The larval development of newts (*Triturus*) takes place here, as does that of tadpoles. Some species of toads, for example Red- and Yellow-bellied Toads (*Bombina*) stay in the shallows even as adults, seeking a hiding place on dry land only during the winter. The Edible Frog (*Rana esculenta*) also stays by the water all the time, leaping into it in a flash when danger threatens.

Birds requiring an aquatic environment also possess certain adaptations. Their legs are short but strong and the toes are equipped with broad webbing. Some diving birds have legs located at the very rear of their body to serve as oars that propel them swiftly along in pursuit of underwater prey. The greatest number of bird species is to be found on large lakes and ponds which are bordered by thick vegetation to provide the birds with ample places of concealment. In damp meadows near water shorebirds (Charadriiformes) build their nests, as do various species of duck and other birds. Thickets on islands or near water are sought out by waders (Ciconiiformes) which build their nests in the branches of trees and shrubs, often forming large colonies. Cormorants (*Phalacrocorax*) are also to be seen in such places. The dense vegetation in shallows and at the water's edge is where rails (Rallidae) and warblers (*Acrocephalus*) congregate. The Great Crested Grebe (*Podiceps cristatus*) and Little Grebe (*Podiceps rufi-*

Fig. 31. The Edible Frog (*Rana esculenta*) perches on aquatic plants.

collis) conceal their floating nests amid reed-mace or reeds. Also found here is the Black-headed Gull (*Larus ridibundus*). Reedbeds provide shelter for large flocks of songbirds to roost in at night before their migratory flight south in the autumn.

Certain mammals are able to swim, having long ago moved from dry land to water and adapted to the new environment. They, too, have webbed feet to help them to swim. One such specialist is the beaver, whose flattened tail serves as a rudder.

Fig. 32. When it occurs in large numbers, the Musk Rat (*Ondatra zibethica*) can do considerable damage to the dams of ponds with its several-metre-long corridors.

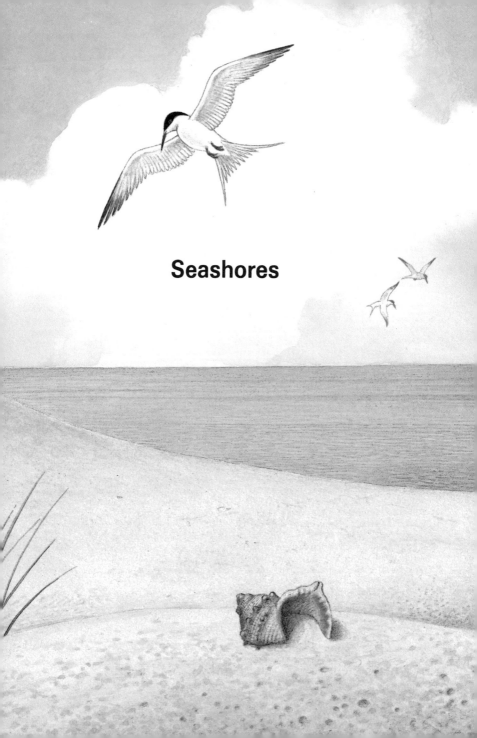

Seashores

Seashores are marked by great diversity. Rocky shores are common, with cliffs rising straight up from the water. Low plateaux, regularly washed over by water and constantly pounded by the surf, bear evidence of marine life. Amid the shells and cases of animals cast up on the shore by the sea, one may find the thalli of algae and seaweeds, torn by the surf from the submerged rocks on which they grow, for example *Xanthoria*, *Lecanora* and the minute shrub-like *Ramalina*.

Salty shores, where the seawater continually soaks into the sandy soil, have a richer flora. Among the first to become established in these sandflats were the glassworts (*Salicornia herbacea* and *Salicornia prostrata*). Related to these herbaceous plants are Herbaceous Seablite (*Suaeda maritima*), *Suaeda prostrata*, Saltwort (*Salsola kali*) and *Basia hirsuta*. Sea Rocket (*Cakile maritima*) grows in salty soil from the surf line to the sand dunes. Very common in such habitats is the salt-tolerant (halophilous) and sand-tolerant (psammophilous) Common Saltmarsh Grass (*Puccinellia maritima*), which forms characteristic stands together with other halophilous species — Mud Rush (*Juncus gerardii*), Sea Rush (*Juncus maritimus*) and Sea Club-rush (*Bolboschoenus maritimus*). Sea Milkwort (*Glaux maritima*) stands up well to flooding by salt water, as well as to burial in sand. Halophilous plants are well adapted to the extreme conditions of their environment: they contain a greater concentration of salt in their cell plasma than other plants so that the greater osmotic pressure inside the cells enables them to absorb salt water more readily. For inland plants this salty, damp environment would seem extremely dry; they would be unable to absorb the water that is so saturated with salt and would suffer from both thirst and hunger. Furthermore, halophilous plants have fleshy stems and leaves and the special construction of their epidermis prevents the excessive evaporation of water.

Another type of coast landscape is spreading sandflats. A typical feature of these sandy coasts is the pronounced and continuous movement of the sandy substrate, caused by the wind. Sand is poor in nutrients, water readily seeps to great depths and the sand is a poor conductor of heat. Plants growing in these sandflats live in an unnourishing and extremely cold environment which hampers their absorption of water via their roots. Winds generally blow in from the sea, carrying the sand away from the shore to form sand dunes. On the leeward side of an obstacle, such as a stone, a clump of plants or a small heap of shells, the sand blown by the wind piles up and the dune gradually becomes bigger. Plants then grow up through the small dune or else new plants become established there, creating a new obstacle, and the dune thus increases in height as well as breadth. It is then shifted farther from the shore by the wind, most of the salt in the sand is washed out by rainwater and a secondary dune is formed. Decomposed plant remnants and the calcareous rubble from the shells of marine animals enrich this secondary dune with calcium and other elements; the sand becomes richer in nutrients and the resulting humus finally enables the growth of more demanding plants. Those that thrive here include Sand Couchgrass (*Elytrigia juncea*), Sea Aster (*Aster tripolium*), Sea Plantain (*Plantago coronopus*), Sea Pink (*Armeria maritima*), Sea Holly (*Eryngium maritimum*) and Scentless Mayweed (*Matricaria maritima*), along with grasses such as Lyme Grass (*Elymus arenaria*) and the related *Ammophilla arenaria*.

On dunes and salt-free sand farther away from the shore one may find plants with much more demanding requirements, such as Sand Sedge (*Carex arenaria*). On such firmed sands even shrubs such as Sea Buckthorn (*Hippophaë rhamnoides*) and Creeping Willow (*Salix repens*) may grow. Sands held firm by the roots of herbaceous plants and shrubs no longer shift, thus making it possible even for trees to grow there, for example the Scots Pine (*Pinus sylvestris*), a familiar inland tree that thrives in sandy soils where it forms typical pine woods.

The sea provides food for countless animals. Every day in these limitless expanses millions of tonnes of minute plankton, algae, crustaceans, molluscs and other animals serve as food for fish. In their turn the fish become food for pinnipeds and fish-eating seabirds.

High up on the seaside cliffs the gannets (*Sula bassana*) build their nests. Gannet colonies may be found on the coasts of England, Scotland, Ireland, Iceland and Brittany. Rocky islands off the northern and western coasts of Europe are the breeding grounds of the Razorbill (*Alca torda*) and the plentiful Guillemot (*Uria lomvia*). One of the most interesting seabirds is the Puffin (*Fratercula arctica*), whose European population numbers several million birds.

Gulls and terns are also common inhabitants of rocky coasts and islands. Thanks to protective measures, the Kittiwake (*Rissa tridactyla*), which forms large closed colonies, has recently even moved into ports where it builds its nest on the windowsills of tall buildings. Many species of graceful terns (Sterninae) nest on large sandy or stony beaches; here the Sandwich Tern (*Sterna sandvicensis*) forms dense colonies numbering many thousands of birds.

Numerous marine invertebrates are found on the seashore, such as crustaceans (Crustacea), molluscs (Mollusca), echinoderms (Echinodermata) and small fish left stranded in little pools or depressions in rocks when the tide ebbs. Some, for instance crabs (Brachyura), are very active on the damp sand at low tide, where they forage for food. At ebb tide flocks of birds converge on such places to feast. These include primarily gulls and terns, herons (Ardeidae) and also shorebirds (Charadriiformes), chiefly plovers (Tringinae) and sandpipers (Calidrinae). The robust Oystercatcher (*Haematopus ostralegus*), a handsome black and white bird with a red beak, cannot escape notice. It runs about in small groups on sandy beaches and shallows seeking food. When it comes upon a mollusc it pries the shell open with its beak and devours the succulent meat inside.

A typical mammal found off the coasts of Europe is the Common Seal (*Phoca vitulina*), which inhabits the coastal waters of the north Atlantic and is occasionally seen in the western Baltic. Sometimes it even strays up rivers and has been spotted 700 km inland up the Elbe.

Fig. 33. Seashores abound in countless species of crabs that feed on animal and plant remnants. This picture shows *Cancer pagurgus* and a typical plant of the North Sea coast—Thrift or Sea Pink (*Armeria maritima*).

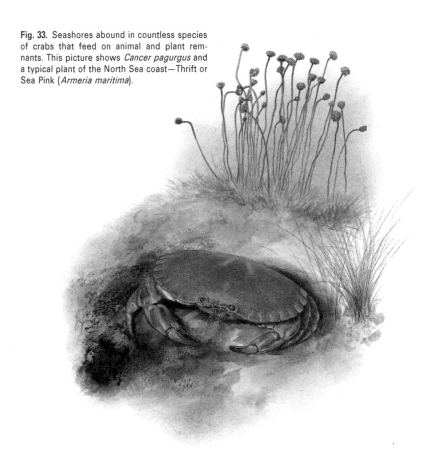

Fungi

The fungi with which we are most familiar are mushrooms with typically shaped caps, such as the Edible Boletus, Orange Cap Boletus, Chanterelle, Parasol Mushroom and toadstools. However, fungi also include yeasts, rusts, smuts and mildew. What all these organisms have in common is that they completely lack the green colouring matter called chlorophyll, by means of which green plants are able to make food through the action of sunlight. Fungi must obtain their food supply by other means. Saprophytic fungi take nourishment from organic compounds that result from the decay of dead organisms. Parasitic fungi obtain nourishment from green plants or else they may be parasitic on animals including humans. Some species of fungi live in a mutually beneficial, or symbiotic, association with other plants; such a symbiotic

Fig. 1. The striking Edible Boletus is one of the most sought-after mushrooms.

association of the mycelium of a fungus with the roots of a seed plant is termed a mycorrhiza.

Saprophytic fungi are usually ground plants, but some, such as the saprophytic bracket fungus *Fomes fomentarius,* also grow on the wood of fallen trees. The thin-walled mycelium of these fungi absorbs water and, with it, the dissolved nutrients from decomposed humus, as well as the decaying bodies of dead plants and animals.

The mycelium of parasitic fungi invades the tissues of the living plants from which it obtains nourishment. This, of course, weakens or even completely destroys the host plant. Parasitic pests of trees are mainly the Honey Fungus (*Armillaria mellea*), some *Pleurotus* and many bracket fungi (Polyporaceae).

Mycorrhitic fungi are the ones we know best and the ones most eagerly sought by mushroom pickers. *Suilus luteus* grows beneath pine trees, *Suilus grevillei* lives symbiotically with larches. *Boletus edulis, Boletus pinophilus* and *Boletus aestivalis* were all named after the tree with the roots of which their mycelium lives in a symbiotic association that is beneficial to both the fungus and the tree. The fibres of the mycelium envelop the tips of minute rootlets, penetrate their cells, from which they absorb certain substances, and in return transfer other substances into these cells.

Many fungi are important agents in the food industry. All types of fermentation, be it in the making of beer, wine or vinegar, or in the leavening of dough, are made possible by the action of microscopic fungi known as yeasts. Some yeasts cause undesirable fermentation, for example the clouding of beer, others may even cause skin diseases in people and animals.

Other fungi (moulds) may cause food and other products to become mouldy, for example spoiling camera film in the tropics. Others, as pathogenic organisms, may cause disease in animals and people. Some moulds give cheeses their specific smell and taste during the ripening process. These moulds are mainly members of the genus *Penicillium,* such as *P. camembertii, P. gorgonzola, P. roquefortii.* Ranking high on the list of useful moulds are those that produce antibiotics such as penicillin (*P. notatum* and *P. chrysogenum*), patulin (*P. patulum*) and griseofulvin (*P. griseum*) which has a fungicidal effect.

There are fungi that are edible and tasty, some that are inedible, unappetizing or bland, others that are revoltingly bitter, and some that are extremely poisonous. Boletus mushrooms, most of which are edible and very tasty, also include several inedible species, for example

Fig. 2. *Tylopilus felleus* is often mistaken for an edible mushroom. It can be readily identified, however, by the prominent network on the stipe and also by its sharp burning taste — tasting just a tiny piece suffices!

Boletus albidus and *B. calopus,* as well as species that vary from slightly to extremely poisonous — *B. luridus, B. satanas.* On the other hand, among toadstools, which are generally inedible and which also include the deadly *Amanita virosa* and the Deathcap (*A. phalloides*), one will find species that are extremely tasty, for example the Blusher (*A. rubescens*). The tastiest of the lot is *A. caesarea,* highly prized as far back as the days of the ancient Romans but nowadays, alas, very rare.

Fig. 3. *Macrolepiota rhacodes* can be readily distinguished from *Macrolepiota procera* by the pronounced colour reaction of the flesh, which turns orange-red to brownish-red when pressed or cut. Both parasol mushrooms are edible.

Some lower fungi are dangerous pests of important crops. Particularly harmful to vineyards, especially in damp, warm summer weather, is *Plasmopara viticola*. This pest was introduced into Europe from America in the mid-nineteenth century. In the first years, before the application of an effective pesticide, it caused great worry to vintners by making the grapes shrivel, turn

a leathery brown and fall prematurely. Also introduced into Europe from America, at the beginning of the nineteenth century, was the potato blight caused by *Phytophtora infestans*. Affected leaves first develop dark spots and later a white coating on the underside; the potato tubers become dry, leathery and mummified.

Some fungi may be harmful in one respect and beneficial in another. Ergot (*Claviceps purpurea*) is harmful in grain crops because it is poisonous, but is beneficial in that its alkaloids may be used in the pharmaceutical industry in the preparation of valuable medicines. *Apiocrea chrysosperma* is harmful to various boletus mushrooms, in particular *Xerocomus chrysenteron*. The related *Byssonectria luteovirens* attacks russulas and other gill fungi. *Morchella* and *Helvella* sp. number among their relatives not only *Rhytisma acerinum* but also the dangerous *Monilinia furstigena* which causes a disease of fruit that spreads from rotting apples and pears to ripening fruits. The diseased fruits then fall or else remain, dried and mummified, on the tree throughout the winter. If the infected fruits are not burned, the disease spreads and attacks the branches which, in the case of cherry trees, will then die back.

Common to all fungi are two types of spore production. In the fruiting body of Ascomycetes there are sac-like structures called asci, in which the propagating bodies, or spores, are formed. Basidiomycetes produce spores at the end of special cells called basidia. In gill fungi these form on the edge of the lamellae (gills); in tube fungi they form inside the tubes.

The thallus of fungi is generally fibrous. Fungal filaments, called hyphae, form a mycelium from which small propagating organs or large fruiting bodies grow.

The classification of fungi into families is based on the identification of features on the fruiting bodies and on the structure and production of spores.

Fig. 4. Development of the fruiting body of the Stinkhorn (*Phallus impudicus*). The spores are dispersed by flies that lick the malodorous, slimy layer on the cap.

Division: **Fungi**—Mycophyta

Class: Ascomycetes

Subclass: Protoascomycetidae

Family: Saccharomycetaceae

1 *Saccharomyces cerevisiae*. Unicellular fungus, known as yeast, visible only under microscope. Of considerable economic value as it is used to leaven dough. Other species are used to ferment wine, cider and beer. In the wild it lives on fruits and other parts of many plants. Propagates by budding; the dividing cells mostly remaining together and forming branched strings.

Family: Taphrinaceae

2 *Taphrina pruni* (syn. *Exoascus pruni*) ('bladder plum'). Attacks fruits of plum-trees causing them to grow large, lop-sided and bladder-like. *T. deformans* ('peach-leaf curl') causes the leaves of peaches and almonds to curl and swell, finally turning bright red. Dense bunches of twigs — witches brooms — are formed on trees attacked by *T. insititiae*. Related species of this fungus cause similar deformations on birches and hornbeams. The mycelium grows through branches or fruits of host plant and terminal cells develop into asci with spores on surface. Asci grow so close to each other that they appear as fine hoar frost on branches or fruits of afflicted plants.

Subclass: Euascomycetidae

Family: Clavicipitaceae

3 Ergot *Claviceps purpurea*. Parasitic on seeds of grasses, particularly rye. Infection is caused by spores producing hyphae which consume ovary and form a black, horny, seed-like sclerotium. This falls to ground and winters in soil. Red-stalked fruiting bodies (*ascophores*) with club-like tips grow from them the following year and produce more spores which are dispersed by wind or insects when the grasses or grain crops are flowering. Ergot is deadly poisonous; its alkaloids are used in the preparation of valuable medicines.

Family: Phacidiaceae

4 *Rhytisma acerinum* ('tar spot'). Parasitic on maple leaves. Forms irregular to rounded, conspicuously large, black, yellow-bordered spots on upper surface of leaves. In spring these black fruiting bodies produce asci full of slender spores. Parasitic also on sow-thistle leaves. Related *Rhytisma punctatum* grows parasitically on sycamore and another member of the genus causes spots on willow leaves.

Family: Morchellaceae (syn. Helvellaceae)

5 Morel *Morchella esculenta.* Fruiting body consists of cap and stalk. Cap mostly ovoid or globose, up to 8 cm high, yellowish to brownish, with irregular, deep and broad cavities that do not form continuous rows, rather recalling a crumpled honeycomb. Well-known spring mushroom, grows in April and May in open deciduous or mixed forests but also in old gardens, parks and yards. Edible only when young.

Old fruit bodies, in which decomposition of albumins takes place, may cause serious poisoning.

Family: Helvellaceae

6 *Gyromitra esculenta.* Brown to dark brown hollow cap, irregularly lobed and wrinkled, up to 10 cm. wide. Stalk whitish to yellowish, hollow, sometimes wrinkled on surface and shorter than cap. Grows in spring in sandy pine-woods, also in other coniferous forests. Sensitivity of man to it varies; it is poisonous to some, even deadly. Therefore, this fungus should never be eaten. Related species *Gyromitra gigas* with lighter cap may be eaten without danger after scalding.

Class: Basidiomycetes

Subclass: Heterobasidiomycetidae

Family: Pucciniaceae

1 *Puccinia graminis*. Parasitic on cereals as well as on barberry. Rusty patches of powdery spores on under surface of barberry leaves. Spores spread by wind on to cereals or other grasses where they germinate. On leaves of these plants so-called summer spores are formed during the growing season. In summer rust spreads by these spores and causes infection of neighbouring plants. At the end of growing season black patches of winter spores form; they overwinter and the following spring each one germinates to produce a basidium with four stalked spores. These are spread by wind and again infect barberry leaves. The sequence of various spore types and alternation of host plants is characteristic of many species of rusts.

Subclass: Homobasidiomycetidae

Order: Hymenomycetales

Family: Corticiaceae

2 *Stereum hirsutum*. Grows on trunks and stumps of deciduous trees. The stemless, shell-like fruiting bodies are yellowish-grey and somewhat leathery, often with a paler zoned striping; the surface varies from soft velvety to shaggy felt in texture. Under surface grey-yellow when dry, reddish in wet weather. A similar species, *Stereum sanguinolentum*, has fruiting bodies with greyish surface. Turns blood-red when injured.

Family: Polyporaceae

3 *Trametes versicolor*. Somewhat fleshy to leathery fruiting bodies form fan-shaped, often overlapping clusters, ornamented with concentric dark and light stripes of brown, grey, orange or yellowish velvety hairs; whitish beneath. Abundant on stumps and decayed trunks of deciduous trees and shrubs, also on dry branches. Related species *Trametes zonatus* has no conspicuous striping. Both species are inedible.

1

2

3

4 *Polyporus squamosus.* Young fruiting bodies convex, older ones widely expanded with a depressed centre; stalk (stipe) short and thick. Whitish to brownish-yellow, roughly circular cap thinly covered with darkish, mostly brown, relatively large scales. Flesh white, whitish to yellowish or slightly brown. Grows on branches, trunks, roots and stumps of deciduous trees, especially nut-trees, individually or in groups, from spring to winter. Young, crisp and still not leathery fruiting bodies edible. Strikingly cucumber-like, floury taste.

5 *Grifola sulphurea* (syn. *Laetiporus sulphureus*). Fruiting bodies fleshy, juicy when young, later tough and brittly crumbling. Cap flat against the tree, usually in tufts densely set one above another. Young fruit bodies bright sulphur yellow, mature even orange, old ones brownish. Grows abundantly on stumps, branches and trunks of deciduous trees in woods but also in parks and gardens. Edible when young, but has a slightly acid, woody taste and seldom eaten.

4

6 *Phellinus igniarius.* Hoof-shaped fruit bodies on trunks of poplars, willows and other trees where they often grow to large size. Cap flat against the tree without stipe, consists of layers; upper surface greyish to blackish. Fruit bodies of this fungus and of its relative *Fomes fomentarius* served once as fuel. In poor mountainous regions fruiting bodies of the latter used to be processed into fine, leathery sheets from which caps and waistcoats were made.

5

6

Family: Hydnaceae

1 *Sarcodon imbricatus* (syn. *Hydnum imbricatum*). Shallow, funnel-shaped cap with rim inrolled when young, 6—18 cm wide, brownish to grey-brown, thickly covered with large, black-grey scales, thickest in centre. Underside of cap thickly covered with greyish to brownish bristles. Grows in coniferous woods, especially pine-woods, in late summer and autumn. In places used for preparing soups and sauces. Only young specimens are suitable, old ones tough.

Family: Clavariaceae

2 *Ramaria flava* (syn. *Clavaria aurea*). Edible species with dense coral-like tufts of fruiting bodies. Distinguishable from other inedible *Ramaria* species by yellow colour of branches which do not turn red on bruised spots. The stalk and flesh are white. In places, especially in warm regions, it occurs abundantly in forests at

beginning of autumn and end of summer. Related *Sparassis crispa* is edible. Its fruiting body formed by flattened undulate branchlets weighs up to several kilograms.

Family: Boletaceae

3 *Boletus felleus* (syn. *Tylopilus felleus*). May easily be mistaken for edible boletus. Differs from it by more striking olive-brown network on stipe. Under surface pinkish, when bruised turning rusty brown. Hot bitter taste, quite inedible, even if not poisonous. Abundant forest mushroom, especially in coniferous woods in higher altitudes; in lowlands and deciduous woods occurs only occasionally.

4 Edible Boletus *Boletus edulis*. Most sought after and most frequent of three similar boleti. Pine boletus and oak boletus are differentiated, apart from colouring, by symbiosis with roots of different trees. Stipe of edible boletus has white network in upper part and the smooth cap is pale brown; more frequent summer oak boletus has network with large mesh on whole of stipe; pine boletus has fine, thick network. Edible boletus is found especially in pine-woods from July to October, from lowlands to mountains; oak boletus from spring to September in deciduous forests, occasionally under other trees; pine boletus grows during summer as well as in autumn in sandy pine-woods, rarely in other woods in lower altitudes.

5 *Boletus luteus* (syn. *Ixocomus luteus*). Chocolate brown to brownish-yellow cap with easily peelable, membranous skin. In wet weather stickily slimy; shiny and smooth when dry. Young fruit bodies have cap connected with stalk by a membranous skin (volva). After the cap has burst through, the remains of volva appear as a ruff-like ring on the stipe. Stipe above ring whitish-yellow, with a darker speckling. Found in grassy places at outskirts of pine forests, usually during whole summer and autumn, from lowlands to mountains. Excellent edible species.

6 *Boletus chrysenteron.* Cap of young fruiting bodies dark brown, smooth, of older ones yellow-brown with an irregular pattern of reddish cracks. Stalk relatively thin, dirty yellow to yellow-brown with touch of red. Under surface yellow, later olive, taking on a blue tint when bruised. Frequent summer and autumnal mushroom. Grows in all woods, more abundant in pine-woods, from lowlands to foothills. Frequently sought after but not very valuable due to considerable fragility.

6

5

4

Family: Boletaceae

1 *Boletus scaber.* Fleshy cap greyish to dark brown, often cracked in dry conditions, pulp watery whitish, early becomes soft; under surface greyish to buff, also soon becoming soft. Stalk long, tough, whitish to brownish-grey, fibrous, covered with tiny blackish scales, flesh when cut turns faintly rosy. In summer and autumn found frequently under birches or aspens.

2 *Boletus aurantiacus.* Fruit body with dark orange to maroon cap. Stipe long, tough, white to greyish, at first covered with whitish, later with reddish to brownish flaky scales. White flesh turns greyish to black. Occurs abundantly in woodland of various types but usually under aspen and birch. Grows from summer to autumn from lowlands to mountains. A similar species, *Boletus testaceoscaber,* has lighter, rather orange cap; young fruiting bodies have blackish scales on stipe.

Family: Cantharellaceae

3 Chanterelle *Cantharellus cibarius.* Young fruit bodies with a convex cap: as it matures, the margins grow up to form a shallow funnel shape. Whole fruit bodies almost yolk yellow, flesh whitish to yellowish. Found from summer to autumn very abundantly in coniferous woods, most frequently in pine-woods. Sought after for preparing fried dishes and pickling in vinegar.

Family: Agaricaceae

4 *Agaricus campestris.* Young fruit bodies have elongated globose cap, later fibrous, brownish and scaly. Whitish flesh; the gills beneath pinkish, maturing to chocolate brown. Whitish stalk with conspicuous ring encircling it in upper third. Never has sheath at base of stalk as is characteristic of deadly poisonous species such as Fool's Mushroom (*Amanita verna*) and

4

5

6

Avenging Angel (*Amanita virosa*). Both differ from *Agaricus campestris* by always having white gills and the fact that they grow largely under deciduous trees. *Agaricus campestris* is found in grassy places, mostly out of woods. In forests, especially spruce-woods, it is replaced by Horse Mushroom (*Agaricus arvensis*).

Family: Lepiotaceae

5 Parasol Mushroom *Lepiota procera*. Stalk up to 35 cm high; cap at first convex, sometimes with small central swelling or umbo, later widely expanded, brownish with torn scales on surface. Flesh and gills white or whitish. Bulbous based stalk has a loose ring. Grows from summer to autumn in spruce-woods but also in other conif-

erous or mixed forests and in grassy places from lowlands to mountains. Commonly prepared in various ways for its attractive meaty flavour.

Family: Tricholomataceae

6 St. Georges Mushroom *Tricholoma gambosum*. Popular spring delicacy; grows from April in grass or sparse woods under deciduous trees and shrubs. Cap whitish, yellowish to brownish, gills white or grey-yellow. Short cylindrical whitish stipe. Flesh has a mealy taste and smell. Young fruiting bodies easily mistaken for poisonous *Rhodophyllus sinuatus* (syn. *Entoloma lividum*) which, however, does not grow until summer and has salmon-pink gills when mature.

Family: Russulaceae

1 *Russula cyanoxantha*. Cap violet, green, violet-green or greenish with violet tint. Flesh whitish, gills white to yellowish, flexible and not brittle, unlike other members of this genus. Grows abundantly in summer and autumn in mixed or deciduous woods, from lowlands to foothills. Suitable mainly for preparing soups and sauces and for pickling in vinegar in a mixture containing boleti.

2 Sickener *Russula emetica*. Strikingly red cap hardly confusable with edible mushrooms. Young fruiting body has convex cap, old ones flattened, often shallowly concave in centre. Gills and stipe white to light yellowish, flesh whitish. May cause vomiting if eaten raw. Edible when cooked, but best avoided. Found from summer to autumn in all woods with acid soils, especially in mixed and coniferous forests.

3 Saffron Milk Cap *Lactarius deliciosus*. Young fruiting bodies have convex cap, in maturity expanded, concave in centre, red-orange, as a rule with several dark, mostly green, concentric circles. When cut, flesh releases orange milk, gills become greenish on bruising. Grows mainly in autumn in grassy places in coniferous woods, especially in young spruce-woods. Commonly pickled in vinegar for its characteristic spicy taste. It can hardly be confused with inedible *Lactarius torminosus* which exudes white milk and mostly grows under birches.

Family: Amanitaceae

4 Death Cap *Amanita phalloides*. Most poisonous European mushroom. Yellow-green, pure green or brown-green cap is convex at first, later flattened. Stipe, flesh and gills whitish to greenish. Stipe with white skirt-like ring has a cup-shaped base and a conspicuous whitish to greyish sheath, torn at tips. Grows quite abundantly in summer and autumn in deciduous or mixed woods in warmer regions, in coniferous forests especially under pines. Inconspicuous, rather sweetish, treacherous taste. Contains at least two deadly poisonous substances.

5 Blusher *Amanita rubescens*. Fleshy cap is rose to maroon with brownish warty scales. When cut, the flesh is reddish, gills whitish with pink tint. Strong, slender stalk with swollen base. Beneath the cap there is flared whitish to grey-rose ring, usually thickly grooved on upper side. Distinguishable from similar inedible toadstools by reddening of pulp and by ring grooving. *Amanita rubescens* grows in summer and autumn from lowlands to mountains in all types of forests, especially under spruces.

6 Fly Agaric *Amanita muscaria*. Much less poisonous than Death Cap or Avenging Angel, being of rather intoxicating character. Cap ornamented with whitish or yellowish warty patches on coral-red surface. Flesh and gills whitish to yellowish, stalk white, with concentric rings of volva remains at base. Ungrooved wide ring under cap. Summer to late autumn in coniferous and birch woods.

Family: Coprinaceae

1 *Coprinus micaceus.* Abundant mushroom, growing in gregarious clusters. Occurs on stumps near human dwellings, in gardens, orchards, parks and forests. Cap firstly ovoid, later bell-shaped, often sprinkled with minute, shiny granules. Gills at first white, soon turning grey, later dark brown. Stalk thin, white, without ring. Ripe fruit bodies tend to disintegrate or 'melt' into slimy black substance. Similar *Coprinus* species may be encountered especially near or on old compost and manure heaps etc.

Order: Gasteromycetales

Family: Sclerodermataceae

2 Earth Ball *Scleroderma aurantium* (syn. *S. citrinum*). Roughly spherical fruiting bodies 3—10 cm. in diameter, sit on the surface of usually peaty soil. Flesh at first whitish, when cut turns pink with violet tint. Young fruiting bodies edible: later become hard and crack into darker scales disclosing the brighter cortical layer. Inside filled with violet-blackish, later black flesh. Finally turns into a black pasty matter that dries up into greyish dust, full of spores. Grows in woods, more often on sandy soils, from summer to autumn.

Family: Lycoperdaceae

3 Warted Puffball *Lycoperdon perlatum* (syn. *L. gemmatum*). Narrowed bases of pear-shaped fruiting bodies grow from soil. Surface of young body whitish or creamy, yellowish with pointed warts. Ripe fruiting body smooth with irregularly round aperture on top; when pressed or stepped on, a cloud of brownish spores is puffed out of this opening. Summer and autumnal, growing from lowlands high up to mountains, in meadows, pastures and spruce-woods, often in great numbers. Young fruit bodies with white flesh edible.

4 *Bovista plumbea.* Young fruiting bodies almost globose, slightly compressed on top; outer surface whitish, inside pure white. Ripe ones dark grey, filled with brown dust-like spore mass; when pressed, spores fly out through oval opening on top. In summer and autumn found abundantly in grassy places, at the edges of meadows and pastures and on the outskirts of forests, from lowlands to mountains. Edible when young; has excellent delicate taste.

Family: Geastraceae

5 *Geastrum fimbriatum.* Young fruiting bodies more or less globose; in maturity outer layer cracks into four ray-like segments which turn inside out thrusting up the ovoid fruiting 'capsule' on a short stem-like neck. Grows in summer and autumn from lowlands to mountains with other species of earth-stars, often in groups, especially in spruce-woods. Unsuitable for eating.

Family: Phallaceae

6 Stinkhorn *Phallus impudicus.* Conspicuous for its appearance and in maturity also for the disgusting smell of decaying flesh. Slightly reminiscent of morel with long, cylindrical stalk and conical, pitted cap. Globular fruiting bodies rather resemble small puffballs when young as they are covered with white-skinned jelly-like layer. In mature specimens only conspicuous sheath at stalk base remains of this layer. Stalk up to 25 cm high, thickly and shallowly porous. Cap covered with olive greenish slime which attracts insects that normally feed on carrion. Grows from summer to autumn in deciduous woods and in gardens on humus-rich soil. Mature fruiting bodies inedible because of bad odour.

6

Lichens

Lichens are also called lichenized fungi. In lichens a fungus tissue lives in a symbiotic association with an alga. This dual association is different from the saprophytic, parasitic or symbiotic properties of fungi.

Even though both fungi and lichens can live independently, albeit with difficulty, it is only when the hyphae of fungi are joined with the cells of algae that the typical thallus of a lichen is formed. The symbiotic association of fungus and alga is also of physiological importance. Although the fungus takes the products of photosynthesis from the alga, it also provides the latter with water and essential salts. Symbiosis is distinguished by certain products of the metabolism, for example lichen acids, which neither the fungus nor the alga is able to produce by itself — these are formed in the thallus or plant body of the lichen.

In most lichens the fungal component, called the mycobiont, is generally composed of ascomycetes; in tropical regions it also contains basidiomycetes. The algal component, phycobiont, may consist of green algae, especially Chlorococcales, or blue-green algae, for example colonies of *Nostoc* or *Chrococcus* sp. Despite their great diversity of shapes, lichens may be roughly divided into three groups: having a crusty thallus, laminar thallus or forked thallus. The internal structure of lichens is also very diverse but usually the fungal component prevails. The tangled hyphae of the fungus form a dense outer layer. Beneath this is a looser layer of fungal fibres and algae, then a loose layer of fungal fibres and often, on the bottom, another layer of thickly intertwined fungal fibres from which individual fibres or clumps of fibres grow into the substrate on which the lichen lives.

The propagating bodies of the fungus are important in the classification of lichens, because the alga remains in a vegetative state. This explains why lichens are called lichenized fungi. The fungal component may be classified according to the fruiting body in the system of fungi, but the lichen thallus can be formed only if the fungus spores develop into fibres that meet up with the respective alga.

Lichens may be found in widely diverse situations and on varied substrates. They commonly grow on the bark of trees, on rotting wood, on rocks, boulders and walls. Individual species sometimes have special requirements, some growing only on limestone rocks, others only on siliceous substrates. Some lichens may be found high up in the mountains, others in lowland country; some species prefer sunny locations, others need habitats that are shaded and damp. Different species grow on broad-leaved

Fig. 1. The striking *Usnea florida* cannot escape notice. It is an extremely sensitive indicator of atmospheric pollution in the mountains.

Fig. 2. The thalli of the various species of *Cladonia* differ in shape as well as colour. *Left: Cladonia sylvatica; right: Cladonia coccifera.*

trees and on the bark of conifers. Most European lichens are extremely sensitive to atmospheric pollution.

Lichens growing on the bark of fruit trees are considered harmful for they may have a detrimental effect on the respiration of the tree as well as promoting dampness and the presence of harmful insects. In Scandinavia ground lichen, especially Reindeer Moss (*Cladonia rangiferina*), are eaten by reindeer, in deserts they may serve as food for people. In the Bible we are told of the 'manna' that was miraculously supplied to the Israelites on their journey through the desert — possibly the thalli of *Lecanora esculenta* that had been uprooted and blown there by the wind.

Roccella tinctoria, which grows on the Mediterranean coast, *Ochrolechia tartarea* and *O. parella*, lichens of the tundra, yield compounds that are used to make the colouring matter litmus and orcein. Lichens also yield polysaccharides and alcohol. They are used in the perfume industry in some countries, and some species even produce substances with antibiotic properties. Lichens also contain several specific compounds that are not found in other organisms.

Fig. 3. A young fruiting body of *Evernia prunastri* growing on the bark of a tree.

75

Division: **Lichens**—Lichenes

Class: Ascolichenes

Family: Buelliaceae

1 *Rhizocarpon geographicum.* Appears as yellow-green, black striated patches on non-limestone rocks. Irregularly lobed thalluses form striking designs resembling maps. Thin, corticular thallus contains in addition to algal cells also hyphae of an Ascomycetes. (Basidiomycetes are a component of tropical lichens.) Tiny fruit bodies of fungal component are black with multicellular spores. Grows mainly in mountains, most often on granite boulders.

2 *Cladonia arbuscula* (syn. *C. sylvatica*). Very abundant species, resembling Reindeer Moss from which it differs especially in colouring; it is yellow-green or straw-yellow, its podetia are narrower and slightly brownish at the shoot ends. Fungal component sometimes forms tiny maroon thalluses on twig tips. Grows in similar places as reindeer moss, together often forming extensive carpets.

3 Reindeer Moss *Cladonia rangiferina.* Forms conspicuous whitish or greyish bushes, abundantly branched. Twigs bent to one side, with brownish tips. Often grows in great quantity in dry pine-woods and on heathland, from lowlands to mountains. Can survive long periods of drought; in rain takes in moisture very quickly again.

4 *Cladonia fimbriata.* 1—3 cm high cups, olive or grey-green on upper side, whitish on under side, grow from a basal scaly podetium. Fungal component forms short-stalked, brownish fruit bodies on margins of cups. Cup surface covered with powdery segments, containing alga cells wound around with fungal hyphae. Grows on dry sites, in open woods, heathlands, on decayed stumps and mossy rocks from lowlands to mountains. Related species have fungal fruit bodies scarlet-red and cup rims strikingly notched.

Family: Peltigeraceae

5 *Peltigera canina.* Thallus broadly lobed, sometimes with lobes up to 5 cm wide, upper side grey-white or brownish, finely felt-like, underside whitish, covered with numerous bunches of fungal rhizoids. Fruiting bodies of fungal component brown, tubular, erect at end of lobes. Common lichen from lowlands high up to mountains. Grows in sunny spots, on mossy rocks, on putrefying trunks as well as in meadows.

Family: Parmeliaceae

6 *Hypogymnia physodes* (syn. *Parmelia physodes*). Probably the most frequently found lichen. Its rosette-like thallus is greyish to grey-green on upper surface, dark brown to black on underside, bordered with white. Fruiting bodies of fungal component appear only rarely. Grows abundantly from lowlands to foothills. In suitable places forms extensive coatings on tree trunks and branches. Also grows on stumps, dead trunks, less often on rocks and earth.

7 Iceland Moss *Cetraria islandica.* Thallus chestnut to dark brown, sinuately branched, spiny margined, ascending, up to 10 cm high, or more. Grows on moorland and heathland and in forests and peat-bogs; indicator of poor soils.

Family: Usneaceae

8 *Evernia prunastri.* Grows from lowlands to mountains on bark of deciduous trees, old shrubs, also on trunks of felled trees, in orchards, parks, gardens and open woods; abundant everywhere, rare only on rocks. Soft thallus is many-branched, often more or less pendent, grey-green to yellow-green, lighter on underside, white-spotted edges and upper side. Similar species, *Evernia furfuracea,* with black-violet underside of thallus, grows in similar places and on rocks and walls at higher altitudes.

Family: Teloschistaceae

9 *Xanthoria parietina.* Brightly coloured thalluses are light to orange-yellow, arranged in rosettes, forming neat patches on trees, rocks and walls. Dish-like fruiting bodies of fungal component are very frequently seen. Grows from lowlands to mountains, but particularly near the sea.

Bryophytes—Mosses and Liverworts

Mosses and liverworts (Bryopsida, Marchantiopsida) are green, mostly ground-dwelling plants that have much in common with other higher green plants, having spore-bearing pteridophytes and gymnosperms as well as angiosperms. They contain chlorophyll and so are capable of photosynthesis, the product of this process being the starch found in liverwort oil. However, their external resemblance to higher plants is deceptive. A moss plant does not have true roots, only underground root-like structures called rhizoids. Even its stem is not a true stem

Fig. 1. *Polytrichum commune* is the most robust European moss, reaching a height of 40 cm. The capsule is closed by a lid covered by a calyptra that falls at maturity.

Fig. 2. Section of the capsule of *Polytrichum commune*. Beneath the lid are locules separated by partitions and filled with spores.

Fig. 3. The stem as well as the branches of *Sphagnum palustre* are covered with minute leaves.

for it has few differentiated tissues, lacks true vascular bundles and the leaves are generally composed of only a single layer of cells. Sometimes the thallus is not differentiated into a stem and leaves at all, as in Anthocerotopsida and some liverworts. The propagating and reproductive organs, on the other hand, resemble those of pteridophytes.

Monoecious species have both male and female sex organs in the same individual; dioecious species have male reproductive organs in one individual and female organs in another. Following fertilization, an asexual sporophore develops, connected to the plant by a stalk through which it draws nutritive substances. This filamentous stalk is terminated by a capsule containing spores. On germination, each spore produces a protonema from which the plant proper grows — this is called the sexual stage.

Bryophytes have no medicinal or edible uses by people. However, clumps of moss do have an extremely beneficial effect on the amount of water in the soil. Mosses have no roots and thus absorb very little moisture from the soil; furthermore, they prevent excessive evaporation of water from the soil. Sphagnums (Sphagnidae) are also important for many other reasons. They grow on poor soils in districts with great amounts of rainfall, or with plenty of underground water. Sphagnums will grow only above the water level; below it they die and partially decompose, forming a small layer of peat every year. In a single year they grow up to 1 cm above ground, and in that same period the layer of peat is increased by an equal amount below the water level because of the inability of decomposition to take place without the access of air. This process has been going on for centuries, which should give one some idea of the great depth of the layers of peat that have formed on high moors. Other, undemanding plants that grow in these localities also contribute to the formation of peat, for example sedges (*Carex*), cotton-grass (*Eriophorum*) and rushes (*Juncus*).

Extracted peat is a very important product. In gardening it is used to lighten the soil. In health hydros it is used in peat baths and body packs. Natural moors are reservoirs of water for the creation of rivers, and these also have a determining effect on the climate.

Bryophytes may be found in widely diverse situations. Liverworts generally grow in damp and shady places, but are also found on rocks, in dry soil and on the bark of trees. Some even grow in ponds, for example *Riccia fluitans*. Stubble

Fig. 4. The reproductive organs of *Marchantia polymorpha* are on stalks; the female ones are star-shaped, the male organs umbrella-shaped. Vegetative propagation is by tiny bodies embedded in shallow cups.

and damp fields are the preferred habitat of *Anthoceros punctatus*, the thalli of which are marked with black dots — mucilaginous cells inside which the blue-green alga *Nostoc* lives in symbiosis.

Mosses also occur in diverse localities, on tree trunks and stumps, on rocks, on walls and roofs and in woodland as well as meadow soils. They include species that form floating clumps in woodland streams, such as *Fontinalis antipyretica*, as well as ones that grow in bogs, at the edge of water and in many other places.

It is estimated that there are some 25,000 species of bryophytes. Their differentiation into families is based on the morphology of the capsules and on the anatomical structure of the leaves.

Division: **Mosses and Liverworts**—Bryophyta

Class: **Liverworts**—Hepaticopsida

Family: Marchantiaceae

1 *Marchantia polymorpha*. Lamellar thallus broadly ribbon-shaped, forked, ground hugging. The upper side has conspicuous air chambers just beneath the surface, each having a breathing pore. Dioecious plant with sexual organs on stalked discs; male discs irregularly lobular, female ones star-shaped. Vegetative propagation by special tiny bodies (*gemmae*) embedded in shallow cups. Forms dark green coatings everywhere in moist places; particularly in gardens and greenhouses. Grows from lowlands to mountains in sunny or semi-shaded places.

Class: **Mosses**—Bryopsida (syn. Musci)

Subclass: Sphagnidae

Family: Sphagnaceae

2 *Sphagnum palustre*. Requires plenty of light as do majority of bog-mosses. Forms soft pale green carpets. Stems 10—40 cm high with clustered side branches rosetted towards the tips; more frequently than in other bog-mosses stem bears round brown capsules at apex which explode on ripening. All members of this genus are important for creation of moss peat.

Subclass: **True Mosses**—Bryidae

Family: Polytrichaceae

3 *Polytrichum commune*. Stout moss whose simple, erect stems can reach a length of 25 cm. Sharply notched leaflets thickly overlap and cover stem during dry spells, standing out and apart in wet weather. Red stalk about 10 cm long. Large capsule covered with hairy, yellow to reddish brown calyptra. Grows in mountains, hill country, heathland, along forest streams and in clearings. Tiny relative *Polytrichum formosum* is more frequent in lowlands. Its leaves stand apart even during dry conditions.

Family: Dicranaceae

4 *Dicranum scoparium.* Erect stems up to 10 cm high, thickly set with sickle-bent, blunt leaflets, finely notched at tip. Stems 2—4 cm high, reddish, with brown, cylindrical, slightly bent capsule having a long-beaked reddish lid. Cap overlaps from lid to capsule. A moss of coniferous woods, growing abundantly on ground, tree stumps, trunks, boulders and rocks, from lowlands to mountains.

Family: Ditrichaceae

5 *Ceratodon purpureus.* Erect stems, sparsely covered with narrow, finely pointed leaves, having inrolled margins; they twist up together in dry weather. Stalk shiny dark red, erect at first, but leaning over horizontally as the capsule ripens. Cap overlaps lid and covers over half of capsule. Grows abundantly from lowlands to mountains, on burnt ground, in clearings, on heathland, rocks and walls.

Family: Leucobryaceae

6 *Leucobryum glaucum.* Forms dense rounded hummocks of distinctive grey-green foliage. Stems bear entire leaves with upturned rim that lack a central rib. Dioecious moss, only very rarely fruitful; female plants have dark purple stems 1—2 cm high. Grows in moist woods and on moorland.

Family: Funariaceae

1 *Funaria hygrometrica*. Grows on bare ground, heathland, walls and roofs, and is one of the first colonizers on burnt ground. Simple stems are not more than 3 cm high, upper leaves rolled and bud-like when dry, short-pointed and entire. Sporophyte stalk is yellow to red, twisted, nodding at the tip with a grooved brown capsule.

Family: Bryaceae

2 *Bryum argenteum*. Tiny moss forming pale to silvery-green cushions. Stems only 1—2 cm high with ovate and pointed leaves. Pendent capsule is red-brown, elongated cylindrical to ovoid, with small pointed lid; the short (about 1 cm) stalk is also red. Grows from lowlands to foothills but is more frequent in lower altitudes on walls, rocks, along roads, among paving-stones and in similar places. It is one of the very few mosses found in big cities.

Family: Mniaceae

3 *Mnium punctatum*. This and other species of *Mnium* are frequent from lowlands to high up in mountains. Reddish stems are up to 5 cm high with relatively large, almost rounded leaves which are covered with pellucid dots. Stalk 2—4 cm high, usually reddish, at top yellow, with drooping or horizontal capsule. Capsule with elongated and sharply beaked lid and a shiny brown cap. Grows abundantly in moist woods, on bank of forest streams and in mountains. Often fertile.

5

6

Family: Hypnaceae

4 *Pleurozium schreberi* (syn. *Hypnum schreberi*). Stems red, up to 15 cm long, ascending, pinnately branched, in two regular rows; branches at top recurving. Leaves overlapping, convex, broadly ovate, with double veins; those on branches are smaller than on main stems. Dioecious, fertile only in places. Then a thin, corrugated red stalk with elongated, curved capsule develops on female plant. Grows not only in coniferous and mixed forests but also in meadows, on grassy slopes and rocks where acid conditions are found.

Family: Hylocomiaceae

5 *Hylocomium splendens.* Stems red, up to 20 cm long, rigid, bi- to tripinnately branched, conspicuously flattened. Main stem leaves sessile, overlapping, ovate, elongated, abruptly tapering to long points; margins of upper third finely serrate; leaves of branches oval, smaller, abruptly tapering to a fine point, serrate. Dioecious species; female plant up to 4 cm high, with pendent, ovoid capsules. Grows in forests, on grassy slopes, among rocks overgrown with vegetation and in meadows. Often fertile.

Family: Rhytidiaceae

6 *Rhytidiadelphus triquetrus.* Reddish stems are densely leaved, up to 15 cm long, erect or semi-prostrate, irregularly branched. Leaves lanceolate, pointed, spreading, in upper part finely serrate and grooved. Dioecious plant, stalk about 2—5 cm high, sinuously corrugated, red. Capsule shortly ovate, pendent, red, with warty navel-shaped lid. Common in shady places in mixed forests, especially on limestone in spruce-beech growths; also on grassy slopes, sand dunes and sometimes on moorland.

Pteridophytes—Clubmosses, Horsetails and Ferns

The Ginkgo (*Ginkgo biloba*) could be considered a 'living fossil' for it has been part of the world's flora for 200 million years. Even further back, in the Palaeozoic era, the typical palaeophytic formations were 'carboniferous forests', composed of tree-like clubmosses, horsetails and ferns. Over the long period of 350 million years, these sporophytes evolved, died out or adapted to the change from life in water and bogs to life on dry land.

The pteridophytes changed over time. Their tree-like forms were replaced by low herbaceous plants that were sometimes even prostrate but nevertheless retained many of their distinguishing features. First and foremost of these is their manner of propagation in a damp environment.

The plant bodies of clubmosses, horsetails and ferns are the asexual phase, which is entirely independent of the sexual phase. These plant bodies are already clearly differentiated into a root, stem and leaves and hence also have a relatively complicated morphological and anatomical structure. Running throughout the entire body, a conductive system of vascular tissues distributes water and food around the body. Be-

sides leaves which manufacture food, the plants also have leaves called sporophylls that develop sporangia. Sometimes the spore-bearing leaves are arranged in a cone-like cluster.

Pteridophytes, then, are ancient sporophytes that evolved in the Palaeozoic period and apparently attained the peak of their development in the Carboniferous period. We shall deal with the more common present-day examples of European clubmosses, horsetails and ferns later in this book, but here let us take at least a passing look at some of the rarer and less conspicuous groups. Growing among the Palaeozoic, extinct clubmosses were tree-like sigillarias and lepidodendrons. Many had leaves with a short tongue (lingula) on the upperside and this same feature may still be found on present-day selaginellas, moss-like plants that grow in mountains. Another group survived only in damp places or directly in water. These are the rare *Isoëtes*, with awl-shaped leaves less than 20 cm long, that are found growing on the floors of mountain lakes.

You would not find such curious groups among the horsetails, but if you came across a mass of *Equisetum telmateia*, in which most of the plants will be nearly 2 m high, you would probably get a better, albeit remote, idea of what the tree-like ancestors of present-day species looked like.

Present-day ferns are not as large as their ancestors. In the tropics, however, they still find conditions favourable for the growth and development of immensely large fronds. Such ferns — up to 20 m high, with leaves up to 3 m long — are to be found in Australia (*Alsophila*) and South America (*Cyathea*). However, ferns also include among their number dwarf species only 5 cm high, more like a liverwort or moss in appearance, that grow on rocks. They are aptly named *Hymenophyllum*, meaning membranous-leaved, for their leaves are composed of only a single layer of cells.

Last but not least, ferns also include plants that long ago gave up life on dry land and went back to living in water. Many people are acquainted with the water-fern *Salvinia* as a plant grown in aquariums. Only in an aquarium, hardly ever in the wild, will you see the popular *Marsilea*. In special aquarist shops one may also purchase *Azolla caroliniana*, which spreads rapidly by vegetative means, soon covering the surface of the aquarium with its leaves.

Fig. 1. *Isoëtes lacustris* is a rare relict of extinct Palaeozoic pteridophytes that grows on the floor of mountain lakes.

Fig. 2. The young leaves of Common Brake (*Pteridium aquilinum*) are characteristically spirally coiled, opening into coarse flat fronds when they mature. Clearly evident in a cross-section of the stem is the typical pattern of the cavity with its vascular bundles.

Division: **Vascular Plants**—Tracheophyta

Sub-division: Pteridophytina

Class: **Clubmosses**—Lycopodiopsida

Family: Lycopodiaceae

1 Stag's-horn Clubmoss *Lycopodium clavatum.* Creeping stems of up to 1 m long, forked into shorter erect stalks. Leaves linear lanceolate, entire to irregularly notched, hairy. Spore-bearing spikes arranged usually in pairs on thin stalks with tiny, sessile leaflets. Sporophylls widely ovate, with colourless, soft spicule. Grows in open forests, on heathland and among rocks in mountains, from lowlands to mountains. Sporangia ripen from June to August.

Family: Huperziaceae

2 Fir Clubmoss *Lycopodium selago* (syn. *Huperzia selago*). Erect, tufted, branched stems up to 25 cm high. Leaves erect, spreading, soft, linear-lanceolate, entire. Sporangia do not form terminal spikes; they are placed mostly in upper part of stem on sporophylls, similar to other leaflets. Often produces bulbils in leaf axils at the end of branches. Grows in humid, shady woods, among rocks and on ledges, particularly in mountains. Sporangia mature from July to October.

Class: **Horsetails**—Sphenopsida (syn. Equisetopsida)

Family: Equisetaceae

3 Common Horsetail *Equisetum arvense.* Species with two types of stems: spring stem terminates in spore-bearing spike, summer stem sterile. Spring stems are 10—20 cm high, yellowish to brownish, with cylindrical, slightly inflated, light green, notched sheaths. Spore-bearing spike up to 3 cm long, brownish; after spores are released in March and April, spring stems die. Summer stems about 50 cm high, with distinct ribs. Both stems and branches have ribbed brownish sheaths. Common weed in fields and gardens, by the roadside and in open woods from lowlands to mountains.

4 Wood Horsetail *Equisetum sylvaticum.* Stems of two types: spring stem up to 50 cm high, at first wax-pink, during ripening of sporangia turns green, later resembles summer stems. These grow almost simultaneously with spring stems; are regularly branched, branches are slender and pendent and further branched. Sheaths slightly inflated, funnel-shaped, teeth tinted with red. Grows gregariously in moist places in forests from lowlands to mountains on poor soils. Sporangia ripen from April to June.

1   2

5 Water Horsetail *Equisetum fluviatile.* Robust stems over 1 m high with fine ribs, often unbranched and shiny, submerged parts maroon. Sessile sheaths glossy, lower ones reddish, upper green with black, awl-shaped teeth bordered with white. Spore-bearing spike short and ovoid. Sporangia mature from May to July. Grows from lowlands to mountains, in wet places, bogs, and on muddy banks of rivers and lakes.

Class: **Ferns**—Filicopsida (syn. Polypodiopsida)

Subclass: Ophioglossidae

Family: Ophioglossaceae

6 Adder's Tongue Fern *Ophioglossum vulgatum.* Small fern, about 8—20 cm high, with underground rhizome and one single leaf. Sterile part of leaf leathery, ovoid, entire, yellow-green and mat-shiny; spore-bearing part with sporangia, arranged in two parallel rows close together. Sporangia ripen from June to August. Grows in marshy and mountain meadows, and moist clearings in woods, more frequently on limestone. A very small form (*O. lusitanicum*) is found on grassy cliff tops in the Channel Isles and Scilly Isles and in Mediterranean regions.

4

5

3

6

Family: Ophioglossaceae

1 Common Moonwort *Botrychium lunaria.*
Small fern up to 5—15 cm or more high. Sterile
part of single leaf simply pinnate, spore-bearing
part bi- to tripinnate. Sterile part composed of
4—7 or more pairs of fan-shaped, entire or sca-
lopped, leathery segments. Spore-bearing part
long-stalked, terminating with sporangia arranged in two rows on linear segments. Sporangia yellow-brown, later of cinnamon shade,
ripen from May to June. Grows from lowlands
to high up in the mountains, in meadows, pastures and among rocks; generally of localized
distribution.

Subclass: Polypodiidae

Order: Polypodiales

Family: Matteuciaceae

2 Ostrich Fern *Matteuccia struthiopteris* (syn.
Struthiopteris germanica). Fan up to 150 cm

high, sterile leaves, grows from robust rhizome.
Blades simply pinnate, segments fine, linear-
lanceolate. Spore leaves only 50—60 cm high,
grow in centre of sterile fronds and have segments at first rolled, later unrolled. Sori ripen
from June to August. Grows in moist places,
along streams and rivers, in forests, from lowlands to mountains. Also cultivated for ornament.

Family: Blechnaceae

3 Hard Fern *Blechnum spicant.* A fern with
leaves of two types; the sterile ones over-win-
tering, leathery, pinnately divided to mid-rib.
Segments dark green, linear-lanceolate, entire.
Non-leafy sporophylls, growing from centre of
tuft, are longer, erect, up to 40 cm high, with interrupted pinnate to linear segments, bearing
sori which ripen from July to September.
Grows, often gregariously, in woods, on moors,
heaths, mountain grassland and among rocks.

Family: Aspidiaceae (syn. Dryopteridaceae)

4 Male Fern *Dryopteris filix-mas.* Robust fern over 1 m high, with rusty-scaly rhizome. Leaf stalks bearing pale brown scales. Leaf blade deeply pinnately divided, pinnules dark green, lighter on underside, with toothed margins. Large sori adhere to mid-rib of pinnules; indusia kidney-shaped. Sporangia ripen from June to September. Grows in shady woods, among boulders and in hedgerows, from lowlands to mountains.

5 Beech Fern *Thelypteris phegopteris* (syn. *Phegopteris polypodioides*). Long-stalked leaves, up to 10—30 cm or more high, grow from long rhizome. Blades simply pinnate, lanceolate leaflets deeply pinnately lobed, more or less hairy. Conspicuous backward slant of lowest pair of leaves and fusion of lowest pinnules with mid-rib aid in identifying this fern. Sori rounded, light brown, on border of pinnules; no indusia. Sporangia ripen in June and July. Grows in moist, shady woods, among rocks and on banks of forest streams, from lowlands to mountains.

Family: Athyriaceae

6 Brittle Bladder Fern *Cystopteris fragilis.* Long-stalked fronds, 8—25 cm or more high, grow from short rhizome. Fragile, dark brown petioles usually shorter than bipinnate blades, with deeply lobed and notched leaflets; sori in two rows either side of pinnule mid-rib. Sporangia ovoid pointed, ripening from June to September. Grows on walls, rocks and screes, also in shady woods, from lowlands to mountains. Only found in the north and west of Great Britain.

4

5

6

Family: Athyriaceae

1 Lady Fern *Athyrium filix-femina.* Leaves 20—100 cm or more high, with stalk and mid-rib often purplish and bearing a few chaffy scales. Grows from short, dark brown, scaly rhizome. Freshly green, bi- to tripinnate leaves with alternate, lanceolate, long-pointed leaflets; pinnules ovate to lanceolate, toothed. Margins of pinnules with crescent or kidney-shaped sori; sporangia ripen from July to September. Grows abundantly and often gregariously from lowlands to mountains, in moist forests, and shady places on acid soils.

Family: Aspleniaceae

2 Forked Spleenwort *Asplenium septentrionale.* Small evergreen fern, 4—15 cm high, short, black-brown scaly rhizome and narrow blades, black-brown at base. Blades have slender, forked pinnules. Sori cover almost whole under surface of pinnules. Sporangia ripen from June to October. Grows in sunny places, in cracks of acid rocks, rarely on walls, from lowlands to mountains. Rare in Britain.

3 Wall Rue *Asplenium ruta-muraria.* Long-stalked evergreen leaves, bipinnate, dark green, up to 3—12 cm high, grow from creeping rootstock. Pinnules obovate to lanceolate with crenate or dentate margins. Linear, coalescent sori ripen from June to October. Grows in cracks of rocks, walls, and screes, almost always on limestone, from lowlands to mountains. Related Maidenhair Spleenwort, *A. trichomanes*, has leaves simply pinnate and oval or oblong pinnules.

4

5

Family: Pteridaceae

4 Bracken *Pteridium aquilinum.* A deciduous fern up to 2 m high with stout cylindrical petioles up to 1 m long, which grow from thick, black, creeping rhizomes. Blades triangular bito tripinnate, light green, lanceolate to oblong pinnules, lobed at the base, with marginal sori. Sporangia ripen from July to September. Grows gregariously in open woods, especially pinewoods, and on heath and moorland, usually on acid soils, from lowlands to mountains. This fern and its subspecies are distributed all over the world; important cosmopolitan species.

Family: Polypodiaceae

5 Common Polypody *Polypodium vulgare.* Long-petioled evergreen leaves, pinnately divided into alternate, lanceolate and entire, somewhat leathery blunt-tipped pinnules, grow from creeping rhizomes. Two rows of relatively large, rounded sori without indusia on under surface of pinnules. Sporangia ripen from May to September. Grows in woods, on shady, mossy rocks, and on trunks and branches of deciduous trees.

Order: Salviniales

Family: Salviniaceae

6 Water-fern *Salvinia natans.* Tiny floating 'fern'. Stem 5—15 cm long, bears leaves in whorls of three of which two are always floating, short-stalked with undivided blade, tufted with hair-like papillae on upper surface; third leaf transformed into numerous, root-like submerged segments. Sporangia of two types: small male and large female ones, closed in sporocarps. Ripen in August and September. Grows locally, in lakes and slow flowing rivers, mainly in central and southern Europe. Often grown as aquarium plant.

Grasses
and Grass-like Plants

Grasses are a typical example of plants found growing in large communities — in savannahs in tropical regions, in pampas, steppes or prairies in the temperate zone. In Europe, grasses are a familiar sight in the semi-cultivated and cultivated meadows of lowland districts, in mountain meadows and in rolling pastureland. Grasses are distributed throughout the world, from the tropics to the arctic regions of both north and south, from seacoasts to mountain

Fig. 2. Detail of a spikelet of Sweet Vernal-grass: awnless lemma, spiny palea, two feathery stigmas and two pendulous stamens with versatile anthers (most grasses have three stamens).

peaks, in deserts as well as in forests. They are one of the largest families of flowering plants, comprising an estimated 10,000 species.

Grasses are members of the Poaceae family — monocotyledonous herbaceous plants with fibrous roots. The stems, or culms, are unbranched, usually hollow, jointed, cylindrical and firm. Only occasionally do they become woody, for example in bamboo stems used as walking sticks or fishing rods. The leaves of grasses are alternate, without a stalk and sheathed; sometimes there is a small leaf-like outgrowth called the ligule at the point where the leaf blade emerges from the sheath. The inflorescences, often very dense, are composed of spikelets. The fruits are grains, one-seeded achenes with a pericarp closely adhering to the seed coat (testa).

Grasses are important as fodder for domestic animals, in the fresh as well as dried state. For people also they are an important source of food. Rye, wheat, oats, barley, maize, rice and millet are the best-known grasses that are grown as cereals for their starchy grains, which are ground in mills into flour or eaten whole, for example rice. Besides starch, gluten and proteins, spirits, starch sugar, dextrin, vegetable oil and other products are also obtained from grains. Today barley grains are less often used to make flour because barley bread is less tasty than wheat bread and rapidly becomes hard. Barley groats, grits and meal, however, are still popular, and barley is used in the preparation of

Fig. 1. A flowering tuft of Sweet Vernal-grass (*Anthoxanthum odoratum*).

Fig. 3. Detail of a spikelet showing awnless lemma and palea, two feathery stigmas and three stamens.

three-sided stems and those of the rush family (Juncaceae) often have leaves with an undifferentiated upper and under surface. The members of these two families also differ from true grasses in their flowers and fruits. Rushes bear capsules; sedges achenes. Of course, reedbeds composed primarily of the Common Reed (*Phragmites australis*), one of the most robust of European grasses, often contain damp-loving sedges and rushes, and other species of sedges, and perhaps also the Field Woodrush (*Luzula campestris*), often intermingle with the numerous true grasses in drier meadows and pastures.

malted coffee substitutes. However, most barley is now made into malt for use in brewing beer (the grains are allowed to germinate and are then lightly roasted). Oats are used to make ground or rolled oats for oatmeal and muesli. Millet was formerly cultivated much more widely. Nowadays it is used only rarely, mostly as bird-seed.

Many alcoholic beverages are dependent on cereals. What would beer be without malted barley or whisky without rye? Japanese sake and Malaysian arak are well-known alcoholic beverages that are made from rice. Maize, too, is fermented for use in making alcoholic beverages.

Grasses are also sugar-yielding herbaceous plants, the most familiar being sugarcane (*Saccharum officinarum*). Sugar is prepared from the juice obtained from the crushed cane. Excellent Jamaican and Cuban rums are obtained through the distillation of molasses and cane syrups following their fermentation.

The leaves of some grasses have cells that contain fragrant essential oils. *Cymbopogon nardus*, for example, is cultivated in Java, Malaysia and elsewhere for its high concentration of citronella oil, other species of *Cymbopogon* yield other essential oils, and some are used in perfumery.

There are certain common European grass-like plants which, though not true grasses, can readily be mistaken for them because of their resemblance in appearance and habit of growth as well as their occurrence in large masses— namely sedges (*Carex*) and rushes (*Juncus*). These, however, do not have jointed stems. Plants of the sedge family (Cyperaceae) have

Fig. 4. A flowering branching panicle of Common Quaking Grass (*Briza media*).

Subclass: **Monocotyledones**—Butomidae

Family: **Rush**—Juncaceae

1 Field Woodrush *Luzula campestris*. Perennial, tufted herb, up to 15 cm high, with erect stems and shortly creeping rhizomes. Linear leaves have sparse but long white hairs. Tiny flowers in few-flowered panicle, usually nodding. Tepals six, brown, equally long, lanceolate, pointed, with a membranous border. Flowers from March to June. Grows in meadows, open woods and on grassy banks and lawns from lowlands to mountains. The similar hairy woodrush (*L. pilosa*) is larger, with distinctly stalked flowers in a lax cyme and rather more hairy leaves. It is usually found in woods and hedgerows only.

2 Soft Rush *Juncus effusus*. Perennial herb almost 1 metre high, densely tufted. Erect stems filled with spongy pith. Leaves grow direct from rhizome, cylindrical, resembling stems. Inflorescences apparently lateral, emerging below the top of the stem. The apparent stem tip is, in fact, a cylindrical bract. Small, six-lobed flowers are brownish. Flowers from June to August. Grows in damp meadows and near water from lowlands to mountains. *Juncus conglomeratus* is similar, but inflorescence is a dense, rounded head. Jointed Rush (*J. articulatus*) has distinct stem leaves and a terminal, open inflorescence. Toad Rush (*J. bufonius*) has very slender branched stems, and filamentous leaves.

Family: **Sedge**—Cyperaceae

3 Common Cottongrass *Eriophorum angustifolium*. Perennial grassy herb, sparsely tufted, up to 50 cm high, with erect stems. Leaves grooved, narrowly linear, slender pointed. Stalked ovate spikelets in pendent clusters of 3 to 5; tiny lanceolate bracts with white membranous border. Perianth of numerous fine bristles which elongate and become white and cottony after flowering. Flowers in April and May. Grows in bog pools on heaths and moorland and in acid fens, from lowlands to mountains.

4 Bulrush *Schoenoplectus lacustris*. Perennial herb 1—3 metres high, with thick, creeping rhizomes and rounded stems. Sheathed leaves with linear triangular blades. Spikelets in large terminal clusters; glumes broadly ovate, often fringed. Fruit a trianglular ovoid nut. Flowers from May to July. Grows in wet soil and near or in water at lower altitudes, often gregariously.

5 Wood Club-rush *Scirpus sylvaticus*. Perennial herb up to 1 metre high, sparsely tufted, with short rhizomes and usually erect stems. Leaves widely linear, flat, rough on margins. Dense, large, well-branched inflorescence of sessile spikelets in clusters. Glumes ovate, entire, greenish-brown. Nuts broadly ovoid. Flowers from June to August. Grows in damp meadows, ditches, and on river or lake banks from lowlands to mountains.

6 Common Sedge *Carex nigra*. Perennial herb up to 70 cm high, with creeping rhizomes and triangular stems, rough textured in upper part. Flat, linear, grey-green leaves often rolled when dry. Spikelets in terminal raceme, the topmost ones male, lower ones female. Black-brown glumes obovate, with two stigmata each. Flowers in May to July. Grows in wet meadows and near water, from lowlands to mountains.

7 Spring Sedge *Carex caryophyllea*. Perennial herb 20—40 cm high, with branched rhizome and slender, bluntly triangular stems. Leaves flat, keeled, stiff, rough textured. Spikelets close together, sessile; sometimes lowest one distant and short-stalked; male spikelet terminal; others female. Glumes rusty brown, glossy with green mid-rib. Nut ovoid, triangular, brownish. Flowers in April and May. Grows in dry grassland and margins of woods, particularly on limestone, from lowlands to foothills. At least 100 species of sedges grow in central Europe.

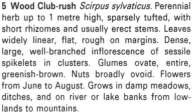

Family: **Grass**—Gramineae (syn. Poaceae)

1 Feather-grass *Stipa capillata*. Perennial herb, densely tufted, up to 80 cm high, with erect stems. Bristly leaves grey-green, rough on margin. Panicles greenish, spikelets with shortly awned glumes, lemma with wavy awns, up to 15 cm long. Flowers in July and August. Grows on sunny, grassy and stony slopes in lower altitudes of milder regions. Common Feather-grass (*S. pennata*) has straight awns and silvery white hairs. It is sometimes grown in gardens but not recorded as a genuine escapee in Britain.

2 Meadow Fescue *Festuca pratensis*. Perennial tufted herb, up to 80 cm high, with erect stems. Leaves narrowly linear, upper side rough, underside smooth. Panicles sparse and open; spikelets up to 10-flowered. Flowers have three stamens with pendulous anthers on long slender filaments; two stigmata; lanceolate glumes, lemma usually awnless. Flowers in June and July. Grows in meadows and other grassy places from lowlands to mountains.

3 Annual Meadow-grass *Poa annua*. Annual or short-lived perennial herb, up to 30 cm high, branched. Ascending or erect stalks, rooting at lower nodes. Blades slightly rough on margins. Open, often one-sided panicle with few-flowered spikelets. Bottom glume single-veined, upper one three-veined, both smooth, lemma has dry-membraneous margin similar to palea. Flowers almost all year round. Grows in lawns, pastures, on wasteland, and as a weed of farms and gardens, almost everywhere.

4 Common Meadow-grass *Poa pratensis*. Perennial, tufted herb, up to 80 cm high, with shortly ascending or erect, smooth, rounded stalks and creeping stolons. Blades flat or rolled, stem leaves usually erect and stiff. Open erect panicles of 3- to 5-flowered spikelets. Glumes equal, lemmas five-veined, hairy at base. Flowers in May to July. Grows in meadows and other grassy places, and on dunes, from lowlands to mountains.

5 Quaking-grass *Briza media*. Perennial, tufted herb, up to 50 cm high, with short, branched rhizome. Slender, smooth, erect stalks. Flat blades, stem ones short, rough on margin. Open sparse panicles of drooping, quaking spikelets often of purplish hue, broadly ovoid. Glumes asymmetrically obovate, keeled, lemma inflated, with a paler border. Flowers in May and June. Grows in all kinds of grassy places, from lowlands to mountains.

4

7

5

1

2

3

6 Cock's-foot *Dactylis glomerata*. Perennial, densely tufted herb, up to 1 metre high with stout rough stalks. Broad flat blades rough on margins and veins. Spikelets in dense, often one-sided panicles. Glumes unequal, lemmas keeled, pointed. Flowers from May to August. Grows in most grassy places and in open woods, from lowlands to mountains.

7 Crested Dog's-tail *Cynosurus cristatus*. Perennial, tufted herb up to 60 cm high with erect, smooth stalks. Narrowly linear leaf blades, rough at tip. Panicles dense and spike-like, one-sided. Almost sessile spikelets arranged in two rows; sterile spikelets, formed only of lemmas, have a comb-like arrangement; fertile ones are three- to four-flowered, with short awns. Flowers in June and July. Grows in meadows and other grassy places, from lowlands to mountains.

6

Family: **Grass**—Gramineae

1 Blue Mountain-grass *Sesleria albicans* (syn. *S. caerulea* and *S. calcarea*). Perennial, tufted herb up to 40 cm high with stalks leafy only in lower part. Blades with distinctly cartilaginous border, rough, flat. Two scaly bracts beneath short spike-like inflorescence. Spikelets glistening blue-grey, rarely yellowish, usually with two flowers. Shortly awned glumes, toothed tipped lemmas, paleas with two terminal teeth. Flowers from March to June. Grows in hill pastures and on stony slopes, usually on limestone, in foothills and mountains.

2 Perennial Rye-grass *Liloum perenne*. Perennial, densely tufted herb, with erect stalks, up to 50 cm high. Smooth, flat linear leaves. Spikelets arranged in an open two-ranked spike. Each spikelet flattened, with 8—11 florets. Single glume longer than half of spikelet, lemmas shortly pointed. Flowers from May to September. Grows in most grassy places, from lowlands to foothills. Much sown as a fodder crop and for rough lawns.

3 Common Couch *Agropyron repens*. Perennial herb with far-creeping, stiff rhizomes and erect stalks, up to 150 cm high. Leaf blades sparsely veined. Slender spike two-ranked, rhachis rough. Spikelets compressed, three- to five-flowered, with equal, veined glumes and shortly awned lemmas. Flowers from June to September. Pernicious weed of farms and gardens; grows in fields, on wasteland and in hedgerows, from lowlands to mountains.

4 Barren Brome *Bromus sterilis* (syn. *Anisantha sterilis*). Annual herb, somewhat tufted, up to 90 cm high, with stiff stalks. Flat leaf blades rough on margins. Large, open, spreading panicles, with pendulous, narrowly wedge-shaped spikelets. Each spikelet up to six-flowered, often flushed dull purple; awn-like pointed glumes and lemma with awn up to 3 cm long. Flowers in May and June. Grows on wasteland, by roadsides and as a farm and garden weed, at lower altitudes.

5 Tufted Hair-grass *Deschampsia cespitosa*. Perennial, densely tufted herb, up to 2 m high, with rough stalks. Leaf blades flat, rough on upper surface, smooth beneath, with sharp ribs. Large, open panicles with arching or lax branches. Spikelets two- or three-flowered, short-stalked, usually violet-tinted; blunt, membranously bordered glumes and shortly awned, toothed lemmas. Flowers from June to August. Grows in damp meadows and open woods from lowlands to mountains. Wavy Hair-grass (*D. . flexuosa*) has bristly leaves and very distinct lemmas.

6 Yorkshire Fog *Holcus lanatus*. Perennial herb of tufted habit, up to 1 metre high, softly short-hairy, with erect or asceding stems. Leaves flat, sheaths inflated. Panicles spreading only during flowering; two- to three-flowered stalked spikelets with coarse bristly glumes and tiny lemmas with awns not projecting beyond the upper glume. Flowers from June to September. Growns in meadows, open woods and waste places, from lowlands to mountains.

2

3

4

Family: **Grass**— Gramineae

1 Sweet Vernal-grass *Anthoxanthum odoratum.* Perennial herb, densely tufted and sweetly aromatic, with erect, smooth stalks, up to 50 cm high. Leaves with flat, usually hairy blades. Panicles spike-like compressed. Spikelets yellow-green, very shortly stalked, bearing 2 sterile and one hermaphrodite florets; lanceolate glumes, lemmas awned, hairy; two stamens only. Flowers in May and June. Grows in dry meadows, pastures, open woods, heaths and moors, from lowlands to mountains. Contains coumarin, which provides the new-mown hay smell.

2 Wood Small-reed *Calamagrostis epigeios.* Perennial herb, tufted and robust, up to 2 m high, with erect, reedy, grey-green stalks. Leaf sheaths and blades rough. Dense, well-branched panicles. Spikelets stalked, greenish or brownish with violet tint. Awl-pointed glumes, lemmas three-veined, membranous, awned and with a basal tuft of hairs. Flowers in July and August. Grows in damp open woods, ditches and fens, mainly in lowlands.

3 Meadow Foxtail *Alopecurus pratensis.* Perennial herb up to 1 metre high, loosely or compactly tufted, with short rhizomes and erect, smooth stalks. Leaf blades flat, rough, the sheaths somewhat inflated. Dense, cylindrical, spike-like inflorescence. Spikelets very shortly stalked; pointed glumes fused together at their bases, the keeled back silky-hairy, lemma almost the same length as glumes, with protruding awn. Flowers in May and June. Grows in damp meadows and other grassy places, from lowlands to mountains. Related *Alopecurus aequalis* is much smaller, with whitish anthers, turning orange.

5

1

6

4 Timothy *Phleum pratense.* Perennial herb up to 1 metre high, densely tufted, with erect stalks. Leaf blades very rough. Dense grey-green, spike-like inflorescence, with almost sessile spikelets. Glumes whitish dry-membranous, on greenish keel bristly hairy and shortly awned; white-membranous lemma, violet anthers. Flowers from June to August. Grows in meadows and other grassy places from lowlands to foothills, more frequent in lower altitudes. Extensively sown for hay and forage.

5 Mat-grass *Nardus stritla.* Perennial, densely tufted herb, up to 30 cm high, with short rhizomes and erect slender stems. Grey-green leaves, filiform, prickly pointed, with conspicuous basal sheaths. Flowering spike sparse, one-sided, spikelets single-flowered. Glumes miss-

ing, lemma with short rough awn; three stamens, one stigma. Flowers in May and June. Grows on heaths and moors, sometimes locally abundant, from lowlands high up into mountains, usually on acid soils.

6 Common Reed *Phragmites communis.* Perennial robust herb up to 3 metres high, with tough, long-creeping rhizome and erect, grey-green stems. Conspicuously double-ranked leaves of sterile shoots; blades flat, rough beneath, gradually tapering to point. Large, dense panicles; spikelets grey, sometimes purple-tinted with long silky hairs. Unequal glumes, lemmas long-pointed, awnless. Flowers from July to September. Grows in marshes, swamps and shallow water, often gregariously, forming extensive colonies.

Herbaceous Plants

Fig. 1. In the Common Dandelion (*Taraxacum officinale*) one may often see inflorescences at all stages of development on a single plant.

When you hear that the banana is a robust herb and, on the other hand, that whortleberry and cranberry are shrubs, you may be surprised. Herbs cannot have trunks, can they? And as for whortleberry and cranberry, what kind of shrubs are they? What actually is the difference between herbaceous and woody plants?

Herbs are annual, biennial and plural-yearly to perennial plants with a non-woody stem that does not thicken and dies at the end of the growing season. In the case of plural-yearly and perennial herbs in temperate regions, their underground parts — roots, rhizomes, tubers or bulbs — live over from season to season and make new growth the following year. Woody plants, on the other hand, have woody stems — trunks in the case of trees, stems and twigs in the case of shrubs and sub-shrubs. Semi-shrubs have stems that become woody, but their tips or young sections die and fall. All woody plants grow thicker with age. Because bananas, which are perennial and thus grow for a long time, have stems that are not woody and do not thicken and their seeming 'trunks' are merely the remains of leaf sheaths pressed closely together, they are neither trees nor shrubs but robust herbs, the largest in the plant realm.

The life forms of herbs may be divided into four groups. Annual herbs germinate, grow, flower and bear fruits within a single growing season. They include numerous weeds that must complete their life cycle within a single year, for example Common Poppy (*Papaver rhoeas*) and Cornflower (*Centaurea cyanus*).

Biennial herbs germinate and produce only a basal leaf rosette or the first vegetative structures the first year, passing the winter in this phase. Then, in the second year, they continue growth, produce flowers and bear fruit. Examples are Mullein (*Verbascum*) and Foxglove (*Digitalis purpurea*), as well as certain winter crops, such as cereals sown in the autumn, mainly wheat.

Plural-yearly herbs also first germinate and form vegetative organs and then overwinter in this phase. However, a plural-yearly herb may remain in this state for several more growing seasons or else may form further vegetative structures. Not until the last year of its life does it flower, produce seeds and then die. Most people are acquainted with the agaves that are cultivated for ornament, especially the American species *Agave americana*, which forms large rosettes of succulent leaves edged with prickly spines along their entire length and with a larger terminal spine at the tip. Agaves live in this state for many years, sometimes even do-

Fig. 2. Flowering Field Poppy (*Papaver rhoeas*) with a bud enclosed by the calyx and a ripening capsule with a dried remnant of the stigma.

103

zens, and only then do they produce an inflorescence on the huge axis, after which they die; in other words they flower only once in their lifetime, at the end of their life cycle. European plants that have a similar life cycle are the broomrapes (*Orobanche*). For several years they live as parasites on their host plant, forming only underground vegetative structures. Then, all of a sudden, they flower and die within a single year.

The last group are perennial herbs that live for several years, producing flowers and seeds each year. They die down to ground level for the winter and grow again the following year from their underground parts — roots, rhi-

zomes, bulbs or tubers — which have survived the cold season unharmed below ground. Examples are certain campions of the genus *Silene*, such as Nottingham Catchfly (*Silene nutans*), *Silene otites*, Moss Campion (*Silene acaulis*), Maiden Pink (*Dianthus deltoides*), German Pink (*D. cartusianorum*) and Ragged Robin (*Lychnis flos-cuculi*).

Among the most remarkable of the aquatic perennial herbs are plants related to Europe's water-lilies (*Nymphaea* and *Nuphar*), such as *Victoria amazonica* (syn. *V. regia*) from the Amazon River region and *V. cruziana* from the Paraná River region. Both are grown in hothouses in Europe and their 2-m leaves are

Fig. 3. Longitudinal section of the head of a dandelion. The involucral bracts are green, the yellow strap-shaped florets are longer towards the edge of the inflorescence.

Fig. 4. On the flower head of the Ox-eye Daisy (*Leucanthemum vulgare*) one can clearly see the two types of florets of certain composite flowers. Unlike the dandelion, for example, the outer florets are ligulate, the inner florets tubular.

Fig. 5. A leaf of Common Sundew (*Drosera rotundifolia*) with long-stalked, sticky glands and short digestive glands.

and Sikkim at elevations of 5,600 m. *D. glomerata* and *D. lasiophylla* grow at elevations of 6,000 m; *Ermania koezlii* was collected in Kashmir at an altitude of 6,300 m above sea level. These undemanding and hardy plants also hold a further record — that of conquering the Arctic. *Draba groenlandica* was found by the Koch fjord in northern Greenland as far north as 82° 48′ latitude North; *Braya purpurascens* occurs in Grinell Land at the eastern tip of Ellesmere Island in northern Canada, at 83° 24′ latitude North.

However, how many people will ever have the opportunity to look for drabas in the mountains of Kashmir or near the North Pole? On the other hand, wo can all admire the largest fruits in the plant realm in our own gardens! *Cucurbita maxima* is not native to Europe; it hails from Central America. Sometimes grown is its large-fruited

Fig. 6. Cowslips (*Primula veris*) are a common sight in spring in open woods.

among the largest in the plant realm. The fragrant flowers measure 35 cm. They open in the late afternoon and close again towards morning. They are a delicate pink at first. Once pollinated, they close immediately; when they open again the following afternoon they are coloured a reddish-pink. These beautiful nocturnal flowers are far above average in size but still cannot begin to compare with *Rafflesia arnoldii* of Sumatra. This is a parasitic plant whose fleshy flowers measure up to 1 m in diameter, have a circumference of 3 m and may weigh over 5 kg — truly the largest flowers known to botany.

At the other end of the scale, the smallest flowering dicotyledonous plant is a member of the Loranthaceae family. This is *Arceuthobium minutissimum* which lives as a parasite on the Himalayan pine *Pinus griffithii*. This miniature parasite lives beneath the bark of the tree, displaying only its 2—3-mm-long flowering stems.

P. griffithii grows at elevations of about 3,000 m, but other small herbs have climbed twice as high. Heading the list of plants that have conquered the Himalayas are members of the mustard family (Brassicaceae). *Braya oxycarpa* and *Draba altaica* grow in western Tibet

In central Europe, too, there are rarities among the herbaceous plants. Leaves that are turned edgewise, in the north-south direction, with leaf surfaces facing east and west, are an unusual characteristic of Prickly Lettuce (*Lactuca serriola*) which grows in sunny waste places.

Even in Europe one may come across plants that are carnivorous, although these are quite rare nowadays. Most familiar is the Common Sundew (*Drosera rotundifolia*). Less familiar is the Common Butterwort (*Pinguicula vulgaris*) which has a basal rosette of oblong-ovate leaves with edges curled upward and an upper surface covered with numerous stalked glands that secrete a sticky fluid on which small insects become caught. Even some aquatic, rootless herbs have leaves adapted for capturing and digesting insects. These are the bladderworts (*Utricularia*) which have minute translucent follicles

Fig. 7. The fleshy outgrowths on the seeds of Sweet Violet (*Viola odorata*) are a favourite food of ants which contribute to the spread of the violets by dispersing the seeds.

variety *gigantea*, with fruits measuring up to 80 cm in diameter and weighing 100 kg. In the European garden it is impossible to provide this plant with tropical, damp, warm conditions throughout the year, as in its native land, where fruits have measured up to 150 cm in diameter and weighed up to 125 kg! These berries are the largest of all known fruits.

Having mentioned one member of the gourd family (Cucurbitaceae), let us take a look at a few more. There is no need to describe the Cucumber (*Cucumis sativus*) or the Sugar Melon (*Melo saccharinus*). However, *Ecbalium elaterium* might catch your attention in the Mediterranean region and might even give you a bit of a fright during an evening stroll. This trailing or climbing herbaceous plant has fleshy leaves and oblong to ovoid fruits that, when ripe, break off with a loud pop when touched, ejecting their seeds and mucilaginous pulp far from the plant.

Fig. 8. The terminal leaf of Meadow Vetchling (*Lathyrus pratensis*) is modified into three twining tendrils by means of which the plant attaches itself to the stems of grasses or other plants.

Fig. 9. The pollination mechanism of Sage (*Salvia officinalis*). Normally the style with bifid stigma, as well as the stamen, is pressed to the flower's domed upper lip. An insect, trying to get to the nectar at the bottom of the corolla tube, presses its body against the outgrowth on the stamen, thereby tilting the stamen and the stigma. The pollen from the stamen spills onto the body of the insect while pollen that has been brought by the insect from another flower is pressed onto the stigma.

amid their thread-like leaf segments. The bladder has a small opening encircled by irritable ciliae and furnished with a lid that only opens inward, thereby blocking the escape of any small aquatic insects or crustaceans trapped inside. The inside walls of the bladder are covered with four-branched glandular hairs and nearer the mouth there are stalked glands that secrete digestive substances and also absorb the decomposed organisms. Observing the minor dramas of captured insects on the leaf of a sundew or bladderwort may cause one to reflect on the ingenious equipment with which nature has provided plants in order that they may obtain essential nutrients that are lacking in nitrogen-poor soils and nutrient-poor water.

The realm of herbaceous plants is extraordinarily rich and diverse. To discuss their useful and medicinal properties in detail would require more than one book.

Herbaceous Plants

Class: **Angiospermous Plants**—Magnoliopsida

Subclass: **Dicotyledones**—Magnoliidae

Family: **Waterlily**—Nymphaceae

1 White Waterlily *Nymphaea alba.* Perennial aquatic herb with stout, creeping rhizome. Long-petiolate leaves, narrowly cordate, have circular blades, floating on water surface. Flowers large, cup-shaped, petals white, of the same length as four green sepals. Stamens have linear filaments. Flowers from June to August. Grows in lakes and ponds, at low altitudes; often cultivated.

2 Yellow Waterlily *Nuphar lutea.* Aquatic plant with stout perennial rhizome, similar to white waterlily. Long-petiolate leaves with ovate-oblong blades are leathery, smooth, floating on water surface. Flowers yellow, strongly fragrant, with disc-like stigma. Fruits are bottle-shaped, pulpy capsules. Flowers from June to August. Grows in lakes, ponds and slow flowing rivers at lower altitudes. Related Least Yellow Waterlily (*N. pumila*) has smaller flowers, slightly fragrant, with a somewhat lobed stigma.

Family: **Buttercup**—Ranunculaceae

3 Marsh Marigold *Caltha palustris.* Perennial, hairless herb 30—40 cm high with fibrous roots, erect stems, sometimes ascending and rooting. Bottom leaves petiolate, top ones sessile, blades cordate, rounded to bluntly triangular, toothed and glossy. Flowers yellow, glossy, with 5—8 golden yellow petals. Fruit a cluster of beaked follicles. Flowers from March to July. Grows by the waterside, in damp meadows and ditches, from lowlands to mountains.

4 Globe Flower *Trollius europaeus.* Robust perennial herbs with erect stems, 30—60 cm high, and terminal, solitary flowers. Leaves deeply palmately lobed with 3—5 segments, each deeply cut and toothed; lower leaves long-petiolate, upper ones sessile. Large flowers up to 3 cm in diameter, globose, light to golden yellow, composed of 5—15 petaloid sepals. Fruit a cluster of beaked follicles. Flowers in May to July. Grows in wet meadows in foothills and mountains; in places extinct through over-picking, therefore it deserves strict protection. Hybrids of this and Asiatic species with orange flowers are cultivated in gardens.

5 Common Baneberry *Actaea spicata.* A somewhat foetid perennial, poisonous herb with erect, unbranched stems, 30—60 cm. high. Basal leaves bi- to tripinnate, leaflets ovate, pointed and toothed. Small flowers, yellowish-white, in long-stalked terminal racemes. Fruit a glossy black berry. Flowers in May and June. Grows im shady, deciduous forests from hills to mountains; in lowlands only rarely.

6 Columbine *Aquilegia vulgaris.* Perennial herb, up to 50 cm high. Leaves composed of 3—9 somewhat glaucous leaflets, ovate, deeply to shallowly lobed; upper stem leaves smaller and less divided. Flowers long-stalked, pendent, blue-violet, rarely white or pink; sepals flared, coloured, petals elongated into curved spurs. Garden varieties of various colouring. Flowers from May to July. Grows in deciduous woods from lowlands to highlands. Much and long-cultivated in flower gardens, along with some equally pretty Siberian and North-American species.

Family: **Buttercup**—Ranunculaceae

1 *Aconitum vulparia* (syn. *A. lycoctonum*). Poisonous, variable perennial herb with fibrous root system and widely branched stem, up to 1 metre high. Leaves palmately parted, segments 3—5 wedge-shaped, downy or smooth. Inflorescences of branched racemes, with well-spaced yellow, hairy flowers with long, cylindrical helmet-shaped spur. Flowers from June to August. Grows in deciduous woods and thickets from highlands to mountains. Sometimes cultivated.

2 Common Monkshood *Aconitum napellus.* A poisonous, perennial herb, with tuberous roots and erect, branched inflorescences. Leaves palmately divided, 3—5 lanceolate to widely linear segments. Dark violet flowers in dense racemes, the 'helmet' almost of the same height and width. Flowers from June to August.

Grows in moist woods and on banks of streams; also cultivated in gardens; occasionally becoming naturalized. Related Lesser Monkshood (*A. variegatum*) with 'helmet' much taller than its width grows in similar places in mountains. Both strictly protected.

3 *Delphinium elatum.* Perennial herb up to 150 cm high, with simple stem, branched only at the inflorescence. Basal, long-petiolate leaves, smooth on the upper side, downy beneath, deeply palmately parted into widely wedge-shaped, deeply cut segments. Flowers dark blue to blue-violet, long-spurred, in dense raceme. Flowers in June and July, in original mountain habitats till September. Grows along mountain streams. Hybrids with this and two other species have given rise to the giant border delphiniums of gardens.

4 Larkspur *Consolida regalis* (syn. *Delphinium consolida*). Annual plant with erect stem, up to 50 cm high and branched only in upper half. Leaves much divided into linear segments; bracts linear, shorter than flower-stalks. Flowers in branched racemes, usually blue, spur reddish. Hairless follicles. Flowers from July to September. A field weed in southern Europe at lower altitudes; grown in gardens. This and the related species *C. ambigua* have given rise to the popular garden larkspurs.

5 Wood Anemone *Anemone nemorosa*. Up to 25 cm high herb with thin rhizome and solitary basal leaves. Stem simple, unbranched, with 3 petiolate leaves. Each leaf trifoliate, the segments bi- to trilobed. Flowers solitary, long-stalked, with usually six white tepals with pink flush outside. Hairy achenes with curved beak. Flowers from March to May. Grows in deciduous woods, thickets and damp meadows; almost common. Related Yellow Wood Anemone (*A. ranunculoides*) has yellow flowers and almost sessile leaves.

6 Snowdrop Wind-flower *Anemone sylvestris*. Herb up to 35 cm high with creeping rhizome and rosette of leaves. Leaves palmately 3—5 parted, segments toothed. Stem leaves divided into 5 oblong, lanceolate, deeply toothed segments. Flowers usually solitary, long-stalked, white, with five widely ovate tepals, hairy outside. Hairy achenes. Flowers from April to June. Grows on sunny, bushy slopes, in open woods, mostly on limestone soils, from lowlands to foothills, in milder regions. A protected plant.

Family: **Buttercup**—Ranunculaceae

1 *Anemone narcissiflora.* A variable tufted perennial. Stem up to 40 cm high, hairy; basal leaves palmately 3—5 parted, each segment deeply toothed. Floral bracts usually in 3- to 5-lobed whorl. Flowers arranged in a several-stemmed umbel, erect; tepals white, sometimes flushed purple. Achenes hairless. Flowers from May to July. Grows in mountain meadows of the Alps and other central-European mountains. Poisonous plant, strictly protected.

2 Alpine Anemone *Pulsatilla alpina.* Up to 30 cm. high herb with branched rhizome, rosette of basal leaves and several simple, hairy, single-flowered stems with whorl of bracts. Basal leaves long-petiolate, stem ones shortly petiolate, with deeply dissected segments. Flowers long-stalked, with 6 white tepals often flushed outside with pink or violet; sometimes yellow. Achenes have long, hairy awn to aid dispersal by wind. Flowers from May to August. Grows on rocky mountain slopes, in meadows and amongst knee-pine. Strictly protected, similar to other pulsatillas.

3 Pasque Flower *Pulsatilla vulgaris.* A variable species with large flowers in shades of purple and violet. Illustrated species has stem up to 50 cm high. Basal leaves develop as the first flowers fade. They are long-petiolate, at first densely hairy, later thinly hairy, simply or twice pinnate, each leaflet deeply dissected; floral bracts divided into narrowly linear segments. Flowers with 6 tepals outside silky hairy, at first tulip-shaped, later opening wide, light to misty violet. Flowers from March to May. Grows on grassy slopes, on limestone soils. Also cultivated as rock-garden plant and occasionally escaping.

4 Fair Maids of France *Ranunculus aconitifolius.* Perennial, robust herb up to 1 metre high or more, with short rhizomes and a well-branched stem. Basal, long-petioled leaves are palmately five-parted, the segments lobed and deeply serrate; stem leaves similar to basal ones, mostly sessile. Flowers white, with 5 pe-

4

5

6

tals. Achenes shortly beaked. Flowers from May to August. Grows in mountain forests, along streams and in knee-pine. Poisonous.

5 Meadow Buttercup *Ranunculus acris*. Poisonous perennial herb, up to 1 metre high. Basal leaves long-petiolate, palmately five-parted, segments lanceolate, dissected and toothed. Stem sometimes with spreading hairs. Stem leaves similar to basal ones, upper leaves cleft into linear segments. Flowers with 5 glossy golden yellow petals. Achenes shortly beaked. Flowers from May to September. Grows abundantly in meadows and moist grassy places.

6 Creeping Buttercup *Ranunculus repens*. Perennial plant with erect flowering stems up to 50 cm long, and creeping stems rooting at the nodes. Basal leaves trifoliate, each leaflet petiolate, lobed and toothed; stem leaves similar to basal ones, upper leaves sessile, cleft into lanceolate or linear segments. Flowers glossy golden yellow with 5 petals. Achenes smooth, with curved beak. Flowers from May to August. Grows abundantly in wet meadows, fields, along banks of streams and ponds; also a garden weed.

Familly: **Buttercup**—Ranunculaceae

1 Water Crowfoot *Batrachium aquatile* (syn. *Ranunculus aquatilis*). Perennial aquatic plant with floating, smooth, branched stem to 1 m. Submerged petiolate leaves much divided into linear, forked segments which collapse after being taken out of water. Leaves floating on water surface are long-petiolate, rounded to reniform, cordate, palmately three-to five-lobed. Long-stalked flowers above water surface, with 5 white petals. Achenes wrinkled, bristle tipped. Flowers from June to September. Grows in lakes and ponds at lower altitudes. Related River Crowfoot (*B. fluitans*) has much longer segments to submerged leaves; segments of Rigid-leaved Crowfoot (*B. circinatum*) do not lose shape when taken out of water.

2 Noble Liverleaf *Hepatica nobilis* (syn. *H. triloba, Anemone hepatica*). Perennial herb with shortly creeping rhizome and single-flowered stems. Leaves trilobed, leathery, softly hairy on underside. A whorl of 3 calyx-like bracts immediately beneath the flower. Flower stalks hairy; flowers with 6—10 tepals, blue to light or dark violet, less frequently rosy or whitish. Achenes without appendages. Flowers in February to April. Grows in deciduous groves and bushy places from lowlands to foothills; locally abundant only. A protected plant.

3 Lesser Celandine *Ficaria verna* (syn. *Ranunculus ficaria*). Perennial herb with tubers among fibrous roots. Smooth stem up to 20 cm high. Basal and stem leaves petiolate, cordate, rounded to reniform, scalloped to notched,

4

5

6

smooth, glossy. Some forms have tiny tubers in axils of basal leaves. Flowers solitary, with 8—12 tepals of glossy yellow. Achenes small, ovoid. Flowers from March to May. Grows commonly in open woods, meadows, ditches and along banks.

4 Spring Pheasant's Eye *Adonis vernalis*. Poisonous perennial plant, up to 40 cm high, with thick rhizome. Erect stem scaly at base. Leaves sessile, up to four cleft into linear segments. Flowers solitary, large, of 10—20 narrowly elongated bright glossy yellow petals. Flowers in April and May. Grows on sunny slopes, bushy ravines and in pine-woods, as a rule on limestone soils. Occasionally cultivated for ornament. Strictly protected plant.

5 Summer Pheasant's Eye *Adonis aestivalis*. Annual herb up to 50 cm high with erect, little branched stem. Basal leaves petiolate, upper ones sessile, as a rule cut into many linear seg-

ments. Flowers individual, smallish, petals red, rarely pale yellow, at base usually with a black spot. Achenes smooth, oblong-ovoid, beaked. Flowers from May to July. Grows as field weed at lower altitudes in milder regions.

6 Upright Clematis *Clematis recta*. Perennial herb up to 1.5 m high, with erect, non-climbing stems. Basal stem leaves simple, upper ones odd-pinnate, leaflets ovate to lanceolate, entire, petiolate. Flowers arranged in terminal panicles; white, composed of 4 petal-like sepals. Achenes have long, hairy style. Flowers in June and July. Grows on bushy slopes, in open woods and meadows, at lower altitudes, mainly on limestone soils. The climbing, white to green-white flowered Traveller's Joy (*C. vitalba*) of Europe (including Britain) and northern Africa is more abundant and flowers from July to September. Many exotic species and cultivated varieties and hybrids are grown in gardens.

Family: **Buttercup**—Ranunculaceae

1 French Meadow-rue *Thalictrum aquilegiifolium*. Robust herb up to 1 metre or more high with erect stem, branched in the upper part, grooved and hairless. Leaves bi- to tripinnate, leaflets obovate, lobed, smooth and grey-green, resembling those of columbine. Flowers in dense corymbose panicles; no petals and the small whitish sepals soon falling; stamen filaments violet, thickened. Ovaries and achenes long-stalked, pendent. Flowers from May to July. Grows in moist forests and thickets and by the waterside from foothills to mountains. Similar but much smaller Lesser Meadow-rue (*T. minus*) has yellow stamens and greenish sepals.

Family: Aristolochiaceae

2 Asarabacca *Asarum europaeum*. Perennial evergreen herb with branched, scaly rhizome. Stems prostrate, each lateral shoot usually with two long-petiolate, reniform, entire, glossy deep green leaves. Fleshy bell-shaped flowers with 3 lobes brownish outside, dark violet within, are hidden by leaves. Flowers from March to May. Grows in humid groves and among bushes from lowlands to mountains.

3 Birthwort *Aristolochia clematitis*. Foetid perennial herb with erect, unbranched stems, up to 50 cm or more high. Leaves alternate, long-petiolate, rounded cordate. Flowers in small groups in axils of leaves; at first erect, later drooping. Corolla tubular, slightly curved, swollen at base, dull yellow. Capsule pear-shaped. Flowers in May and June. Grows in thickets, in hedges and vineyards at lower altitudes, in temperate regions. Formerly cultivated as a medicinal plant and later escaping to become naturalized.

4

5

6

Family: **Poppy**—Papaveraceae

4 *Papaver alpinum.* Perennial tufted herb, with unbranched flowering stems up to 20 cm high. Leaves petiolate, simply pinnate, segments linear to linear-lanceolate, deeply lobed, grey-green. Flowers white or yellow, calyx, with black bristles, falls off as flower expands; petals widely obovate. Seed-heads small, obovate with a flat top. Flowers in July and August. Grows on screes and among rocks at high elevations of the Alps and Carpathians.

5 Field Poppy *Papaver rhoeas.* Annual herb with erect, simple or little branched stems, bristly, leafy, up to 1 metre high. Leaves pinnate, segments deeply lobed and toothed, lower ones petiolate, upper sessile and bristly. Solitary flowers on long stalks with bristles; drooping in bud, erect in bloom. Calyx green, bristly, falling as flower opens. Corolla of 4 bright red petals; stigma usually ten-lobed. Seed-heads obovate, flat topped. Flowers from May to September. Grows as weed in fields and gardens, on spoil heaps and wasteland, from lowlands to foothills in temperate regions; locally abundant, elsewhere missing.

6 Greater Celandine *Chelidonium majus.* Perennial herb releasing orange latex when cut. Stem up to 60 cm high, erect and branched. Leaves somewhat hairy, lower ones petiolate, odd-pinnate, upper leaves sessile, deeply cut; segments lobed and toothed, underside grey-green. Flowers in umbels, yellow, petals soon falling. Capsule linear. Flowers from May to October. Grows in open woods, thickets and hedgerows, from lowlands to foothills.

1

2

6

Family: **Fumitory**—Fumariaceae

1 Common Fumitory *Fumaria officinalis.* Annual, grey-green herb, up to 30 cm high, with erect or ascending stem, branched and leafy. Leaves petiolate, bipinnate; petiolate leaflets palmately parted into linear segments. Flowers in upright racemes, small and narrow, rosy red, dark purple at tip; tiny sepals persistent. Fruits globular, single-seeded. Flowers from May to October. Grows commonly as weed in fields, gardens and on wasteland from lowlands to foothills.

2 *Corydalis cava.* Perennial herb up to 30 cm high, with hollow-topped underground tuber and erect stem, as a rule with two leaves. Leaves cut into several lobed leaflets. Flowers in erect raceme, bracts under flowers entire; corollas rosy-purple, yellow-white, spurred. Capsules long and narrow, beaked. Flowers from March to May. Grows in woods and thickets, from lowlands to foothills. Related *Corydalis fabacea* has pendent, few-flowered raceme while *Corydalis solida* has palmately lobed bracts beneath the flowers.

Family: Cruciferae (syn. Brassicaceae)

3 Charlock or **Wild Mustard** *Sinapis arvensis.* Annual plant up to 50 cm high with erect, little branched stem, irregularly hairy. Leaves mostly unparted, irregularly toothed, lower ones lyre-shaped, pinnatisect. Flowers have expanded, yellow-green sepals, corollas yolk-yellow, of four petals. Seed pod, either somewhat hairy or not at all, with short beak. Flowers from June to October. Grows fairly abundantly as field weed in lower altitudes. Related *Sinapis alba*, cultivated for seeds, has stem leaves lyre-like, pinnatisect to pinnately divided.

4 Wild Radish *Raphanus raphanistrum.* Annual herb with erect, slender, bristly stem. Leaves petiolate, lower ones lyre-shaped to pinnately lobed, unequally dentate; top leaves often undivided and irregularly toothed. Petals sulphur-yellow, violet-veined, sepals erect. Fruit is a pod

118

3

4

5

or loment, dehiscent, with beaked last segment. Flowers from June to October. Grows fairly abundantly as weed in fields and on wasteland. Related Radish (*R. sativus*) with flowers white or violet-tinted and non-dehiscent loment is cultivated as vegetable.

5 Hoary Cress *Cardaria draba.* Perennial, grey-downy herb, up to 50 cm high. Basal leaves ovate, stem ones usually shallowly toothed, clasping, arrow-shaped. Flowers in branched, crowded racemes, corollas white. Siliqua (pod) heart-shaped with long, persistent style. Flowers from May to July. Grows as weed in fields, on wasteland and trenches. Native of eastern Mediterranean, today abundantly naturalized, especially in milder regions.

6 Field Pennycress *Thlaspi arvense.* Annual hairless herb, up to 30 cm high, after bruising gives out a foetid smell. Stems slender, leaves distantly toothed, dentate, arrow-shaped, stem clasping. Flowers in erect racemes; calyx yellow-green, corolla white. Siliquas large, flat, ovately rounded, with wide rim, deeply dissected. Flowers from May to October. Commonly grows as weed in fields, fallows and on wasteland.

Family: Cruciferae

1 Shepherd's Purse *Capsella bursa-pastoris.*
Annual to biennial herb, up to 50 cm high, stem
often branched. Basal leaves pinnatisect to almost entire, arranged in rosette, stem leaves
clasping. Many-flowered inflorescences;
flowers small, white, occasionally petal-less. Siliquas roughly triangular with many small seeds.
Flowers from February to November, sometimes whole year round. Grows as common
weed in fields, gardens, on wasteland and along
paths from lowlands to mountains.

2 Perennial Honesty *Lunaria rediviva.* Perennial
plant up to 140 cm high, with creeping rhizome
and erect, unbranched stem. Leaves petiolate,
cordate, upper ones triangular, toothed. Flowers
light violet, rarely whitish. Siliquas large, elliptical, tapering to both ends, with membranous
partition and stiff valves. Flowers from May to
July. Scattered on screes, in open mountain forests and in ravines from foothills to mountains.
Protected plant. Cultivated Honesty (*L. annua*),
native of eastern Mediterranean, has sessile upper leaves and large, broad siliquas.

3 Golden Alison *Alyssum saxatile.* Evergreen
sub-shrub with oblanceolate, grey-felted leaves.
Stems up to 30 cm high, upright, few-leaved. Inflorescence branched; flowers in dense corymbs; petals shallowly lobed, golden yellow,
siliquas hairless. Flowers in April and May.
Grows on sunny rocks. Also cultivated as rock-
garden plant.

4 Mountain Alison *Alyssum montanum.* Perennial sub-shrub, 10—20 cm high. Stems and grey-
green leaves have grey hairs which are
branched and distinctly star-shaped under lens.
Lower leaves obovate or spatulate, upper ones
oblanceolate. Flowers in simple racemes; sepals as well as petals soon fall, corollas golden
yellow. Raceme during fruition much elongated,
siliquas almost round. Flowers from April to
June. Grows on rocks, dry and sunny slopes,
sandy places and margins of pine-woods at
lower altitudes, in warm regions.

1

2

5 Common Whitlow-grass *Erophila verna*. Tiny, annual, only 2—10 cm high with basal rosette of leaves and simple, leafless, filamentous stem. Leaves elliptic or lanceolate, entire or toothed. Few-flowered inflorescences; upper side of sepals hairy, margins white or light violet, membraneous. Petals distinctly cleft, white; siliquas elliptic to almost rounded, without style. Flowers from March to May. Grows gregariously in places from lowlands to mountains, on slopes, in fields, meadows, fallows, and on walls.

6 Lady's Smock *Cardamine pratensis*. Perennial herb, 20—40 cm high, with short rhizome and erect, hollow stem. Basal leaves in rosette, odd-pinnate, with up to 8 pairs of ovate leaflets, angularly toothed. Stem leaves pinnately divided, with linear, usually entire segments. Flowers often in dense racemes, lilac or violet-tinted, distinctly violet-veined. Anthers yellow; siliquas linear without beak. Flowers from April to June. Grows abundantly in damp meadows, from lowlands to mountains. Related Bitter Cress (*C. amara*) has rather weak, semi-decumbent stems and white flowers with violet anthers.

121

Family: Cruciferae

1 Common Winter-cress *Barbarea vulgaris*. Biennial, almost hairless herb up to 50 cm high. Lower leaves lyre-shaped, pinnately lobed, terminal leaflet broadly ovate, somewhat lobed or toothed; base of leaf stem clasping. Racemes dense, branched; flowers golden-yellow, petals almost double length of sepals. Siliquas erect on short stalks. Flowers from May to July. Grows in meadows, ditches, along streams, and also in fields and on wasteland.

2 *Hesperis matronalis*. Perennial, robust herb, up to over 1 metre high, hairy. Lower leaves oblong-ovate to lanceolate, upper ones smaller, almost sessile, all distantly toothed. Raceme long, sometimes branched; flowers large, fragrant, usually violet, rarely reddish or white, petals somewhat shallowly toothed. Siliquas cylindrical, up to 10 cm long. Flowers from May to July. Grows wild in the Mediterranean; often cultivated and becoming naturalized on waste ground, along hedges, in thickets and open woods.

3 Garlic Mustard or **Jack-by-the-Hedge** *Alliaria petiolata* (syn. *A. officinalis*). Biennial herb, smelling of garlic when bruised. Stems erect, often branched at the top. Lower leaves long-petiolate, cordate, irregularly sinuate toothed; stem leaves shortly petiolate, ovate to triangular, irregularly toothed. Flowers small, white; siliquas long, stalked, erect. Flowers from April to June. Grows in open woods, thickets, in hedgerows and on wasteland, abundant from lowlands to foothills.

1

2

3

Family: **Mignonette**—Resedaceae

4 Wild Mignonette *Reseda lutea.* Perennial herb with erect stems, little or not branched, up to 50 cm high. Leaves once pinnately cut into linear segments, with wavy margins. Flowers in dense racemes, during fruition becoming elongated. Each floret yellow-green, with 6 narrow petals, the 4 upper ones lobed. Upright oblong capsules. Flowers from May to September. Grows on grassy slopes and waste ground and as weed of cultivated land at lower altitudes in milder regions. Garden Mignonette (*R. odorata*), a North-African species, is cultivated in gardens; it has almost undivided leaves, reddish anthers and pendent fruits.

Family: **Rockrose**—Cistaceae

5 *Helianthemum chamaecistus* (syn. *H. nummularium*). Procumbent, evergreen, hairy shrublet 10—20 cm high. Leaves oval or oblong-ovate, densely white, hairy beneath. Inflorescence a few-flowered raceme, flowers large, 2—2.5 cm in diameter. Two minute outside sepals linear, three inner ones larger, ovate. Corolla of five yellow, rarely yellowish white petals. Flowers from June to October. Grows on sunny grassy slopes and in open scrub, from lowlands to mountains.

Family: Silenaceae (syn. Caryophyllaceae)

6 Corn Cockle *Agrostemma githago* (syn. *Lychnis githago*). Annual plant with erect stem up to 1 metre high, grey hairy. Leaves opposite, linear-lanceolate, hairy. Long-stalked flowers solitary; calyx bell-shaped, with five slender lobes; corolla red-purple, petals obovate. Capsules ovoid with black, reniform, poisonous seeds. Grows as weed in cereal crops in lower altitudes; formerly more abundant. Native probably of eastern Mediterranean.

4

5

6

Family: Silenaceae

1 Ragged Robin *Lychnis flos-cuculi.* Perennial plant up to 80 cm high. Stems of two sorts; decumbent and leafy and erect flowering. Opposite leaves narrowly to oblong lanceolate, entire. Open dichasial inflorescence; calyx bell-shaped, with 5 triangular teeth. Petals rose-red, cleft into four linear segments. Capsule broadly ovoid. Flowers from May to July. Grows in damp meadows, marshes, fens and open wet woods, from lowlands to mountains.

2 *Lychnis alba* (syn. *Silene alba, Melandrium album*). Annual to perennial herb, up to 1 metre high, softly downy, stems erect, branched. Lower leaves petiolate, oblanceolate, upper ones lanceolate to elliptic, sessile, all opposite. Flowers arranged in open dichasia. Flowers dioecious, stalked, opening in afternoon, slightly fragrant, calyx bell-shaped, inflated, with 5 pointed teeth; petals white, lobed. Capsule widely ovoid, enveloped in persistent calyx. Flowers from June to September. Grows in hedgerows, meadows, on waste and cultivated land, from lowlands to foothills. Related *Silene dioica* (syn. *Melandrium rubrum*) has red flowers and hairy stems.

3 Red German Catchfly *Lychnis viscaria* (syn. *Viscaria vulgaris*). Perennial plant up to 50 cm high, with smooth stem, having sticky zones beneath each pair of the upper leaves. Bottom leaves oblong-lanceolate, upper ones linear-lanceolate, all opposite, often with red tint. Inflorescence an interrupted spike-like panicle of axillary cymes. Calyx tubular, reddish, corolla bright red; ovoid capsules. Flowers from May to July. Grows in pastures, on stony slopes and dry rocks, from lowlands to foothills; very rare in Britain.

4 Moss Campion *Silene acaulis.* Perennial plant, cushion-like, densely leafy with numerous stems, only 2—4 cm high. Leaves spreading, linear, pointed, sessile. Flowers solitary, short-stalked. Calyx narrowly bell-shaped, petals bright to dark rose; capsules stalked, ovoid. Flowers from June to September. Grows on stony slopes and ledges, screes and among rocks above forest zone in mountains of western and central Europe.

5 Bladder Campion *Silene vulgaris* (syn. *S. cucubalus*). Herb up to 50 cm high, perennial, grey-green and smooth. Leaves elliptic lanceolate, entire, lower ones almost, upper leaves distinctly sessile. Flowers arranged in corymbose cymes, lower ones with long stalks, upper flowers short-stalked. Calyx inflated, ovoid, strikingly net-veined, yellowish green or with tint of purple. Petals usually white, deeply bilobed. Capsules broadly ovoid. Flowers from June to September. Grows on grassy slopes, by the roadside, on margins of woods, and on cultivated land, from lowlands to mountains.

6 Nottingham Catchfly *Silene nutans*. Up to 50 cm high, perennial, with erect and unbranched stems. Lower leaves spathulate, upper ones with short petioles, lanceolate to linear-lanceolate, with short hairs. Inflorescence a lax panicle of dichasial cymes, glandularly hairy; flowers long-stalked, more or less drooping. Calyx cylindrical, petals whitish, deeply bilobed. Capsules ovoid. Flowers from May to August. Grows on sunny slopes, among rocks, at outskirts of woods and on screes, from lowlands to foothills.

4

5

6

Family: Silenaceae

1 German Pink *Dianthus carthusianorum.* Perennial, tufted herb, over 25 cm high, with slender flowering stems and short, leafy, non-flowering ones, little branched. Leaves linear, fused at the base into a short sheath, pointed, stiff, rough on margins. Inflorescence a dense corymbose head, flowers almost sessile, bracts under calyx leathery, brown to red-brown, bluntly obovate, with awn-like point. Calyx cylindrical, smooth with maroon tint; petals purple-red, with toothed tip; capsules narrow oblong. Flowers from June to September. Grows on grassy, stony dry slopes and field boundaries.

2 Maiden Pink *Dianthus deltoides.* Perennial, sparsely tufted herb, with prostrate leafy stems and erect flowering ones. Leaves linear-pointed, opposite, roughly hairy on margins. Flowers long-stalked, solitary, bracts under calyx membranous. Calyx cylindrical, sometimes reddish; petals carmine-red, toothed at tip; conspicuously bristled and white-dotted at base. Flowers from June to September. Grows in dry pastures, banks and field boundaries, from lowland to foothill country. Some related species, e.g. Carnation (*D. caryophyllus*) and China Pink (*D. chinensis*), are cultivated in gardens.

1

2

3

3 Soapwort *Saponaria officinalis.* Perennial robust plant, up to 75 cm high, erect, usually with finely downy stem, branched only in upper part. Leaves ovate to elliptic, pointed, sessile, three to five-veined. Flowers pink, sometimes white, in terminal corymbs. Calyx usually light green, hairy; petals blunt or square tipped. Capsules oblong ovoid. Flowers from June to September. Grows in hedgerows, by streams and in open moist woods, from lowlands to foothills. A double-flowered form is sometimes cultivated and becomes naturalized on banks and wasteland.

4 Greater Stitchwort *Stellaria holostea.* Perennial, sparsely tufted plant with creeping rhizome and erect, square stems, up to 30 cm high. Leaves spreading, narrowly lanceolate, pointed, opposite, underside and margins rough. Flowers in an open, terminal, few-flowered dichasia. Petals white, double the length of calyx, almost deeply bilobed. Flowers from May to September. Grows in hedgerows, on bushy slopes and in open woodland from lowlands to foothills. Related Common Chickweed (*S. media*) has much smaller flowers and petals of the same length as calyx.

5 Field Mouse-ear *Cerastium arvense.* Perennial herb, sparsely tufted, up to 30 cm high, with numerous stems creeping or ascending, with sterile leafy shoots. Leaves narrowly oblong to linear-lanceolate, pointed, hairy. Flowers in lax dichasia. Sepals hairy, with whitish membranous margins; petals double the calyx length, white, bilobed. Flowers from April to July. Grows in dry grassland and on banks, from lowlands to mountains.

6 *Cerastium holosteoides* (syn. *C. vulgatum*). Perennial tufted herb up to 30 cm high, with ascending, flowering stems and semi-prostrate, leafy, sterile shoots. Leaves oblanceolate to elliptic, bluntly pointed, with short hairs. Flowers in open dichasia. Petals slightly longer than calyx, small, white, bilobed. Flowers from May to October. Grows by the roadside, on dunes, in dry meadows and on grassy slopes, from lowlands to mountains.

node, silvery membranous. Flowers in a small terminal cyme; flower stalks nodding, after fertilization again erect, and elongated when capsule is mature. Petals pink, usually shorter than sepals. Flowers from May to September. Grows in sandy or gravelly soils, from lowlands to foothills.

Family: **Violet**—Violaceae

2 Sweet Violet *Viola odorata*. Perennial herb with short, thick rhizomes and long prostrate stolons. Basal leaves ovate-orbicular, cordate, sparingly hairy. Stems up to 10 cm high, with widely ovate stipules, entire or glandular fringed. Fragrant flowers blue-violet or white, rarely pink; petals whitish at base, the lowest one spurred; calyx has appendages which are much shorter than the spur. Flowers in March and April. Grows in woods, thickets and hedgebanks at lower altitudes; often cultivated in gardens. Related Heath Violet (*V. canina*) is distinctly hairy and has narrower leaves, and unscented flowers with a whitish spur.

3 Common Violet *Viola riviniana*. Perennial plant with short rhizome and basal rosette of leaves. Stems erect, usually 10—15 cm high. Leaves long-petiolate, ovate-orbicular, deeply cordate, crenate; stipules lanceolate, deeply fringed. Flowers large, various shades of blue-violet, spur paler. Calyx with angularly rounded

Family: Stellariaceae (syn. Alsinaceae)

1 Sand Spurrey *Spergularia rubra*. Annual or biennial plant, somewhat tufted, decumbent or ascending. Stems 5—25 cm long; leaves narrowly linear, sharply pointed, shorter than stem internodes. Stipules ovate, fused around the

5

6

appendages. Flowers in April and May. Grows in open woods, hedgebanks, heaths, pastures and among rocks, from lowlands to mountains. A very variable species; the smaller forms distinguished as *V. riviniana* ssp. *minor*.

4 Heartsease or **Wild Pansy** *Viola tricolor*. Annual or perennial herb, usually tufted, up to 20 cm high, with branched, erect or ascending stem. Leaves petiolate, ovate to lanceolate; stipules deeply lobed. Flowers on long stalks; lanceolate sepals have blunt to rounded appendages. Petals often double calyx length, two upper ones mostly violet, others light yellow, or entirely blue-violet or yellow; spur longer than calyx appendages. Flowers from May to September. Grows in fields and meadows, on wasteland, from lowlands to foothills. Related Field Violet *V. arvensis* has much smaller light yellow flowers, the calyx and corolla of equal length. *Viola* × *wittrockiana* is the cultivated hybrid garden pansy with large flowers of varied colours.

Family: **Goosefoot** —Chenopodiaceae

5 Good King Henry *Chenopodium bonus-henricus*. The only perennial goosefoot; stem up to 50 cm or more high, unbranched. Petiolate leaves triangular, with pointed basal lobes and a wavy margin. Globose clusters of flowers arranged in dense, terminal, leafy, pyramidal panicle. Flowers have minute five-lobed perianth which enfolds the base of the tiny ovoid capsule. Flowers from May to August. Grows abundantly near human dwellings and by roadsides from lowlands to foothills. Related Sowbane (*C. hybridum*) and especially Stinking Goosefoot (*C. vulvaria*) are slightly poisonous and distinctly malodorous.

6 Shining Orache *Atriplex nitens*. Annual herb up to 150 cm high, with branched stems. Leaves triangular, lobed, on upper surface glossy, dark green, on underside silvery grey with a mealy coating. Inflorescence drooping, especially during fruiting. Pair of enlarged bracts in which fruit is enclosed, is rhomboid, entire, longer than fruit stalks. Minute flowers are greenish. Flowers from July to September. Grows on wasteland and by roadsides at lower altitudes. Related Common Orache (*A. patula*) has rhomboid-lanceolate to linear-oblong leaves and floral bracts with one or two small teeth on each side.

Family: **Knotgrass**—Polygonaceae

1 Sheep's Sorrel *Rumex acetosella.* Perennial plant, often with red tint; stem up to 25 cm high, decumbent or erect. Lower leaves long-petiolate, hastate, upper ones linear-lanceolate. Inflorescence a small branched raceme; flowers have small greenish perianth; during fruition this enlarges and more or less encloses the fruit. Flowers from May to August. Grows on heaths and pastures, and as a weed in fields and gardens from lowlands to foothills.

2 Common Sorrel *Rumex acetosa*. Over 50 cm high, perennial. Lower stem leaves narrowly ovate, arrow-shaped, with pointed basal lobes. Stipules fused as a fringed sheath. Inflorescence a branched raceme; flowers have green perianth. Inner segments rounded cordate with tiny, round swelling, enlarging during fruit development; outer segments reflex back. Flowers from May to July. Grows in light woodland clearings, in damp meadows, and by roadsides, from lowlands to mountains. Eaten in salads and sauces. Related Curled Dock (*R. crispus*) has a triangularly ovate fruiting perianth and the lower leaves with waved and curled margins.

3 Bistort or **Easter-ledges** *Polygonum bistorta*. Perennial herb with thick rhizome and simple stems up to 1 metre high. Basal leaves long petiolate, ovate, pointed, entire, stem leaves triangular-ovate, sessile. Inflorescence a dense terminal spike, individual flowers rosy, rarely whitish. Flowers from May to July. Grows in damp meadows, pastures and by roadsides, often in dense colonies or clumps, from lowlands to mountains. *Polygonum persicaria* has leaves with large, horseshoe-shaped maroon blotch.

4 Knotgrass *Polygonum aviculare*. An annual, decumbent plant with branched stem, up to 50 cm long, often forming dense mats. Leaves elliptic, spathulate, lanceolate or linear with membranous stipules, fused into sheaths, usually lacerated. Flowers in clusters of one to six in leaf axils; perianth whitish, often pink tinted; enlarging during fruition and becoming red. Flowers from May to October. Grows in waste places, by roadsides, along paths and as farm and garden weed, from lowlands to hills.

5 *Polygonum convolvulus*. Annual, prostrate or twining, with angular stems up to 1 metre long. Leaves ovate-acuminate to triangular, arrow-shaped. Flowers in an interrupted, terminal raceme; perianth of 5 segments, the outer two somewhat keeled. Flowers from July to October. Grows as field and garden weed, and on wasteland at lower altitudes.

Family: **Nettle**—Urticaceae

6 Hop *Humulus lupulus*. Twining, perennial, dioecious plant with coarsely hairy stems, 2—6 metres long. Stipules triangular-ovate; leaves opposite, long-petiolate, lower ones palmately three- to five-lobed, cordate, upper leaves more shallowly lobed to ovate, all boldly toothed. Male flowers in axillary panicles, female ones in ovoid, cone-like spikes. Fruiting heads pendent, pale greenish-yellow, their scales covered with golden-yellow glands. Flowers from July to August. Grows in hedgerows, amongst scrub, and at edges of woodland at lower altitudes. Has been cultivated since 8th century in fields for flavouring beer.

6

131

Family: **Nettle**—Urticaceae

1 Small Nettle *Urtica urens*. Annual herb, 10—30 cm high, with erect, little branched stems. Leaves ovate to elliptic, serrate. Erect inflorescences of the same length as petioles or shorter; tiny flowers have light green perianth. Fruit a tiny ovoid nutlet. Whole plant covered with stinging hairs; sharply 'burns' on touch. Flowers from June to September. Grows abundantly as weed in fields and gardens, on wasteland and by rubbish tips at lower altitudes.

2 Stinging Nettle *Urtica dioica*. Robust, perennial, dioecious herb with a far-creeping rhizome. Stems erect, rarely branched, up to 150 cm tall. Leaves petiolate, ovate, cordate, pointed, serrate. Male inflorescences spreading or pendent panicles, longer than leaf petioles; female always drooping and longer. Perianth greenish, nutlet ovoid. Whole plant covered with stinging hairs, but sometimes without. Flowers from June to October. Grows as a farm and garden weed on waste ground, in thickets, damp woods, ditches and in hedgerows, from lowlands to mountains.

Family: **Sundew**—Droseraceae

3 Common Sundew *Drosera rotundifolia*. Perennial herb, forming solitary or tufted rosettes. One to several erect stems, 10—20 cm high, usually red tinted, bearing a few-flowered spike of tiny, white flowers. Leaves rounded and fleshy, long-petiolate, reddish, with long, glandular hairs; fruit is a capsule. Flowers in July and August. Grows in bogs and wet peaty places, on moors and heaths, from lowlands to mountains. Grows in sites with soil poor in nitrogenous substances; acquires missing compounds from bodies of insects. Sensitive, glandular hairs exude sticky liquid which traps insects; special glands secrete substances for digesting soft parts of insects body.

1

2

3

4

5

6

Family: **Crassula**—Crassulaceae

4 Orpine or **Livelong** *Sedum telephium*. Perennial herb with thick rootstock and erect stems up to 50 cm high. Leaves ovate to oblong-lanceolate or obovate, toothed, tapered to sessile base, alternate, opposite or in whorls of three, fleshy grey-green. Inflorescence flattened and compact, composed of numerous cymes; sepals 5, green, corollas reddish purple. Flowers from July to September. Grows among rocks, on hedgebanks, walls, and in light dry woods from lowlands to mountains.

5 Wall Pepper *Sedum acre*. Perennial, mat-forming plant, 5—10 cm high, with prostrate, much branched stems. Leaves widely ovate to ovoid triangular, blunt, sessile, thickly set and usually overlapping, having a sharply burning taste. Inflorescence a few-flowered cyme; flowers short-stalked, corollas bright yellow, star-shaped. Flowers in June and July. Grows on sunny slopes, among rocks, in sandy places, on wasteland, walls and dunes, from lowlands to foothills.

6 *Sempervivum soboliferum*. Perennial herb with leaves arranged in a dense basal rosette. Leaves ovate, reddish brown at tip, margins shortly bristled. Flowering stems glandular-hairy, up to 20 cm high, thickly leaved. Calyx also glandular, sepals red-tipped. Petals six, pointed, greenish yellow. Flowers in July and August. Grows on rocks, stony slopes and walls, from lowlands to mountains. Protected plant. Common Houseleek (*S. tectorum*), bearing rosy flowers, and other species are cultivated in gardens.

Family: **Saxifrage**—Saxifragaceae

1 Meadow Saxifrage *Saxifraga granulata*. Perennial, somewhat tufted plant, up to 40 cm high, with basal rosettes and stems usually branched. Overwinters as a cluster of small bulbils from the axils of the basal leaves. These leaves are reniform, cordate, glandular-hairy, usually with large crenations. Stem leaves almost sessile, much smaller. Inflorescence a loose terminal cyme. Flowers shortly glandular, petals white, at least three times longer than calyx. Capsules ovoid or sub-globose. Flowers in May and June. Grows in well-drained grassland and on margins of woods at lower altitudes.

2 Livelong Saxifrage *Saxifraga paniculata* (syn. *S. aizoon*). Perennial herb with stiff, grey-green leaves in numerous basal rosettes. Basal leaves obovate to ligulate, serrate; the margins with small glands which secrete calcium carbonate.

Stem up to 30 cm tall, leaves small, ligulate, finely serrate. Inflorescence open, paniculate, corollas white, often red-dotted. Capsules globose. Flowers in June and July. Grows scattered on rocks, screes and stony barrens in mountains. Many related species grow in Alps, some of them cultivated in gardens.

3 Grass of Parnassus *Parnassia palustris*. Perennial herb with few-leaved basal rosette and stems 10—20 cm high. Basal leaves long-petiolate, ovately cordate, smooth. Single-flowered stems with one sessile clasping leaf. Flowers of five white petals; five gland-fringed staminodes alternate with five stamens. Capsule ovoid. Flowers from June to September, in lowlands much later than in mountains. Grows in damp meadows and on heaths and moors from lowlands to foothills, in mountains, in peaty meadows and among wet rocks.

4

5

Family: **Rose**—Rosaceae

4 Wood Goatsbeard *Aruncus dioicus* (syn. *A. sylvester*). Perennial, clump-forming herb up to 2 metres high, with erect, smooth stems. Leaves long-petiolate, two or three times pinnate, the leaflets ovate to lanceolate, shortly petiolate to almost sessile, pointed and unequally toothed. Inflorescence a large, dense, terminal panicle, composed of numerous minute, unisexual or dioecious cream-white flowers. Fruits are tiny brown follicles. Flowers in July. Grows in damp mountain forests and thickets and often naturalized by roadsides, from hilly country to mountains.

5 Meadowsweet *Filipendula ulmaria*. Perennial, clump-forming plant up to 150 cm high, with short rhizomes and erect, stiff, seldom branched stems. Leaves odd-pinnate, with double-toothed ovate leaflets, terminal one larger, palmately three- to five-lobed. Flowers in large, dense, terminal cymes, creamy-white, fragrant. Flowers from June to September. Grows in swamps, marshes, fens, damp or wet woods, and in lowlands and foothills. Dropwort (*F. vulgaris*) thrives in dry habitats, is smaller and has a tuberous rootstock.

6 Marsh Cinquefoil *Potentilla palustris* (syn. *Comarum palustre*). Perennial, woody-based herb up to 1 metre high. Leaves odd-pinnate with 5—7 oblong, toothed leaflets, dark green above, hairy on veins and grey-green beneath. Flowers in sparse terminal cymes, the five-lobed calyx outside green, inside red-purple. Petals smaller than calyx lobes, deep purple, stamens dark red; achenes ovoid. Flowers in June and July. Grows in fens, bogs, marshes, and by water, from lowlands to foothills.

Family: **Rose**—Rosaceae

1 Silverweed *Potentilla anserina.* Perennial herb with thick rhizome and creeping, rooting stems, up to 50 cm long. Leaves odd-pinnate, with 7—12 pairs of main leaflets alternating with pairs of much smaller ones. The large leaflets oval, serrate, underside silky, white-felted. Golden yellow flowers solitary, on slender stalks; sepals 5, ovate. Flowers from May to August. Grows in waste places, in pastures, on paths, roadsides and banks, from lowlands to foothills. Related Creeping Cinquefoil (*P. reptans*) has palmate leaves with 3—7 obovate leaflets.

2 Golden Cinquefoil *Potentilla aurea.* Perennial herb with thick rhizome. Stems ascending, up to 25 cm long, growing from axils of basal rosette leaves. Leaves palmate, with 5 oblong to obovate leaflets toothed at the top; margins and undersides silvery and silky hairy on veins; upper side smooth and glossy. Flower stalks long and hairy, flowers rich yellow with a darker base. Flowers from June to September. Grows in mountain meadows and on rocky slopes.

136

3 *Potentilla tabernaemontani* (syn. *P. verna*). Perennial mat-forming plant with much branched rhizome and numerous prostrate shoots, often rooting at the nodes. Leaves long-petiolate, palmate, with 5 somewhat hairy, toothed, wedge-shaped to obovate leaflets. Stalked flowers with shallowly notched yellow petals. Flowers from March to June. Grows on sunny, grassy slopes, in sandy places and among rocks from lowlands to foothills. Related Hoary Cinquefoil (*P. argentea*) has leaflet margins recurved and undersides white-felted similarly to stems.

4 Tormentil *Potentilla erecta*. Perennial herb with short, thick, branched rootstock and erect or ascending leafy stem, up to 30 cm long. Basal leaves petiolate, stem ones almost sessile, usually trifoliate; leaflets wedge-shaped, obovate, toothed, lobed stipules large and conspicuous. Flowers slender, stalked, small, with 4 rounded, faintly notched yellow petals. Flowers from June to August. Grows on heaths, heather moors and in rocky and grassy places, from lowlands to mountains.

5 White Cinquefoil *Potentilla alba*. Perennial herb with much-branched rhizome and numerous flower stems, about 10 cm high, from axils of basal leaves. Leaves palmate, with 5 lanceolate leaflets, finely toothed at tip; upperside dark green, underside silvery, silky-hairy. Flowers white; sepals of the same length as epicalyx. Achenes hairy. Flowers from May to July. Grows in dry woods, meadows and on grassy slopes at lower altitudes, in milder regions.

6 Wild Strawberry *Fragaria vesca*. Perennial tufted herb with branched rhizome and creeping, rooting stolons. Stems up to 20 cm high emerge from axils of leaves. Leaves trifoliate, leaflets obovate to ovate, toothed, lateral ones sessile. Flower stalks have appressed hairs, flowers are white; ripe strawberries sub-globose to bluntly conical, red. Flowers in May and June. Grows in woodland clearings, open woods, on bushy slopes, banks and hedgerows, from lowlands to mountains. Related *Fragaria moschata* is larger, has flower stalks with spreading and lateral leaflets shortly petiolate. Fruits whitish, on sunny side red flushed.

5

6

Family: **Rose**—Rosaceae

1 Mountain Avens *Dryas octopetala*. Plant with woody stems forming cushion-like tufts, several centimetres high. Leaves petiolate, ovate-oblong, with rounded teeth, leathery, on underside white, upper surface dark green, glossy. Flowers solitary on erect, up to 10 cm long stalks; petals 7—10, white, obovate. Achenes have long, hairy appendages and resemble those of Pasque Flower. Flowers from June to August. Grows on rocks, screes, and grassy slopes in mountains and by the sea, predominantly on limestone soils.

2 Common Avens *Geum urbanum*. Perennial tufted herb, up to 50 cm high, with thick rhizome and basal rosette of leaves. These are petiolate, odd-pinnate, with lanceolate lateral and broadly ovate to orbicular terminal leaflets, irregularly double-toothed. Stem leaves trifoliate or trilobed. Flowers erect, calyx after flowering reflexing; petals yellow. Achenes bristly hairy with a sharp hook on the modified style. Flowers from May to August. Grows in open woods, thickets, along hedgerows and on wasteland, from lowlands to foothills.

3 Water Avens *Geum rivale*. Perennial plant up to 1 metre high, with thick rhizome. Stems erect, hairy, often red flushed. Basal leaves in a rosette, long-petiolate, lyre-like, pinnate, terminal leaflet large, rounded, trilobed; lateral leaflets ovate, all hairy and toothed. Stem leaves are trifoliate. Flowers drooping; calyx purple, petals orange-pink; after fertilization flowering stem erect. Achenes hairy, with a stalked hook. Flowers in May and June. Grows in wet meadows, marshes, streamsides and damp woods, from hilly country to mountains.

4 Common Agrimony *Agrimonia eupatoria*. Perennial plant up to 1 metre high, hairy, with thick rhizome. Stem little branched. Basal leaves odd-pinnate, leaflets elliptic, toothed; stem leaves smaller, with few leaflets. Flowers short-stalked, arranged in simple, erect raceme; corollas small, yellow; calyx hairy, with numerous deep grooves and bearing hooked spines. Flowers from June to August. Grows on hedge banks, along field boundaries, by roadsides and on bushy and grassy hills, from lowlands to foothills.

5 Great Burnet *Sanguisorba officinalis* (syn. *Poterium officinale*). Perennial herb up to 1 metre high, with thick rhizome and erect, branched stems. Basal leaves odd-pinnate in basal tufts; leaflets shortly petiolate, oblong-ovate, toothed, upper side glossy dark green, under side blue-green, hairless. Floral heads oblong-ovoid, dull crimson; flowers very small, without petals. Flowers from July to September. Grows fairly abundantly in damp meadows, from lowlands to foothills. *Sanguisorba minor* grows in well-drained hill grassland, has globose, reddish green heads, and leaflets widely ovate with green undersides.

6 Common Lady's Mantle *Alchemilla vulgaris.* Perennial herb, with a thick, somewhat woody rhizome and tufts of basal leaves. Stems ascending or erect, 10—30 cm high, hairy to smooth. Petiolate basal leaves rounded or reniform, palmately lobed and toothed. Flowers without petals, yellow-green, in open panicles; sepals either smooth or hairy. Flowers from May to September. Grows in meadows, pastures, along brooks and at outskirts of woods, from lowlands to mountains.

Family: Fabaceae (syn. Papilionaceae)

1 Common Lupin *Lupinus polyphyllus*. Perennial plant up to 150 cm high. Stems leafy, erect, unbranched. Leaves petiolate, palmate, with cuneate, elliptic, hairy leaflets. Pea-shaped flowers in dense, upright racemes; corollas blue or blue and white. Pods large, hairy and many-seeded. Flowers from June to August. Native of North America; at one time cultivated as forage for farm animals and for green manuring in gardens. Also grown for ornamental purposes and often going wild. South-European species are sometimes cultivated as forage, having white or yellow flowers.

2 Common Melilot *Melilotus officinalis*. Biennial herb with erect, branched stems up to 1 metre high, angular, usually smooth. Leaves petiolate, trifoliate, with oblong-elliptic, toothed leaflets, the central one distinctly petiolate; stipules lanceolate, entire. Dense axillary stalked racemes bearing tiny yellow drooping flowers. Pods ovoid, smooth and black. Flowers from June to September. Grows in fields, wasteland and by roadsides, from lowlands to hilly country. Related White Melilot (*M. albus*) has white flowers.

3 Lucerne *Medicago sativa*. Perennial herb, up to 80 cm high, with erect, smooth stems and trifoliate leaves; leaflets narrowly obovate, central one distinctly petiolate. Flowers purple, rarely whitish, in dense, short racemes. Pods spirally twisted, two to three turns. Flowers from June to September. Native of eastern Mediterranean and western Asia; long cultivated for forage and often well naturalized. Related Sickle Medick (*M. falcata*) is native of central Europe, has yellow flowers and sickle-shaped pods. Hybrid populations are often encountered.

4 White Clover *Trifolium repens*. Perennial herb with creeping, rooting stems, ascending at the tips, up to 30 cm long. Leaves long-petiolate, trifoliate, leaflets sessile, obovate to obcordate, finely toothed at tip, with lighter angled band towards the base. Flower heads globose; florets white or pink; after flowering light brown. Flowers from May to September. Grows in meadows, lawns and ditches. Cultivated as a fodder crop.

5 Red Clover *Trifolium pratense*. Perennial herb almost 50 cm high, with erect, little-branched stems. Leaves in basal tuft are trifoliate and long-petiolate; leaflets sessile, obovate to elliptic, entire, usually with a whitish or red-brown crescent-shaped spot on upper surface. Stem leaves smaller, sessile. Flower heads globose to ovoid, flowers purple-pink or pale red, rarely whitish. Flowers from June to September. Grows in meadows, by the roadside and in forest clearings, from lowlands to mountains. Often cultivated for forage. Cultivated *Trifolium incarnatum* has striking cylindrical heads. Tiny Haresfoot Trefoil (*T. arvense*) has small hairy heads and palest pink flowers.

1

6 Kidney Vetch *Anthyllis vulneraria*. Perennial herb with hairy stem, up to 30 cm high, ascending to erect. Odd-pinnate basal leaves; 11–15 leaflets, elliptic to linear-oblong, terminal one much larger than lateral ones. Globose flower heads singly or in clusters. Flowers light yellow to reddish. Flowers from May to August. Grows on sunny grassy banks and slopes.

4

6

2

3

5

Family: Fabaceae

1 Common Birdsfoot Trefoil *Lotus corniculatus.*
Perennial herb, well-branched rhizome, decumbent or ascending stems, up to 30 cm long, distinctly angular. Leaves odd-pinnate, the 5 leaflets smooth, entire, broadly ovate to lanceolate, underside grey-green. Flowers short-stalked, in 3—10 flowered umbels, corollas intense yellow, outside usually reddish. Flowers from May to September. Grows in pastures and on grassy and bushy slopes from lowlands to mountains. Related Marsh Birdsfoot Trefoil (*L. uliginosus*) has hollow, round stems, larger inflorescence and grows in moist habitat.

2 Common Crown Vetch *Coronilla varia.* Perennial, robust herb with numerous stems, decumbent or ascending, often climbing, branched, up to 1 metre long. Leaves odd-pinnate, the 9—17 leaflets shortly petiolate, oblong elliptic with a short point. Long-stalked inflorescence erect; white, pink or purple flowers in 10—20 flowered umbels. Pods slender, breaking up into one-seeded sections. Flowers from June to August. Grows on field boundaries, bushy slopes and by the roadside, from lowlands to foothills. Slightly poisonous.

3 Sainfoin *Onobrychis viciifolia.* Perennial, robust herb, scattered with hairs, up to 50 cm. high, with stiff, erect stem. Leaves odd-pinnate, the 11—25 leaflets obovate to linear-oblong. Racemes ovoid to cylindrical, flowers bright red or pink, the standard petal purple-striped. Pods short, flat, one-seeded. Flowers from May to July. Commonly cultivated forage since 16th century; often becomes locally naturalized. Found along field boundaries, by the roadside and on dry slopes at lower altitudes.

1 2 3

4 Bush Vetch *Vicia sepium*. Perennial herb with branched rhizome and erect or climbing stem up to 50 cm high. Leaves pinnate, terminated in branched tendril; the 10—18 leaflets ovate to elliptic, mucronate, and pointed. Flowers in threes to sixes in axils of leaves; corollas pale purple, calyx teeth unequal, shorter than calyx tube. Flowers from May to August. Grows in hedgerows, thickets, open woods and meadows, from lowlands to mountains. Related Common Vetch (*V. sativa*) has larger flowers in groups of one to three in the leaf axils. Large forms cultivated as forage and well naturalized by roadsides and on waste ground.

5 Tufted Vetch *Vicia cracca*. Perennial herb with strong, creeping rhizome and angular, softly hairy stems, up to 1 metre or more high. Pinnate leaves terminate in branched tendril; the 12—30 leaflets oblong to linear-lanceolate, underside usually hairy. Inflorescence a 10- to 40-flowered, one-sided raceme, stalked, almost as long as leaves; corollas blue-violet, rarely whitish. Pods short-stalked. Flowers from June to August. Grows in hedgerows, thickets, along field boundaries and in grassy places, from lowlands to mountains.

6 Hairy Milk Vetch *Oxytropis pilosa*. Perennial herb 15—30 cm high, densely hairy. Erect, ascending stems bear odd-pinnate leaves with narrowly lanceolate leaflets. Dense inflorescence an elongated raceme; flowers light yellow. Pods linear with white hairs. Flowers in June and July. Grows on sunny grassy slopes at lower altitudes, in milder areas.

4 5 6

143

Family: Fabaceae

1 Earth-nut Pea *Lathyrus tuberosus.* Perennial, hairless, grey-green herb with creeping rhizome and tuberous, thickened roots. Stems climbing, up to 1 metre long, square. Leaves with one pair of obovate leaflets and branched tendril. Long-stalked inflorescences bear a few-flowered raceme; flowers fragrant, light purple, standard crimson. Flowers from June to August. Naturalized in Britain in fields and hedgerows especially on calcareous soils, at lower altitudes. Related Annual Sweet Pea (*L. odoratus*) with large flowers of various colours is native of southern Europe and cultivated in gardens.

2 Narrow-leaved Everlasting Pea *Lathyrus sylvestris.* Perennial, robust plant with long, creeping rhizome. Numerous stems are ascending or climbing, up to 3 metres long, keeled or winged. Leaves with branched tendril, the 2 leaflets linear-lanceolate, petioles widely winged. Axillary, long-stalked inflorescences, with 3—8 rose-pink flowers. Pods to 8 cm long, winged. Flowers in July and August. Grows in open woods, on bushy slopes and in hedgerows from lowlands to foothills. Related Meadow Vetchling (*L. pratensis*) is much smaller with attractive yellow flowers.

3 *Lathyrus vernus* (syn. *Orobus vernus*). Perennial herb with erect, self-supporting stems up to 40 cm high. Pinnate leaves bright green, without tendrils, the 2 or 3 pairs of leaflets ovate and long-pointed. Inflorescence a few-flowered raceme. Flowers red-violet, later blue-green, wings with blue tint. Flowers in April and May. Grows in open woods, from lowlands to foothills.

4 Milk Vetch *Astragalus glycyphyllos.* Perennial herb with decumbent or ascending, hairless stems, sometimes creeping, up to 1 metre long. Leaves odd-pinnate, the 11—21 leaflets oblong-elliptic. Axillary, stalked inflorescences in racemes, shorter than leaves; flowers creamy-white, tinged greenish. Pods linear, sickle-shaped. Flowers in June and July. Grows in open woods, thickets and rough grassy places, from lowlands to foothills. Related Alpine Milk Vetch (*A. alpinum*) has light blue flowers and violet-red keel.

Family: **Geranium**—Geraniaceae

5 Bloody Cranesbill *Geranium sanguineum*. Perennial herb with thick, creeping rhizome. Stems ascending, up to 50 cm long, hairy. Basal leaves die early; stem ones are opposite, petiolate, deeply palmately lobed into five to seven narrow segments, which are further cut or lobed. Solitary, axillary, long-stalked flowers have 5 purple-crimson petals. Flowers from June to August. Grows in open bushy places, on stony slopes and in grassland, at lower altitudes.

6 Herb Robert *Geranium robertianum*. Annual or biennial herb, red-tinted, hairy, somewhat foetid. Erect or decumbent stems up to 40 cm long. Leaves palmately lobed, petiolate leaflets once or twice pinnately dissected, segments toothed. Rose-pink flowers in pairs; corollas less than 15 mm in diameter. Flowers from May to October. Grows in open woods, on screes and walls, from lowlands to mountains. Wood Cranesbill (*G. sylvaticum*) has purple flowers; Meadow Cranesbill (*G. pratense*) has violet-blue and *Geranium phaeum* brown or black-purple flowers. All have strikingly beaked fruits.

3

4

5

6

Family: **Geranium**—Geraniaceae

1 Common Storksbill *Erodium cicutarium.* Annual or biennial herb with erect or inclined stems, hairy, up to 25 cm long. Basal, long-petiolate leaves in rosette, upper ones are shortly petiolate; all leaves odd-pinnate, segments pinnatisect, hairy. Inflorescence a several-flowered, stalked umbel with rose-violet corollas; downy, long-beaked fruits follow. Flowers from April to October. Grows in fields, waste places, dry grassland and downs, from lowlands to mountains.

Family: **Oxalis**—Oxalidaceae

2 Common Wood Sorrel *Oxalis acetosella.* Perennial tufted herb up to 10 cm high. Leaves and long-stalked flowers grow directly from stiff, creeping rhizome. Leaves trifoliate, leaflets sessile, obcordate and entire, underside usually reddish. Flowers white, veined lilac or purple. Fruit an explosive capsule. Flowers in April or May. Grows in damp forests or thickets and among rocks from lowlands to mountains. Introduced, yellow-flowered species: Upright Yellow Wood Sorrel (*O. europaea*) with leaves in whorls and Procumbent Yellow Wood Sorrel (*O. corniculata*) with prostrate stems and alternate leaves often purple-flushed.

Family: Linaceae

3 Flax *Linum usitatissimum.* Annual herb, up to 50 cm high with erect, leafy stems. Leaves linear-lanceolate to linear, pointed, three-veined, entire. Flowers in cymose inflorescences; corolla of 5 light blue petals. Fruit a globular capsule. Flowers in June and July. Long cultivated for linen fibre; native of Asia Minor; mainly cultivated in foothills. Purging Flax (*L. catharticum*) is a small slender plant with tiny white flowers and forked stems with opposite, obovate leaves.

146

Family: **Rue**—Rutaceae

4 Burning Bush *Dictamnus albus.* Perennial, aromatic plant with whitish, branched rhizome. Erect stems up to 1 metre high, inflorescence reddish glandular. Odd-pinnate leaves, the 9—15 leaflets ovate or lanceolate, finely toothed, with translucent dots; dark green. Flowers in terminal racemes; calyx dark-veined, rarely whitish, petals purple or white, outside glandular hairy, similarly to capsules. Flowers from May to June. Grows only rarely on sunny slopes and forested steppes in temperate regions. Also often cultivated in gardens. Strictly protected plant.

Family: **Milkwort**—Polygalaceae

5 Common Milkwort *Polygala vulgaris.* Perennial, tufted herb. Ascending, erect or decumbent stems up to 25 cm long, usually simple and hairless. Leaves linear-lanceolate, pointed; bracts shorter than flower buds. Flowers are blue, rarely rose or white, with two enlarged sepals. Flat, obcordate capsule. Flowers from May to August. Grows in dry meadows, on grassy slopes and on outskirts of forests. *Polygala amara* has basal leaves in rosette.

Family: **Spurge**—Euphorbiaceae

6 Dog's Mercury *Mercurialis perennis.* Perennial plant with far-creeping rhizome and usually erect, round, unbranched stems. Petiolate leaves dull green, lanceolate to elliptic-ovate, toothed, as a rule with spreading hairs. Unisexual, minute, greenish flowers; pistillate ones long-stalked, solitary or in twos, male flowers in small clusters forming sparse racemes. Capsules globular, bristly. Flowers in April and May. Grows in shady deciduous woods and among rocks from lowlands to mountains. Related Annual Mercury (*M. annua*) has pale green glossy leaves, square, branched stem and almost sessile pistillate flowers.

6

5

4

1

2

3

Family: **Spurge**—Euphorbiaceae

1 Cypress Spurge *Euphorbia cyparissias*. Perennial plant up to 30 cm high, with woody, branched rhizome. Stems tufted, erect, soon leafless at bottom, with red tint; densely leaved above, especially the lateral, non-flowering twigs. Narrowly linear leaves; yellowish bracts, after flowering reddish. Inflorescence a branched umbel with petalless flowers bearing wax-yellow glands. Capsules finely warty. Flowers in April and May. Grows in dry grassland and scrub and by roadsides from lowlands to foothills. All species of spurge have a white milky sap (latex).

Family: Impatientaceae

2 Touch-me-not *Impatiens noli-tangere*. Annual up to 1 metre high with erect stem, thickened at the nodes. Leaves petiolate, alternate, ovate-oblong, pointed, toothed, with glands at the base. Flowers in axillary few-flowered racemes, bright yellow, the mouth red-dotted, drooping, with curved spur. Cylindrical to ovoid explosive capsule. Flowers in July and August. Grows in damp woods and on the banks of rivers and streams, from lowlands to mountains. Related *Impatiens parviflora* has small, erect flowers with straight spur; Siberian plant, introduced to central Europe and now naturalized.

Family: **Mallow**—Malvaceae

3 Common Malow *Malva sylvestris*. Perennial herb with ascending or erect, tough stems, up to 1 metre long. Leaves palmate, petiolate, shallowly 5—7 lobed and toothed. Stalked flowers in small axillary clusters. Calyx flattened, with triangular lobes; corollas rose-purple, striped darker, petals spathulate, notched at tip. Stamen filaments fused into tube. Fruit a disc-shaped schizocarp, when ripe splitting into single-seeded, disc-shaped nutlets. Flowers from June to September. Grows by roadsides, in hedgerows, on wasteland, at lower altitudes of temperate regions.

148

4   5   6

4 Dwarf Mallow *Malva neglecta.* Annual to perennial with decumbent or ascending, branched stems, almost 50 cm long. Long-petiolate leaves, shallowly palmately lobed and toothed, with hairy underside. Axillary, stalked flowers reflexed during fruiting; sepals flat, corollas twice the calyx length, pale lilac to whitish, darker-veined, notched at tip. Fruits smooth. Flowers from June to October. Grows on waste ground, by roadsides and in fields, from lowlands to mountains. Similar Small Mallow (*M. pusilla*) is smaller, lighter green and little branched, with the corollas same length as calyx; fruits wrinkled.

Family: Hypericaceae (syn. Guttiferae)

5 Common St. John's Wort *Hypericum perforatum.* Perennial herb with erect stems, 50 cm or more high, with two longitudinal, narrow ridges and numerous lateral, non-flowering, leafy twigs. Leaves ovate-elliptic, hairless, with conspicuous translucent dots. Flowers arranged in terminal inflorescences; stalks usually dotted with black. Corollas golden yellow, sepals and petals black-dotted; stamens in three bundles. Capsule conical, glandular, dotted. Flowers in July and August. Grows abundantly in woodland clearings, on bushy slopes, by the roadside and in fields, from lowlands to mountains. Related Mountain St. John's Wort (*H. montanum*) has rounded, sparsely leaved stem and fringed glandular sepals.

Family: Lythraceae

6 Purple Loosestrife *Lythrum salicaria.* Robust woody-based perennial up to 1 metre or more high. Erect, hairy stems, sharply square in section. Leaves ovate to lanceolate, base rounded or cordate, sessile, almost hairless. Terminal, dense, spire-like inflorescence. Flowers small, purple, with 6 obovate, waved petals. Fruit a small ovoid capsule. Flowers from July to September. Grows by water, in fens, marshes, swamps and in damp meadows, from lowlands to foothills.

Family: Onagraceae

1 Rosebay Willowherb *Chamaenerion angustifolium* (syn. *Epilobium angustifolium*). Perennial herb up to 1 metre or more high. Erect stems usually smooth and unbranched. Leaves oblong-lanceolate to linear-lanceolate, entire, or with a few distant teeth. Flowers in long dense racemes; calyx dark purple, petals 4, obovate, rose-purple, rarely whitish. Long, slender, cylindrical, downy capsules. Minute seeds, with long white hairs. Flowers in July to September. Grows in woodland clearings, on margins of woods and on wasteland, often gregariously.

2 Broad-leaved Willowherb *Epilobium montanum*. Perennial herb up to 80 cm high; erect or shortly ascending stems, simple or sparingly branched in inflorescence, with appressed hairs in two rows, before flowering usually drooping. Opposite, shortly petiolate leaves, elliptical-ovate, pointed, toothed, usually downy. Flowers in leafy terminal raceme; corollas up to 1 cm, petals notched at tip, pink, dark-veined. Stigma four-lobed, capsules downy and glandular. Flowers from June to September. Grows in woods, in bushy slopes, in hedgerows, on walls and as a weed in gardens, from lowlands high up into mountains. Many related species, e.g. Great Hairy Willowherb (*E. hirsutum*) with flowers up to 2 cm across and softly hairy stem.

3 Common Evening Primrose *Oenothera biennis*. Biennial plant up to 1 metre high. Erect stems, as a rule unbranched. Leaves in basal rosette, lanceolate; stem leaves smaller, alternate, finely toothed. Flowers up to 2 cm in diameter are arranged in terminal, leafy racemes. Lanceolate sepals reflexed, petals obcordate, light yellow. Capsules cylindrical, finely hairy. Flowers from June to August. Native of North America, introduced to Europe and much cultivated in gardens. Now well naturalized in waste places, by the roadside and on banks, from lowlands to foothills.

Family: Trapaceae

4 Water Chestnut *Trapa natans*. Annual herb with long, submerged stem. Leaves of two types: submerged ones pinnately divided, with linear segments; rosette leaves floating on water surface with rhomboid blades, sharply toothed at apex; petioles slightly inflated. Axillary, solitary flowers with 4 small white petals. Fruit is conspicuous small edible nut with oily seed surrounded by the enlarged, woody, spiky, four calyx lobes. Flowers in July and August. Grows in still waters of lower altitudes; formerly more frequent.

Family: Umbelliferae (syn. *Apiaceae*)

5 Field Eryngo *Eryngium campestre*. Perennial herb, robust, spreading, up to 50 cm high, grey-green, with well-branched stem. Leaves bi-pinnate, spire-tipped segments. Flowers in ovoid capitula, bracts and sepals spiny; corollas small, white or purplish. Flowers in July and August. Grows in dry grassy places in milder regions of lower altitudes.

6 Wood Sanicle *Sanicula europaea*. Perennial herb with short, creeping rhizome. Erect, angular stems, up to 40 cm high. Basal leaves petiolate, palmately 3—5 lobed, cordate, the segments again divided and sharply toothed; one or two sessile on flowering stem. Flowers small, arranged in several umbels grouped together. Corolla tiny, white or pinkish with protruding stamens. Flowers in May and June. Grows in deciduous woods, particularly on chalk and limestone, from lowlands to mountains; only locally frequent.

1

2

4

Family: Umbelliferae

1 Masterwort *Astrantia major.* Perennial herb with a somewhat woody rhizome. Erect stems up to over 50 cm high, each with one or two leaves. Basal leaves petiolate, palmate, deeply five- to seven-lobed, segments ovate, toothed; stem leaves more deeply dissected, segments wedge-shaped with trilobed tip. Bracts lanceolate, white or flushed pink. Flowers in simple umbels, corollas white, stamens protruding from flowers. Flowers from June to August. Naturalized in Britain, growing on margins of forests and in meadows in a few places from lowlands to mountains.

2 *Falcaria vulgaris.* A perennial, grey-green herb with erect, much-branched stems. Leaves stiff, doubly trifoliate (each lobe or leaflet again 3-lobed), segments linear-lanceolate, pointed,

sharply serrate. Several small secondary umbels form sparse compound umbels; tiny, white flowers. Flowers from July to September. Grows on dry grassy slopes and on field and meadow margins. Only just naturalized in eastern England and Guernsey.

3 Burnet Saxifrage *Pimpinella saxifraga.* Perennial plant up to 50 cm high, with finely grooved, branched stems. Bottom leaves odd-pinnate, long-petiolate; leaflets more or less deeply lobed, sessile; blades of stem leaves smaller, lobed less or not at all. Inflorescence of compound umbels without bracts. Very small flowers, corollas white, rose or yellowish. Fruit a double, ribbed schizocarp. Flowers from July to September. Grows on grassy slopes, field boundaries, in pastures, and by the roadside, from lowlands to mountains.

152

3   5

6

4 Goutweed *Aegopodium podagraria.* Robust perennial plant, almost 1 metre high, with hollow, angular stems and far-creeping rhizomes. Leaves have stem-sheathing petioles; bottom ones twice, upper leaves simply trifoliate; leaflets ovate, petiolate, lateral ones usually lobed, toothed. Inflorescence of compound umbels without bracts; small white or rose-tinted corollas. Schizocarp brown with paler ribs. Flowers in June and July. Grows on waste ground, in damp woods and ditches; also a common garden and farm weed.

5 Wild Angelica *Angelica sylvestris.* Perennial, robust plant, up to 150 cm high, with thick rhizome. Petiolate leaves have shallowly grooved petioles and inflated sheaths; bottom leaves two to three times pinnate, upper ones smaller and simply lobed; leaflets ovate, almost sessile, toothed. Dense compound umbels without bracts; small white or rosy corollas; three-

ribbed schizocarp, somewhat winged on margin. Flowers from July to September. Grows in damp woods, thickets and hedgerows, from lowlands to mountains.

6 Fine-leaved Water Dropwort *Oenanthe aquatica.* Perennial, well branched, robust herb with erect stems, up to 1 metre or more high, hollow, at base up to 5 cm in diameter. Leaves sheathed, petiolate, three times pinnate; segments lobed and toothed, lanceolate; submerged leaves filamentous. Numerous compound umbels, umbellets with bracts; small corollas white. Schizocarp narrowly ovoid, ridged. Flowers from June to August. Grows near or in water at lower altitudes and in moist places in hilly country. Related Fool's Parsley (*Aethusa cynapium*) has glossy coarser leaves and long slender floral bracts. It is a weed of cultivation on well-drained soils.

153

Family: Umbelliferae

1 Wild Parsnip *Pastinaca sativa*. Robust biennial herb up to 1 metre high; stem with angular grooves, more or less hairy. Odd-pinnate leaves; the leaflets ovate, serrate, lobed to pinnately divided. Secondary umbels on angular stalks, without bracts; small yellow flowers. Schizocarps elliptical, over 0.5 cm large, flattened and winged. Flowers from July to September. Grows on grassy slopes, in meadows and ditches, along roads, from lowlands to foothills, particularly on chalk and limestone. Caraway (*Carum carvi*), grown as a culinary herb, has upper leaves divided into filamentous segments and white flowers. The cultivated parsnip, with a thick fleshy root, is derived from this species.

2 Wild Carrot *Daucus carota*. Biennial herb almost 1 metre high, with erect, branched, hairy stem. Leaves twice or three times pinnate; pinnatisect segments of upper leaves linear. Dense, compound umbels have numerous pinnate bracts with linear segments. Flowers white, sometimes rosy, central umbels usually red or violet. Schizocarp ovoid, with hooked bristles. Flowers from June to September. Grows in dry meadows, field boundaries and on slopes from lowlands to mountains. *D. carota* ssp. *sativus* is the cultivated carrot.

3 Hogweed *Heracleum sphondylium*. Robust perennial herb up to 150 cm, somewhat foetid. Erect, grooved stems bristled and hollow. Large leaves, lower ones having a grooved petiole, upper leaves sessile with inflated sheaths, pinnate; segments asymmetrically lobed to pinnatisect, toothed. Large compound umbels usually without bracts; corollas white or pinkish. Flowers from June to September. Grows in damp meadows, on waste ground, by roadsides, from lowlands to mountains.

Family: **Primrose**—Primulaceae

6 Mountain Tassel-flower *Soldanella montana.* Small perennial herb with creeping rhizome and basal rosette of long-petiolate, reniform, faintly toothed and somewhat leathery leaves. Stems 10—30 cm high, bearing umbels of up to six pendent flowers on finely glandular stalks. Violet-blue flowers, calyx five-parted, corolla bell-shaped. Ovoid capsule, opening through ten blunt teeth. Flowers in May and June. Grows in mountain and foothill forests and mountain meadows.

2

4 *Anthriscus sylvestris.* Perennial, robust plant up to 150 cm high. Grooved, hollow stems usually bare or bristly at bottom. Pinnate leaves with toothed segments; bottom leaves are petiolate, upper ones sheathing and sessile. Long-stalked compound umbels, secondary umbels having bracts. Small flowers with white corollas. Schizocarps glossy, black, oblong-ovoid, pointed. Flowers from April to June. Grows in meadows, hedgerows and by roadsides. Poisonous Rough Chervil (*Chaerophyllum temulentum*) differs from it by fruits which are distinctly ribbed.

Family: Plumbaginaceae

5 Thrift or **Sea Pink** *Armeria maritima.* Perennial plant, 10—50 cm high, with cushions of linear, single-veined leaves, usually with bristled margins. Stems solitary, erect, smooth, with a globular head of rose-pink, occasionally white flowers. Funnel-shaped, persistent, chaffy calyx acts as a wing when the fruit is ripe. Bracts beneath capitulum sometimes red tinted. Flowers from May to October. Grows in sandy places, dunes, on rocks and screes, in meadows and pine-woods, from lowlands to mountains.

6

5

Family: **Primrose**—Primulaceae

1 Cowslip *Primula veris.* Perennial plant, up to 30 cm high. Leaves in basal rosette, wrinkled, hairy beneath, ovate-oblong, with winged petioles. Stem with umbel of several shortly stalked, fragrant flowers. Bell-shaped calyx, corolla yolk-yellow, with an orange spot at the base of each lobe. Corolla tube slightly longer than five-toothed calyx. Flowers from April to June. Grows on banks, in meadows and pastures, from lowlands to foothills.

2 Oxlip *Primula elatior.* Similar to preceding species. Leaves of basal rosette less wrinkled, grey-green on the underside, irregularly toothed. Flowers not scented, with longer stalks. Calyx tubular, corolla pale yellow, larger and flatter than in cowslip. Corolla tube double the length of five-toothed calyx. Cylindrical capsules longer than calyx. Flowers from March to May. Grows in deciduous woods, thickets and damp meadows, from uplands to mountains.

3 Bear's-ear *Primula auricula.* Perennial herb more than 20 cm high, finely and shortly glandularly downy and often somewhat mealy. Basal rosette of almost fleshy leaves with cartilaginous margin, rounded to ovate-obovate, tapering to wide petiole, usually entire, grey-green. Stem bears umbel of yellow, fragrant flowers, having a whitish throat; widely funnel-shaped corollas with the lobes notched at the tip. Capsules ovoid. Flowers from April to June. Grows on limestone rocks in Alps, Carpathians and their foothills; also cultivated. Protected plant.

156

2

6

4

4 Purple Sowbread *Cyclamen purpurascens* (syn. *C. europaeum*). Perennial plant with underground, flatly globose tuber. Leaves in basal rosette are long-petiolate, cordate, rounded, somewhat leathery, shallowly toothed; on upper surface dark green with silvery white patterning, underside carmine. Pendent, pink to carmine, fragrant flowers, the corolla reflexed sharply back. Globose capsule. Flowers from July to September. Grows in deciduous woods and among bushes, usually on limestone soils, only in eastern Bavaria, scattered in neighbouring Austria and southern parts of Czechoslovakia. Protected plant.

5 Yellow Loosestrife *Lysimachia vulgaris*. Perennial herb up to 150 cm high, with creeping rhizome and erect, leafy stems. Leaves opposite, or more frequently in whorls of three, downy, shortly petiolate, ovate-lanceolate, pointed, entire. Golden yellow flowers, calyx and petals sometimes bordered with red. Flowers from June to August. Grows in fens, beside water, and in damp forests from lowlands to foothills.

6 Creeping Jenny *Lysimachia nummularia*. Perennial, creeping herb with stem up to 50 cm long, rooting. Leaves broadly ovate to sub-orbicular, entire. Flowers solitary or in twos in leaf axils; corollas rich yellow, inside dotted with dark red. Capsule globose but seldom forms. Flowers from May to July. Grows in damp meadows, open woods and ditches. Related Wood Pimpernel (*L. nemorum*) has ovate, pointed leaves, flower stalks longer than leaves, with smaller, more starry flowers.

Family: **Wintergreen**—Pyrolaceae

1 Larger Wintergreen *Pyrola rotundifolia.* Evergreen perennial up to 30 cm high. Ascending, triangular stems. Leaves in sparse basal rosette, widely ovate to rounded, petiolate, indistinctly toothed, leathery; stem leaves scale-like, clasping. White flowers in dense, short raceme. Bracts usually of the same length as flower stalks. Open, broadly bell-shaped corolla, petals double the length of lanceolate sepals. Flowers in June and July. Grows in woods and on moors, from lowlands to mountains. Protected plant.

2 One-flowered Wintergreen *Moneses uniflora.* Evergreen perennial, up to 10 cm high. Round, petiolate, finely toothed, leathery leaves in basal rosette. Solitary, drooping flowers are fragrant, on long stalks; yellowish calyx, white corolla. Five-lobed stigma, ovoid capsule. Flowers from May to July. Grows in mossy forests from hilly country to mountains. Protected plant.

Family: **Gentian**—Gentianaceae

3 Spring Gentian *Gentiana verna.* Small evergreen perennial plant, up to 10 cm high. Rhizome bears numerous basal leaf rosettes. Leaves elliptic to oblong-ovate, pointed. Erect, short stems, with one to three pairs of smaller leaves, bear solitary erect flowers; corolla tubular with five brilliant deep blue lobes. Flowers from March to May, in high mountains till August. Grows in meadows and on rocks from hilly country to mountains. Protected. Very rare in Britain. Marsh Gentian (*G. pneumonanthe*) has corollas green-spotted at the throat and slender erect, often branched stems.

4 Spotted Gentian *Gentiana punctata.* Perennial, up to 60 cm high plant with thick, branched rhizome and erect, hollow stem. Ovate to broadly elliptic leaves, pointed and sessile. Flowers in axils of upper leaves, sessile, erect, bell-shaped. Corollas yellow, dotted with dark purple. Flowers in July and August. Grows on barrens, in meadows and mountain pastures of Alps and Carpathians. Great Yellow Gentian (*G. lutea*) is gathered for its bitter roots, although it is protected; it has unspotted golden yellow petals not joined into a tube.

5 *Gentiana acaulis.* Evergreen perennial tufted to mat-forming, up to 10 cm high, with basal rosette of almost leathery, ovate-lanceolate leaves. Short-stalked, large flowers, up to 6 cm long, erect; corolla funnel-shaped, rich blue, of lighter shade at mouth, often dark green spotted within. Grows in Alps and on their foothills in alpine meadows, also on screes and rocks. *G. acaulis* is nowadays considered as obsolete and used for a group of species. Three main species are now recognized: *G. clusii, G. kochiana* and *G. angustifolia.* Trumpet Gentian (*G. clusii*) has stemless flowers; Broad-leaved Trumpet Gentian (*G. kochiana*) has flowers on a short leafy stem and with a bell-shaped calyx; Narrow-leaved Gentian (*G. angustifolia*) is quite similar, but has markedly narrower leaves and deep sky-blue flowers. These species are strictly protected.

6 Willow Gentian *Gentiana asclepiadea*. Perennial herb, up to 80 cm high, often in dense tufts, with erect stems arching at the top. Ovate-lanceolate leaves, long-pointed and sessile. Axillary short-stalked flowers are borne in the upper leaf axils. Corollas funnel-shaped, azure blue, spotted purple within; rarely white. Flowers from July to September. Grows in Alps and Carpathians in woods, and along banks of streams.

Family: **Gentian**—Gentianaceae

1 *Centaurium erythraea* (syn. *C. umbellatum, C. minus*). Annual herb up to 50 cm high. Erect, square stems, forked above. Obovate to elliptic leaves in basal rosette; stem ones smaller and narrower, pointed, sessile, entire. Short-stalked to sessile flowers are pink, rarely whitish, with a five-lobed tubular corolla. Capsules cylindrical. Flowers from July to September. Grows on margins of forests and thickets, in dry meadows and on grassy slopes.

2 Marsh Felwort *Swertia perennis*. Perennial herb up to 50 cm high. Erect stems, often with violet tint. Basal leaves elliptic, petiolate, stem leaves lanceolate, sessile to semi-clasping. Flowers on winged, square stalks, in panicles. Corollas have five lobes, violet to light blue, dotted black-purple, greenish within. Fruit a capsule. Flowers from June to August. Grows in mountains, in peaty meadows and by streams.

Family: Menyanthaceae

3 Bogbean *Menyanthes trifoliata*. Perennial herb up to 30 cm high, with thick, creeping rhizome and erect, leafless flowering stems. Basal leaves, direct from rhizome, have long petioles, trifoliate leaflets almost sessile, obovate. Conspicuous flowers in dense raceme. Corollas broadly funnel-shaped, divided into five fringed lobes, white or pinkish; violet anthers. Capsule broadly ovoid. Flowers in May and June. Grows in marshes, bogs, fens and in ditches, lakes and ponds, from lowlands to mountains.

Family: Apocynaceae

4 Lesser Periwinkle *Vinca minor.* Evergreen perennial with long, creeping, rooting stems. Non-flowering stems are creeping and rooting; flowering ones are short, not more than 20 cm high, erect or ascending. Leathery leaves are opposite, lanceolate to elliptic, entire. Long-stalked flowers are axillary, tubular, with five angular lobes, light blue to blue-violet, rarely white or pink. Fruit formed of two slender, cylindrical follicles, fused at the base. Flowers in April and May. Grows in deciduous woods and thickets, from lowlands to foothills; also cultivated in gardens and becoming naturalized in hedgerows.

Family: **Milkweed**—Asclepiadaceae

5 Swallow-wort *Cynanchum vincetoxicum* (syn. *Vincetoxicum officinale, V. hirundinaria*). Perennial herb up to 1 metre high, poisonous, with rhizome and numerous thick roots. Erect, simple stems with opposite, ovate-lanceolate, entire leaves, hairy on veins beneath. Inflorescences in upper leaf axils, flowers bell-shaped, corollas white, greenish or yellowish, small. Fruit a slender pod-like follicle; seeds have white, silky plumes. Flowers from May to August. Grows on sunny slopes and among rocks, on margins of woods and thickets, more frequently on calcareous soils, from lowlands to foothills in milder regions.

Family: **Convolvulus**—Convolvulaceae

6 Field Bindweed *Convolvulus arvensis.* Perennial, prostrate or twining plant, up to 1 metre long. Rhizomes extensive, penetrating to depths of 5 cm. Stems climb by twisting counterclockwise. Leaves arrow-shaped, entire. Axillary flowers usually solitary, on short stalks, with widely funnel-shaped corollas, white or pink. Flowers from June to September. Grows in fields, on waste ground, roadsides, dunes, and in gardens as a pernicious weed.

1

2 Corn Cromwell *Lithospermum arvense.* Annual herb up to 50 cm high, with erect stems simple or branched towards the top. Leaves lanceolate to obovate, sessile. Inflorescence a leafy cyme; corollas white to bluish, their tubes sometimes with violet tint. Brown, wrinkled nutlets not glossy. Flowers from April to July. Grows as field weed, by roadsides and on wasteland, at lower altitudes. Related *Lithospermum purpureocoeruleum* is perennial, with purple flowers, later turning blue.

3 Common Forget-me-not *Myosotis arvensis.* Annual herb, rarely biennial, up to 40 cm high, with greyish hairs and erect or ascending stems. Oblanceolate, densely hairy leaves. Inflorescence a bractless, dense cyme; flower stalks spreading. Calyx deeply lobed into lanceolate sepals, hairy. Nutlets ovoid, keeled, dark glossy brown. Flowers from August to October. Grows along paths and in meadows, on wasteland, in sandy places, and as weed in fields. Related Yellow and Blue Forget-me-not (*M. discolor,* syn. *M. versicolor*) has fruit-stalks shorter than calyx and corollas coloured according to age of flower, from yellow through to blue.

4 Wood Forget-me-not *Myosotis sylvatica.* Perennial herb up to 50 cm high, fresh green, softly, usually densely haired. Erect stems with obovate to lanceolate leaves. Inflorescence a dense cyme, calyx with thick, hooked hairs; shorter than stalks; during fruition closed. Small corollas are over 5 mm in diameter, azure blue, with a yellow eye. Glossy, black-brown nutlets. Flowers in May and June. Grows in woods and meadows from lowlands to mountains; often cultivated in gardens and several forms known. Related Water Forget-me-not *Myosotis scorpioides* (syn. *M. palustris*) has calyx with appressed hairs, divided only to one third, and an angular stem.

5 Lesser Honeywort *Cerinthe minor.* Biennial, rarely perennial herb, up to 50 cm high, with erect stems. Leaves grey-green, ovate, clasping, lower ones usually white-spotted and warted. Calyx bristly-hairy; sulphur yellow corollas deeply cut into pointed lobes and drooping. Nutlets two-seeded. Flowers from May to July. Grows scattered in pastures, on field boundaries, slopes and along paths in lower altitudes of temperate regions and Alpine foothills.

Family: **Borage**—Boraginaceae

1 Hound's Tongue *Cynoglossum officinale.* Biennial herb up to 80 cm high, with erect, leafy, branched stems. Lanceolate, pointed leaves, basal ones petiolate, stem leaves sessile to clasping, all entire, softly densely grey hairy, especially on under surface. Inflorescence of dense cymes. Corollas small, red-purple, rarely whitish. Nutlets ovate, flattened, margins thickened and bearing short barbed spines. Flowers from May to July. Grows on grassy slopes, field boundaries and by roadsides at lower altitudes of milder regions.

6 Viper's Bugloss *Echium vulgare*. Robust annual or biennial herb up to 1 metre high with spreading bristles. Erect, simple stems. Leaves linear-lanceolate, sessile. Inflorescence dense axillary cyme. Calyx bristly hairy; corolla obliquely funnel-shaped to almost bilabiate, with rounded lobes, at first rose, later blue; rarely white. Nutlets triangular, roughly warted. Flowers from May to October. Grows on sunny grassy slopes, field boundaries, by roadsides and on wasteland from lowlands to foothills; locally abundant.

5

4

1

Family: **Borage**—Boraginaceae

1 True Alkanet *Anchusa officinalis*. Biennial or perennial plant up to 80 cm high, with spreading hairs, rough. Erect much-branched stems with oblong-lanceolate leaves, entire, sessile with rounded base. Dense, short, axillary cymes bear five-lobed flowers, at first reddish, later dark blue-violet, rarely white, dotted. Nutlets brown, flowers from May to September. Grows in pastures, fields, by roadsides, on field boundaries and wasteland, from lowlands to foothills in milder regions. Related Italian Alkanet (*A. italica*, syn. *A. azurea*) has large, light blue corollas.

2 Wrinklenut *Nonea pulla*. Perennial, grey-haired herb up to 50 cm high, with erect, stiff stems. Leaves oblong to lanceolate, top ones semi-clasping, entire, bristled to glandular hairy. Inflorescence of several dense, axillary cymes bearing short-stalked flowers. Calyx bell-shaped, enlarging after fertilization. Corolla tubular, funnel-shaped, brown-violet, rarely yellowish or whitish, tube white. Nutlets ovoid. Flowers from May to August. Grows on field boundaries, by roadsides and on wasteland, often on calcareous soils at lower altitudes of milder regions.

3 Common Lungwort *Pulmonaria officinalis*. Perennial herb, up to 30 cm high. Bottom leaves ovate-cordate, abruptly narrowed into petiole, pointed, usually spotted silvery-white; stem ones almost sessile, ovate to lanceolate. Bracted cymes short and dense. Flowers short-stalked, calyx enlarging after fertilization. Corolla purple-rose to pink, later turning violet-blue. Dark brown nutlets. Flowers from March to May. Grows in light woodland and bushy places from lowlands to foothills.

3

2

Family: Labiatae (syn. Lamiaceae)

6 Common Bugle *Ajuga reptans.* Perennial herb up to 30 cm high, with creeping shoots and long-petioled, obovate basal leaves. Erect, simple, square leafy stems, bearing short-stalked flowers in the axils of leafy, purple-tinted bracts. Calyx bell-shaped with triangular-ovate teeth; corolla violet-blue, rarely pink or white; lower lip deeply three-lobed. Fruit of four smooth brown nutlets. Flowers from May to August. Grows in meadows, thickets and woods from lowlands to mountains. Related Upright Bugle (*A. genevensis*) has no creeping stems, but underground stolons; upper floral bracts are shorter and usually three-lobed, corollas bright blue.

4 Common Comfrey *Symphytum officinale.* Perennial herb with robust, bristly, hairy stems up to 1 metre high. Stems usually well-branched, and keeled or winged. Long tapering, broadly lanceolate leaves with winged petioles. Inflorescence of dense, bracted cymes. Short-stalked flowers purple, rarely rose or whitish. Corolla tubular; calyx with long-pointed lobes. Nutlets brown-grey, glossy. Flowers from May to July. Grows abundantly in damp meadows, on banks and in ditches from lowlands to foothills.

5 *Symphytum tuberosum.* Perennial herb up to 50 cm high, with short bristly hairs. Thickened, tuberous rhizome. Erect, almost unbranched, indistinctly angular stems. Shortly tapering leaves, widely lanceolate with winged petioles. Inflorescence of few-flowered cymes. Flowers yellowish white with short hairs. Corolla tubular, with recurved lobes; calyx deeply cleft. Nutlets cuneoid, brown, wrinkled. Flowers in April and May. Grows from lowlands to foothills in damp woods and thickets, rarely in meadows.

6

165

Family: Labiatae

1 Ground Ivy *Glechoma hederacea* (syn. *Nepeta hederacea*). Perennial herb up to 30 cm high, with long-creeping prostrate stems, rooting at the nodes. Leaves petiolate, reniform to broadly ovate-cordate, having rounded teeth. Axillary flowers usually in twos; calyx tubular, hairy, indistinctly bilabiate; corollas blue-violet with a bilobed upper and trilobed lower lip bearing dark purple pattern. Flowers from April to July. Grows in woods, bushy places, grassy slopes, on wasteland, and sometimes as weed in gardens, from lowlands to mountains.

2 Common Self-heal *Prunella vulgaris*. Perennial herb, somewhat hairy or glabrous, up to 30 cm high, with short leafy rhizomes and ascending, often brown-violet stems. Petiolate, ovate to elliptic leaves, entire or irregularly toothed. Inflorescence of axillary, bracted flowers arranged in short, dense, oblong head. Corollas blue-violet, rarely pink or white; upper lip hooded and bristly-hairy. Glossy nutlets. Flowers from May to September. Grows in pastures, dry meadows, open woods and by the roadside. Related Large-flowered Self-heal (*P. grandiflora*) is more robust and has larger flowers. It is sometimes grown in garden.

3 *Melittis melissophyllum*. Perennial herb up to 50 cm high, with erect stems and soft hairs. Erect, unbranched stems bear cordate-ovate, toothed and pointed leaves. Scented flowers are borne in axils of upper leaves. Corollas long-tubular, white or pink, lower lip rosy, central lobe usually yellow and with deep pink spots. Triangular, smooth nutlets. Flowers in May and June. Grows in open woods and hedgerows especially on limestone soils, at lower altitudes in milder regions. Sometimes cultivated for its distinctive flowers.

4 Large Hemp-nettle *Galeopsis speciosa*. Robust annual herb, up to 1 metre high with branched stems swollen at nodes. Leaves petiolate, ovate, serrate, long-pointed. Flowers in whorls in the upper leaf and bract axils. Corolla longer than calyx, light yellow, central lobe of lower lip violet. Flowers from June to September. Grows in open woods, clearings, bushy places and on wasteland. Common Hemp-nettle (*G. tetrahit*) has smaller light purple or whitish flowers with the lower lip purple-spotted.

4

5

6

5 Black Horehound *Ballota nigra*. Perennial herb up to 1 metre high, stems and leaves grey-hairy. Ovate to orbicular leaves wrinkled, pointed and toothed. Calyx bell-shaped; corolla purple, central lobe of lower lip mottled whitish. Flowers from June to September. Grows on wasteland, edges of fields, among bushes and along hedgerows, from lowlands to foothills.

6 Yellow Archangel *Galeobdolon luteum* (syn. *Lamium galeobdolon*). Perennial plant up to 50 cm high, with far-creeping leafy stolons and erect, simple flowering stems. Leaves petiolate, ovate, pointed, toothed. Flowers in whorls in the upper leaf axils. Calyx bell-shaped with pointed triangular lobes. Corolla yellow with large, hooded upper lip. Nutlets smooth, trigonous. Flowers from April to July. Grows in damp woods and thickets from lowlands to mountains. Related White Dead-nettle (*Lamium album*) lacks stolons and bears white flowers.

Family: Labiatae

1 Spotted Dead-nettle *Lamium maculatum.* Perennial herb up to 50 cm high. Petiolate leaves ovate-cordate to toothed, pointed, usually with a central silvery-white zone. Flowers in whorls in the upper leaf axils. Corollas purple, lower lip dark violet-spotted; tube curved. Triangular-obovoid, black-green nutlets. Flowers from April to September. Grows in open woods, on wasteland and by roadsides. Only naturalized in Britain as an escapee from gardens. Similar Red Dead-nettle (*L. purpureum*) with red-purple flowers, almost straight corolla tubes and plain green leaves is a common annual weed.

2 Hedge Woundwort *Stachys sylvatica.* Perennial herb up to 1 metre high, with creeping rhizomes and erect stems. Leaves long-petiolate, ovate-cordate, toothed and pointed. Flowers in bracted whorls, red-purple or crimson. Flowers from June to September. Grows in damp woods, among bushes and in hedgerows from lowlands to mountains. Related Marsh Woundwort (*S. palustris*) has almost sessile, lanceolate leaves with rounded teeth and pale purple flowers.

3 Wood Betony *Betonica officinalis* (syn. *Stachys betonica*). Perennial herb up to 1 metre high, with erect stems, having long internodes. Leaves petiolate, ovate-oblong, cordate, with rounded teeth; upper ones almost sessile and smaller. Dense oblong inflorescence with linear bracts. Corolla purple-red, tube whitish. Flowers in July and August. Grows in open woods, on hedgebanks and on grassy slopes from lowlands to foothills.

4 Whorled Clary *Salvia verticillata*. Perennial herb up to 50 cm high, hairy and foetid. Basal leaves ovate with rounded teeth, usually fading or dead at flowering time. Stem leaves petiolate, smaller, sometimes pinnately lobed. Inflorescences spike-like, composed of several bracted whorls. Corolla violet, rarely whitish or pink. Flowers from June to September. Grows by the roadside, on grassy slopes and rocky places in the mountains of central Europe, west to Spain; often naturalized elsewhere.

5 Meadow Clary *Salvia pratensis*. Perennial herb up to 50 cm high, with erect stems. Leaves long-petiolate, ovate to oblong-cordate, shallowly lobed with irregular rounded teeth, wrinkled. Inflorescence spike-like, formed of several whorls of blue, rarely pink or white flowers; upper lip of corolla hooded, lower one small and rounded. Flowers from May to August. Grows on dry slopes, in meadows, bushy places, hedge banks and on field boundaries, mainly in milder regions.

6 Pot Marjoram *Origanum vulgare*. Perennial aromatic herb up to 50 cm high with a woody rhizome. Stems erect, leafy. Short-petiolate leaves ovate, almost entire, glandular. Inflorescence a dense corymbose cyme. Flowers rose-purple, rarely white. Nutlets ovoid, smooth, brown. Flowers from July to September. Grows fairly abundantly on sunny grassy slopes, in bushy places, and on margins of forests, mainly in milder regions.

4

6

5

Family: Labiatae

1 *Thymus praecox.* Small carpeting subshrub up to 7 cm tall (in flower). Stems creeping, up to 50 cm long, rooting. Ascending. Flowering stems four-angled, with two opposite sides densely hairy. Leaves suborbicular to oblanceolate with marked venation on under surface. Inflorescences compact, spherical to ovoid. Flowers rose-purple to red, occasionally white. Flowers from May to June. Grows on sunny, grassy or rocky slopes at lower altitudes of milder regions, especially on calcareous soils. *T. serpyllum* has the stems sparsely and evenly hairy all round. It is one of many European species of thyme.

6

4

Family: Solanaceae

3 Deadly Nightshade *Atropa bella-donna.* Perennial herb, glandular-hairy, up to 150 cm high with thick, erect, branched stems. Leaves alternate, or on the flowering stems in unequal pairs; ovate to elliptic, entire, with a winged petiole. Flowers drooping, solitary, seemingly axillary, having bell-shaped corollas, outside brown-purple, inside yellowish. Berries globose, black, subtended by the star-like enlarged calyx. All parts of the plant are poisonous. Flowers from June to August. Grows scattered in woodland clearings, on margins of forests and wasteland from lowlands to foothills.

4 Henbane *Hyoscyamus niger.* Annual to biennial herb, up to 80 cm high, sticky glandular-hairy and foetid. Erect, densely leafy stems bear alternate oblong-ovate, somewhat irregularly lobed leaves, the lower ones petiolate, top ones semi-clasping. Flowers in axils of upper leaves. Calyx bell-shaped, glandular-hairy, prominently net-veined; corolla funnel-shaped, dull yellow, violet-netted. Anthers violet. Capsules with lids contain black-brown seeds. Whole plant poisonous. Flowers from June to October. Grows on wasteland, by roadsides, and on sandy ground, often near the sea, in lowland areas, more frequently in milder regions.

5 Winter-cherry *Physalis alkekengi.* Perennial herb up to 60 cm high, with creeping rhizome. Erect stems somewhat angular, upper part downy. Petiolate broad leaves ovate, usually entire, pointed. Flowers solitary, axillary, stalked; globular lantern-shaped inflated calyx; dull white or yellowish-green corolla. Berries orange, enclosed in the enlarged inflated calyx, both red when ripe. Flowers from May to August. Grows in deciduous woods, bushy places and on waste ground, in central and southern Europe. Cultivated and escaping here and there.

6 Black Nightshade *Solanum nigrum.* Annual herb up to 60 cm high. Erect or decumbent branched stems. Leaves widely ovate or rhomboid, shallowly lobed or with a sinuate margin. Flowers in small leafless cymes. Corollas white, with 5 spreading pointed lobes. Berries usually black, rarely greenish or yellowish. Flowers from June to October. Grows as weed in fields, gardens and on wasteland from lowlands to foothills. Related Bittersweet or Woody Nightshade (*S. dulcamara*) is a semi-climbing shrub with violet flowers and yellow anthers fused into a cone, protruding from reflexed corolla; berry translucent red. Both species poisonous.

2 Corn Mint *Mentha arvensis.* Perennial herb up to 50 cm high, often purple-tinted, aromatic, with underground rhizomes. Decumbent or ascending stems are densely leafy. Leaves narrowly to broadly ovate, toothed. Inflorescence of several axillary whorls. Calyx with triangular teeth. Corolla lilac to blue-purple. Flowers from June to October. Grows in damp fields, ditches, and in open wet woods from lowlands to foothills. Peppermint (*Mentha × piperita*), a hybrid of Water Mint and Spearmint (*M. aquatica × M. spicata*) is often cultivated for flavouring.

Family: **Snapdragon**—*Scrophulariaceae*

1 Common Mullein *Verbascum thapsus*. Biennial herb up to 2 m high, covered with dense whitish-felted hair. Leaves in basal rosettes obovate to oblong; stem ones lanceolate, with winged stalks that run down the stem. Light yellow flowers in a spire-like panicle; corollas up to 2 cm in diameter. Filaments of two longer stamens smooth, those of three shorter ones hairy. Flowers from July to September. Grows on hedgebanks, sunny slopes and wasteland, from lowlands to foothills. Related Large-flowered Mullein (*V. thapsiforme*) has flowers up to 4 cm in diameter, and filaments of bare stamens are double the anther length.

2 White Mullein *Verbascum lychnitis*. Biennial herb up to 1.5 metre high, with short hairs. Oblong to lanceolate basal leaves have small rounded teeth or are entire; stem leaves almost sessile, ovate, pointed. Inflorescence a narrow erect panicle; flowers white or yellow; stamen filaments of almost equal length, white-woolly. Flowers from June to August. Grows in waste places, on sunny slopes, forest margins and by roadsides, from lowlands to foothills. Related Dark Mullein (*V. nigrum*) has bottom leaves usually cordate and filaments of stamens violet-woolly.

3 Purple Mullein *Verbascum phoeniceum*. Biennial herb up to 1 m high, with stem usually densely glandular. Leaves of basal rosette ovate, stem ones sparse, cordate and sessile. Flowers in terminal raceme; dark violet corollas up to 3 cm in diameter. Flowers from May to July. Grows scattered at outskirts of forests, on bushy, sunny slopes and in sandy places at lower altitudes in milder regions. Cultivated in Britain and occasionally escaping.

4 Toadflax *Linaria vulgaris.* Perennial herb up to 40 cm high, usually unbranched. Alternate, sessile leaves linear-lanceolate, entire, grey-green. Flowers in dense terminal raceme; corollas snapdragon-like, sulphur yellow, with palate of lower lip orange; corolla tube with long spur. Ovoid capsule. Flowers from June to October. Grows abundantly in fields, on wasteland, by roadsides and among rocks from lowlands to foothills. Sometimes a weed of gardens. Tiny Alpine Toadflax (*L. alpina*) is grey, decumbent, with leaves in whorls; violet flowers have lower lip with orange palate.

5 Field Cow-wheat *Melampyrum arvense.* Annual herb up to 40 cm high, downy. Opposite, lanceolate leaves; bottom ones entire, upper leaves have several long, large teeth at the base. Flowers in dense spike, bracts purple. Corollas tubular bilabiate, pink, with yellow throat and deep pink lips. Flowers from May to September. Grows in fields, on slopes and margins of woods, mainly in the lowlands. Rare in Britain. Related Crested Cow-wheat (*M. cristatum*) has reddish crested bracts, smaller yellow and purple flowers and grows mainly in open woods.

6 Common Cow-wheat *Melampyrum pratense.* Annual herb up to 50 cm high with spreading branches. Linear-lanceolate to narrowly ovate, entire leaves. Flowers arranged in a sparse, one-sided spike, the lower ones well spaced. Calyx lobes unequal, pointed; corollas whitish to lemon yellow, with a narrow mouth. Flowers from May to September. Grows in forests and in clearings, from lowlands to mountains. Wood Cow-wheat (*M. sylvaticum*) has triangular-lanceolate sepals and yellow to orange-yellow flowers with wide open mouths.

4

5

6

Family: **Snapdragon**—Scrophulariaceae

1 Germander Speedwell *Veronica chamaedrys.*
Perennial herb up to 25 cm high, little branched.
Prostrate or ascending stems have hairs in two
rows. Leaves are opposite, ovate to elliptic,
toothed. Sparse floral racemes in axils of upper
leaves; corollas sky-blue with a white eye. Capsules obcordate, shorter than calyx. Flowers in
May and June. Grows on field boundaries and
grassy banks, in meadows, open woods and
among bushes. Thyme-leaved Speedwell (*V.
serpyllifolia*) has white or pale blue flowers and
rounded to oblong leaves.

2 Common Speedwell *Veronica officinalis.* Perennial herb with rooting prostrate stems up to
30 cm long. Finely serrate leaves elliptic to
ovate or obovate, shortly petiolate, toothed. Racemes form in upper leaf axils. Flowers light
violet to lilac. Capsules obcordate, glandular.
Flowers from June to August. Grows in dry
woods, clearings and on heaths and moors. Bux-
baum's Speedwell (*V. persica*) has stalks longer
than ovate, toothed leaves and sky-blue and
white flowers formed singly in leaf axils.

3 Spiked Speedwell *Veronica spicata.* Perennial herb, up to 50 cm high, downy, on top
glandular. Leaves opposite, oval or ovate, blunt,
toothed along the sides. Flowers in dense, terminal racemes; corollas violet-blue. Obcordate,
glandular capsules. Flowers from June to August. Grows in rocky places, on sunny grassy
slopes, in pastures and on field boundaries from
lowlands to foothills, mainly in milder regions.
Rare in Britain.

4 Yellow-rattle *Rhinanthus minor.* Annual herb with a simple or branched stem up to 60 cm. Leaves linear-lanceolate with rounded teeth. Inflorescence a terminal bracted raceme. Calyx inflated; corolla yellow, hooded, just protruding from calyx. Flattened capsules hidden in calyx. Flowers from May to July. Grows scattered as field weed, in meadows and heaths, from lowlands to mountains.

5 Lousewort *Pedicularis sylvatica.* Perennial herb with decumbent stems, only at tip ascending, up to 20 cm high. Alternate, pinnately lobed leaves, the segments toothed. Inflorescence a few-flowered terminal raceme. Inflated, unequally five-toothed calyx; corollas pink. Flowers from May to July. Grows scattered in damp meadows and on moors and heaths from lowlands to mountains.

6 Yellow Foxglove *Digitalis grandiflora* (syn. *D. ambigua*). Perennial herb up to 1 metre high. Erect stems glandular-hairy. Alternate leaves, bottom ones oblanceolate, upper leaves ovately lanceolate, sessile. Flowers in one-sided, dense raceme. Corollas tubular, bell-shaped, somewhat flattened and lobed, light yellow outside, brown-netted inside. Flowers in June and July. Grows in clearings, on overgrown rocky slopes, and in open woods from hilly country to mountains. Grown in gardens and very rarely escaping.

Family: **Plantain**—Plantaginaceae

3 Ribwort *Plantago lanceolata.* Perennial herb up to 45 cm high, with deep green leaves in basal rosette and simple, erect flowering stem. Leaves lanceolate, sometimes obscurely toothed. Grooved stem and dense, ovoid to cylindrical spike. Corollas brownish with white anthers. Capsule with ovoid lid. Flowers from May to September. Grows as a weed in meadows, fields, pastures, by roadsides, on wasteland, from lowlands to mountains. Related Hoary Plantain (*P. media*) has elliptic to ovate hoary leaves, round stems and filaments of stamens light violet.

Family: Orobanchaceae

1 Toothwort *Lathraea squamaria.* Perennial whitish or pinkish parasitic herb, up to 25 cm high. Stout branched rhizome with fleshy, white scale leaves. Erect stem is fleshy, unbranched, with a few scale leaves. Flowers in one-sided, dense raceme, at first drooping at tip. Corollas tubular, bilabiate, dull purple, lower lip reddish. Capsules explosive, with large seeds. Flowers from March to May. Grows in deciduous woods at lower altitudes; parasitic on roots of deciduous trees, especially hazel and elm.

2 Red Broomrape *Orobanche alba.* Perennial yellowish parasitic herb up to 30 cm tall. Slender stems unbranched, thickened underground, glandular hairy. Stem bracts ovate-lanceolate; flowers in sparse raceme with reddish bracts. Calyx bilabiate. Corolla tubular, curved, labiate, upper lip dark glandular-hairy purple-tinged, rest of corolla whitish. In Britain flowers reddish throughout. Flowers in June and July. Grows on sunny grassy slopes, mainly in milder regions; parasitic on thyme and other members of the Labiatae.

4 Great Plantain *Plantago major*. Perennial herb up to 30 cm high. Broadly ovate to elliptic leaves in basal rosette narrow abruptly to a cordate base and winged petiole. Erect stems bear a long, dense, narrow spike of small yellowish white flowers; anthers lilac, turning to dull yellow, filaments whitish. Capsules broadly ovoid with lids. Flowers from June to October. Grows as a weed in pastures, fields, on wasteland and by roadsides, from lowlands to mountains.

Family: **Madder**—Rubiaceae

5 Field Madder *Sherardia arvensis*. Annual herb with slender, generally prostrate stems, up to 30 cm long, branched and square. Leaves in whorls of 4—6, with tiny prickled hairs, lanceolate to elliptic, pointed, single-veined. Inflorescence a few-flowered umbel terminating the branches. Corollas with 4 narrow cross-like lobes. Fruit of 2 obovoid mericarps. Flowers from June to October. Grows as a weed in fields, on wasteland and by roadsides, from lowlands to foothills, more frequently on calcareous soils.

6 Woodruff *Galium odoratum* (syn. *Asperula odorata*). Perennial herb up to 40 cm high, with far-creeping rhizomes and erect, square, smooth flowering stems. Leaves lanceolate to elliptic, with marginal prickles, tip usually with small hard point, in whorls of up to 6. Flowers in terminal, long-stalked cymes. Corollas small, white, funnel-shaped, with 4 blunt lobes. Double mericarp has hooked bristles. Flowers in May and June. Grows in deciduous woods and among bushes, from lowlands to mountains.

4

5

6

Family: **Madder**—Rubiaceae

1 Goosegrass or **Cleavers** *Galium aparine*. Annual herb with stems bearing hooked bristles, prostrate or climbing, square, up to 120 cm long. Leaves in whorls of 6—8, linear, oblanceolate, margins with small, curved bristles. Flowers in stalked, axillary cymes; four-parted corollas very small, whitish, with spreading lobes. Double mericarps with small white hooks. Flowers from June to October. Grows in hedgerows, thickets, on wasteground and in fields, and at outskirts of forests, from lowlands to mountains.

2 Lady's Bedstraw *Galium verum*. Perennial herb with creeping rhizome and prostrate to erect, angled stems, up to 60 cm long or more, branched at the top. Leaves narrowly linear, single-veined, in 8—12 whorls. Bright yellow cross-shaped flowers in dense terminal panicles. Flowers from May to September. Grows abundantly in meadows, on sunny grassy banks, field boundaries, in hedgerows and on dunes. Low-growing *Galium cruciata* has unbranched stems with spreading white hairs and three-veined ovate-elliptic, hairy leaves; flowers pale yellow.

3 Hedge Bedstraw *Galium mollugo*. Perennial herb up to 1 metre long with decumbent, ascending or erect stems, often climbing, square, smooth. Leaves linear to obovate, edge finely prickly, tip pointed. White cross-shaped flowers in long, terminal panicles. Corolla lobes prolonged into slender point. Double mericarps wrinkled. Flowers from May to September. Grows in meadows, on field boundaries, in hedgerows, at outskirts of forests and on dunes, from lowlands to mountains.

178

Family: Loniceraceae

4 Danewort *Sambucus ebulus*. Perennial herb, malodorous, poisonous, up to 150 cm high with erect, grooved stems. Leaves petiolate, odd-pinnate, leaflets 7—13, sharply serrate, oblong-lanceolate. Dense flat-topped, panicle-like cymes bear small 5-petalled, white or pale pink flowers; anthers violet. Fruits are glossy black globose drupes. Flowers in June and July. Grows in woodland clearings, margins of forests, among bushes and in hedgerows, from lowlands to foothills. Related species are woody plants.

Family: **Valerian**—Valerianaceae

5 Smooth-fruited Cornsalad *Valerianella dentata*. Annual herb up to 30 cm high, with erect, repeatedly forking stems, usually with single flower in forks of branches; further flowers in terminal heads. Tiny bluish white flowers; calyx margin with one tooth longer than others.

Leaves spathulate, blunt, opposite, sometimes toothed at the base. Flowers from June to September. Grows in fields, wasteland, on rocky slopes and old walls, from lowlands to foothills. Related Common Cornsalad (*V. locusta*) has forked branches without flowers and entire leaves.

6 Common Valerian *Valeriana officinalis*. Perennial herb up to 1 metre high, with stout erect stems and shortly creeping rhizomes. Pinnately divided leaves, bottom ones petiolate, upper leaves sessile. Flowers in dense cymose head with usually two main branches. Corollas white or pink, tubular, with 5 lobes. Achenes conical with crown of pappus. Flowers from June to September. Grows in damp meadows, and in bushy places from lowlands to mountains. Smaller Marsh Valerian (*V. dioica*) has almost entire, ovate to spathulate basal leaves, stem ones pinnately lobed, and unisexual flowers.

Family: **Scabious**—Dipsacaceae

1 Teasel *Dipsacus fullonum* (syn. *D. sylvester*). Biennial herb up to 200 cm high with robust, angled stems, prickly on the angles. Basal leaves in rosette, oblong to elliptic, stem ones lanceolate, opposite, fused at base, prickly on margins and central rib. Stalks of inflorescences densely prickly, flowers in a dense ovoid head, rose-purple, rarely whitish. Involucral bracts linear, pointed, prickly, longer than head. Flowers in July and August. Grows in open woods and thickets, on stream banks and wasteland, in ditches and by the roadside, usually at lower altitudes. *D. fullonum* ssp. *sativus* is cultivated for napping cloth. It has larger heads and stiff, spiny floral bracts.

2 Field Scabious *Knautia arvensis*. Perennial herb almost 1 metre high with spreading hairs and erect stems. Basal rosettes of somewhat grey-green leaves, oblanceolate to obovate, stem ones pinnately lobed, segments lanceolate. Long-stalked flowering heads; corollas bluish-lilac, rarely pink, whitish or yellowish; outer florets with 2 enlarged petals. Achenes ovoid, hairy, with a crown of persistent calyx lobes. Flowers in July and August. Grows in meadows, on field boundaries, grassy slopes and margins of forests from lowlands to mountains.

3 Yellow Scabious *Scabiosa ochroleuca*. Perennial herb up to 50 cm high, with erect stems. Leaves of basal rosettes obovate, lyre-shaped, pinnately lobed, terminal lobe toothed; stem leaves with linear, toothed segments. Long-stalked flower heads; outer florets with 2 enlarged petals. Light yellow corollas; calyx bristly hairy, at first reddish. Flowers from July to October. Grows on sunny slopes, field boundaries, rocky slopes and margins of forests, in lower altitudes of milder regions. Sometimes grown in gardens.

2   3   1

Family: **Campanula**—Campanulaceae

4 Peach-leaved Bellflower *Campanula persicifolia*. Perennial plant up to 1 metre high, with shortly creeping rhizome and erect stems. Glossy, smooth leaves are shallowly toothed; basal ones lanceolate to oblanceolate, top ones narrowly lanceolate. Flowers up to 4 cm long, in an open raceme. Corolla broadly bell-shaped, blue-violet to white, with 5 broad lobes. Erect capsules with three basal openings. Flowers from June to September. Grows in woods, thickets and on bushy slopes, from lowlands to mountains. Often cultivated in Britain and escaping; well naturalized in a few places.

5 Clustered Bellflower *Campanula glomerata*. Perennial herb up to 40 cm high, usually with downy hairs and erect stems. Basal leaves petiolate, ovate-cordate, stem ones sessile, lanceolate, toothed. Sessile flowers in terminal and/or axillary heads; corollas erect, bell-shaped, dark blue to blue-violet, less frequently white. Flowers from June to September. Grows on bushy or grassy slopes, in open woods and clearings from lowlands to mountains. Several forms are grown in gardens.

6 Alpine Bellflower *Campanula alpina*. A perennial herb up to 15 cm high, with basal rosette of hairy, oval leaves, toothed at the tips. Stem leaves lanceolate, usually toothed, rarely entire. Drooping flowers on hairy stalks; corollas broadly bell-shaped, light blue, with recurved lobes, woolly hairy on margins. Flowers in July and August. Grows on screes and among rocks in mountains. In the Alps accompanied by Bearded Bellflower (*C. barbata*) with larger, pale violet-blue flowers having prominently woolly hairy corolla lobes.

4   5   6

Family: **Campanula**—Campanulaceae

1 Spiked Rampion *Phyteuma spicatum*. Perennial herb up to 80 cm high, with erect stems. Long-petioled bottom leaves are cordate-ovate, with rounded teeth; stem leaves lanceolate. Flowers in dense, cylindrical head; corollas whitish-yellow, tubular; petals linear. Capsule ovoid, with two openings. Flowers from May to July. Grows in deciduous woods and thickets, from lowlands to mountains. Rare in Britain. Related Round-headed Rampion (*P. orbiculare*) has dark blue flowers in globose heads.

2 Common Sheepsbit *Jasione montana*. Biennial herb with erect hairy stems up to 50 cm high. Basal leaves, linear to oblong, hairy, mostly withered at flowering time; stem ones smaller with wavy margins. Flowers in globose heads, bracts triangular-ovate, pointed. Corollas bright blue, rarely rosy or whitish; petals linear. Capsule ovoid. Flowers from June to August. Grows in grassy places, dunes, on rocky slopes and on cliffs, especially on non-calcareous soils, from lowlands to foothills.

Family: Compositae (syn. Asteraceae)

3 Chicory *Cichorium intybus*. Perennial herb, up to 150 cm high, with a milky sap. Stiff, erect, branched stems. Basal leaves petiolate, in rosette, oblanceolate, irregularly lobed, bristle beneath; stem leaves sessile, upper ones lanceolate. Inflorescence a capitulum, involucral bracts in two rows. All florets strap-shaped, five-toothed at the tips, blue, rarely rose or whitish. Achenes without hairs, crowned with short scales. Flowers from July to October. Grows by roadsides on waste ground and in pastures, from lowlands to foothills. Much cultivated for roots (chicory) and as salad vegetable (chicons).

4 Mouse-ear Hawkweed *Hieracium pilosella.* Perennial herb with long, leafy stolons and leafless, single-headed flowering stems, up to 30 cm high. Leaves in basal rosette linear to obovate-oblong, white hairy floccose beneath, sparingly so above. Linear involucral bracts grey-green, hairy on margins. All florets ligulate, five-toothed, yellow, outer ones reddish, striped. Achenes purple-black, with pappus. Flowers from May to October. Grows in meadows, on grassy slopes and banks, and by roadsides, from lowlands to mountains.

5 *Hieracium aurantiacum.* Perennial herb up to 50 cm high, with creeping stolons and erect stems. Leaves of basal rosette oblong to lanceolate, hairy, glandular, woolly hairy beneath. Flower heads in a terminal cluster covered with black-based glandular hairs. Capitula have dark orange florets. Flowers from June to August. Grows in mountain meadows of central Europe. Sometimes grown in gardens and escaping; can become an aggressive weed.

6 Common Dandelion *Taraxacum officinale.* Perennial herb with a milky latex-like sap, 20—40 cm high. Leaves of basal rosette are angularly, pinnately lobed, either deeply or shallowly. Leafless stems with single capitula; outer involucral bracts linear, spreading or reflexed; inner ones erect and longer; strap-shaped florets golden yellow. Achenes with pointed tubercles, beaked, crowned by parachute-like pappus. Flowers from April to September. Common in meadows, pastures, lawns, by roadsides and as field weed, from lowlands to mountains.

Family: Compositae

1 Prickly Lettuce *Lactuca serriola*. Biennial herb up to 150 cm high, with a milky sap and prickly hairs. Bottom stem leaves pinnately lobed and toothed; upper leaves lanceolate, clasping. Leaf blades vertical, usually in a north-south plane (Compass Plant). Capitula in large panicles; all florets strap-shaped, yellow. Achenes with small points and stalked pappus. Flowers from July to September. Grows on wasteland, banks, dunes and walls at lower altitudes in milder regions. Related *Lactuca sativa* is cultivated as a salad vegetable.

2 Giant Cat's-ear *Hypochoeris uniflora*. Perennial herb up to 40 cm high, with erect stems bearing a solitary capitulum, usually leafless. Leaves of basal rosette lanceolate, toothed, coarsely hairy. Large capitula up to 5 cm in diameter, the involucre bearing soft blackish hairs; florets yellow. Achenes beaked, crowned with pappus. Flowers from July to September. Grows in mountain meadows, in rocky places and in clearings of knee-pine.

3 Greater Goatsbeard *Tragopogon dubius*. Biennial herb up to 50 cm high, with erect, branched and leafy stem. Leaves linear-lanceolate, sharply pointed, usually grey-green. Stems thickened and hollow beneath capitula. Solitary capitula with yellow florets. Involucral bracts longer than outer florets. Achenes up to 4 cm long, with spiny projections and stalked pappus. Flowers from May to July. Grows on sunny, grassy slopes, field boundaries and by roadsides at lower altitudes of milder regions.

4 Common Vipersgrass *Scorzonera humilis*. Perennial up to 40 cm high, with brownish-black rhizome and erect, simple, almost leafless stems, usually with single capitulum. Basal leaves petiolate, linear-lanceolate, woolly hairy when young, later smooth. Capitula with a bell-shaped involucre and yellow florets. Achenes ribbed and crowned with pappus. Flowers in May to July. Grows in damp meadows, on moors and in open forests, from hilly country to mountains. Rare in Britain. Related Purple Vipersgrass (*S. purpurea*) has lilac flowers and linear leaves.

5 Hemp Agrimony *Eupatorium cannabinum.*
Perennial, robust herb up to 150 cm high with
erect, leafy stems. Leaves short-petiolate, hairy,
opposite, three- to five-lobed and toothed.
Dense inflorescences, small, few-flowered capitula, narrowly cylindrical involucre. Florets pink
or whitish tubular, with five corolla lobes.
Achenes black, crowned with pappus. Flowers
from July to September. Grows in damp open
woods, on banks, in ditches and marshes, from
lowlands to mountains.

6 Golden-rod *Solidago virgaurea.* Perennial
herb up to 75 cm high. Stems erect, simple,
leafy. Basal leaves obovate to oblanceolate, petiolate, toothed; upper ones lanceolate, sessile.
Small yellow capitula arranged in dense, erect
raceme or panicle. Outer ligulate florets longer
than involucre, disc florets tubular. Achenes
downy, crowned with pappus. Flowers from July to October. Grows in open woods, among
rocks, in hedgerows, on cliffs and dunes, from
lowlands to mountains. A very variable plant
with several distinct forms varying from 5 to 75
cm in height.

6

4

5

Family: Compositae

1 Daisy *Bellis perennis.* Perennial herb up to 10 cm high. Leaves in basal rosette, obovate to spathulate, widely toothed. Erect stems with single capitula. Conical receptacle hollow, involucral bracts lanceolate, blunt. Disc florets tubular, yellow; ray ones ligulate, white, often red-tinted at the tip. Flowers from March to November. Grows in grassy places from lowlands to mountains. Large-flowered forms are cultivated, some with 'double' flower heads (all florets ligulate).

2 Alpine Aster *Aster alpinus.* Perennial herb up to 20 cm high. Erect, unbranched stems with single capitula, few-leaved. Three-veined, hairy, entire leaves; basal ones spathulate, stem leaves lanceolate, sessile. Capitula up to 4 cm in diameter, involucral bracts lanceolate, hairy. Disc florets yellow, tubular, ray ones strap-shaped, violet-blue, rarely rose. Flowers from June to August. Grows in rocky, stony places or on grassy slopes in mountains. Also grown in gardens.

3 *Erigeron canadense.* Annual or biennial plant, up to 1 metre high, with erect, densely leafy, simple stems and a large paniculate inflorescence. Leaves lanceolate; bottom ones petiolate, upper leaves sessile. Tiny capitula with membranous bordered involucral bracts. Disc florets yellowish white, tubular; ray ones dirty white, slightly longer than involucral bracts. Fruit is an achene. Flowers from July to October. Native of North America but extensively naturalized on wasteland, by roadsides, on dunes and walls. Also a weed of farmland and gardens.

4 Blue Fleabane *Erigeron acer*. Biennial to perennial herb, up to 30 cm high, with erect, reddish, leafy stems, all coarsely hairy. Leaves usually entire, bottom ones obovate-lanceolate, petiolate; upper leaves lanceolate, sessile. Capitula at the end of upper lateral branches, 1 cm in diameter; cylindrical involucre has linear bracts with grey hairs. Central florets whitish to yellow-green, tubular; outer ones short-ligulate, filamentous, slightly longer than central flowers, purple. Flowers from June to September. Grows particularly in limestone areas, on dry, grassy slopes, dunes, banks and walls, from lowlands to foothills.

5 Cat's-foot *Antennaria dioica*. Perennial evergreen plant with stolons up to 20 cm high, with stems and leaves white-woolly beneath. Basal leaves spathulate, stem ones lanceolate to linear. Separate-sexed capitula in close terminal cluster, stalked; involucral bracts overlapping, chaffy in texture, whitish or pink; florets usually whitish. Flowers in May and June. Grows in hill pastures, rocky places, in open pine-woods and on heaths and moors, from foothills to mountains.

6 Edelweiss *Leontopodium alpinum*. Perennial herb up to 20 cm high, thickly white woolly hairy. Erect simple stems sparsely leaved. Basal leaves in rosette, oblanceolate, petiolate, entire; stem ones alternate, smaller. Small hemispherical capitula grouped at end of stem into a dense cluster, surrounded by star-like unequal bracts which are lanceolate and white-felted; florets tiny, yellowish white. Flowers from June to September. Grows in mountain pastures, on limestone rocks and screes in central and south-eastern Europe. Protected plant in some countries.

4

5

6

Family: Compositae

1 Wood Cudweed *Gnaphalium sylvaticum.* Perennial herb up to 50 cm high, erect, simple leafy stems. Single-veined, entire leaves on upper surface downy or bare, underside grey-felted; bottom ones lanceolate, upper leaves linear. Small capitula clustered in axils of upper leaves; involucral bracts bordered light brown. Tiny florets narrowly tubular, pale brown. Flowers from July to September. Grows in open woods, clearings and on heaths and moors, from lowlands to mountains.

2 *Inula britannica.* Perennial herb up to 60 cm high, with appressed hairs and erect, leafy stems. Hairy basal leaves oblong-ovate to lanceolate, toothed or entire; upper ones sessile, cordate and clasping. Capitula solitary or in groups of up to four at end of branches. Widely ovoid involucre, bracts linear-lanceolate, glandular-hairy. Florets yellow, central ones tubular, outer ones long ligulate. Flowers from July to September. Grows scattered in damp meadows, ditches, streamsides and damp woods, from lowlands to hilly country. Probably now extinct in Britain.

3 Common Cocklebur *Xanthium strumarium.* Annual, grey-green herb, up to 75 cm high, with a stout, sparsely leaved stem. Leaves cordate triangular, lobed and toothed. Axillary capitula unisexual; male ones with several flowers, greenish female capitula have two flowers enclosed in spiny involucral bracts. Achenes enclosed in spiny, woody involucre. Flowers from July to October. Native of South America, introduced and established on wasteland, by roadsides and on tips, usually at lower altitudes in temperate regions.

4 Tripartite Bur-marigold *Bidens tripartita*. Annual herb up to 60 cm high, with maroon-tinted, much branched stems. Opposite, petiolate stem leaves three- to five-lobed, segments lanceolate, toothed. Capitula solitary at ends of branches; outer involucral bracts enlarged and leafy, inner ones ovate, brownish. Disc florets yellow, ray ones absent. Achenes obovoid, flattened, edges barbed, with two to three straight barbed awns. Flowers from July to October. Grows in ditches, by ponds and rivers and in damp meadows, from lowlands to foothills. Related Nodding Bur-marigold (*B. cernuus*) has larger nodding capitula.

5 Corn Chamomile *Anthemis arvensis*. Annual herb, up to 50 cm high. Erect, much-branched stems. Twice or three times pinnately divided leaves, segments linear. Solitary, long-stalked capitula; receptacle conical, bearing lanceolate, pointed, chaffy awns. Disc florets yellow, tubular, ray ones white, ligulate. Achenes truncate ovoid, without pappus. Flowers from May to October. Grows in fields, on waste ground and by roadsides from lowlands to foothills.

6 Stinking Mayweed *Anthemis cotula*. Foetid annual herb, up to 50 cm high, with much-branched stems. Leaves twice to three times pinnately divided, with narrowly linear, toothed segments. Solitary stalked capitula, bracts of involucre with wide membranous rim. Tubular disc florets yellow, ray ones ligulate, white. Achenes lop-sided, ovoid, ribbed, without pappus. Flowers from June to October. Grows in fields, on wasteland and by roadsides, from lowlands to foothills.

Family: Compositae

1 Gallant Soldier *Galinsoga parviflora.* Annual herb up to 70 cm high, with erect, branched, leafy stems. Leaves opposite, ovate, pointed, sharply toothed. Small capitula in terminal, leafy clusters. Tubular disc florets yellow, ray ones shortly ligulate, white. Achenes with scaly pappus. Flowers from May to October. Native of South America, introduced to Europe and now a familiar weed in fields, gardens and on wasteland, from lowlands to foothills. Related Hairy Galinsoga or Shaggy Soldier (*G. ciliata*) is similar, but more or less densely covered with long hairs.

2 Sneezewort *Achillea ptarmica.* Perennial up to 60 cm high, with woody creeping rhizome and erect, leafy stems. Leaves linear-lanceolate, sessile, sharply toothed. Capitula in a loose terminal cluster, involucral bracts bordered with

dark brown. Central florets whitish, surrounded by up to 12 ligulate flowers of the same length as involucre. Flowers from July to September. Grows on heaths, in ditches and damp meadows from lowlands to foothills. Double forms are often cultivated in gardens.

3 Yarrow *Achillea millefolium.* Perennial up to 50 cm high, with far-creeping stolons and erect flowering stems. Leaves twice to three times pinnate, segments linear-lanceolate, spreading. Small capitula in dense flattened corymbs. Disc florets creamy, surrounded by up to five ligulate ray florets coloured white, sometimes pink or cerise. Flowers from June to October. Grows in meadows, pastures, woodland clearings, among rocks and by the roadside from lowlands to mountains. Pink- and cerise-flowered forms are grown in gardens.

5

6

4

4 *Matricaria recutita* (syn. *M. chamomilla*). Annual herb, up to 50 cm high, pleasingly aromatic with branched stems. Leaves alternate, sparse, up to three times pinnately divided into narrow, linear segments. Individual long-stalked capitula at end of upper branches, disc florets yellow and tubular, ray ones white and ligulate, soon reflexing backwards. Receptacles of capitula hollow, conical. Achenes ovoid, ribbed, without pappus. Flowers from March to August. Grows as a weed in fields, gardens and by roadsides, from lowlands to foothills, mainly in milder regions. Once much cultivated as a medicinal herb and still used as a substitute for true Chamomile.

5 Pineapple Weed *Matricaria matricarioides*. Annual herb, up to 30 cm high, sweetly aromatic, with branched, densely leafy stems. Sessile leaves up to three times pinnately divided into linear-lanceolate segments. Flower stalks short, thickened at top; involucral bracts with translu-

cent membranous rim. All florets yellow-green, tubular. Receptacles hollow, conical. Achenes ovoid, truncate, ribbed, pappus absent. Flowers from June to August. Native of north-eastern Asia, introduced and now a common weed of cultivated land, roadsides, wasteland and along paths, from lowlands to foothills.

6 Scentless Mayweed *Tripleurospermum maritimum* ssp. *inodorum*. Annual or biennial herb, up to 50 cm high, with erect stems usually branched only on top. Leaves up to three times pinnately divided into narrowly linear segments. Long-stalked capitula. Disc florets yellow, tubular; ray ones white, ligulate. Achenes ovoid, truncate, ribbed, without pappus. Flowers from June to October. Grows in fields, fallows, on wasteland and by roadsides, from lowlands to foothills. *T. maritimum* ssp. *maritimum* is perennial and more or less prostrate, growing only near the sea.

Family: Compositae

1 Tansy *Tanacetum vulgare* (syn. *Chrysanthemum vulgare*). Perennial, with creeping rhizomes and erect stems up to 1 metre high. Leaves twice pinnately divided, segments lanceolate, toothed; pleasingly aromatic when bruised. Numerous capitula in dense corymbs. All florets yellow, tubular, five-lobed. Achenes ovoid, crowned with a short membranous cup. Flowers from July to September. Grows by the roadside, on wasteland, and in hedgerows, from lowlands to mountains. Formerly much grown as a medicinal and pot-herb.

2 Ox-eye Daisy *Chrysanthemum leucanthemum*. Perennial herb up to 70 cm high, with erect, simple stems, occasionally sparsely branched. Bottom leaves simple, spathulate, petiolate, shallowly lobed and toothed; upper ones oblong-lanceolate, sessile, clasping. Long-stalked capitula; disc florets yellow, tubular, ray ones white, ligulate. Achenes obovoid, grooved. Flowers from June to October. Grows in meadows, on grassy slopes, banks, and by the roadside.

3 Wood Chrysanthemum *Chrysanthemum corymbosum*. Perennial up to 1 m high, with erect, densely leafy stems. Bottom leaves petiolate, stem ones sessile, all pinnately lobed, the segments double-toothed. Capitula in corymbs. Disc florets yellow, tubular, ray ones white, narrowly ligulate. Flowers from June to August. Grows in open woods and among bushes, on sunny slopes, from lowlands to mountains, mainly on limestone, in milder regions.

4 Mugwort *Artemisia vulgaris*. Perennial herb up to 120 cm high, with erect, stiff, branched stems. Leaves pinnately lobed, underside thinly white-felted, segments lanceolate to oblong,

1

2

3

lobed, toothed, upper leaves simply pinnate with entire segments. Small capitula arranged in long, dense, pyramidal panicles. Minute, tubular florets reddish-brown. Flowers from July to September. Grows on waste ground, by roadsides and in hedgerows, from lowlands to mountains.

5 Coltsfoot *Tussilago farfara*. Perennial herb, up to 25 cm high, with creeping rhizome and erect, simple stem, bearing single capitulum. Basal tufts of leaves develop after flowering period. Leaves long-petiolate, rounded, polygonal, shallowly 5—12 lobed, cordate, shallowly black-toothed, underside grey-felted. Scale leaves on flowering stems ovate, numerous, yellowish.

Capitula solitary; bracts linear, sometimes with red tint. Yellow florets, disc ones tubular, ray ones linear-ligulate. Achenes cylindrical, ribbed, with crown of pappus. Flowers in March and April. Grows in fields, on wasteland, on banks and in ditches, from lowlands to mountains.

6 Purple Coltsfoot *Homogyne alpina*. Perennial evergreen herb up to 15 cm high with thin creeping rhizome. Stems with thick, grey hairs are erect, bearing a single capitulum, usually with two ovate, sessile, clasping leaves. Long-petiolate leaves in basal tufts are almost leathery, cordate-orbicular or reniform, shallowly sinuate toothed. Capitula with linear bracts; florets pale violet, slightly longer than involucral bracts. Achenes cylindrical, ribbed, crowned with pappus. Flowers from May to July. Grows in mountain forests, meadows and on barrens. Very rare in Great Britain, being found in Scotland only and even there not native.

4

6

5

Family: Compositae

1 Common Butterbur *Petasites hybridus* (syn. *P. officinalis*). Perennial herb up to 1 metre high, partly dioecious. Thick, branched rhizomes strikingly aromatic if bruised or cut. Erect, simple flowering stems often violet-tinted. Basal leaves long-petiolate, cordate, angularly rounded to reniform, bluntly toothed. Lanceolate stem bracts clasping, bottom ones sheathed. Capitula in dense racemes, during fruition elongated; involucres flushed purple. Florets pink, seemingly bisexual, tubular, five-lobed, pistillate ones shortly tubular. Achenes cylindrical, with pappus. Flowers in April and May. Grows gregariously on river and canal banks, in ditches and damp meadows from lowlands to mountains.

2 White Butterbur *Petasites albus*. Perennial herb up to 80 cm high, with far-creeping rhizome. Very similar to preceding species. Stem and scales light green. Leaves in basal rosette rounded, reniform, cordate, angularly lobed, sharply toothed, grey-felted to smooth on underside. Florets yellowish-white, seemingly bisexual; five-lobed, pistillate ones shortly tubular. Flowers in April and May. Grows in open woods, along streams and on wasteland, from foothills to mountains; in higher altitudes more frequent and often gregarious.

3 Mountain Arnica *Arnica montana*. Perennial herb up to 50 cm high, with far-creeping rhizome. Erect stems glandular hairy, usually with only one capitulum. Basal rosette leaves ovate, entire; stem ones opposite, oblong-lanceolate. Involucral bracts lanceolate; florets orange-yellow, disc ones tubular, ray ones ligulate. Achenes with a crown of pappus. Flowers in June and July. Grows in meadows, forest glades and on margins of peat-bogs from foothills to mountains, mainly at higher altitudes. Protected plant in some countries.

4 Austrian Leopards-bane *Doronicum austriacum*. Perennial herb up to 150 cm high, with short rhizome and angular, erect, hairy stems bearing several capitula. Basal leaves petiolate, ovate-cordate, toothed; stem ones elongated, cordate to auriculate, clasping. Long-stalked capitula with linear-lanceolate involucral bracts. Florets yellow, disc ones tubular, ray ones long-ligulate. Achenes of central flowers with pappus, outer ones without. Flowers in July and August. Grows in open woods and river banks, from foothills to mountains.

5 Common Ragwort *Senecio jacobaea*. Perennial up to 1 metre high, with erect, densely leafy stems branched in upper part. Basal leaves pinnately lobed, stem ones usually sessile, smaller. Capitula in flattened compound corymbs; florets yellow, disc ones tubular, ray ones ligulate. Flowers from July to September. Grows on grassy slopes, in meadows, on margins of forests and by roadsides, from lowlands to foothills.

6 *Senecio nemorensis*. Perennial herb up to 150 cm high, usually hairy. Stem leaves oblong-ovate to lanceolate, stalkless, semi-clasping, toothed, underside downy. Capitula in flattish compound corymbs. Florets pale yellow, disc ones tubular, surrounded by five ligulate ray ones. Achenes with long pappus. Flowers from May to July. Grows in forests and clearings from foothills to mountains.

6   4   5

Family: Compositae

1 Lesser Burdock *Arctium minus*. Biennial herb up to 1.5 m high, with erect, stout, much-branched stems, woolly-hairy. Leaves petiolate, ovate-oblong, cordate, entire or shallowly toothed, on underside thinly grey-felted. Capitula in racemes, involucral bracts with sharply hooked tips. Tubular, red-violet florets. Achenes ovoid, without pappus. Flowers from July to September. Grows in light woodland, on wasteland and by roadsides from lowlands to foothills.

2 Musk Thistle *Carduus nutans*. Biennial herb up to 1 metre high, with winged, spiny stems. Leaves elliptic, cottony-hairy, pinnate-lobed, with a spiny toothed margin. Capitula solitary, nodding, long-stalked; involucral bracts spine-tipped, webbed with cottony hairs. Florets tubular, red-purple. Achenes grey, smooth, with a light spherical pappus. Flowers from July to September. Grows on sunny grassy slopes, in pastures and by the roadside, from lowlands to foothills.

3 Welted Thistle *Carduus acanthoides*. Biennial plant up to 1 metre high, with winged, spiny stems. Leaves lanceolate, pinnate-lobed, the margins wavy and set with spines. Capitula on short, erect, winged spiny stalks; involucral bracts spiny. Florets red-purple. Flowers from June to September. Grows in pastures, on wasteland and by roadsides, from lowlands to foothills, especially in milder regions.

4 Creeping Thistle *Cirsium arvense*. Biennial plant up to 1 metre high or even taller with erect, leafy stems and far-creeping rhizomes. Leaves oblong-lanceolate, pinnately lobed, spiny toothed, upper ones smaller and sessile. Capitula in terminal clusters, sometimes violet-tinted; bracts pointed or shortly spined. Imperfectly dioecious pale purple florets. Achenes ovoid with long white pappus. Flowers from July to September. Grows on wasteland, as field and garden weed, in forest clearings and by roadsides, from lowlands to mountains. Spear Thistle (*C. vulgare*) is a biennial herb, with spiny-winged stems, and the leaves thinly grey-felted beneath.

5 Marsh Thistle *Cirsium palustre*. Biennial herb up to 1.5 m high, with little branched spiny winged stems. Basal leaves sometimes red-tinted, oblanceolate; stem leaves pinnate-lobed with winged bases, spiny-toothed. Capitula in crowded leafy clusters, somewhat cottony hairy and purple tinted; florets red-purple. Flowers from July to September. Grows in marshes, damp meadows, woodland clearings and in hedgerows from lowlands to mountains.

6 Cabbage Thistle *Cirsium oleraceum*. Perennial herb up to 120 cm high with erect, distantly leaved, rarely branched stems. Softly spiny leaves, bottom ones deeply pinnately lobed with toothed segments, upper leaves smaller, cordate, sessile. Capitula in clusters subtended by enlarged yellowish bracts. Yellow-white florets. Flowers from June to September. Grows in damp meadows, marshes, open moist woods and by streams, from lowlands to foothills. Naturalized in a very few places in Britain.

5

3

6

Family: Compositae

1 Brown-headed Knapweed *Centaurea jacea.*
Perennial herb up to 50 cm high, with erect,
branched stems, sparsely leaved. Upper leaves
oblanceolate, sessile, with one or two large
teeth. Capitula solitary at end of branches,
bracts with distinct dry-membranous, fan-
shaped appendages. Florets red-purple.
Achenes ovoid, grey, glossy, without pappus.
Flowers from June to October. Grows in grassland and waste places from lowlands to mountains. Only naturalized in a few places in southern Britain. Greater Knapweed (*C. scabiosa*) has
pinnate-lobed leaves and larger heads. It is
found in grassy places and by roadsides
throughout lowland Britain.

2 Cornflower *Centaurea cyanus.* Annual or
overwintering herb up to 60 cm high, with erect,
branched stems. Leaves lanceolate, the basal
ones often with narrow pinnate lobes. Capitula
solitary at ends of branches, cottony hairy, central one with narrow-toothed appendages. Central florets violet, marginal ones much larger,
spreading, bright blue, rarely whitish or rosy.
Achenes with a brush-like crown of stiff hairs.
Flowers from June to October. Grows in cornfields and waste places. Formerly a common
weed of cornfields throughout Europe, but now
on the decline where good farming practices
prevail.

3 Mountain Cornflower *Centaurea montana.*
Perennial herb up to 60 cm high, with erect,
little-branched stems. Leaves lanceolate, entire,
underside cobwebby hairy, upper surface
smooth, stem leaves sessile with winged bases.
Stalked capitula often solitary, bracts with
black, short-toothed border. Central flowers violet, outer ones larger, blue, sometimes rose or
white. Flowers from May to October. Grows in
mountain meadows and forest clearings, from
foothills to mountains. Grown in gardens in Britain and sometimes escaping.

4 Stemless Carline-thistle *Carlina acaulis.* Perennial plant with usually very short flowering stems, only a few centimetres tall. Leaves in basal rosette pinnate-lobed and spiny toothed. Capitula solitary, over 15 cm in diameter; outer involucral bracts leaf-like, inner ones linear, upper surface silvery glossy, underside yellowish, in sunshine widely expanded, in wet weather rolled tightly closed. Tubular, whitish or pinkish florets. Achenes with hairs. Flowers from July to September. Grows scattered in dry pastures and on stony slopes from lowlands to foothills.

5 Common Carline-thistle *Carlina vulgaris.* Biennial herb up to 50 cm high, with erect, purplish, cottony hairy stems. Under surface of leaves cobwebby woolly, later bare, oblong-lanceolate, with undulate margins densely spiny toothed. Basal leaves in rosette, dying before flowering starts. Stem leaves cordate, sessile, the topmost ones transformed into bracts. Capitula terminate lateral branches; inner involucral bracts straw-yellow, spreading and resembling ray florets. Florets purple. Achenes with short hairs and crowned with pappus. Flowers from July to September. Grows on sunny grassy slopes and banks, particularly on limestone, from lowlands to mountains.

6 Great Globe-thistle *Echinops sphaerocephalus.* Perennial herb up to 2 m high, with robust, woody, white-woolly stems. Bottom leaves petiolate, stem ones sessile, lanceolate, pinnate-lobed and spiny toothed. Single-flowered, narrow capitula aggregated into dense globose heads. Florets bluish or white, tubular. Achenes oblong-ovoid, with a cup-like crown of partly fused hairs. Flowers from June to August. Grows on forest margins, in vineyards, quarries, on river banks and wasteland, and by roadsides, in lower altitudes of milder regions. Grown in gardens in Britain and sometimes escaping.

3

5

4

Orchids, Lilies and Related Plants

Without doubt, the most striking plants are those that belong to the order Orchidales. Everyone has marvelled at the exotic tropical orchids in florists' windows or in the glasshouses of botanical gardens. It is amazing to find flowers with so many bizarre shapes and widely diverse colour combinations in a single family. One must realize, of course, that the plants belonging to the orchid family (Orchidaceae) are estimated to number as many as 25,000, making it the largest family in the whole plant kingdom.

Orchids have an extremely wide range of distribution. Although they grow mainly in damp tropical forests, their range reaches far into the Arctic and extends from coastal rain forests high up into the mountains.

Just as their habitats are marked by great diversity, so is the structure of their bodies, their manner of obtaining nourishment and their life forms. European orchids are mostly green autotrophic ground orchids, with only occasional supplementation of their diet by saprophytic means. Practically all species are mycorrhizal. Only a few central European species lack chlorophyll and are entirely saprophytic, for example *Neottia, Corallorhiza, Epipogium* and several others. Tropical orchids are mostly epiphytic, which means that they grow on other plants, usually on tall trees, although a few genera are ground plants.

Many European orchids have underground tubers. Those belonging to the genus *Orchis* (which gave the whole family its name), have a typical pair of tubers, while the tubers of *Dactylorhiza* orchids and some others are digitately lobed. The food reserves in the tubers enable the plants to survive cold winter months or periods of drought. These reserves are more readily and more quickly transformed into nourishing substances than starch. Epiphytic orchids also have tubers, but these developed from stems, not from roots, and can thus reproduce by vegetative means. A common feature of epiphytic orchids is their aerial roots, through which respiration takes place and through which atmospheric moisture, which is nearly 100 per cent in tropical rain forests, is absorbed. Some epiphytic orchids have no leaves whatsoever, their function having been taken over by the aerial roots which are rich in chlorophyll.

Fig. 1. One of the loveliest European orchids, Lady's Slipper (*Cypripedium calceolus*). The conspicuously inflated, originally upper, lip assumes its position at the bottom as the flower develops.

The flowers of orchids exhibit perhaps the greatest diversity of shape of all plants. Usually there are several to dozens of blossoms on a single plant; sometimes they grow in clusters that hang in drooping racemes from the crowns of the trees on which tropical epiphytic orchids grow. These may form garlands up to 4 m long, as in the species *Renanthera lowii* of New Guinea. The European orchids with the largest flowers are Lady's Slipper (*Cypripedium calceolus*), with a flower up to 9 cm long, and *Himantoglossum hircinum*, with a flower up to 5 cm long, strap-shaped and twisted, with a violet-spotted lip. All the other European orchids have much smaller flowers; those of some species of *Epipactis, Listera, Spiranthes* and *Herminium* are extremely small and inconspicuous. The interesting and diverse shapes of the flowers of certain *Ophrys* species fully justify the names given to the respective plants: *O. insectifera, O. sphecodes, O. fuciflora* and *O. apifera*.

The flowers of orchids are extremely interesting. Before they open, the flower-peduncle is twisted round a full 180 degrees, so that the spurred, lip-shaped, upper perianth segment becomes the bottom segment. Only rarely are the pollen grains free, mostly they are in a coherent cluster, called a pollinium, with a sticky pad at the end of a stalk. The pollinia adhere to the bodies of insects that visit the flower, so that when they visit another, the pollinia are transferred to its stigma, thereby pollinating the flower.

Orchid seeds are the smallest and lightest in the plant realm and their number is the greatest. Of the European species the smallest number is produced by *Coeloglossum virida* — only about 1,330! The ovary of the South American orchid *Cychnoches ventricosum*, on the other hand, contains more than four million seeds! Despite this astounding quantity the chances of the development of a new plant are extremely small, for the seed must find conditions that are suitable for its germination and most orchids, including tropical species, require a mycorrhizal association to obtain their nourishment.

In no other family have so many hybrids been developed by selective breeding than in the case of orchids. In the continual quest for ever-new combinations of colour and form, not only have breeders crossed numerous species of the same genus but also some belonging to different genera. The genus *Cattleya* alone, which numbers 60—70 species, has more than 5,000 hybrids. As for the Indomalaysian genus *Vanda*, its species and varieties have been successfully crossed with members of eleven other genera.

Fig. 2. The flowers of Flowering Rush (*Butomus umbellatus*) adorn waterside meadows and wet places.

Numerous varieties have been developed among the popular orchids of the genera *Dendrobium, Catasetum, Cymbidium, Oncidium, Odontoglossum, Laelia, Phalaenopsis, Miltonia, Stanhopea* and dozens of others.

Despite the fact that all species of orchids are on the list of protected species in Europe, they are declining in number every year due to the disappearance of their natural habitats through land reclamation and runoffs from fields treated with chemicals. Even tropical orchids are not safe from human activity, for a portion of the tropical forest in the Amazon region, central Africa and south-east Asia is irretrievably lost every hour as a result of the unscrupulous felling of trees whose crowns contain orchids that have climbed there in search of light and air.

In addition to the lily family (Liliaceae), the order Liliales also comprises garlic, onion, Lily-of-the-Valley, crocus, snowdrop and snowflake. As with orchids, we are more likely to be acquainted with the cultivated plants than with those that grow in the wild. The lily family includes lilies (*Lilium*), fritillaries (*Fritillaria*), tulips (*Tulipa*), *Erythronium, Gagea, Lloydia* and several other genera. These appear to be common and familiar plants but we do not know all of them as well as we know the cultivated ones, for example *Lilium candidum*, native to the Lebanon, southern Syria and neighbouring regions, and the east-Asian species *Lilium regale* and Tiger Lily (*L. tigrinum*). Probably loveliest of all is the Turk's-cap Lily (*L. martagon*) with its pendulous, light purple, dark-spotted Turk's-cap flowers with recurved petals. I know of a dappled glade where dozens of these flowers, their protruding stamens tipped with dark orange anthers, glow brightly in the shafts of sunlight.

The same is true of fritillaries. We are more apt to be familiar with the Crown Imperial (*Fritillaria imperialis*), native to Iran and Afghanistan, which is widely grown for its large yellow or brick-red flowers, but who can boast having seen the unusual flowers of Snake's Head (*F. meleagris*) in the wild? The unbelievable regularity of its brown and violet checkerboard pattern is one of the small miracles of the flora of damp meadows.

Dog's-tooth Violet (*Erythronium dens-canis*) is also familiar to us as a garden plant, but in southern Europe one may come across it in the wild, its pink, brown-spotted flower rising from between two marbled leaves. In central Europe Dog's-tooth Violet is a rare relict of Tertiary period flora and, as such, is on the list of rigidly protected species in several localities in Austria, Czechoslovakia and Switzerland, where its distribution occasionally extends from the southern regions of its range.

Most familiar of all the plants of this group are the tulips, grown in a wide range of varieties and hybrids. Garden tulips are classed under the heading *Tulipa gesneriana* and their popularity, cultivation and spread throughout Europe is fairly recent, dating from the sixteenth century, although they were cultivated in the Middle East as far back as the tenth century. Also popular are the low-growing, early-flowering, botanical tulips such as *T. greigi, T. fosteriana* and *T. kaufmanniana*, native to central Asia.

All plants of the lily family may be seen only rarely in the wild and for that reason they are on the list of protected species. We must all be content with the beauty of their cultivated

Fig. 3. Autumn Crocus (*Colchicum autumnale*) flowers in the autumn and again in the spring of the following year.

forms as it is an offence to gather bulbs or tubers in the wild. Wild plants should be left where they belong, to enhance the beauty of their natural surroundings.

Plants of the order Butomales are aquatic or bog plants. The order Pandanales comprises solely bog plants with a typical globose or cylindrical inflorescence (spadix), for example Lesser Reedmace (*Typha angustifolia*), a robust plant that grows on the banks of still stretches of water.

The order Arales is extremely diverse. It includes Sweet Flag, Bog Arum and duckweeds (Lemnaceae). It is native to India but has long since been naturalized throughout Europe, where it is a common plant.

The simplest and smallest of all flowering plants belongs to the duckweed family. This is Rootless Duckweed (*Wolffia arrhiza*), a tiny, rootless aquatic plant with a body consisting of minute (1.5 mm) thalli without vascular bundles and without stomata. The male flower is concealed in a minute hollow on the upperside. This consists solely of a single stamen. In the same tiny hollow the female flower grows, consisting of a single pistil. Rootless Duckweed grows in southern and western Europe, was introduced into central Europe and is sometimes grown in aquariums. In south-east Asia it is cultivated for its high concentration of proteins and its thalli are being experimentally processed as food for manned space flights of long duration.

Fig. 4. The perianth segments of the pendulous flowers of Turk's-cap Lily (*Lilium martagon*) are conspicuously curved upward.

Family: **Orchid**—Orchidaceae

1 Large White Helleborine *Cephalanthera damasonium.* Perennial herb up to 45 cm high with slender leafy stem, scaly at bottom. Leaves ovate to lanceolate. Flowers 3—12 in a loose spike. Cream-white tepals, bracts usually longer than ovary. Flowers in May and June. Grows scattered in deciduous woods, from lowlands to foothills. Related Red Helleborine (*C. rubra*) has rose to purple flowers and stem glandularly downy above.

2 Common Helleborine *Epipactis helleborine* (syn. *E. latifolia*). Perennial herb up to 60 cm high, with erect stems, downy above. Broadly ovate green leaves mostly spreading, sessile, clasping, on under surface downy. Raceme one-sided, elongated, many-flowered. Each flower at first drooping, straightening up while flowering. Inner tepals greenish and dull purple-brown. Flowers from July to September. Grows in forests from lowlands to mountains. Related Dark-red Helleborine (*E. atrorubens*) has ovaries densely glandular downy, flowers dark purple, fragrant, and whole plant is purple-tinted; protected in some countries.

3 Lesser Butterfly Orchid *Platanthera bifolia.* Perennial herb almost 30 cm high, with tuberous rootstock and erect, hollow stems. Basal leaves, two opposite widely elliptic; stem bears up to three small, leafy bracts. Open spike of white, spurred, fragrant flowers. Flowers in June and July. Grows in open woods, among bushes and sometimes on heaths, from lowlands to mountains.

4 Fragrant Orchid *Gymnadenia conopsea* (syn. *Habanaria conopsea*). Perennial herb up to 40 cm high, with lobed tubers and erect stems. Leaves grey-green, narrowly oblong-lanceolate, bottom ones close to each other. Floral spike has lanceolate bracts, often with purple margins. Purple, rarely whitish tepals; spurs of double length. Conspicuously twisted ovary. Flowers from May to July. Grows scattered in open woods, meadows and on grassy slopes from lowlands to mountains, usually on limestone.

5 Green-winged Orchid *Orchid morio.* Perennial herb up to 25 cm high with undivided, globose tubers and green stem. Leaves grey-green, lower ones lanceolate, upper ones smaller and narrow. Flowers in short terminal raceme, purple, rarely whitish, green-veined. Helmet-like perianth, lip red-purple, dark-spotted; spur thick, cylindrical. Flowers from April to June. Grows in dry meadows and on grassy slopes, from lowlands to foothills. Related species of *Ophrys* have lip without spur but with striking design, simulating bee, bumblebee or other insect body.

6 Broad-leaved Marsh Orchid *Dactylorchis majalis* (syn. *Dactylorhyza majalis*). Very variable perennial herb up to 40 cm high, with finger-like divided tubers and erect, hollow stems. Leaves oblong-lanceolate, shortly sheathed, dark green, sometimes black-brown spotted. Dense floral spike; flowers reddish to purple, with spotted outer petals, lip purple-red, three-lobed, spur shorter than ovary. Flowers from May to July. Grows in damp meadows, fens, marshes, dune hollows, from lowlands to foothills. Several forms are now given specific rank, *D. praetermissa* and *D. purpurella* being the most noteworthy.

7 Lady's Slipper *Cypripedium calceolus*. Perennial downy herb up to 50 cm high, with shortly creeping rhizome and erect stems, scaly at base. Only three or four leaves, alternate, ovate, prominently ribbed. Flowers solitary, or less frequently two, in axil of upper leaf. Lip light yellow, red-dotted, tepals maroon; three-lobed stigma. Flowers in May and June. Grows scattered in deciduous woods on calcareous grounds from lowlands to mountains. Almost extinct in Britain. Protected plant in some countries.

Family: Lily—Liliaceae

1 White False Helleborine *Veratrum album.*
Perennial herb, with stout erect leafy stems, up
to 150 cm high. Underside of leaves downy,
pleated, widely elliptical, upper ones lanceolate,
some in whorls of three. Flowers in dense, long
panicles, greenish-white or yellowish, bottom
ones bisexual, upper flowers mostly male. Cap-
sular fruits many-seeded. Flowers from June to
August. Grows in mountain meadows, pastures
and in rocky places, from foothills to mountains.

2 Meadow Saffron *Colchicum autumnale.* Perennial, poisonous herb with a large corm often
deeply buried. Basal, oblong-lanceolate leaves
develop in spring together with maturing capsule. Flowers pale purple, long-tubular, with 6
oblong, spreading tepals. The three-celled
ovary below ground; capsule ripens above
ground in spring. Flowers from August to November. Grows in damp meadows and open
woods, from lowlands to foothills.

3 Martagon or **Turk's Cap Lily** *Lilium martagon.*
Perennial herb with robust erect stems up to
1 metre high, and a scaly bulb. Leaves obovate-lanceolate pointed, mostly in whorls of
5—10. Flowers in open racemes, stalked and
nodding; tepals with reflexed tips, dull purple,
brown-spotted, sometimes white. Fruit an ovoid
ridged capsule. Flowers from June to August.
Grows in deciduous woods, thickets and pastures, more frequently on limestone soils, in
mountains. Protected plant in some countries. In
Britain often grown in gardens, escaping, and
now well naturalized in a number of wooded
areas.

4 Ramsons *Allium ursinum.* Perennial herb up
to 50 cm high with a bulbous rootstock and leafless stems. Basal leaves, two to three only, elliptic to lanceolate, long-petiolate. Umbellate inflorescence ensheathed while immature in two
or three bracts. Flowers up to 1 cm across, star-
shaped, with 6 pointed lobes, perianth white.
Fruit a flattened, 3-lobed capsule. Flowers from
April to June. Grows scattered in deciduous
woods, from lowlands to mountains, often gregariously. Related Crow Garlic (*A. vineale*) has
narrowly linear leaves and dense heads of bulbils and purple-red flowers; sometimes bulbils
only.

5 *Allium flavum.* Perennial herb up to 50 cm
high, with ovoid bulbs. Hollow channelled
leaves narrowly linear, grey-green. Spathe composed of two unequally long bracts. Stamens
project from bell-shaped, yellow perianth. Cap-

sules triangularly ovoid. Flowers from June to
August. Grows on sunny slopes, among rocks,
and in sandy places at lower altitudes of south-
eastern Europe. Related *Allium suaveolens* with
rosy flowers grows in the Alps.

6 May Lily *Maianthemum bifolium.* Perennial
herb up to 15 cm high with thin, creeping rhizome and erect stems, usually with two shortly
petiolate, cordate-ovate, pointed leaves.
Stalked racemose inflorescence bears small,
white starry flowers with 4 perianth lobes. Fruit
a small, red, globose berry. Flowers from May
to July. Grows in woods and among bushes
from lowlands to mountains. Very rare in Britain.

7 Common Solomon's Seal *Polygonatum multiflorum*. Perennial plant up to 80 cm high, with thick, creeping rhizome and smooth, rounded stems arching at the top. Leaves alternate, ovate to elliptic, bare. Axillary flowers usually in clusters of 2 to 5, pendulous. Perianth of six fused tepals, narrowly tubular, greenish white. Fruits are globular, blue-black berries. Flowers in May and June. Grows in shady woods and among bushes, from lowlands to foothills. Related Angular Solomon's Seal (*P. odoratum*) has angular stems and flowers solitary or in twos. *Polygonatum verticillatum* has narrowly lanceolate leaves in whorls. All species poisonous.

1

4   5

3

to August. Grows in deciduous and mixed forests and glades, from lowlands to mountains.

Family: Iris—Iridaceae

3 Yellow Flag *Iris pseudacorus.* Perennial herb up to 1.5 m high with thick, shortly creeping, branched rhizome and erect flowering stems branched at the top only. Leaves sword-shaped. Long-stalked flowers; perianth segments in two whorls of 3; outer tepals ovate, recurved, yellow, with violet-brown veining; inner tepals erect, obovate, yellow, shorter than crown-shaped stigma arms. Capsule bluntly triangular ovoid. Flowers in May and June. Grows in or close to water, rivers, ponds, lakes and ditches, mainly at lower altitudes. Related Siberian Iris (*I. sibirica*) has blue-violet flowers and linear leaves. Not native to Britain, but much cultivated in gardens and occasionally escaping.

Family: Amaryllidaceae

4 Snowdrop *Galanthus nivalis.* Perennial herb up to 20 cm high with brown-scaly bulb. Two basal leaves linear, grey-green, blunt, scale-sheathed at base. Erect stem with solitary pendent flower in axil of membranous bract. Outer perianth whorl consists of three obovate-ob-

Family: Lily—Liliaceae

1 Lily-of-the-Valley *Convallaria majalis.* Perennial, poisonous herb, up to 20 cm high, with creeping rhizome. Usually two petiolate leaves with sheathing scales at base, elliptic-lanceolate, entire. Erect stem, flowers in one-sided raceme, short-stalked, drooping, very fragrant, white or occasionally pinkish. Perianth broadly bell-shaped, consists of six short tepals. Fruits are sub-globose red berries. Flowers in May and June. Grows in open deciduous woods and among bushes, from lowlands to mountains.

2 Herb Paris *Paris quadrifolia.* Perennial herb up to 30 cm high, with creeping rhizomes and erect stems. Obovate-lanceolate leaves in one whorl of four. Flowers stalked, solitary, the perianth in whorls of four. Outer tepals lanceolate, green; inner ones narrowly linear, yellow-green. Eight stamens with anther connective awl-like. Fruits black globose berries. Flowers from May

2

6

7

long, white tepals, inner three are shorter, blunt
and shallowly notched, with green spot near tip.
Flowers in February and March. Grows in woods
and hedgerows from lowlands to mountains.

5 Spring Snowflake *Leucojum vernum.* Perennial herb up to 30 cm high, with globose bulbs
and 3 or 4 linear, dark green basal leaves.
Drooping flowers solitary or in twos. All 6 tepals
are equally long, white, with yellowish green
spot at the tip. Flowers from February to April.
Grows in shady deciduous woods, forest glades
and damp meadows from lowlands to mountains. Often cultivated but rarely escaping.

Subclass: **Monocotyledones**—Butomidae

Family: **Flowering Rush**—Butomaceae

6 Flowering Rush *Butomus umbellatus.* Perennial herb up to 150 cm high, with creeping rhizomes and erect flowering stems. Basal tufts of
leaves are sheathed, triangular at base, expand-
ing to a linear blade. Pink flowers in many-
flowered terminal umbels. Six obovate tepals, 3
smaller than the rest, and 6—9 stamens. Fruits
a cluster of small ovoid follicles. Flowers from
June to August. Grows in ditches and on margins of water bodies, from lowlands to foothills.

Family: **Water-plantain**—Alismataceae

7 Common Water-plantain *Alisma plantago-
aquatica.* Perennial herb up to 1 metre high,
with short, thickened rhizome and erect stems.
Submerged leaves (when present) linear, those
above the water are long-petiolate, prominently
ribbed, broadly ovate, pointed. Flowers in well-
branched, whorled panicle; both sepals and petals in threes; petals obovate, pale white, lilac
or rarely pink. Fruit a doughnut-shaped schizocarp. Flowers from June to September. Grows
in shallow water and on banks of ponds, lakes,
canals, slow flowing rivers, and in ditches, from
lowlands to foothills. Related Arrowhead (*Sagit-
taria sagittifolia*) has arrowhead-shaped leaves,
larger, fewer, white flowers and petals with
black-violet spot at base.

Family: **Pondweed**—Potamogetonaceae

1 Broad-leaved Pondweed *Potamogeton natans.* Perennial submerged aquatic herb with stem up to 1 m long or more in deep water. Floating leaves long-petiolate, elliptic, pointed, cordate. Submerged leaves linear. Tiny, greenish flowers, without petals, in erect, cylindrical spikes, emerging above water surface. Flowers from June to August. Grows in lakes, ponds, rivers and ditches, from lowlands to foothills.

Family: **Arum**—Araceae

2 Sweet Flag *Acorus calamus.* Perennial iris-like herb up to 1 metre high, with thick, fragrant rhizomes. Sword-shaped leaves arranged in two ranks. Triangular stems with a bract similar to leaf continuing in stem direction. Minute flowers in apparently lateral spadix, with 6-lobed, green-yellow perianth. Fruits do not mature in northern Europe. Flowers from June to August. Grows near and in water, from lowlands to foothills. Native of southern Asia and northwestern U.S.A., introduced about 400 years ago and naturalized in Europe.

3 Bog Arum *Calla palustris.* Perennial aquatic herb, up to 30 cm, with hollow, green rhizome. Leaves broadly ovate-cordate. Axillary stems bear short, cylindrical, short-stalked spadix. Minute yellow-green flowers without a perianth. Fruits are red berries. Flowers from May to August. Grows in pools, bends of rivers and peatbogs from lowlands to foothills, rarely at higher altitudes, in central and northern Europe. Naturalized only in Britain.

4 Lords-and-Ladies or **Cuckoo-pint** *Arum maculatum.* Perennial plant, almost 50 cm high, with short tuberous rhizome and erect stem. Leaves long-petiolate, triangular ovate to arrow-shaped. Spathe cyathiform, whitish or greenish, rarely red-tinted inside, with violet blotches. On spadix, lowest are female flowers, above them male ones; above these ring of sterile, bulb-like thickened 'flowers' modified into thick bristles; spadix tip violet-brown or yellowish. Fruits are red, poisonous berries. Flowers in April and May. Grows in open deciduous woods, in hedgerows and on hedgebanks, from lowlands to foothills.

Family: **Bur-reed**—Sparganiaceae

5 Branched Bur-reed *Sparganium erectum* (syn. *S. ramosum*). Perennial aquatic herb up to 50 cm high with thick, spreading rhizomes. Stiff, erect leaves, triangular in section. Erect robust stems, with terminal stiff panicle. Flowers in globose heads, unisexual, bottom ones female, upper ones male; perianth much reduced, 3-lobed. Fruit ellipsoidal, shouldered yellow-brown nut. Flowers from June to August. Grows in shallow water and on mud or wet soil from lowlands to foothills.

Family: **Reedmace**—Typhaceae

6 Lesser Reedmace *Typha angustifolia*. Perennial herb up to 3 metres high, with extensively creeping rhizome and rigid erect, round stems. Erect, linear leaves not more than 1 cm wide. Inflorescence composed of two separate cylindrical spadices, one above the other; bottom one has female flowers, upper one male florets. Bottom spadix is narrow, red-brown. Unisexual flowers without any perianth. Fruits stalked with long pappus-like hairs. Flowers in June-July. Grows in water and wet soil, from lowlands to foothills. Related Great Reedmace (*T. latifolia*) has leaves up to 2 cm wide and spadices united one above other, bottom one dark brown and thick. This is much more common in Britain than *T. angustifolia*.

Family: Lemnaceae

7 Ivy Duckweed *Lemna trisulca* (a). Tiny perennial, aquatic herb, floating just beneath water surface. Leaf-like thalli ovate lanceolate, petiolate, branching from the middle. Flowering plants rare, smaller and floating. Grows in stagnant waters at lower altitudes. **Common Duckweed** *(L. minor)* (b) has floating thalli round to broadly ovate, usually growing gregariously. **Great Duckweed** (*L. polyrhiza*) (c) has roundly ovate thalli with reddish underside, each with bundle of rootlets.

Trees and Shrubs

Woody plants are plants with stems that are, or become, woody and thicken secondarily. They may be deciduous or evergreen and include trees and shrubs as well as sub-shrubs ranging from huge forest giants to such tiny shrubs as the whortleberry and cranberry.

Trees are long-lived plants. Often we can only estimate the age of large oaks or lime trees. On the cross-section of the trunk of a felled tree one can count the annual rings, each produced by a single year's growth. This is quite laborious and, of course, it cannot be done in the case of

Fig. 1. A twig of Scots Pine (*Pinus sylvestris*) with male (*left*) and female (*right*) cones. *Below*, a ripe cone with fallen seeds.

Fig. 2. Male flowers of the Beech (*Fagus sylvatica*).

living trees. The true age of a living tree is scientifically determined in a quite different way. A bore is drilled in the trunk of the tree and a sample of the wood removed; once healed, the minute scars on the bark are practically unnoticeable.

In central Europe the only truly old trees are yews (*Taxus*), some believed to be over two thousand years old. Yews have a very slow rate of growth, their trunks increasing by only 0.5—1 mm in diameter each year. Larches rarely reach the age of 600 years, and as for oaks, 500 years is a record. Even the fantastically twisted, hollow trunks of the olive trees (*Olea*) that are cultivated in the Mediterranean region, are no more than a hundred years old.

On the other hand, North America has trees that were alive at the time of the growth of the civilizations of the ancient Egyptians and Sumerians. Still growing today in the White Mountains of California are specimens of the ancient Bristlecone Pine (*Pinus aristata*), less than 10 m high, their trunks' remnants deformed by gales and winds, yet with living green branches. With the aid of radiocarbon dating, probes have revealed that the famed Giant Sequoias (*Sequoiadendron giganteum*), hitherto believed to be the oldest living organisms (about 3,200 years old), are much younger than the Bristlecone Pine. The wood of the dead trunks of these pines remains undecayed, making it possible to date these remnants, and it has been determined that they are between 6,200 and 7,100 years old!

Fig. 3. An inflorescence of Small-leaved Lime (*Tilia cordata*).

Although the giant sequoias rank second in terms of age, they rank first in another respect, in that they are the largest and most massive of all existing plants. One Giant Sequoia, called 'Father of the Forest', was the tallest tree ever measured. It reached a height of 135 m and the trunk measured 12 m in diameter at ground level. The present-day record is held by 'General Sherman' in the Sequoia National Park. This tree is 83 m tall, measures 11 m in diameter at ground level and is more than 8 m in diameter 3 m above ground level; in other words this tree represents 1,400 cu m of wood. Currently, the tallest plant in the world is one American Coastal Redwood (*Sequoia sempervirens*), which reaches a height of 112 m. It grows in California's Redwoods State Park.

Competitors in height with these giant trees were the eucalypts (*Eucalyptus*). Earlier records gave their greatest height as being more than 150 m, but experts on Australian flora consider this improbable. According to present-day measurements eucalypts reach a maximum height of less than 100 m. However, they do have an extraordinarily rapid rate of growth, making as much as 3 m in height per year. Their wood is very dense, firm and highly prized.

The most primitive existing angiosperms are ever-green woody plants growing on the islands of Fiji in the Pacific. There, in 1934, the American A. C. Smith discovered a 14-m-high tree with unusual fruits. Its leaves are also unusual in the Pacific region. Not until 1941 did Otto Degener bring to the USA sufficient material, including flowers, according to which Smith and Bailey described a new family and new genus, consisting of a single species which they named *Degeneria vitiensis.* The discovery of this woody plant greatly contributed to a realistic idea of the general character of the very first angiosperms.

The most primitive flowering plants also include the members of the Winteraceae family, comprising six genera and approximately 60 species, found in the South Pacific region, and other families of the order Magnoliales. Certain species of the magnolia family (Magnoliaceae) are also grown in Europe's parks and gardens. Magnolias (*Magnolia*) have large, striking, fragrant flowers that often open before the leaves. Also grown in parks is the North American Tulip Tree (*Liriodendron tulipifera*) with its large, orange-spotted flowers. These woody plants also possess certain primitive features and are also related to the very first flowering plants.

Fig. 4. A fruit-bearing twig of Common Ash (*Fraxinus excelsion*).

The cranberry and whortleberry have already been mentioned as examples of the smallest woody plants. Also related to them are the heathers (*Calluna*) and heaths (*Erica*). The Tree Heath (*Erica arborea*), however, is a true shrub, 3—5 m high, which, in the Mediterranean region, is a woody component of the evergreen maquis. Below ground it has globose or tuberous roots of extremely hard reddish-brown wood which, because of its resistance to heat and fire, is used in the manufacture of tobacco pipes and briars.

The commonest trees and shrubs are discussed in greater detail on the following pages. They hold no records of size or age, but that does not make them any the less interesting.

Fig. 5. Branches of Broom (*Sarothamnus scoparius*) showing the typical flowers of papilionaceous plants.

Fig. 6. The hip, the aggregate fruit of the Dog Rose (*Rosa canina*), has long-haired fruits (achenes) enclosed in a fleshy receptacle.

2 Silver Fir *Abies alba*. Tall, stout tree up to 45 m or more, with pyramidal to cylindrical crown. Young shoots with fine, grey-brown tomentum, gradually changing into whitish, grey-green, smooth or scaly bark. Blunt, flat needles, with two white stripes beneath arranged in two rows, adhere to twig by disc-like bases. After they fall the twig remains almost smooth. Fir is monoecious, flowers from May to June. Male flowers have orange yellow anthers. Female flowers are borne on upper side of preceding year's stronger twigs and develop into erect cones, disintegrating at maturity. Grows in mountain or foothill woods and forms important component of beech-fir forests. Often planted. In parks cultivated in various forms, together with related species from North America, Asia and southern Spain.

Sub-division: **Gymnosperms**—Gymnospermae

Class: **Coniferous plants**—Coniferopsida

Family: Taxaceae

1 Yew *Taxus baccata*. Broad-headed tree up to 20 m, either in the open or as an understorey tree, mainly on chalk or limestone. Abundantly planted in many cultivated forms, often in parks. Grows slowly; therefore annual rings are very dense and even old trees are rarely very big. Only coniferous tree with resin canals. Wood and needles contain poisonous alkaloid toxin. Dioecious tree, flowers in March and April. Male cones grow in axils of needles and have shield-shaped stamens. Female cones have one ovule ripening into seed, enveloped in fleshy red cupule; only this is not poisonous.

3 Norway Spruce *Picea abies* (syn. *P. excelsa*). Tall tree up to 60 m or more, with shallow roots and slender pyramidal crown; young bark light brown, older greyish or maroon, scaly, changing into cracked bark. Branches in regular whorls, with pointed needles; when these fall they leave peg-like protuberances on twigs. Spruce is dioecious; flowers in April and May. Male flowers grow on preceding year's twigs; at first they are red, later yellowish and ovoid. Pendent female flowers at end of branches in upper part of crown are reddish before pollination. Mature cones also are pendulous and do not disintegrate. Originally native of mountain and foothill forests but generally planted also at lower altitudes; in many cultivated forms commonly planted in parks together with some North-American species. This is the popular Christmas tree of central Europe and Britain.

4 European Larch *Larix decidua*. A deep-rooting tree up to 45 m tall with spreading branches that droop at the tips in mature specimens. Grey-brown bark later becomes thick and irregularly scaly. The soft light green needles in clusters on shortened lateral shoots are of annual duration. Flowers from April to June; male flowers globose, sulphur-yellow, female ones red, ripening in autumn to small ovoid-globose cones. Larch is a mountain conifer, and needs high light intensity. For its valuable timber it is abundantly cultivated even at lower altitudes, especially on margins of coniferous woods and in parks. The evergreen Douglas Fir (*Pseudotsuga menziesii*) is also planted in woods. The pendent cones have trifid scales which project like three-pointed tongues; needles with two white stripes give out pleasant smell when crushed. Also cultivated in parks; native of western North America.

3

4

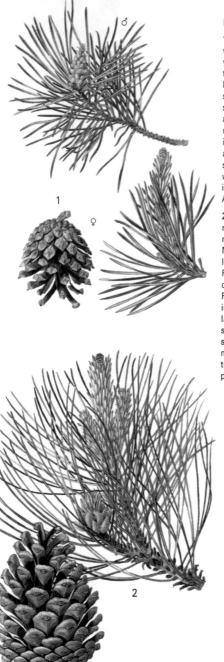

Family: Pinaceae

1 Scots Pine *Pinus sylvestris.* A tree up to 40 m, with a globose to flattened crown. Bark of young twigs green, later turning rusty; old trunks have a fissured, reddish-brown or grey-brown bark. Needles arranged in pairs on short shoots. Flowers from May to June; male flowers sulphur-yellow, female ones arranged individually or in twos or threes at ends of branches, reddish, ripen in two years. Originally grown in lowlands and hills, on sandy soils, rocks and heather moors. Commonly planted in poor, sandy soils. The Weymouth Pine (*P. strobus*) with grey-green, long needles in clusters of five, is often cultivated in parks; it is native to North America.

2 Austrian Pine *Pinus nigra.* A variable species ranging in height from 25—45 m, sometimes more. Bark rough, greyish to dark brown. Needles longer than in Scots Pine, 8—15 cm long, dark green, stiff and sharply pointed. Flowers in June and July. Male flowers cylindrical, yellowish, stamens with pink connective. Female flowers red to light violet during flowering, pruinous, ripen as late as third year into large, glossy, yellow-brown cones with seed-scales of dark brown beneath. Grows from limestone foothills of eastern Alps up to Mediterranean region. Often planted in dry forests of central Europe. Also cultivated for ornamental purposes in parks.

3 Mountain Pine *Pinus mugo.* A broad, bushy shrub with irregularly branched trunk, or small tree with erect trunk and pyramidal crown. Mountain pine grows either as knee-pine in central-European mountains above tree line or as bog-pine on peat soils and in hilly country. Needles arranged in pairs, slightly twisted, rich green, under lens distinctly toothed. Male flowers yellow, with conspicuously large stamen connective. Female flowers on ends of shoots, red to light violet. Knee-pine flowers from June, bog-pine as early as May. Cones ripen third year, are conically ovoid to globose. Of compact conical habit is the Arolla Pine (*P. cembra*), reaching 20—25 m in height. Needles usually in fives and cones containing large edible seeds; a native of Alps and Carpathians.

Family: Cupressaceae

4 Juniper *Juniperus communis.* A very variable species, ranging in size from a prostrate shrub to a small tree with conical crown up to 10 m or more tall. Needles stiff, prickly pointed, grey-green, in trimerous whorls; white stripe on upper side. Dioecious flowers; male flowers axillary, ovate, yellowish; female ones individual, greenish. Flowers in April and May. Fruit matures into short-stalked, berry-like cone formed by three fleshy, fused seed scales; at first green, second year blue-black with a whitish 'bloom'. Forms undergrowth of coniferous forests, especially pine-woods, also occurs on slopes and in pastures. Protected in many countries. Savin (*J. sabina*) with scaly, sessile needles, and several American and Asian species, is also often cultivated.

Flowering Trees and Shrubs

Class: **Angiospermous Plants**—Magnoliopsida

Subclass: **Dicotyledones**—Magnoliidae

Family: **Barberry**—Berberidaceae

1 Common Barberry *Berberis vulgaris.* Shrub up to 2.5 m, with smooth bark and alternate leaves. Clusters of obovate sharply serrated leaves with short petioles arise in axils of branched spines (modified leaves). Yellow fragrant flowers in pendent racemes. Stamens sensitive to touch. Flowers during May and June. Fruit a red berry. Grows on sunny slopes and open groves from lowlands to foothills; most commonly seen in hedgerows in Britain. Also cultivated in various garden forms.

Family: Loranthaceae

2 Mistletoe *Viscum laxum.* Semi-parasitic evergreen shrub, of spreading habit up to 1 m in diameter in crowns of coniferous trees, especially pines. Branches by repeated forking; twigs brittle. Leaves opposite, yellow-green, longish obovate, entire, leathery texture. Tiny unisexual flowers are borne in small clusters in forks of branches. Fruits yellowish-white, globose berries. Flowers from March to April; berries mature as late as December. Stouter White Mistletoe (Common Mistletoe in G.B.) (*V. album*) with larger white berries, grows on a wide range of deciduous trees.

Family: **Elm**—Ulmaceae

3 European White Elm *Ulmus laevis* (syn. *U. effusa*). Robust tree with wide crown up to 35 m. Leaves with short petioles, sharply serrate, smooth above, usually hairy beneath. Flowers arranged in clusters on long stalks; anthers reddish. Achenes have wide cilious border, notched at tip. Flowers in March and April. Grows in meadows and moist forests; often also planted. Related Wych Elm (*U. glabra*) grows in woods, from hilly country to foothills, while *Ulmus carpinifolia* (syn. *U. campestris*) grows in river valleys; both species have flowers in sessile clusters.

5

4

Family: **Rose**—Rosaceae

4 Wild Raspberry *Rubus idaeus*. Branches somewhat thorny in lower parts, otherwise hairy to smooth. Leaves odd-pinnate, sharply toothed, underside white; terminal leaflet largest, sometimes rounded. Flowers white, arranged in pendent cymes. Fruits a cluster of red druplets — raspberries; easily separate from the plug-like receptacle when ripe. Flowers in June and July, sometimes later. Grows abundantly on heaths and hills, scrub and open woods. Often cultivated in gardens for its fruit.

5 Bramble *Rubus fruticosus*. A very variable species according to some authorities, split up into hundreds of microspecies. Native to woods, scrub, heaths, open hillsides and hedgerows. Most important common features: thorny branched stems and compound, mostly palmate leaves with 3—5 leaflets. Flowers white or pink. Globose druplets ripen to purple-black, pruinose blackberries. The related, smaller, thin-stemmed *Rubus caesius*, growing along roads, field margins, paths, has mainly trifoliate leaves and fruits with a waxy white 'bloom'.

6 Dog Rose *Rosa canina*. A variable spreading shrub up to 3 m tall; best known and most abundant of all wild central-European roses, characterized by arching, spiny branches. Leaves pinnate, with 5 to 7 ovate to elliptical, sharply serrate, smooth leaflets. Flowers solitary or in small clusters at end of branchlet. Sepals glandular on margins, outer ones usually cleft. Corollas white, flushed pink. Fruit an ovoid hip. Flowers from May to July. Grows in thickets on slopes, in hedgerows and forest margins from lowlands to foothills. The similar *Rosa dumetorum* has hairy leaflets and petioles.

6

1

Family: **Rose**—Rosaceae

1 Alpine Rose *Rosa pendulina* (syn. *Rosa alpina*). Widely expanded shrub up to 2 m tall, with pendent branches, sparsely covered with fine spines; upper branches are usually spineless. Leaves pinnate, with 7 to 11 elliptic, sharply serrate leaflets, dark green above, somewhat hairy underside. Flowers solitary, rarely in small clusters, on long stalks. Flowers purple-red; hips bottle-shaped, pendent, red. Flowers from May to July. Grows in hill and mountain forests and on bushy slopes.

2 Blackthorn or **Sloe** *Prunus spinosa*. Densely branched thorny shrub or small tree up to 4 m. Leaves elliptic, smooth, obovate with glandular margins. White flowers in small clusters often in profusion, before the leaves. Fruits are globose drupes, dark purple when ripe, usually with a waxy white 'bloom'. Flowers in March and April. Grows abundantly on sunny slopes, in hedgerows, at the edge of forests and in clearings from lowlands to foothills.

3 Gean or **Wild Cherry** *Prunus avium*. Tree up to 20 m or more tall, with widely expanded crown and smooth, grey branches. Entire, ovate leaves have two small, reddish, globose glands at base; blades serrate, smooth above, hairy beneath. Flowers white, opening from April to May. Fruit a globose drupe, yellow or red, sweet, with agreeable but slightly bitter taste. Found in woods, thickets and hedgerows, often on limestone or chalk soils. The cultivated sweet cherry is derived from this species.

4 Bird Cherry *Prunus padus*. Large shrub or tree up to 15 m with glossy brown branches. The leaves are obovate, abruptly pointed, finely serrate with two spherical glands on petiole. Flowers white, in pendent racemes; drupes small, black, astringent. Flowers and leaves give out pleasant bitter-almond smell. Flowers open in April and May. Grows in woods, scrub, and in hedgerows at lower altitudes. Sometimes forms of this tree are planted in parks and gardens.

5 *Cotoneaster integerrimus*. A low, spreading shrub with reddish branchlets. Leaves small, with short petioles, entire, rounded, smooth above, hairy beneath. Flowers in small clusters, somewhat pendent. Calyx maroon, persistent; corollas white or pink flushed, stamens red; fruits subglobose, red. Flowers in April and May. Grows on sunny, bushy, stony or rocky slopes, in open woods and steppes, from lowlands to foothills. Many Asiatic species are cultivated as ornamental shrubs, e.g. *Cotoneaster horizontalis*, *C. microphyllus*, and the tree-sized *C. frigidus*.

6 Midland Hawthorn *Crataegus laevigata* (syn. *C. oxyacanthoides*). Shrub or small tree up to 10 m, with red-brown, spiny branches. Leaves shallowly lobed and serrate. Flowers arranged in flattened clusters, stalks white or sometimes rosy. Globose to ovoid, red fruits (haws) have two stones each. Flowers in May and June. Grows wild in woods, on bushy slopes and in hedgerows. Several red, pink and double-flowered forms are cultivated in parks and gardens.

6

2

1

5

Family: **Rose**—*Rosaceae*

1 Wild Pear *Pyrus communis.* Broadly pyramidal tree, sometimes with spiny branches up to 15 m tall. Leaves with long petioles are ovate, pointed, finely serrate, glossy. Flowers, arranged in rounded corymbs, have long stalks. Corollas white or rarely pink-flushed. Fruits pear-shaped or globose, mature seeds black. Flowers in April and May. Grows wild in deciduous forests, on thickets and hedgerows at low altitudes. An allied species, *P. cordata*, is more bushy and spiny with smaller fruits. All the cultivated varieties of pears are derived from *P. communis*, which some authorities claim to be of multiple hybrid origin.

2 Crab Apple *Malus sylvestris.* Small tree up to 10 m tall. Young branches woolly, hairy, later more or less smooth. Leaves ovate, serrate, finely toothed. Petioles half of blade length. Flowers in small corymbs, pink in bud opening white; anthers yellow, lower half of styles fused together. Fruits almost globose, mature seeds brown. Flowers in May. Grows wild in hedgerows and woods. Cultivated apple-trees (*M.* × *domestica*) have no spiny branches; leaves are densely hairy on under surface, upper surface scattered with hairs; considered to be of ancient hybrid origin.

3 Mountain Ash or **Rowan** *Sorbus aucuparia.* A spreading tree up to 15 m or more tall, with felted winter buds. Leaves odd-pinnate, leaflets sessile, elongated, lanceolate, sharply serrate, hairy on underside. Flowers creamy white, arranged in wide, flattened, branched corymbs. Fruits red, berry-like, globose, slightly larger than pea. Rowan grows wild in open woods and on grassy and rocky slopes from lowlands to mountains; often planted in avenues.

4 Common Whitebeam *Sorbus aria.* A large shrub or small tree up to 15 m or more tall, with glossy, red-brown branches. Leaves irregularly serrate to shallowly lobed, under surface white, petals woolly at base. Fruits orange to reddish with yellow pulp. Flowers in May and June. Grows on sunny slopes and in open woodland from lowlands to mountains. Related Wild Service Tree (*S. torminalis*) has sharply pinnately cut leaves almost hairless beneath and fruits, yellow-brown, spotted with darker lenticels.

Family: Fabaceae (syn. Papilionaceae)

5 Broom *Sarothamnus scoparius* (syn. *Cytisus scoparius*). Shrub with angular green branches up to 2 m or more tall. Alternate leaves with short petioles composed of 3 lanceolate to obovate leaflets, silky hairy beneath. Flowers solitary or in small clusters, bright yellow. Style spirally twisted, protruding from keel, pods black, explosive when ripe. Flowers in May. Grows, often gregariously, at forest margins, sandy and stony slopes at lower altitudes, excluding limestone soils.

6 German Greenweed *Genista germanica.* Small shrub up to 40 cm or more, with ascending or erect, hairy, thorny branches. Leaves are ovate-lanceolate, pointed, and hairy. Flowers yellow, in leafy racemes at tips of shoots. Pods black-brown, hairy, exploding when ripe. Flowers from May to July. Grows in dry woods, especially pine-woods and in open sites on sandy soils from lowlands to foothills. Related Dyer's Greenweed (*G. tinctoria*) has thornless stems and hairless pods.

3

4

Family: Fabaceae

1 *Cytisus nigricans.* Deciduous shrub up to 2 m tall, with erect, green, hairy branches. Petiolate leaves of three pointed, obovate, dark green leaflets, paler beneath. Yellow flowers in bractless racemes turn black when dried. Pods brown-black, smooth. Flowers from May to August. Grows on sunny slopes, among rocks and in dry woods from lowlands to foothills. Related Common Laburnum (*Laburnum anagyroides*), a tree up to 7 m tall with pendent racemes of large, yellow flowers, is often cultivated.

2 Spiny Rest-harrow *Ononis spinosa.* Subshrub up to 40 cm or more, with ascending or erect branches, mostly spiny, with one or two rows of hairs. Leaves of three leaflets, each narrowly obovate and serrate. Flowers pink, calyx bilabiate, hairy. One-seeded pods of the same length as or longer than calyx, softly hairy. Flowers from June to September. Grows in rough grassy places, field boundaries and on sunny slopes in lower altitudes of temperate regions. Related Common Rest-harrow (*O. repens*) is thornless, creeping or decumbent subshrub with underground rhizomes.

3 False Acacia *Robinia pseudoacacia.* Tree up to 27 m tall with deeply fissured bark. Leaves petiolate, odd-pinnate, stipules transformed into strong, curved thorns. Leaflets petiolate, oval to elliptic, entire. Flowers white, occasionally flushed pink, fragrant, in pendent racemes. Pods strongly flattened, hairless. Flowers in May and June. Native of North America, since 18th century planted in avenues together with other North-American species with pink or violet-rose flowers.

Family: Platanaceae

4 *Platanus hispanica* (syn. *P.* × *acerifolia*). Abundantly cultivated hybrid of eastern and western plane-trees, planted only rarely in parks. Robust tree up to 40 m with striking scaly fawn and grey bark peeling in flakes. Illustrated species differs from its parent species by hairless underside of leaves; central lobes usually longer than their base width; globose inflorescences arranged mostly in strings of one to four. Oriental Plane (*P. orientalis*), native of eastern Mediterranean, has narrower lobes and inflorescences arranged in strings of up to six. Buttonwood or 'Sycamore' (*P. occidentalis*), native of North America, has leaves hairy on underside, central lobes wider and inflorescences in ones and twos. Plane-trees flower in May.

Family: **Hazel**—Corylaceae

5 Hornbeam *Carpinus betulus.* Tree up to 30 m tall, with grey, smooth bark and glossy, brown branches. Leaves narrowly oblong, doubly sharply serrate. Male and female catkins cylindrical, female ones erect, with flowers in axils of trilobed bracts; male pendulous. Ovary, with two red stigmata, develops into a nut, attached to the trilobed bract which enlarges and acts as a wing for wind dispersal. Flowers from April to May. Grows in woods and hedgerows at lower altitudes, also planted for coppicing, hedging and as a specimen tree.

6 Hazel *Corylus avellana.* Tall, well-branched shrub up to 6 m. Leaves petiolate, glandular, obovate to rounded, doubly serrate, with short hairs. Male inflorescences are catkins up to 5 cm long, female ones bud-like with two filamentous, red stigmata. Fruit is small nut enveloped in enlarged bracts, with white seed and cinnamon-brown seed coat. Flowers from January to April. Grows fairly abundantly in open woods and on sunny slopes from lowlands to mountains. Once much planted for coppicing. The cob nut of commerce is a form of this species.

4

5

6

Family: **Walnut**—Juglandaceae

1 Common Walnut *Juglans regia*. Robust tree up to 30 m tall, with grey bark; branchlets at first green-brown, later ash-grey. Leaves odd-pinnate, with usually 5 to 7 pairs of obovate or elliptic, entire, smooth leaflets. Male catkins pendulous on previous year's twigs, female flowers at tips of new twigs with two lobed stigmata. Fruit globose to ovoid drupe with tough, somewhat fleshy exocarp and stony endocarp; seed coat membranous, lobed seed white.

Flowers in April and May. Native of south-eastern Europe and Asia Minor. Often cultivated for its edible nuts.

Family: **Birch**—Betulaceae

2 Silver Birch *Betula pendula* (syn. *B. verrucosa*). Slender elegant tree up to 25 m tall with straight trunk and white bark, transversely peeling in paper-thin bands; bark deeply fissured at base. Leaves usually rhomboid to triangular, ovate, with pointed tip, smooth, doubly serrate except base. Male as well as female catkins pendent, anthers yellow, stigmata purple. Seeds (nutlets) winged, wings wider than nutlet. Flowers in April and May. Grows abundantly in forests, on slopes and heathland, often planted. Related birch, *Betula pubescens*, has less pendent branches and leaves and twigs hairy when young.

3 Alder *Alnus glutinosa*. Tree up to 20 m or more tall, with slender, dark grey trunk with fissured bark; young branchlets glandular. Leaves broadly obovate, with notched point, doubly toothed, smooth, rich green; young ones sticky. Male catkins with red scales, female ones long-stalked, ovate, maturing to brown, cone-like fruits. Wingless achenes. Flowers in March and April. Grows in moist meadows and near water. Related Grey Alder (*A. incana*) has pointed leaves, grey-green on underside, downy; bark light grey and smooth.

Family: **Beech**—Fagaceae

4 Beech *Fagus sylvatica*. Robust tree up to 30 m or more, with slender trunk and smooth, pale grey bark. Buds long, slender, pointed, with red-brown ciliate scales. Leaves petiolate, almost entire, broadly ovate, pointed, with ciliate margins. Male flowers in long-stalked, pendent clusters; perianth red-brown. Female flowers in pairs are at ends of new twigs, enclosed in green cup. These mature red-brown and open by four valves. Fruits are triangular nuts or beech-mast. Flowers in April and May. Grows fairly abundantly from lowlands to highlands. Several forms are known, including red, purple and copper-leaved and the fern-leaved beech with deeply cut leaves.

5 Sweet Chestnut *Castanea sativa*. Tree up to 30 m or more, dark grey-brown bark often with spiral fissures. Leaves short-petiolate, oblong, lanceolate, stiff, sharply serrate. Flowers in erect spike-like clusters; female ones at the bottom, individual or in threes, enclosed in globose, prickly barbed cupule; male florets whitish, forming bulk of spike. Fruit — chestnuts — dark brown, glossy, leathery skin, with single seed. Flowers in July. Native of southern Europe; often planted for edible seeds and in parks for ornament. Naturalized in some territories, e.g. Carpathians and southern Britain where it was once extensively coppiced for fencing.

Family: **Poplar and Willow**—Salicaceae

6 White Poplar *Populus alba*. Rapidly growing suckering tree up to 25 m, with pale grey bark. Leaves ovate, orbicular, notched to deeply 5-lobed, undersides felted with white hairs. Male catkins long and thick, female ones shorter; flowers with two red styles and yellow stigmata. Long-haired seeds. Flowers in March and April. Grows in forests and near rivers; also much planted. Related Black Poplar (*P. nigra*) is often planted in avenues, mainly the Italian form with columnar crown.

Family: **Poplar and Willow**—Salicaceae

1 Aspen *Populus tremula.* A suckering tree up to 20 m tall, with bark at first smooth, yellow-grey, later black-grey and fissured. Young twigs smooth or shortly hairy, buds sticky. Leaves almost round to rhomboid, shallowly notched. Long catkins with bracts palmately cut, anthers before releasing pollen red; purple stigmata in twos. Downy seeds. Flowers in March and April. Grows in open, moist places in woods, clearings, hedgerows, from lowlands to mountains.

2 Goat Willow *Salix caprea.* Large shrub or small tree up to 10 m tall. Leaves petiolate, ovate-oblong to obovate, pointed, narrowed or rounded at petiole, entire or irregularly toothed, upper side more or less hairy, under side felted with persistent grey hairs. Dioecious catkins appear before the leaves; male ones erect, thick, long silvery-haired, flowers with yellow anthers; female catkins similar, but are less hairy and remain grey-green, elongate when ripe and shed tiny seeds in cotton wool-like hair. Flowers from March to May. Grows abundantly at edges of forests, in clearings, on slopes, along brooks and in hedgerows from lowlands to mountains.

3 *Salix purpurea.* Shrub or small tree up to 3 m tall with thin, flexible and tough branches. Leaves shortly petiolate, obovate-oblong to linear oblanceolate, pointed, finely serrate, entire at petiole; somewhat blue-green above, glaucous beneath. Male catkins have stamens fused to filaments; red anthers, after pollination turning black; female catkins shortly conical. Flowers in March and April. Distinctive by having leaves and buds in sub-opposite pairs. Grows along streams and rivers and in wet meadows from lowlands to foothills. Also cultivated together with Osier (*S. viminalis*).

Family: **Beech and Oak**—Fagaceae

4 Common Oak *Quercus robur* (syn. *Q. pedunculata*). Robust tree up to 30 m or more tall with widely expanded, irregular crown; old branches strong, tortuous, old trunk has brownish-grey, deeply fissured bark. Buds ovoid, brown. Leaves shortly petiolate, pinnately lobed, blades cordate at petiole, hairy when young, soon becoming smooth, leathery, usually with five pairs of lobes. Male flowers in pendent catkins, female ones sessile, globular, in cupule; stigmata red. Acorns in twos to fives on long stalks. Flowers in April and May. Forms main component of oak-woods from lowlands to foothills. At one time commonly planted.

5 Durmast Oak *Quercus petraea* (syn. *Q. sessiliflora*). Differs from preceding species by ovoid crown, long-petiolate leaves, wedge-shaped blades at petiole and sessile acorns. Both species often hybridize and many trees are difficult to identify. In places the hybrid is more abundant than parent species. North-American *Quercus borealis* with red autumn leaves and *Quercus coccinea* with scarlet leaves are cultivated in parks; both have leaves larger than the native species and with bold, sharply pointed lobes.

6 Hairy Oak *Quercus pubescens*. Usually shrub with often distorted trunk and cracked bark. Young twigs and buds white-haired. Leaves obovate, pinnately lobed, blades wedge-shaped or cordate at petiole, lobes rounded or pointed, felted with grey hairs on both sides when young. In maturity upper surface almost smooth. Acorns long ovoid, pointed, in felted cupule. Flowers in April and May. Grows mainly on limestone soils, on sunny slopes in lower altitudes of warm regions.

Family: Simaroubaceae

1 Tree of Heaven *Ailanthus peregrina* (syn. *A. altissima*). Robust tree up to 35 m or more; young branches reddish, hairy. Leaves up to 1 m long, odd-pinnate, reddish when young. Leaflets lanceolate with one to three glandular teeth at base. Tiny flowers yellow-green, arranged in large panicles; fruit winged, sometimes bright red. Flowers in June and July. Native of eastern Asia; cultivated as ornamental tree and often planted. Sometimes becomes naturalized.

Family: **Milkwort**—Polygalaceae

2 Box-leaved Milkwort *Polygala chamaebuxus* (syn. *Chamaebuxus alpestris*). Small sub-shrub, rarely above 20 cm. Stems decumbent, ascending, often rooting. Leaves almost sessile, persistent, evergreen, leathery, smooth, entire, oval, with a small point. Flowers arranged singly or in small groups in leaf axils; winged sepals white, sometimes buff-yellow or carmine. Petals yellow, reddening at tips after fertilization. Fruit a capsule. Flowers from March to September. Grows among rocks and in open forests, mainly pine-woods, on mountain slopes.

Family: Celastraceae

3 Spindle Tree *Euonymus europaea*. A shrub up to 3 m or more; young branches green, somewhat four-winged, smooth. Leaves petiolate, lanceolate to ovate, pointed, smooth. Flowers in axillary clusters; petals greenish. Square pink capsule with orange seeds. Flowers in May and June. Grows at outskirts of forests, on slopes and in hedgerows from lowlands to foothills. Several forms are cultivated in gardens.

Family: Hippocastanaceae

4 Common Horse-chestnut *Aesculus hippocastanum*. Robust tree up to 25 m or more; young branches brown, buds large and sticky. Leaves palmate, compound with 5—7 leaflets, each obovate, up to 20 cm long and irregularly toothed. Flowers in dense, pyramidal panicle, petals white, spotted with red and yellow. Fruit a somewhat spiny capsule with one or two glossy, dark brown seeds. Flowers in May and June. Native of Albania and Greece, but commonly cultivated in avenues, parks and gardens. Related species have red or rosy flowers.

1
2
3

Family: **Maple**—Aceraceae

5 Sycamore *Acer pseudoplatanus*. Tree up to 30 m or more with broad crown and scaly bark. Leaves deeply palmately lobed and toothed; grey-green on underside, sometimes reddish flushed on both sides. Flowers yellow-green, in pendent panicles. Fruit a double samara with propeller-like wings. Flowers in May and June. Native of central and southern Europe but well naturalized elsewhere. Grows fairly abundantly from lowlands to mountains in deciduous forests. Several forms are planted in parks and gardens.

6 Norway Maple *Acer platanoides*. Tree up to 30 m, with fissured scaly bark; young twigs release milky juice. Leaves palmate with 5—7 pointed lobes and blunt teeth; in autumn turns yellow or reddish. Corymbs of bright yellow-green flowers are erect, appearing before the leaves unfold. Fruit much flattened double samara with long, parallel wings. Flowers in March to May. Grows fairly abundantly from lowlands to mountains in deciduous woods. Several forms are often cultivated (some with purple or variegated leaves) in parks and gardens.

233

Family: **Maple**—Aceraceae

1 Common Maple *Acer campestre*. Shrub or small tree up to 15 m or more; twigs sometimes with corky ridges. Leaves palmate, with 3 to 5 lobes, entire or bluntly toothed. Flowers yellow-green, downy, in small, erect, corymbose panicles. Fruit a hairy double samara with small blunt wings. Flowers from May to June. Grows in hedgerows on bushy slopes and in open forests mainly at lower altitudes.

Family: Rhamnaceae

2 Alder Buckthorn *Frangula alnus*. Smooth-barked shrub up to 5 m with slender branches. Leaves alternate, shortly petiolate, elliptic, entire, under side hairy when young. Small greenish flowers in axillary clusters; fruit a berry-like, black-violet, three-seeded drupe. Flowers in May and June. Grows in moist forests and near water, from lowlands to mountains. Related *Rhamnus catharticus*, usually with spiny branches, finely serrate opposite leaves and a more bushy habit grows on bushy slopes and in hedgerows on well-drained soils.

Family: **Lime**—Tiliaceae

3 Small-leaved Lime *Tilia cordata*. Tree up to 25 m tall with long-petiolate leaves, asymmetrically cordate, smooth above, on under side greyish, with tufts of rusty hairs in vein-axils. Flowers yellow-white, flower stalk bearing a large ligulate bract. Fruit a globose capsule, the bract persisting as a wing for wind dispersal. Flowers in early July. Grows in deciduous woods from lowlands to foothills; also often planted in parks and avenues.

4 Large-leaved Lime *Tilia platyphyllos*. A robust tree up to 30 m with black-brown bark. Leaves petiolate, cordate, usually asymmetric, dark green above, pale green beneath, somewhat hairy. Flowers white-yellow; capsule with three to five ribs, sub-globose. Flowers in late June. Grows in deciduous woods and on stable screes. Planted in parks and gardens, sometimes with other species; Silver Lime (*T. tomentosa*), having leaves white felted beneath; and the similar but pendulous branched *T. petiolaris*.

3

4

6

Family: Elaeagnaceae

5 Sea Buckthorn *Hippophaë rhamnoides.* Spiny shrub up to 3 m tall with dense branches, silvery-scaly when young. Leaves alternate, linear-lanceolate, entire, under surface silvery-scaly. Flowers greenish, in axillary clusters; male and female on separate plants. Fruits orange-red, rarely yellow, brown-dotted berries. Flowers from March to May. In Europe native only on sandy, gravelly river banks and stony slopes. In Britain on dunes and cliffs by the sea. Often planted for showy fruit, and as a hedge or windbreak near the sea.

6 Oleaster *Elaeagnus angustifolia.* Shrub, less frequently small tree, usually with spiny branches. Leaves alternate, shortly petiolate, narrow-lanceolate, upper side grey-green, under side silvery white. Tubular flowers silvery yellowish, fragrant. Fruits are pale amber-yellow berries. Flowers in May and June. Native of Mediterranean; often cultivated in parks and gardens. Not to be confused with the allied *E. argentea* (syn. *E. commutata*) with wider leaves, pendent flowers and silvery berries.

235

Family: Thymelaeaceae

1 Mezereon *Daphne mezereum*. Deciduous shrub up to 1 m, mostly with erect, little branched stems. Leaves alternate, lanceolate to oblanceolate, blunt-pointed, smooth, pale green. Strongly fragrant rosy-purple flowers appear before the leaves in lateral clusters. Fruits are globose, orange-red, poisonous drupes. Flowers from February to April. Grows in deciduous woods from lowlands to mountains. *Daphne cneorum* with terminal flowers and evergreen leaves grows at foot of Alps. Both species often cultivated. More common in Britain is the evergreen Spurge Laurel (*D. laureola*), with glossy dark green, oblanceolate leaves and yellow-green flowers from the leaf axils of the shoot tips.

Family: Araliaceae

2 Ivy *Hedera helix*. Evergreen climber up to 30 m with stems that cling by pads of short adhesive roots. Leaves leathery, opposite, long-petiolate, smooth, glossy, of two basic forms: non-flowering branches have leaves palmately three- to five-lobed, flowering ones have entire leaves, ovate to lanceolate. Flowers with five petals, greenish, arranged in rounded umbels. Fruit a globose, black berry. Flowers in September and October. Grows from lowlands to mountains in forests and thickets, climbs rocks and tree trunks. Flowers and fruits only at the top of its support. Many forms of varying leaf shape and colour are often cultivated for ornament.

Family: **Dogwood**—Cornaceae

3 Cornelian Cherry *Cornus mas*. Shrub or small tree up to 8 m. Leaves opposite, shortly petiolate, ovate to elliptic, pointed, with flattened hairs. Profuse yellow flowers in corymbs before leaves unfold. Fruits are oblong-ovoid red drupes. Flowers from February to April. Grows on bushy slopes and in open forests at lower altitudes. For long cultivated in parks and gardens for its distinctive early flowers.

4 Dogwood *Cornus sanguinea* (syn. *Svida sanguinea*). Shrub of bushy habit up to 3 m tall, with dark red branches especially during the winter. Leaves opposite, petiolate, ovate or oval, pointed, smooth. Flowers white in flat cymes, followed by black drupes. Flowers in May and June. Grows abundantly in deciduous woods, on bushy slopes and in hedgerows from lowlands to foothills. Related *Cornus alba*, with underside of leaves grey-green and hairy and bright red winter stems, a native of North America, is often cultivated.

3

4

Family: **Heath**—Ericaceae

5 Rusty-leaved Rhododendron *Rhododendron ferrugineum.* Small shrub up to 1 m tall. Tough, evergreen leaves are oblong-lanceolate, glossy, underside covered with rusty brown scales; margins inrolled. Flowers dark rose. Flowers from May to July. Grows on rocky slopes of Alps and in open woods on lower slopes. Related Alpenrose (*R. hirsutum*) with somewhat paler flowers and bristly margins of leaves, green on both sides, grows mainly in calcareous Alps. Many North-American and Asian species and especially their hybrids are cultivated in parks and gardens.

6 Marsh Tea or **Wild Rosemary** *Ledum palustre.* Low evergreen shrub to 1 m tall, with curious spicy fragrance. Young branches rusty hairy. Leaves alternate, sessile, linear to oblong, entire, the margins inrolled, under side rusty felted. Flowers fragrant, white, in dense terminal umbels; fruit an oblong capsule. Flowers from May to July. Grows in peatbogs, mossy rocks and at outskirts of wet forests from lowlands to foothills. Avoids limestone soils. Native of northern Europe and Asia. Poisonous, formerly used for protection against moths. In some areas now exterminated; a protected plant in certain countries.

5

6

Family: **Heath**—Ericaceae

1 Heather or **Ling** *Calluna vulgaris*. Low shrub up to ¹/₂ m, rarely to 1 m tall, sometimes decumbent, rooting and densely leafy. Leaves very small, linear, overlapping, with margins inrolled; glabrous or densely grey hairy in some forms. Flowers in one-sided racemes, drooping, pale purple, sometimes darker or white. Fruit a capsule. Flowers from July to October. Grows abundantly on acid soils, in places dominant over vast areas — heaths and moors — also in open woods, on rocks, and in sandy places, from lowlands to mountain slopes.

2 *Erica carnea*. Decumbent, well branched, small evergreen shrub to 30 cm tall, with ascending, densely-leaved branches. Leaves linear, in whorls, smooth and glossy. Flowers in dense one-sided racemes. Stalked flowers drooping, rose-red, with narrow, bell-shaped carollas; capsule cylindrical. Flowers from December to May. Grows on screes, among rocks and in pine-woods, in the Alps and on their lower slopes. Many forms also cultivated. Related *Erica tetralix* has pink flowers in umbels and hairy leaves; *Erica cinerea* has flowers in dense racemes in summer.

Family: Vacciniaceae

3 Cowberry *Vaccinium vitis-idaea*. Low, densely branched evergreen shrub to 30 cm with creeping shoots and erect twigs. Leaves alternate, obovate, the apex rounded or with a short point, slightly inrolled, margin dark green, glossy above, gland dotted beneath. Flowers in short terminal drooping racemes, corollas white or light rosy, bell-shaped. Fruit a berry, globose, red and glossy. Flowers from June to August. Grows in dry forests, especially pinewoods, on heaths, moors and peat-bogs, from hilly country to mountains.

4 Common Bilberry *Vaccinium myrtillus.* Low, densely branched deciduous bush with creeping stems and erect branches up to 60 cm tall. Leaves alternate, ovate, pointed, finely serrate, smooth, bright green, borne on green, angled twigs. Flowers solitary in leaf-axils, stalked, drooping; corolla globose, palest green with rosy flush. Mature berries globose, black, with a waxy 'bloom'; edible and tasty. Flowers from April to July. Grows abundantly in forests, from lowlands high up to mountains; in Britain mainly on heaths and moors, locally abundant, but only on acid soils. Related Cranberry (*Oxycoccus quadripetalus*), with evergreen leaves and prostrate stems and the corollas deeply four-parted, grows on peat-bogs.

Family: **Olive**—Oleaceae

5 *Forsythia suspensa.* Shrub up to 3 m tall, with long, pendent branchlets, hollow, angled and warty. Leaves simple or trifoliate, ovate, irregularly serrate, mostly unfold later than flowers. Flowers in lateral clusters before the leaves; bright yellow, bell-shaped with four lobes. Fruit a capsule. Flowers in March and April. Native of eastern China, but frequently cultivated in parks and gardens.

6 Common Privet *Ligustrum vulgare.* A semi-evergreen to deciduous shrub up to 3 m or more. Leaves opposite, shortly petiolate, lanceolate, entire, mostly pointed, bright green. Flowers in terminal, erect panicles; corollas cream-white and funnel-shaped. Fruit a glossy, black berry. Flowers in June and July. Grows on bushy slopes, in hedgerows and open woods, mainly at lower altitudes. Sometimes grown in hedges. The Japanese *L. ovalifolium*, a taller, more robust species with elliptic leaves, is now a popular hedging shrub.

5

6

Family: **Olive**—Oleaceae

1 Common Ash *Fraxinus excelsior*. Broad-headed tree up to 25 m tall. Branches grey-green, buds black-brown, broadly ovate. Leaves opposite, odd-pinnate; leaflets sessile, ovate to lanceolate, long-pointed, finely and sharply toothed, smooth. Flowers tiny, purplish, without petals, in axillary panicles before the leaves. Fruits are narrow, elongated, glossy samaras on slender, pendent stalks. Flowers from April to May. Grows fairly abundantly in woods, meadows, on screes, and in hedgerows, from lowlands to mountains. Also often planted, particularly the weeping form.

Family: **Nightshade**—Solanaceae

2 Bittersweet or **Woody Nightshade** *Solanum dulcamara*. Climbing deciduous subshrub up to 2 m, sometimes taller, with petiolate, entire, ovate, often pinnatifid leaves. Flowers in drooping panicles at end of branches. Corollas blue-violet with reflexed petals. Anthers yellow, a central yellow cone. Fruit a drooping, red, elliptical berry. Flowers from June to September. Grows fairly abundantly in thickets, hedgerows, woods and waste places, from lowlands to foot-hills.

Family: Loniceraceae

3 Common Elder *Sambucus nigra.* A shrub or small tree up to 10 m, with branchlets filled with white pith. Leaves odd-pinnate; leaflets ovate to elliptic, pointed, toothed, except at base. Inflorescence a large, flat-topped cyme with creamy flowers having a rank fragrance. Fruits are black, glossy druplets. Flowers in June and July. Grows abundantly in thickets, forests, on debris and along hedges from lowlands to foothills. Inflorescence and fruits edible and tasty, leaves poisonous.

4 Scarlet-berried Elder *Sambucus racemosa.* Shrub up to 4 m, with branchlets having yellow-brown pith. Leaves odd-pinnate, leaflets ovate to elliptic, finely toothed, on under side finely and thinly scalloped. Inflorescence a dense ovoid panicle with flowers greenish yellow. Red druplets. Flowers from April to May. Grows in clearings and at outskirts of woods, from foothills to mountains. Several forms, with deeply cut or golden leaves, are grown in parks and gardens.

5 Guelder Rose *Viburnum opulus.* A deciduous shrub or small tree up to 4 m tall. Leaves palmate with three to five lobes, sharply pointed and irregularly toothed. Inflorescences flat, cymose; inner flowers small, bell-shaped, hermaphrodite, whitish; outer flowers large, round, white and sterile. Mature drupes subglobose, red. Flowers in May and June. Grows fairly abundantly at woodland margins, in thickets and hedgerows, from lowlands to mountains. Several forms are cultivated in gardens and parks; one (the snowball tree), has all sterile flowers in globose heads. Related Wayfaring Tree (*V. lantana*) with oval leaves, felt-like on under side, and without showy sterile florets, grows in more open places, especially on chalk and limestone.

6 Snowberry *Symphoricarpos rivularis.* A deciduous suckering shrub about 2 m tall. Leaves oval, entire, rarely lobed. Flowers in small racemes; corollas bell-shaped, small, white with rosy tint. Fruit a white berry with spongy flesh. Flowers from June to August. Native of North America; commonly cultivated in woods for game birds, often becomes wild. Also often grown in gardens.

5

4

6

Gastropods and Bivalves

Gastropods (Gastropoda) are the best known of the molluscs. They may be found in woods, meadows, fields, gardens and often also in houses, in cellars and other damp places. They do not find dry conditions congenial, which is why they generally leave their damp hiding places only after dusk falls and dew has formed on the vegetation, or during the daytime after a rainfall.

The body of gastropods is divided into three parts — a head, foot and asymmetrical visceral sac. Many species have a shell, usually coiled in a spiral, inside which they can retreat. Some species, however, are without a shell. Gastropods are differentiated, according to their means of respiration, into three groups or subclasses: Pulmonata, Prosobranchia and Opistobranchia.

Best known are the Pulmonata, which have attained their greatest development on dry land. Only a few species inhabit fresh water, and a small number occur in the sea. The main distinguishing feature of pulmonate gastropods is the lung chamber, consisting of a dense network of branching blood vessels immediately beneath the fine skin of the mantle cavity, whose inner wall absorbs oxygen and releases carbon dioxide. The breathing hole (spiracle), through which air enters the cavity, is quite visible, for example in slugs, and can be opened and closed by the animal.

The shell of pulmonate gastropods is variously shaped and variously developed. As a rule, it is spirally coiled, but is sometimes only dish-shaped. In slugs, the remnants of the vestigial shell are found underneath the shield.

Commonest and most conspicuous are the gastropods of the order Stylommatophora, which have literally 'stalked' eyes. These are located on two long, retractable tentacles and look like black dots at the ends of the tentacles when they are extended. Below these tentacles are two further, shorter tentacles that can also be retracted. Stylommatophorous gastropods live on dry land but seek out moist locations. Some species have shells, others are without a shell. Some shells are conical-ovoid, such as the shell of Succinea, others are longish and spindle-shaped, for example Clausilia. The mouth of the shell is generally narrowed. Helicidae have spherical to flattened shells, often beautifully coloured as in the genus Cepaea. Helicidae, which are hermaphroditic, possess a special calcareous structure, sometimes

Fig. 1. *Cepaea nemoralis* has a beautifully coloured shell. The basic colouring may be different shades of yellow to reddish, striped with rich, dark brown bands.

called an 'arrow of love', which they use during copulation to pierce the body of their partner. Being hermaphrodites, one of them plays the role of the male and the other the role of the female, with only the latter being fertilized. The one that was the 'male' partner in this case, however, may be the 'female' partner in further acts of copulation.

Of all the members of the Helicidae family, the best known is the Edible Snail (*Helix pomatia*) whose shell may measure over 5 cm in diameter, thus making it one of the largest species. It is unjustly believed to be harmful by gardeners. In truth, not only are gardens undamaged by this snail, in fact they benefit from its presence because it feeds on and destroys many weeds. The worst that can be said of it is that it used to be partially harmful in the vineyards of southern Europe. The Edible Snail stays within a very limited area; often it will not even cross a path between two garden beds and may readily be lifted from a vegetable patch and placed elsewhere. During long dry periods, snails conceal themselves in a shady spot. There they retreat inside their shells and close the opening with a special membrane of hardened mucus. This enables them to survive the period of drought. During the winter they hide in loose soil, slowly digging their way into the earth using the edge of the shell. Once in the ground they form a hard and thick calcareous lid (operculum) which is porous, thus enabling the animal to breathe. In spring the snail presses the lid out and climbs out of the ground up into the air again. In many countries the flesh of the snail is considered a delicacy and this has been responsible for its disappearance in many places. For that reason it has been placed on the list of protected species. Nowadays snails are cultivated for food on special snail farms. Their flesh is tastiest in spring when it does not contain the calcareous salts required to form the operculum.

Also numerous are the 'naked' gastropods (slugs) without a shell, mainly members of the families Arionidae and Limacidae. These slugs have a dorsal shield at the front end of the body. In the Arionidae the spiracle is located on the lower right-hand edge of the front half of the shield; in the Limacidae it is located behind the midway point.

Fig. 2. The Roman or Edible Snail (*Helix pomatia*) is the largest European terrestrial mollusc.

Of the gastropods belonging to the order Basommatophora, which mostly comprises freshwater species, best known are the Lymnaeidae and Planorbidae. Lymnaeidae have a shell up to 6 cm high, a broad foot and a short head. They travel over the surface of the water by sliding along on the underside of a thin layer of mucus. They feed on algae and on decaying as well as fresh aquatic vegetation. Their eggs are deposited in cases on aquatic plants. In dry periods they form an operculum to prevent their bodies from drying out.

Planorbidae have a disc-like shell and a small head and foot. Their thread-like tentacles are extremely long. Unlike all other freshwater molluscs, these gastropods have red-coloured blood.

Prosobranchia gastropods have an operculum at the back of the foot with which they close the mouth of the shell when they retreat inside. The best known (*Viviparus*) have long tentacles. In males the right tentacle is thicker and is used as an organ of copulation. These gastropods are viviparous, which means that they produce living young.

Opistobranchia occur only in the sea and the main feature they have in common is that the gills are located behind the heart. The shells are often reduced or entirely absent.

Bivalves (Bivalvia) have a bilaterally symmetrical body consisting of only a trunk and a foot; the head is greatly reduced. They are devoid of a radula and tentacles and are generally also without eyes, whose function has been taken over by certain spots on the body that are sensitive to light. The soft body is enclosed by a mantle which secretes a substance that forms a paired shell consisting of two parts — a right and a left half. These are connected on the dorsal side via a strong elastic ligament. The two halves of the shell are usually equal in size and shape, which is dish-like. In some species, however, the valves are different, one being larger and more concave than the other and often with a patterned surface. Some bivalves are firmly attached to the substrate, to which the bottom half of the shell is cemented fast. In many species a thick layer of mother-of-pearl is formed on the inner side of the shell. On the dorsal side, at the apex, the two halves of the shell are joined by a ligament and often fasten by means of toothed edges which form a sort of interlocking system. The animal closes the shell halves by means of strong muscles.

Fig. 3. The Forest Slug (*Arion subfuscus*) is easily recognized by the traces of yellowish to orange slime it leaves behind it. It likes to feed on mushrooms.

Fig. 4. The Pearl Mussel (*Margaritana margaritifera*) inhabits small cold rivers and clear streams. It has disappeared from polluted waters in many places and is becoming increasingly rare.

In most bivalves the sexes are separate. In some species, however, their sex may change, sometimes several times, during their life cycle so that at certain periods they function as males, at others as females. The fertilized eggs develop into larvae.

Bivalves live only in water, most in the sea and only a small number in fresh water. There are some 25,000 species of bivalves worldwide. In the fresh waters of central Europe there are slightly more than 30 species. Bivalves are very important commercially. Many species are a common food in maritime regions and they are also shipped to inland countries where they are considered a great delicacy. The shells of many bivalves, even some freshwater species, yield mother-of-pearl, and certain species are highly prized as the source of precious pearls.

One of the best known marine bivalves is the Common or Edible Oyster (*Ostrea edulis*). The two parts of its shell are asymmetrical, the larger being deeper and thicker and firmly attached to the substrate, the smaller forming a lid to the cup. Because the oyster lives permanently in one spot, its foot has atrophied. The oyster grows to 8—10 cm and is able to reproduce when one year old. It forms large colonies.

Fig. 6. The marine gastropod *Natica millepunctata*.

Fig. 5. Great Ram's Horn (*Planorbarius corneus*) is found in pools, ponds, lakes and slow-flowing waters.

Class: **Gastropods**—Gastropoda

Family: **Amber Snails**—Succineidae

1 *Succinea putris*. Distributed in Europe, western and northern Asia. Common mainly in lowlands. Frequents lake- and pond-sides, ditches and marshes. Height 16—22 mm (in Danube basin up to 27 mm high and 13 mm wide). Life span up to 3 years. Lives on fresh and decaying vegetation. In pairing, one partner plays male and other female role. Each individual lays 50—100 eggs on damp ground. Spends winter and dry part of summer in crevices or among rotting leaves.

2 *Succinea pfeifferi*. Distributed in Europe and cool parts of Asia and northwest Africa. Occurs in low-lying country, lives on reeds and in waterside mud. Often found in large numbers on floating plants. Height 12—15 mm, width about 7 mm. Transparent shell. Similar biology to preceding species.

Family: Pupillidae

3 *Abida frumentum* Inhabits southern Europe and warm parts of central Europe. Frequents dry, grassy slopes. Height 6—10 mm, width 3 mm. Likes damp rocks, trees and other plants.

Family: Enidae

4 *Zebrina detrita*. Distributed over central, western and southern Europe, and south-western Asia. Common in limestone regions. Frequents warm spots. Plain-coloured or brown-striped shell. Height 18—25 mm, width 9—10 mm. Life span from 4 to 5 years. Shell often covered with dried slime and hardened soil.

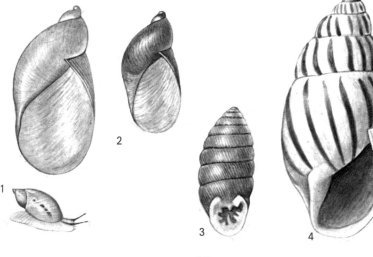

1

2

3

4

Family: Clausiliidae

5 *Laciniaria biplicata.* Distributed in central Europe, southern England, north-eastern France, Belgium; northern limit Sweden. Several subspecies. Very variable. Height 17—19 mm, width 4 mm. Inhabits forests, gardens, parks and hillsides, lives on tree-trunks, rocks, walls, etc. Usually produces live young, which take 5—10 months to develop. Life span about 3 1/2 years.

6 *Laciniaria turgida.* Inhabits eastern part of central Europe (chiefly the Carpathians), but exact distribution not known. Very variable. Height 12—17 mm Fusiform, transparent, glossy shell. Smaller shells at higher altitudes. Lives mainly in damp mountain forests; is especially abundant in thickly overgrown valleys, but also encountered in drier places. Several very similar species distributed all over Europe.

7 *Clausilia dubia.* Distributed in central, western and northern Europe as far as Sweden. Mainly inhabits mountains and rocky hills. Frequents rocks, ruins, walls, etc. Height 11 to 16 mm, width about 3 mm. Variably grooved. In winter hides under moss or fallen leaves.

Family: **Slugs**—Arionidae

8 Red Slug *Arion rufus.* Inhabits central and western Europe. Found in damp woods and meadows. Length 12—15 cm. Very large respiratory aperture. Variable colouring, from all shades of orange and brown to black. Black forms in colder areas, abundant local incidence of red forms in places. Border of foot usually red. Omnivorous. Often found on dead animals or excreta. Lays 300—500 eggs in piles, under stones, in moss, etc. Self-fertilization also observed.

9 Forest Slug *Arion subfuscus.* Distributed over whole of Europe. Chiefly inhabits lowland and mountain forests. Length 4—7 cm. Variable colouring. Basic colour yellow to reddish-yellow; back brown, sides often striped. Foot yellowish-white. Produces yellow or orange slime. Most frequently found on mushrooms, behind bark of tree-stumps, etc. Also eats fruit and parts of plants.

Family: Keeled Slugs—Limacidae

1 Great Greyslug *Limax maximus.* Distributed in southern and central Europe; extends to England and south of Scandinavia. Found in gardens, parks, cellars, etc. Variable colouring, often in association with differences in temperature. Length up to 15 cm. Frequently raids vegetable stocks in cellars, etc., but also eats other gastropods. When pairing, both partners hang twisted round a rope of slime attached to a twig. Active mainly at night and in damp weather.

2 Ash-blackslug *Limax cinereoniger.* Inhabits almost whole of Europe. Found mainly in deciduous woods in hilly and mountainous regions. Lives near trees, behind bark, under stones, etc. Colouring very variable (some specimens white), but mantle and foot always dark. Life span 3 years. Partners intertwine during pairing. Self-fertilization also known.

Family: Helicidae

3 *Helicodonta obvoluta.* Distributed in southern and central Europe and south-eastern England. Inhabits forests on warm limestone slopes. Lives under stones, leaves, etc. Forms white, parchment-like operculum in dry weather. Height 6 mm, width 13 mm. Thin-walled, discoid shell, hairy in young specimens.

4 *Helicigona lapicida.* Inhabits central and western Europe. Lives on damp rocks and tree-trunks in beechwoods. Often found on walls of ruins. Height 8.5 mm, width 17 mm. Shell partly transparent.

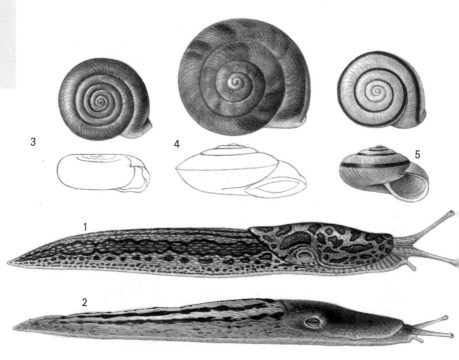

5 *Helicigona rossmässleri.* Inhabits the Carpathians. Lives on rocks and tree-trunks in damp forests. Commonest at altitudes of 800—1,400 metres above sea level. Attains 10—13 mm. Several tens of similar species occur in the Alps and mountains of central Europe.

6 White-lipped Snail *Cepaea hortensis.* Distributed over central and western Europe. Frequents damp spots in open woods, in gardens and at foot of rocks, etc. Shells of variable colouring; some specimens plain yellow or reddish, others striped. Width 15—25 mm, height 16 mm.

7 *Cepaea nemoralis.* Distributed in central and western Europe and Baltic coast. Lives in open woods and gardens and near human communities. Height 17—18 mm, width 20—24 mm. Basic colouring: different shades of yellow or red; usually striped with rich dark brown bands.

8 *Cepaea vindobonensis.* Inhabits eastern and south-eastern Europe; extends to the Alps and Danube and Vltava basins. Found primarily on limestone slopes, on outskirts of forests, etc., secondarily in vineyards and on banks. Width 19—25 mm, height 17—18 mm. Basic colour whitish to yellow; always striped.

9 Roman or **Edible Snail** *Helix pomatia.* Distribution area from south-eastern England across central Europe to Balkans. Is found today in places where it did not live originally. Inhabits open deciduous woods and thickets, chiefly in warm, low-lying country or hills. Frequents chalky regions. Often found on walls of ruins, etc. Height and width 40 mm; it is the largest European snail. Mean life span up to 6 years. Vegetarian. Pairing time May to August. After 6—8 weeks, each individual lays 20—60 eggs 5—6 mm in diameter in pits in the soil. In dry weather the shell is closed with a slimy secretion which looks like parchment when dry and ensures several months' survival. In winter a chalky operculum is added. Hibernates from October to April.

6

7

8

9

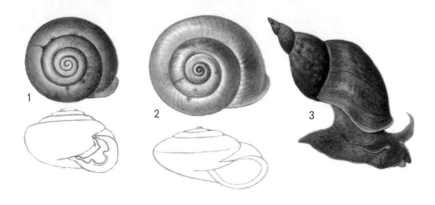

Family: Helicidae

1 *Isognomostoma personatum.* Distributed over central Europe, mainly the Alps, Pyrenees, Carpathians and German uplands. Does not occur in lowlands. Usually frequents rubble, hides under fallen trees and often under stones. Height about 6 mm, width 9—10 mm. Easily identified by three teeth on narrow aperture of rough, hairy shell.

2 *Zenobiella umbrosa.* Inhabits eastern Alps, German uplands, western Bohemia and Slovakia. Inhabits damp forest valleys, bogs and dense vegetation at foot of rocks, etc. Likes to climb tall plants where it can be found on leaves. Width of shell 9—13 mm, height 6—7 mm. Thicker shells in limestone areas.

Family: **Pond Snails**—Lymnaeidae

3 Great Pond Snail *Lymnaea stagnalis.* Its range of distribution includes whole of Europe, Morocco, northern Asia, North America. Lives in stagnant water at low altitudes. Has elongate, ovoid, pointed shell 45—60 mm high and 22—34 mm wide. Feeds on algae and parts of rotting vegetation. Eggs laid in capsules attached to aquatic plants. Life span 3 years.

4 Marsh Snail *Galba palustris.* Distributed over whole of Europe, Algeria, northern Asia and North America. Found in low-lying country in stagnant water, creeks and ditches. Has elongate, ovoid shell with dull lustre and finely grooved surface. Size very variable. Height 20—30 mm, width 10—18 mm. Colouring dark, inner surface usually deep violet.

Family: Planorbidae

5 Ram's Horn *Planorbis planorbis.* Distributed over almost whole of Europe. Found at low altitudes in stagnant and brackish water. Discoid shell about 3.5 mm high and 15—17 mm wide. Red blood. Frequents aquatic plants. Often seen surfacing for air. Feeds on algae, etc. Life span 2—3 years.

6 Great Ram's Horn *Planorbarius corneus.* Distributed over most of Europe except northern regions. Inhabits stagnant or slow-flowing, thickly overgrown water at low altitudes. Width of shell 25—37 mm, height 10—17 mm. Specimens in swamps and ponds small. Shells of young snails covered with bristles.

Family: Pomatiasidae

7 Round-mouthed Snail *Pomatias elegans.* Inhabits warm regions of Europe, particularly southerly areas. Lives under stones, fallen trees, on rocks and walls. Height 10—17 mm, width 8—13 mm.

Family: **River Snails**—Viviparidae

8 Common River Snail *Viviparus viviparus.* Distributed over large part of central Europe. Occurs in pools, ponds, creeks, etc. Lives at bottom in mud. Height 30—45 mm, width 25—35 mm. Specimens with shell of up to 50 mm are known. Has operculum with accretion grooves. Gives birth to live young with small shell. Feeds mainly on algae and organic debris.

9 *Viviparus fasciatus.* Distributed over whole of Europe except most northerly parts. Inhabits large rivers or river-fed reservoirs. Found between stones. Height 28—32 mm, width 22 to 24 mm. Likewise produces live young. Feeds on algae, organic debris in mud and occasionally plankton.

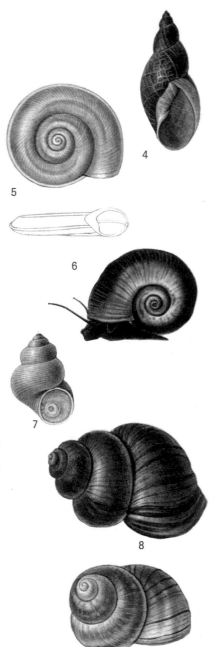

Class: **Bivalves**—Bivalvia

Family: **Freshwater Mussels**—Unionidae

1 *Unio tumidus.* Distributed over practically whole of Europe. Found in slow-flowing lowland rivers, lakes and ponds. Length of shell 70—90 mm. Annually lays up to over 200,000 eggs, incubated 4—6 weeks in female's gills. The hatched larvae (glochidia) hook themselves to fish gills, but after a few weeks drop to the bottom and live in the mud like adult animals. The adult mussel lives on microorganisms and debris.

2 *Anodonta cygnea.* Distributed over almost whole of Europe. Commonest in stagnant lowland waters. Length 170—260 mm. Hermaphroditic, lays up to 400,000 eggs a year. The eggs, produced in the winter, remain several months in the mussel's gills. The hatched larvae attach themselves to fish skin. When fully developed they leave their host and settle in the mud at the bottom. The adult animal lives on microorganisms.

Family: **Freshwater Pearl Oysters**—Margaritanidae

3 Pearl Mussel *Margaritana margaritifera.* Inhabits western, northern and occasionally central Europe. Scattered incidence. Inhabits small, cold rivers and clear streams. Length up to 150 mm, width 70 mm. Thick-walled valves. The small glochidia live as parasites in fish gills. Pearls may be formed in the mantle. Grows very slowly (only a few mm a year), but has life span of up to 80 years. Feeds on microorganisms and debris on bed of streams and rivers.

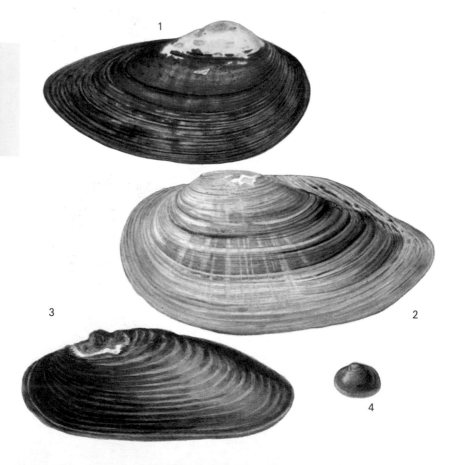

1

3

2

4

Family: **Orb Cockles**—Sphaeriidae

4 *Musculium lacustre*. Distributed over practically whole of Europe. Lives in rivers, streams, ponds and swamps. Common in lowlands. Length 8—14 mm, width 6—8 mm; 3—4 mm thick. Has thin-walled, transparent valves. Hermaphroditic and viviparous. Tolerates long droughts.

Family: **True Oysters**—Ostreidae

5 Edible Oyster *Ostrea edulis*. Distributed over European coasts from North Africa to Arctic Circle. Hermaphroditic, alternation of sexes in same individual. Free-swimming larvae hatch from the eggs. Up to 3 million eggs laid yearly by one oyster. Diet consists of plankton and debris. Collected as delicacy.

Family: **Cockles**—Cardiidae

6 Edible Cockle *Cardium edule*. Its area of distribution includes Atlantic, North, Baltic, Mediterranean and Black Seas. Diameter 3—4 cm. Lives in sand or mud in tidal zone, to depths of 10 metres. Can 'leap' distances of over 50 cm with long, bent foot. Lives on plankton.

Family: **Piddocks**—Pholadidae

7 Common Piddock *Pholas dactylus*. Distributed from Mediterranean to Norway. Tunnels in soft rocks and wood. Length up to 9 cm, width 3.5 cm. Secretes phosphorescent slime. Damages ships, but not seriously.

Family: **Scallops**—Pectinidae

8 *Pecten varius*. Its range of distribution includes Atlantic Ocean from Spain to western Norway and North Sea. Shell 3—7 cm in diameter. Colouring very variable. Adult sessile, young swim by snapping valves together.

Family: **Mussels**—Mytilidae

9 Blue Edible Mussel *Mytilus edulis*. Distributed in Arctic Ocean to North Africa, North and Baltic Seas. Forms large colonies, anchored to base by byssus. Settles in places with strong tides. Length 6—10 cm. One individual can lay up to 12 million eggs a year. Feeds on algae, debris and protozoans. Collected and sold as delicacy. Flesh rich in vitamins A, B, C and D. In many places piles are driven into the sea bed to provide the mussels with a ready-made base.

5

7

6

8

9

Spiders, Scorpions, Centipedes and Millipedes

The arachnids (Arachnidae) form a very large class of arthropods. Some 36,000 species have been described to date. These are divided into nine orders, of which the best known in central Europe are the spiders (Araneida), false scorpions (Pseudoscorpionidea), harvestmen (Opilionidea), and mites and ticks (Acari). Arachnids have four pairs of legs, one pair of chelicerae and one pair of pedipalps. The body is segmented but the segments are often fused together to form larger units. Arachnids live on dry land and in fresh water as well as in the sea. Many species are parasites of animals and humans as well as of plants.

Most familiar to us are the spiders (Araneida). The body of a spider consists of a cephalothorax and abdomen. The head is separated from the thorax by a suture. There are usually eight eyes, less often six or less. At the front of the mouth are claw-like fangs (chelicerae) which are connected to a venom gland. On either side of the mouth are the pedipalps, which resemble legs. The four pairs of legs are located on the thorax. The respiratory organs are either lung chambers or tracheae, sometimes both. The abdomen terminates in a spinneret that produces fine threads out of secretions from silk glands. The sexes are separate; the young that emerge from the fertilized eggs resemble the adults.

Some spider species are aquatic and spin their webs beneath the surface of salty coastal water. Best known of the freshwater species is the Water Spider (*Argyroneta aquatica*).

The best known spiders are the Araneidae. A typical representative of this large family (in central Europe there are more than 50 species)

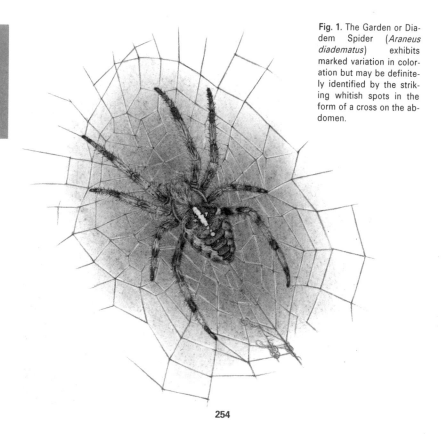

Fig. 1. The Garden or Diadem Spider (*Araneus diadematus*) exhibits marked variation in coloration but may be definitely identified by the striking whitish spots in the form of a cross on the abdomen.

is the Garden or Diadem Spider (*Araneus diadem0matus*). The concentric, outer threads of its web are dotted with tiny drops of a sticky substance. These threads trap and hold insects, while the spider usually sits in the centre of the web in a spot that is not sticky or else lies in wait near the web. As soon as the prey is caught fast, the spider hastens to it and either stuns or kills it with venom from its chelicerae. Then it winds threads round the victim's body and 'stores' it until it decides to feed. When that time comes, the spider injects digestive juices into the insect's body. These dissolve the tissues into a thick liquid which the spider then sucks out. The female usually remains in the same spot throughout her whole life. The male, much smaller in size, approaches the web and woos the female by shaking it. He places reproductive cells inside the female's body with his pedipalps and then departs quickly. It occasionally happens that a careless suitor is seized and devoured by the female. The female lays up to 700 eggs in a cocoon. Young spiders spin silken threads and wait for a breeze to carry them off to a different spot.

The young of other species of spiders (e.g. crab spiders — Thomisidae) spin silken parachutes or balloons on which they are borne far away by the wind.

Centipedes and millipedes belong to the group of tracheates (Tracheata) in which respiration is achieved by means of a system of air tubes called tracheae. These terminate in paired openings on the sides of the body segments and convey oxygen to all the body organs. Tracheates usually have a pair of antennae on their heads. The largest class of tracheates are the insects.

Centipedes (Chilopoda) have an extremely elongated, flat-backed and distinctly segmented body. The body consists of a head with a pair of long antennae and a large number of segments, each of which has a pair of legs. The mouthparts of centipedes consist of one pair of mandibles and two pairs of weak maxillae. The

Fig. 2. The Crab Spider (*Thomisus albus*) lies in wait for insects on a blossom. The splayed forelimbs serve to capture prey.

appendages of the first body segment have evolved into large pincer-like organs containing a venom gland. In central Europe there are more than 50 species of centipedes.

Millipedes (Diplopoda) are arthropods with the body segments fused into pairs so that there are two pairs of legs on each segment. The body is usually cylindrical and has a chitinous covering. The head usually has short antennae and a few simple eyes. The mouthparts consist of a pair of mandibles and a curious formation called a gnathochilarium, formed by the fusion of the maxillae. Millipedes have weak legs. In central Europe there are some 100 species.

Fig. 3. Centipedes (*Dermacentor pictus*) courting.

255

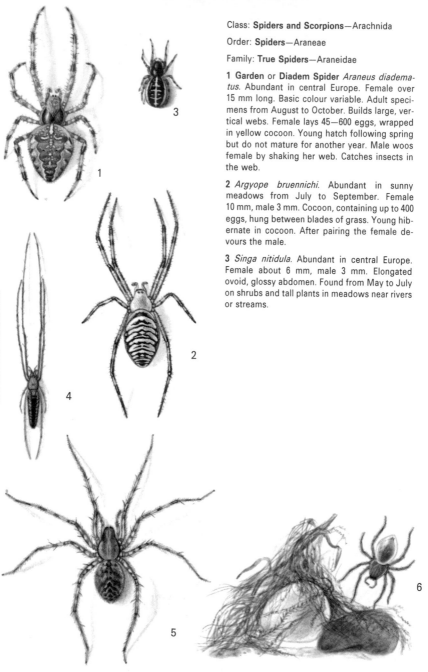

Class: **Spiders and Scorpions**—Arachnida

Order: **Spiders**—Araneae

Family: **True Spiders**—Araneidae

1 Garden or **Diadem Spider** *Araneus diadematus*. Abundant in central Europe. Female over 15 mm long. Basic colour variable. Adult specimens from August to October. Builds large, vertical webs. Female lays 45—600 eggs, wrapped in yellow cocoon. Young hatch following spring but do not mature for another year. Male woos female by shaking her web. Catches insects in the web.

2 *Argyope bruennichi*. Abundant in sunny meadows from July to September. Female 10 mm, male 3 mm. Cocoon, containing up to 400 eggs, hung between blades of grass. Young hibernate in cocoon. After pairing the female devours the male.

3 *Singa nitidula*. Abundant in central Europe. Female about 6 mm, male 3 mm. Elongated ovoid, glossy abdomen. Found from May to July on shrubs and tall plants in meadows near rivers or streams.

Family: Tetragnathidae

4 *Tetragnatha extensa.* Found all over central Europe. Up to 11 mm long. Strikingly elongated body. Builds web in damp spots between grasses and rushes. Attaches egg cocoon to rushes, etc.

Family: Agelenidae

5 House Spider *Tegenaria derhami.* Widespread all over Europe. Length 6—11 mm. Looks much larger because of its long legs. Frequents houses, cattle-sheds, etc. Builds dense, horizontal webs in corners. Can be found whole year round. Lives several years. Catches insects. Female suspends spherical egg cocoon from several webs disguising it with fragments of mortar, etc.

6 Water Spider *Argyroneta aquatica.* Inhabits whole of central and northern Europe. Body length 8—15 mm (male larger than female). The only subaquatic spider. Lives in clean pools. Weaves 'diving-bell' between aquatic plants and fills it with air. Bell also used as receptacle for eggs. Found whole year round. Life span two years.

Family: **Wolf Spiders**—Lycosidae

7 *Xerolycosa nemoralis.* Distributed over whole of central Europe. Length 5—7 mm. Common in woods, especially coniferous. Does not build web. Runs about among stones, pine needles, etc., catching small insects. Found from May to August. Egg cocoon carried attached to tip of female's abdomen. Female also carries young on its body for short time.

Family: Pisauridae

8 *Pisaura mirabilis.* Abundant in low-lying country. Length up to 13 mm. Elongated abdomen, long legs. Found on ground or leaves. Hunts prey. Male woos female with gift of fly; takes advantage of situation while female eats the fly. Does not build web. Female carries egg cocoon in jaws.

Family: **Crab Spiders**—Thomisidae

9 *Diaea dorsata.* Common everywhere in central Europe. Length 5—7 mm. Found on bushes in both coniferous and deciduous forests. Lies in wait for insects, with two pairs of long legs in typical splayed position. Walks sideways. Seen mainly in May and June.

10 *Misumena vatia.* Common in central Europe. Female 10 mm, male only 4 mm. Frequents tall plants and bushes, chiefly in May. Lies in wait for insects in flowers.

9

7

8

10

1

4

2

3

Family: **Jumping Spiders**—Salticidae

1 Zebra Spider *Salticus zebraneus*. Inhabits warm parts of Europe. Length up to 6 mm. Short legs. Appears in sunny spots early in spring. Male performs nuptial 'dance' in front of female. Female weaves nest and then lays eggs in it and guards them.

Family: Eresidae

2 *Eresus niger*. Inhabits warmer parts of Europe. Length 8—16 mm. Female velvety black. Male has red abdomen with 4 black spots. Found in sandy areas, lives in colonies. Scrapes holes 10 cm deep, lined with cobwebs. Erects porch over entrance and builds web traps in vicinity. Hunts tiger beetles. Female lives 3 years, male only one.

Order: **Pseudoscorpions**—Pseudoscorpionidea

3 Book Scorpion *Chelifer cancroides*. Very common. Length 3—4 mm. Lives among leaves, behind bark, in old books, etc. Catches small insects and mites. Spread by flies. Nuptial 'dances'. Female lays 5—18 eggs in pouch on underside of body. Able to spin cocoons.

Order: **Harvestmen**—*Opilionidea*

4 Common Harvester *Opilio parietinus*. Abounds in damp, shady spots. Hunts flies and ants. Males fight at pairing time. Female lays small piles of eggs in damp soil or cracked ground. Young hatch early in spring.

Order: Mites and Ticks—Acari

5 Sheep or **Castor-bean Tick** *Ixodes ricinus.* Inhabits almost whole of Europe. Male 1 to 2 mm, female up to 4 mm (several times larger when engorged). After fertilization and engorgement with vertebrate blood female lays up to 3,000 reddish eggs on ground or between stones. After sucking blood, the 6-legged larvae turn into nymphs, find fresh hosts and moult again to become adult males and females. Total time of development 178 to 274 days.

6 *Trombidium holosericum.* Very common. Length about 2.5 mm. Found on bushes, grass, ground, etc., from spring until autumn. Larvae 6-legged and bright red. Lives mainly on insects' eggs.

7 Common Beetle Mite *Parasitus coleoptratorum.* Occurs over most of Europe. Often found on dung beetles, used by adult female as means of transport to new dwelling-place, manure, compost, etc. Initial diet mouldy or rotting matter, later flies' eggs. Eggs usually unfertilized, but sometimes produce males.

Class: **Centipedes**—Chilopoda

Order: *Lithobiomorpha*

8 *Lithobius forficatus.* Common all over central Europe. Length 20—30 mm. Lives under stones, behind bark, etc., in woods and gardens. Solitary species. Can crawl both forwards and backwards. Bite harmless. Moults as it grows. Lives on insects, spiders, etc. Life span several years.

Class: **Millipedes**—Diplopoda

Order: Oniscomorpha

9 *Glomeris pustulata.* Widespread in central Europe. Length 4.5—14 mm. Resembles woodlouse, also able to curl up. Lives under stones, tree trunks, etc. in open country. Diet rotting leaves. Crawls very slowly. Eggs laid singly, in special nest made by female from damp clay. Life span 7 years.

Order: Opisthospermophora

10 *Julus terrestris.* Very common in central Europe. Length 20—50 mm. Coils itself up when disturbed. Lives under stones and leaves, behind bark, etc. Staple diet decomposing matter. Nocturnal animal. Female lays eggs in piles encased in capsule made of soil and secretion and fitted with ventilating shaft.

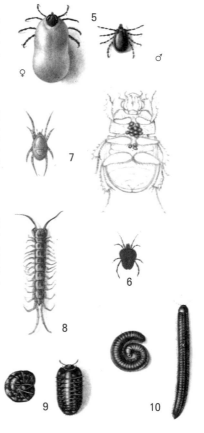

Crustaceans

Crustaceans (Crustaceae) belong to the sub-phylum Branchiata, in which respiration is achieved by means of gills. Crustaceans are mostly aquatic arthropods with two pairs of antennae, the first of which are simple, while the second, shorter pair are forked. The body segments exhibit marked diversity. The sexes are usually separate; only sessile forms, such as barnacles (Cirripedia), and some parasitic species are hermaphroditic. A few are parthenogenetic, that is the young develop from an unfertilized egg, as in water fleas (Cladocera). Some species of crustaceans care for their offspring.

Most crustaceans live in the sea, a smaller number in fresh water and only a few are terrestrial. Reproduction is by means of eggs. In many cases the larvae that hatch from the eggs resemble the adult—such larvae are called nauplii.

Fig. 1. The Common Hermit Crab (*Eupagurus bernhardus*) has a soft, vulnerable abdomen, which it protects by wearing the empty shells of various marine gastropods. When danger threatens, it closes the aperture of the shell with its large claw.

Fig. 2. Colonies of *Balanus tintinnabulum* are found on rocks, mollusc shells and even crabs' claws.

Some groups of crustaceans are important as the mainstay of the diet of numerous fish as well as some cetaceans; others, such as shrimps, lobsters and crabs, are a favourite food of people.

An interesting group of small crustaceans are the branchiopods (Anostraca), which are generally found in still bodies of fresh water. Only *Artemis salina* inhabits salt lakes, but not seas. In many places it forms the basic food of flamingoes. Branchiopods usually occur in small seasonal tracts of water that dry up. They pass the dry period in the egg stage, the larvae hatching as soon as their abode fills with water after a rainfall or after the spring thaw. They grow rapidly, reaching maturity within a short time and laying eggs that will again wait out the period of drought.

Water fleas (Cladocera) are a well-known group of crustaceans that usually live in fresh water. The head is free and the body encased in a translucent bivalvular shell. The second pair of antennae are branched, unusually large and are used for swimming. Water fleas occur in large numbers mainly in still or slow-flowing waters. Live, as well as dried, water fleas are commonly used as food for aquarium fish.

Another interesting group are the barnacles (Cirripedia), which mostly live in the sea. Some species are parasites on other animals. Usually they are hermaphroditic. Free-swimming larvae, known as nauplii, hatch from the eggs. Adult forms are anchored to a base, often a floating object or the body of another animal. The body of the barnacle is protected by a covering, usually consisting of calcareous platelets, in which the animal can enclose itself and thus prevent itself from drying out, for example when stranded by the tide.

The higher crustaceans (Malacostraca) have a constant number of body segments, usually twenty. The head is generally united with the thoracic segments to form a cephalothorax. All body segments, except the last, called the telson, have forked or simple appendages. These crustaceans live in the sea as well as in bodies of fresh water; some groups also live on dry land. Of commercial importance are, first and foremost, the decapods (Decapoda)—crayfish, lobsters and crabs. One feature they have in common is a very thick shell, usually united with the thoracic segments on the dorsal side. The first three pairs of thoracic appendages are converted to mouthparts. The body has five pairs of strong legs, the first three pairs being furnished with claws. The claws of the first pair are usually extremely powerful. In some species one of these claws is much bigger than the other. Crabs (Brachyura) have a short, square abdomen concealed beneath the cephalothorax, and large, occasionally asymmetrical, claws. Many species of decapods are a greatly prized catch in marine fishing.

Fig. 3. The Goose Barnacle (*Lepas anatifera*) does not look in the least like a crustacean. It is completely concealed inside a special shell and firmly anchored by a long, flexible stalk on its dorsal side to a solid object — a rock or stone or even the body of another animal such as a shark or whale.

Class: **Crustaceans**—Crustacea

Order: **Branchiopods**—Anostraca

1 *Branchipus stagnalis.* Common all over central Europe. Length up to 23 mm. Found in wet ditches and pools. Occurs from April to September. Swims upside down. Lives on microorganisms. Female lays eggs in a special pouch on her abdominal segments, carries them a short time and then drops them into the mud. The eggs can survive five years of drought.

Order: **Water Fleas**—Cladocera

2 Common Water Flea *Daphnia pulex.* Abounds in stagnant water. Length about 2 mm. Fertilized hibernated eggs produce only females which reproduce further by unfertilized eggs. Eggs laid by the last generation also give rise to males and the females again lay fertilized eggs.

Order: Thoracica

3 Goose Barnacle *Lepas anatifera.* Lives off coasts from North to Mediterranean Sea. Length 3—4 cm. Locally abundant. Usually occurs in deep water but often found on floating objects. Anchored to base by thick, flexible stalk. Lives on plankton gathered by the gyrating movements of its six pairs of lash-like limbs. Hermaphroditic. Larvae hatch from eggs.

4 Acorn Barnacle *Balanus crenatus.* Inhabits tidal zone of North Sea and western Baltic. Very abundant. Lives in colonies. Attached to base over wide area of body surface. Often found on crabs' claws. Individuals in colonies stranded by tide enclose themselves in their shell, compound of 6 parts, by means of a leathery 'lid'. Size 10—20 mm.

Order: **Sea Lice and Allies**—Isopoda

Family: **Water Lice**—*Asellidae*

5 Hog-slater *Asellus aquaticus.* Plentiful in central and northern Europe. Length up to 13 mm. Lives at bottom of stagnant or slow-flowing water. Female carries the eggs or embryos in a brood pouch on the underside of her thorax. Lives on rotting vegetable debris. If water dries up, burrows in mud.

Family: **Sea Woodlice**—Ligiidae

6 Sea Woodlouse *Ligia oceanica.* Common on coasts from central Norway to Spain. Length up to 28 mm. Found under stones or among seaweed on rocky shores. Runs very quickly and dashes for water if in danger. Leads amphibian existence.

Family: **Land Woodlice**—Porcellionidae

7 Common Woodlouse *Porcellio scaber.* Abundant all over central Europe but has been carried to all parts of world. Length up to 16 mm. Colouring rather variable, but usually marbled. Lives in damp buildings, cellars, cracked walls, behind bark, etc. Large communities common. Breathes by means of gill plates on underside of abdomen. Lives on decomposing matter.

Order: **Flea Shrimps**—Amphipoda

Family: **Freshwater Shrimps**—Gammaridae

8 Common Freshwater Shrimp *Gammarus pulex.* Very common in central Europe. Length up to 24 mm. Inhabits shallow lakes, ponds and streams. Found under stones or among plants. Good swimmer. Mainly vegetarian. Usually winters on sandy bottoms, but often under stones. Sexes separate. Female lays eggs in brood pouch on legs where they are then fertilized. Young remain a short time with female.

Family: Caprellidae

9 *Caprella linearis.* Found off coasts of North and Baltic Seas as far as Kiel. Length up to 20 mm. Flat-sided, thread-like body. Legs terminate in prehensile claws. Frequents algae, seaweed, etc. Crawls swiftly over sea bed in search of prey. Predacious, catches small crustaceans, worms, polyps, etc. Deep red with light red eyes.

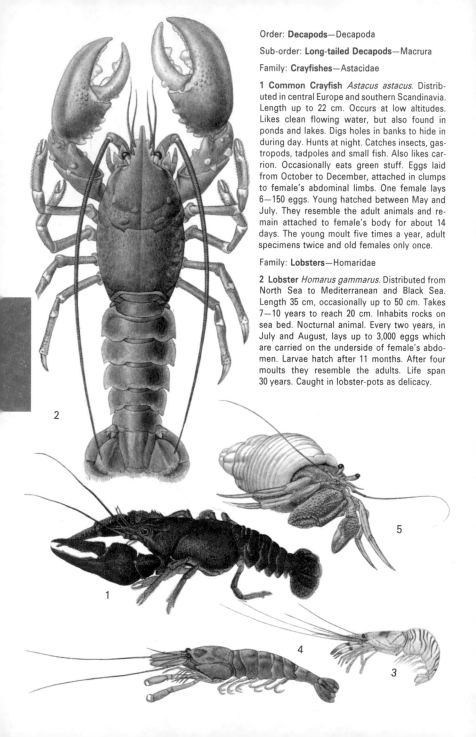

Order: **Decapods**—Decapoda

Sub-order: **Long-tailed Decapods**—Macrura

Family: **Crayfishes**—Astacidae

1 Common Crayfish *Astacus astacus*. Distributed in central Europe and southern Scandinavia. Length up to 22 cm. Occurs at low altitudes. Likes clean flowing water, but also found in ponds and lakes. Digs holes in banks to hide in during day. Hunts at night. Catches insects, gastropods, tadpoles and small fish. Also likes carrion. Occasionally eats green stuff. Eggs laid from October to December, attached in clumps to female's abdominal limbs. One female lays 6—150 eggs. Young hatched between May and July. They resemble the adult animals and remain attached to female's body for about 14 days. The young moult five times a year, adult specimens twice and old females only once.

Family: **Lobsters**—Homaridae

2 Lobster *Homarus gammarus*. Distributed from North Sea to Mediterranean and Black Sea. Length 35 cm, occasionally up to 50 cm. Takes 7—10 years to reach 20 cm. Inhabits rocks on sea bed. Nocturnal animal. Every two years, in July and August, lays up to 3,000 eggs which are carried on the underside of female's abdomen. Larvae hatch after 11 months. After four moults they resemble the adults. Life span 30 years. Caught in lobster-pots as delicacy.

Family: **Prawns**—Palaemonidae

3 Common Prawn *Palaemon squilla.* Lives in North and Baltic Seas. Length 5—6 cm. Frequents seaweed near shore in summer, deeper water in winter. Lives on algae, debris, small crustaceans, etc. Eggs laid in summer. Almost transparent when alive, turns pinky-red when boiled. Delicacy.

Family: **Shrimps**—Crangonidae

4 Common Shrimp *Crangon crangon.* Distributed from North Sea to Mediterranean. Length 4—5 cm. Frequents coastal zone, enters brackish water in summer. Lives on small molluscs, fish roes, etc. Eggs laid April-June and October-November. Delicacy. Does not change colour when boiled.

Family: **Hermit Crabs**—Paguridae

5 Common Hermit Crab *Eupagurus bernhardus.* Distributed from Mediterranean to North Sea where it is very abundant. Length about 3.5 cm. Frequents shore but also found at depths of 450 m on sandy or rocky bottom. Wears marine gastropod shells to protect its soft abdomen. Closes aperture of shell with claw. Lives on small animals and debris. Large numbers of young may be found in shallow water.

Sub-order: **True Crabs**—Brachyura

6 Common Shore Crab *Carcinus maenas.* Its distribution area ranges from Mediterranean to Iceland. Abundant in North Sea, rare in Baltic. Length 5—6 cm, width up to 8 cm. Large well-developed nippers. Can swim short distances. Runs rapidly sideways on sea bed and on land. If stranded by tide, hides under large pebbles or burrows in sand. Lives on remains of different animals and plants.

7 Spider Crab *Macropodia rostrata.* Plentiful in North Sea and Baltic bays as far as Kiel. Also occurs in Mediterranean. Frequents coastal zone to depth of 100 m. Hides in rocks or sand. Length up to 18 mm. Rostrum formed of two long, joined spines. Eats small molluscs, crustaceans, algae, etc.

8 Mitten Crab *Eriocheir sinensis.* Native of rivers of northern China and shores of Yellow Sea. Brought to Europe, now lives in Elbe, Weser and other rivers. Locally abundant. Length up to 7.5 cm. Very wide chelae thickly covered with fine hairs. Travels long distances upstream. Attains adulthood after 4 years and then returns to sea where female lays eggs. Larvae can hatch only in salt water.

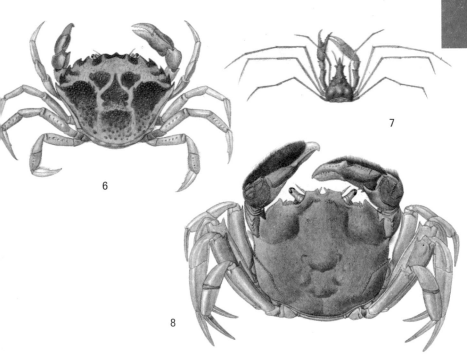

6

7

8

Springtails and Insects

Springtails (Collembola) were formerly classed among insects, but today they are in a separate class by themselves. They are primitive wingless creatures that never possessed even vestigial wings. They occur in large numbers in the ground as well as on the soil's surface in woods and gardens, on trees, leaves and on flowers, and they form large colonies. They usually measure 1—3 mm. Most species jump well, aided by a special forked appendage at the caudal end on the underside of the body. This generally lies folded under the body, facing forward. When suddenly extended, it hurls the springtail up and out. Springtails feed on rotting debris, fungi and the like; some species are also carnivorous.

The females lay eggs several times a year beneath stones and in holes in the ground. The young moult a number of times. Adult forms also moult, often reproducing missing organs, such as antennae or appendages, that have been lost one way or another. Springtails are important soil organisms which contribute to the decomposition of plant substances and thereby to the formation of humus. Some species may cause damage by nibbling parts of green plants. There are some 3,500 known species distributed throughout the world, from the tropics to the regions of permanent snow and ice. In central Europe there are about 400 species.

Insects are arthropods with a body that is divided into three distinct parts: the head, thorax and abdomen. The head generally bears large, compound eyes made up of many small prismatic eyes; however, some species have simple eyes. Attached to the front sides of the head are mobile antennae composed of several segments. The antennae are sensory organs, serving primarily as organs of smell and touch, and they may vary greatly in form. In some species they are thread-like (filiform), in others club-shaped (clavate), comb-like (pectinate), etc.

The mouthparts may be adapted for chewing or else for sucking or licking. Above the mouth opening is the upper lip or labrum, below it is the lower lip or labium, bearing small appendages known as the labial palps. The mouthparts proper consist of a pair of mandibles and a pair of maxillae to which are attached a pair of appendages known as the maxillary palps. Protruding from the mouth opening is a tongue-like appendage known as the hypopharynx.

Fig. 1. Developmental stages of the Swallowtail (*Papilio machaon*). The caterpillars like to feed on dill.

266

Fig. 2. Common Stag Beetles (*Lucanus cervus*) engaged in combat.

The thorax is composed of three segments: the prothorax, mesothorax and metathorax. The second and third segments both bear a pair of wings. Sometimes, however, one pair of wings is reduced, for example in flies, to form minute balancing organs (halteres). Some groups of wingless insects once had winged ancestors and their present wingless condition is an acquired one, for example in fleas. Wingless insects such as fish moths (Thysanura), however, never possessed wings in the first place. In many species of insects the wings are membranous, in others the front wings are thickened and serve to protect the hind wings; wings of this type are termed wing-covers or elytra, for example in beetles.

On the underside of each thoracic segment is a pair of legs, so that insects have six legs altogether. Legs are adapted for jumping, scraping, swimming, holding prey and so on. The abdomen may be of diverse shape, ranging from thread-like to broad and flattened. It is composed of a varying number of segments that look like rings.

The sexes are usually separate. In some species the male and female differ markedly in coloration or size or by having various appendages.

The development of insects is generally achieved by one of two methods: incomplete metamorphosis or complete metamorphosis. In the case of complete metamorphosis, the larvae that emerge from the eggs (caterpillars in Lepidoptera) do not resemble the adult at all. They shed their skin (moult) several times and then turn into a pupa, from which the adult, known as the imago, emerges after a time. In the case of incomplete metamorphosis, the larvae that emerge from the eggs slightly resemble the adult insect but are without wings. These larvae,

Fig. 3. Female Colorado Potato Beetles (*Leptinotarsa decemlineata*) lay orange eggs in piles. The red, black-spotted larvae gnaw the leaves of potato plants, often leaving only the skeleton.

Fig. 4. The caterpillar of the Puss Moth (*Cerura vinula*) has prongs at the tip of the abdomen, from which it extrudes pink filaments to scare foes.

known as nymphs (in some species also as naiads), shed their skin a number of times, looking more like the adult with every moult, until they finally change directly into an adult. This is the basic scheme, but the development of some species or groups of insects is rather more complex.

Winged insects (Pterygota) have wings in the adult stage. In some species the adults have reduced wings, but this is an acquired condition. Fleas, for example, are wingless because they have adapted to a parasitic way of life.

Wings and their shape differ markedly in the various insect groups. In many species the front wings are not adapted for flight but form a hard, protective cover for the hind pair of membranous wings.

The pictorial section of this book does not include members of certain insect orders that occur rarely or are less well known—the enormous number of insect species makes this impossible. Furthermore, the individual orders are not presented according to the zoological system of classification; this has been done to show species that are similar (not related) alongside one another in the colour plates, for the purpose of easier orientation on the part of the reader. For example, springtails and fleas are not related at all, but members of the two groups might readily be mistaken for one another by the layman;

Fig. 5. The larvae of *Perla abdominalis* live in water, on or under stones. They like clear water and are therefore most often found in swift-flowing streams. The adult insects are on the wing from April until June in foothill districts, but fly only short distances.

Fig. 6. The development of a dragonfly (*Aeschna*).

Insects make up the largest group of animals. The number of described species totals nearly a million, but the actual number is much larger.

Insects are divided into two sub-classes: wingless insects and winged insects. Wingless insects (Apterygota) never had winged ancestors and they undergo an incomplete metamorphosis. Fish moths (Thysanura), for example, belong to this group. These are small insects with a body that is narrowed toward the end and terminates in two cerci and a single long median caudal filament. The body is covered with fine scales. The antennae are usually quite long. The legs are slender and break off easily, but will grow again. Fish moths are nocturnal insects. Their development is slow and includes several larval stages. There are some 500 species worldwide; in central Europe there are over 20 species.

the same holds true for snoutflies (Mecoptera) and alderflies (Megaloptera), as well as for leaf beetles (Chrysomelidae) and ladybirds (Coccinellidae). The following are the insect orders found in central Europe, representatives of which appear in the pictorial section.

Mayflies (Ephemeroptera) are small insects with a 3—4-mm-long body. Their forewings are larger than the hind wings, which, however, may be absent in some species. When at rest, the wings are held upright above the abdomen, thus making it easy to distinguish mayflies from

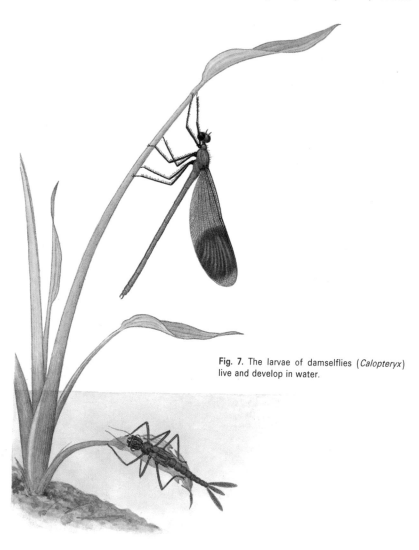

Fig. 7. The larvae of damselflies (*Calopteryx*) live and develop in water.

Mayflies are widely known for their mass occurrence. In summer, when naiads complete their development, millions of mayflies may appear around rivers. Often they fly to streetlamps by the riverside or to lighted windows. Such hordes of mayflies are a sight that is becoming increasingly rare nowadays because they cannot live in polluted waters. There are some 2,000 known species of mayflies in the world; more than 80 are found in central Europe.

Stoneflies (Plecoptera) are smaller to moderately large insects with a wingspan of about 5 cm. There are some 90 species in central Europe. Their metamorphosis is incomplete. Their bodies are elongated and slightly chitinous. The forewings are narrower than the hind wings. Both wings are folded flat against the abdomen when resting. The flight of stoneflies is cumbersome. The mouthparts are usually vestigial in the adults. Development takes place in water where the females lay their eggs cemented to-

Fig. 9. Developmental stages of the Common Fire-bug (*Pyrrhocoris apterus*).

Fig. 8. The larvae of spittle-bugs (Cercopidae) develop in a large mound of froth attached to a plant.

other insects. The abdomen of mayflies is terminated by a pair of long cerci with a third, long caudal filament in the middle. The mouthparts are vestigial in the adults and that is why they do not feed. The metamorphosis of mayflies is incomplete; the developmental stages are called naiads. The larvae of mayflies show little resemblance to the adults and live in water. However, there exists a transitional stage between the naiad and the adult that is not found in any other insects. The fully grown naiad climbs out of the water onto a stem above the surface, where it changes into a sub-imago, greatly resembling the adult and covered with a delicate membranous skin. Only after it has shed this skin is the true adult stage (imago) attained. In some species of mayflies the sub-imago stage lasts only a matter of minutes, in others up to two or three days. The life of the adult is extremely short, usually only a few days.

271

Fig. 10. The female Katydid or Green Grasshopper (*Tettigonia viridissima*) has a long, stout ovipositor with which she deposits as many as 100 eggs in the ground.

gether in a mass. The nymphs live for one to four years under stones in streams and rivers. They are more abundant in faster flowing brooks and streams because they require well-aerated water. They are predacious.

Dragonflies (Odonata) are one of the best-known groups of insects. They brighten riversides, ponds and lakeshores but will often fly quite far from water to meadows, fields and forest clearings. These are large insects with an elongated abdomen and long, relatively narrow wings. They are excellent fliers. The eyes are large. The metamorphosis is incomplete. The eggs develop into larvae (nymphs) lacking any resemblance to the adults. These larvae live in water and are very predacious. They hunt small aquatic insects and crustaceans but will also attack small tadpoles and fish fry. Some nymphs develop into adults within three months, others not until a year to four years after hatching.

The nymphs of dragonflies have a well-developed lower and upper lip round the mouth opening. At the sides are mandibles and maxillae. The lower lip is shaped like a mask that aids in seizing prey. At the end of their development the nymphs climb up out of the water onto a plant stem or some other object, where they change into the adult form.

Dragonflies are predacious and hunt various insects, mostly flies but also lepidoptera, on the wing. There are some 4,700 known species in the world; about 100 species are found in Europe. Dragonflies are divided into two suborders: damsel-flies (Zygoptera) and giant dragonflies (Anisoptera). Damsel-flies have both pairs of wings of almost equal size. These are folded vertically when resting. Giant dragonflies have the hind wings broader than the forewings and the wings are held outspread when resting. Whereas damsel-flies fly relatively slowly, giant dragonflies are swift and skilful fliers.

Cockroaches (Blattodea) are moderately large to large flat-bodied insects, although some species measure only a few millimetres. As a rule, however, cockroaches are over 1 cm long, some tropical species being up to 12 cm long. The three-sided head is bent downward and the mouthparts have greatly developed mandibles. The wings are large, the forewings more chitinized, the hind wings broad and membranous and folded beneath the forewings. Both pairs are laid flat against the body. Even though the wings are well developed, cockroaches are poor fliers. In some species the wings are absent or the females may even be wingless. The legs of cockroaches are long and slender, adapted for fast running.

Cockroaches are nocturnal insects, hiding in cracks and crevices during the daytime. They are omnivorous, but generally prefer plant food. Some species form colonies. The metamorphosis is incomplete. The eggs are enclosed in characteristic purse-like cases called oothecae, which the females carry about for several days until they find a place to conceal them. The larvae moult five to nine times; in some species as often as twelve times. The nymphs resemble the adults but are wingless. Cockroaches are distributed primarily in the tropics, where there are more than 3,500 species; some ten species are found in central Europe. Certain species are common pests in mills, bakeries and the like, and are difficult to get rid of.

Mantids (Mantodea) are thermophilous insects distributed mainly in tropical and subtropical regions, where there are some 2,000 species. Only a single species is found in the warm regions of central Europe. Mantids are moderately large to large insects, some being only 1.5 cm long, others as much as 16 cm long. They are distinguished by the unusual form of the front legs which are adapted for seizing and holding prey. The legs are strong, the coxae extremely long, the femora armed with three rows of sharp spines, and the tibia spiny as well. The mantid seizes its prey between the femur and tibia, piercing it with the spines in several places so that its victim cannot escape. The head is three-sided and bent downward, the mandibles large and strong. The predaciousness of mantids is proverbial. Often the much larger female devours her smaller partner. Mantids have large wings, often covering the entire abdomen. Their flight, however, is cumbersome and they fly only short distances. The metamorphosis is incomplete. The females lay their eggs in oothecae which they fasten to plants and the like. They secrete the case together with the eggs. The oothecae rapidly harden, thus providing good protection for the eggs. The larvae hatch after a long time, are predaceous, and feed on small insects.

Straight-winged insects (Orthoptera) are moderately large to large insects with powerful mouthparts adapted for biting. The hind legs are generally very stout and adapted for jumping. The body is compressed from side to side. The head is bent downward and is furnished with large mandibles. The antennae vary in length; in green grasshoppers, for instance, they are very long and thread-like; in field grasshoppers they are short and thicker. Both males and females have wings. Some species are short-winged; in others the wings are absent in the females or in both sexes. The forewings often differ markedly from the hind wings. Whereas the forewings are usually a nondescript colour that blends well with their surroundings, the membranous hind wings are brightly coloured.

The males (very occasionally also the females of certain species) produce shrill sounds by means of a special organ called the stridulatory organ. Each species produces a specific sound by means of which the male tries to attract a mate. Green grasshoppers produce sounds by rubbing the bases of the forewings together; field grasshoppers by rubbing the hind femora against the edges of the upper wings. Crickets have a large 'chirping' apparatus on the forewings.

The metamorphosis is incomplete. The larvae that hatch from the eggs moult five to six times and resemble the adults. Some species of straight-winged insects are predacious, others herbivorous. The females of green grasshoppers have a large ovipositor. There are more than 25,000 known Orthoptera species in the world, mostly found in the tropics and subtropics. Only some 120 species are found in central Europe.

Earwigs (Dermaptera) are moderately large insects with a flattened, elongated body that is firm and glossy. The long abdomen of both males and females terminates in two forceps-like appendages that are used for seizing and holding prey, in defence, as well as for attack, and also for pulling out the folded membranous wings or when folding them back again in the case of flying species. The forewings are short and leathery, the hind wings long and membranous and elaborately folded three times under the forewings when resting. The legs of earwigs are relatively short and are used for walking.

Fig. 11. Female Potter Wasps (*Eumenes coarctatus*) build fat-bellied, short-necked nests of clay and saliva for their larvae on walls or stones and often also on heather and the bark of trees. To feed the larvae, they capture a small hairless caterpillar, paralyze it and put it into the nest.

Fig. 12. The Red-bearded Fan Wasp (*Ammophi-la sabulosa*) takes similar care of its larvae. It drags the paralyzed caterpillar to the nest at the end of an underground burrow, lays the egg on its body, and firmly fills in the entrance to the nest.

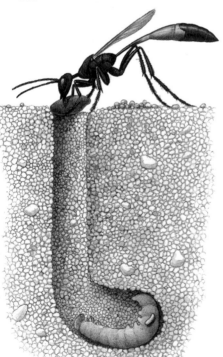

The head projects directly forward and is furnished with thread-like antennae. Earwigs are nocturnal insects. During the daytime they remain concealed in crevices or under bark, emerging to forage for food when dusk falls. They are omnivorous. The metamorphosis is incomplete. The females lay several dozen eggs, covering them with the body until they hatch and protecting them from drying out as well as from fungal attack. They take similar care of the larvae. There are 1,300 known species in the world, about ten species being found in central Europe.

Bird lice or biting lice (Mallophaga) are small, flat-bodied, wingless species, although they had winged ancestors. The head is broader than the thorax and is furnished with well-developed mandibles. The antennae are short, the eyes vestigial or absent. Biting lice are parasites that are found in the feathers of birds or in the fur of mammals. They feed on feathers and hair and often also on dermal scales or occasionally even upon the blood of their host. Their metamorphosis is incomplete. The females lay eggs (nits) that stick to hair or feathers. Nymphs usually take three to four weeks to develop, but sometimes only eight days. There are some 3,500 species in the world; about 130 of these live in central Europe.

Bugs (Heteroptera) form a very large insect order and are to be found in all kinds of environments—in forests, meadows, fields and water, as well as in human dwellings. They are small to

275

Fig. 13. *Cicindela campestris* with prey.

Fig. 14. The Common Sexton or Gravedigger Beetle (*Necrophorus vespillo*) can scrape away the earth under the body of a dead bird until it is completely buried. The female then lays eggs on the body and the larvae feed on the putrefying flesh. *Oeceoptoma thoracica* forages in the immediate vicinity for the dead bodies of the larvae of flies and other insects.

moderately large insects, tropical species usually being larger. The body is greatly flattened dorso-ventrally. The front wings are usually hemelytra, the hind wings are membranous. Some species, however, are wingless. The mouthparts are designed for piercing and sucking. The metamorphosis is incomplete. The larvae resemble the adults but are devoid of wings and are smaller. Some species are troublesome pests of cultivated plants, others are predacious. Some of the predacious species specialize in sucking the blood of warm-blooded animals, including people. Some aquatic species

have extremely long hind legs which are used for rowing. There are some 45,000 known species in the world; more than 1,000 are found in central Europe.

Plant-bugs (Homoptera) are usually small insects with two pairs of membranous wings, often folded roof-wise when resting. Some species are wingless. The mouthparts are designed for piercing and sucking. Homoptera usually suck plant juices. The metamorphosis is incomplete. Of the 53,000 known species, more than 2,000 are found in central Europe. Many species, for example aphids (Aphidoidea) or coccids (Coccoidea), are troublesome plant pests.

Bees, wasps and ants (Hymenoptera) are the most perfectly developed group of insects. The head is free, with the mouthparts adapted for chewing. Most species have greatly developed mandibles, only in some are they modified into a licking-sucking apparatus. The two pairs of membranous wings have both longitudinal and transverse venation. The hind wings are usually smaller. Females have an ovipositor. The metamorphosis of hymenopterous insects is complete. The larvae moult a number of times before changing into a pupa from which the adult emerges after a certain period. They vary greatly in size, some species measuring only 1 mm while others may be giants of 6 cm. This is an extremely large order with more than 150,000 known species distributed throughout the world; more than 10,000 are found in central Europe.

Beetles (Coleoptera) include among their number many small as well as extremely large species. In most species membranous wings are folded beneath thick elytra. The mouthparts are adapted for chewing. The metamorphosis is complete. Beetles are one of the largest insect orders, with more than 350,000 known species distributed throughout the world; some 7,000 species are found in central Europe.

Alderflies (Megaloptera) are moderately large insects with a large forward-projecting head. The wings are short and broad and are folded roof-wise above the abdomen when resting. Their flight is rather cumbersome. The head bears long, thread-like antennae and mouthparts that are adapted for chewing. The meta-

Fig. 16. The larvae of the Giant Ichneumon Fly (*Rhyssa persuasoria*) develop inside the bodies of large wood wasp larvae that live in wood. The female pushes her ovipositor into the wood and lays the egg in the wood wasp larva's body.

morphosis is complete. The larvae live for two years in water, climbing out onto the shore before pupating beneath leaves. The adult emerges from the pupa after about two weeks. Of the 250 known species only three are found in central Europe.

Fig. 15. The nest of a bumble-bee (*Bombus*) in an underground hole.

Snakeflies (Raphidioptera) are moderately large insects with a greatly elongated neck-like prothorax. The head is large, with mouthparts that are adapted for chewing. The wings are richly veined; both pairs are about the same size and are folded roof-wise above the abdomen when resting. The female has an ovipositor. Adults, as well as larvae, live under the bark of trees and are predacious. The metamorphosis is complete. There are some 200 species worldwide; approximately ten species are found in central Europe.

Nerve-winged insects (Neuroptera) are small to moderately large insects with two pairs of

Fig. 18. The Garden Tiger Moth (*Arctia caja*) is one of the loveliest of all moths. Its coloration is extremely variable.

practically identical membranous wings, folded roof-wise when resting. The metamorphosis is complete. Of the 7,000 known species, about 100 are found in central Europe.

Scorpion flies (Mecoptera) are small to moderately large insects with the head prolonged into a deflexed beak, at the end of which are sited mouthparts which are adapted for chewing. The antennae are thread-like. The wings are relatively long. In many species the male has the abdomen curved upward at the tip. The metamorphosis is complete. The eggs are laid in the ground. The larvae have outgrowths on their backs and pupate in the ground. Adults, as well as larvae, feed on small insects. Some 350 known species are distributed throughout the world; about ten species are found in central Europe.

Caddis-flies (Trichoptera) are moderately large insects with translucent wings, the hind wings are usually paler than the fore wings. The antennae are thread-like and very long. Adults are found in the vicinity of water. The metamorphosis is complete. The omnivorous larvae live in water where they build a typical portable case in which the soft hind part of the body is concealed. They also pupate in water. The pupa

Fig. 17. Caddis-flies (Trichoptera) are found near water; the larvae develop in water. The cases in which the larvae conceal themselves are made from small grains of sand, fragments of pine needles, leaves, bits of wood or the shells of small molluscs. The species of caddis-fly can usually be determined by the shape of the case and the material from which it is constructed.

rises to the water's surface before the adult emerges, which is generally at night. Of the 3,500 known species, approximately 250 are found in central Europe.

Butterflies and moths (Lepidoptera) are perhaps the most familiar of the insect orders. They have four wings, usually covered with fine scales. The jaws are converted into a coiled proboscis. The antennae are long and variously shaped, the legs slender. The larvae (caterpillars) have three pairs of thoracic legs, usually four pairs of prolegs and one pair of anal legs

Fig. 19. The female Ant Lion (*Myrmeleon formicarius*) lays eggs in sand. The larvae trap insects, mainly ants, in funnel-shaped pits. The adults are on the wing on July evenings in sandy locations; during the day they rest on bushes.

Fig. 20. The Crane-fly or Daddy-longlegs (*Tipula oleracea*) often flies indoors but there is no need to fear it as it does not bite or sting.

known as claspers. The metamorphosis is complete. These are very plentiful insects, numbering some 110,000 known species worldwide; approximately 4,000 species are found in central Europe.

Two-winged flies (Diptera) are small insects with a body distinctly divided into a head, thorax and abdomen. The head is very mobile. The mouthparts are adapted for sucking, licking or piercing. The compound eyes, composed of numerous small ocelli, are strikingly large. In many species they have a metallic sheen. There are also usually three simple eyes on top of the head. The antennae are generally rather short. Dipterous insects have only one pair of wings, the second pair are modified into club-shaped organs called halteres that function as sensory flight instruments. The metamorphosis is complete. Of the 130,000 species distributed throughout the world, more than 6,000 are found in central Europe.

Fleas (Aphaniptera) are small wingless insects (although they had winged ancestors) with a flat-sided body. The hind legs are adapted for jumping. The mouthparts are designed for piercing and sucking. Fleas are parasites. The metomorphosis is complete. The larvae feed on organic remnants. The pupa matures inside a cocoon made of feathers and hair. There are some 1,600 species worldwide; central Europe is inhabited by some 100 species of fleas.

1

4

3

2

5

Class: **Insects**—Insecta

Order: **Springtails**—Collembola

1 Black Water Springtail *Podura aquatica.*
Common in Europe. Length 1 mm. Wingless.
Found in vast numbers on aquatic plants or directly on surface of streams, puddles, pools,
etc. Scaly body. Jumps by means of forked
caudal appendage. Female lays over 1,300
eggs. Larvae hatch in 12 days. Several generations a year. Lives on rotting vegetable debris.

Order: **Fish Moths**—Thysanura

2 Silverfish *Lepisma saccharina.* Very common.
Length about 10 mm. Often frequents buildings.
Nocturnal insect. Comes out after dark and
looks for scraps. Found in bathrooms and lavat-
ories, behind wallpaper, etc.

Order: **Mayflies**—Ephemeroptera

3 Common Mayfly *Ephemera vulgata.* Widespread in central Europe. Length 14—22 mm.
Black-spotted wings. Larvae live in slow-flowing
water, bent drainpipes, etc. Development takes
2 years. Swarming time May to August. Attracted by light.

4 White Mayfly *Polymitarcis virgo.* Common in
central Europe. Length 10—18 mm. Snow-white.
Larvae live in large rivers. Develops 2 years.
Swarming time August to September. Mass incidence. Adults live only 1—3 days. Female lays
eggs on surface of water. Larvae resemble adult
insects and live on small animals. Fully developed nymphs leave water and moult (sub-
imago). Next moult produces adult insect capable of further reproduction.

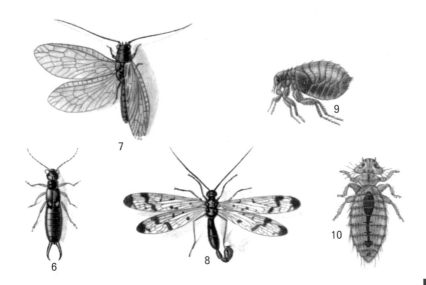

Order: **Stone-flies** —*Plecoptera*

5 *Perla abdominalis.* Common in central Europe. Length 17—28 mm. Found near large ponds and rivers. From April to June, adult insects cling to underside of leaves. Predacious larvae hide under stones on water bed. Mature larvae climb tree trunks, their dorsal skin splits and winged insects emerge. Female lays eggs on surface of water in the evening.

Order: **Earwigs** —Dermaptera

6 Common Earwig *Forficula auricularia.* Distributed all over Europe. Length 9—16 mm. Pincers at tip of abdomen used for defence or for unfolding membraneous wings. Appears from April to October. Female lays piles of eggs in spaces under stones and guards both eggs and wingless larvae. Eats eggs of other insects and parts of plants.

Order: **Alderflies** —Megaloptera

7 Luteous Alderfly *Sialis flavilatera.* Lives all over Europe. Length 19—38 mm. Found near water in May and June. Larvae live in water, eat other insects and their larvae. Pupate in damp soil on bank. Adult insects live only few days. Female lays up to 2,000 eggs on rushes, hatched larvae drop into water. Development takes 2 years.

Order: **Snoutflies** —Mecoptera

8 Scorpion-fly *Panorpa communis.* Found all over Europe. Length about 20 mm. Male has tapering abdomen like scorpion's. Female lays up to 75 eggs in hollows in ground. Caterpillar-like larvae live in moss, etc. Eats vegetable and animal matter. Sometimes sucks wounded insects dry.

Order: **Fleas** —Aphaniptera

9 Human Flea *Pulex irritans.* Lives all over the world. Length about 4 mm. Wingless. Adults parasitic on man. After sucking blood, female lays eggs in crevices etc. Legless larvae live on organic debris in which they also pupate. Female lays 4—8 eggs daily for 3 months. Flea-bites turn red and swell.

Order: **Bird Lice** or **Biting Lice** —Mallophaga

10 Fowl-louse *Menopon gallinae.* Very common in Europe. Length 1—1.5 mm. Wingless. Lives in plumage of fowls, eats feathers, bites skin and sucks blood. Female attaches eggs to feathers. Occasionally, but not for long, can live as parasite on man.

Order: **Snakeflies**—Raphidioptera

1 Snakefly *Raphidia notata*. Distributed all over Europe. Length up to 30 mm. Inhabits woods, especially sunny outskirts. Appears during summer, from April. Female has long ovipositor. Catches insects and spiders. Flat larvae live behind bark and catch insects. Female lays up to 50 eggs on wood.

Order: **Nerve-winged Insects**—Neuroptera

2 Owl-fly *Ascalaphus macaronius*. Lives in warm regions, including central Europe. Length up to 30 mm. Found on sunny slopes etc. Appears in June. Catches small animals on wing. Larvae live on ground, in grass, and catch other insects, especially ants. Pupate in soil.

3 Ant Lion *Myrmeleon formicarius*. Abundant in central Europe. Wing span up to 75 mm. Adult insects live only from June to August. Female lays single eggs in sand. Larvae make funnel-shaped pits, in which they mainly trap ants, sucking them dry with their strong hollow jaws. Pupate in soil in sandy cocoon.

4 Green Lacewing *Chrysopa vulgaris*. Very common. Length about 20 mm. Flies mainly in evening. In autumn often seen at windows. Hunts plant lice. Female lays eggs on long stems near plant lice, on which larvae live 10—24 days before pupating. Two generations a year. Adults of second generation hibernate and are brownish, in spring greenish.

Order: **Cockroaches**—Blattodea

5 Croton Bug or **German Cockroach** *Blatella germanica*. Today distributed over whole of the world. Length 11—15 mm. Runs well but flies badly. Hides during day in buildings. Comes out after dark to look for food. Eats vegetable and animal matter, paper, leather, etc. Likes warmth. Reproduces whole year round. Female lays about 30 eggs in special capsule carried on its abdomen. Capsule shed after 14 days. After hibernating, larvae moult 6 times before maturing to adult insects.

6 Black-beetle or **Oriental Cockroach** *Blatta orientalis*. Found all over Europe. Length 19—30 mm. Inhabits old houses, bakeries, etc. Likes warmth. Occurs whole year round. Nocturnal insect. Lives on both vegetable and animal matter. Female lays eggs in capsules (ootheca). Life span up to 6 years.

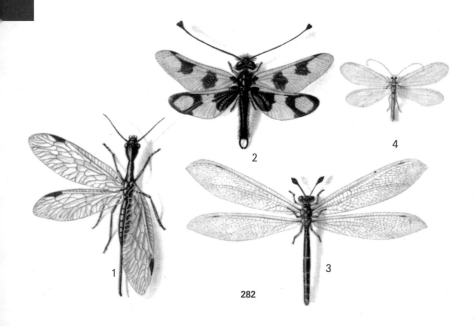

Order: **Mantids**—Mantodea

7 Praying Mantis *Mantis religiosa*. Inhabits only warmest parts of central Europe. Length of male 60 mm, female 75 mm. Lives on bushes. Slow-moving. Appears from June to September. Waits motionless for prey, seizes it with long forelimbs. Lives mainly on insects. In autumn, after pairing, female often devours male. Female lays eggs in capsules attached to twigs. Predacious larvae hatch in spring, mature in August.

Order: **Caddis-flies**—Trichoptera

8 Macro-caddisfly *Phrygaena grandis*. Abundant throughout central Europe. Wing span up to 70 mm. Appears near water from April to August. Female lays piles of eggs on underside of leaves near water surface. Larvae form cases from fragments of plants and pupate in these under water. Imagos emerge en masse, flutter over water and pair.

9 Rhomboid Caddis-fly *Limnophilus rhombicus.* Abundant in central Europe. Length 17 to 44 mm. Appears from May to September. Larvae make case of criss-cross fragments of bark, wood and leaves. Pupates under water. Imago-like pupa bites through cocoon envelope, floats to surface and immediately splits open, releasing adult insect. Adults pair in evening over water. Common fish food.

9

8

5

7

6

3 *Coenagrion puella.* Found everywhere in central Europe. Length 23—30 mm. Male has slim blue body, female greenish. Appears from May to end of September. Flies among reeds and tall grass beside water. Female lays eggs in plants, often submerging completely. Larvae live in stagnant or slow-flowing water. Develop one year. Mature nymph crawls out of water and after one more moult is transformed to adult insect, whose wings and abdomen soon grow to full length.

Sub-order: **Giant Dragonflies**—Anisoptera

4 Giant Dragonfly *Anax imperator.* Scattered over whole of Europe. Length up to 60 mm. Appears from June to August, often far from water. Swift, skilful flier. Catches insects on wing. Larvae live at bottom of stagnant water, are exceptionally predacious and even hunt small fish. Female lays eggs in plants, but does not submerge completely. Development takes one year.

5 Brown Dragonfly *Aeschna grandis.* Widely distributed in Europe. Length 49—60 mm. Green-blue with black spots. Appears from end of June to end of September. Frequents forest clearings, footpaths near ponds and rivers, etc. Develops 2—3 years. Predacious larvae live among aquatic plants at bottom of stagnant water. Often catch small fish or tadpoles.

6 *Gomplus vulgatissimus.* Abundant everywhere in central Europe. Length 33—37 mm. Appears from May to end of July. Flies quickly, catches insects on wing. Female lays eggs in water while flying. Relatively thick-bodied larvae breathe through intestinal gills. Predacious, catch chiefly insect larvae, small tadpoles and newt larvae. Usually take 3 years to develop.

7 *Libellula quadrimaculata.* Widely distributed in Europe. Length 27—32 mm. Appears from May to middle of August. Rapid, apparently aimless, zigzag flight. Catches insects on wing. Female lays eggs in water while flying. Stout, fat larvae live mainly at bottom of small ponds and pools. Development takes 2 years. Form of migration in large numbers over considerable distances observed.

Order: **Dragonflies**—Odonata

Sub-order: **Damselflies**—Zygoptera

1 Blue Damselfly *Calopteryx virgo.* Abundant all over central Europe. Length 34—39 mm. Male has blue wings, female brownish. Frequents flowing water and ponds. Appears from May to August. Female lays eggs in plants under water, often submerging completely to do so. Slim larvae, which take 2 years to develop, have three leaf-like caudal appendages. When fully developed, they crawl out, grip a reed and wait until dorsal skin splits, releasing adult insect.

2 *Calopteryx splendens.* Very common beside both stagnant and flowing water from May to September. Length 33—40 mm. Male has broad bluish band on wings. Larvae live in water. Develop in same way as preceding species.

8 *Libellula depressa.* Abundant local incidence in Europe. Length 22—28 mm. Flat abdomen, sky-blue in male, brownish in female. Appears from May to beginning of August. Found near ponds and rivers but also far from water. Female lays eggs on surface of stagnant water. Larva short, fat and grey-brown. Development takes 2 years. This species also often migrates in large numbers.

Order: **Straight-winged Insects**—Orthoptera

Family: **Green Grasshoppers**—Tettigoniidae

1 Katydid or **Green Grasshopper** *Tettigonia viridissima.* Common all over central Europe. Length 28—35 mm. Long antennae. Adult specimens can fly. Female has long ovipositor. Appears from July to October in lowlands and uplands. Males can often be heard chirping loudly in evening from tall trees, but often also during daytime. Female lays 70—100 eggs in soil. Nymphs live in meadows. Last moult before complete maturation end of July. Larvae and adult insects largely predacious. Catch different insects, occasionally also eat plants.

2 *Decticus verrucivorus.* Abundant in places. Length 22—35 mm. Spotted wings. Lives in grass or clover fields. Appears from June to September. Carnivorous. Nymphs often gregarious.

Family: **Crickets**—Gryllidae

3 Old World Field Cricket *Gryllus campestris.* Distributed over most of Europe. Length 20—25 mm. Lives in dry meadows and slopes in lowlands. Appears from May to July. Digs burrows as hideaways. Solitary, except at pairing time, when male chirps loudly to attract female. Female lays up to 300 eggs in ground with ovipositor. Nymphs hibernate, mature following spring. Lives on vegetable and flesh diet.

4 House Cricket *Acheta domestica.* Originally from Mediterranean region, brought to Europe for laboratory purposes. Length 15—25 mm. Frequents warm places, requires at least 10° C. Diverse diet. Female lays eggs in damp soil, etc., up to 4,000 during its 2 months' life span. According to temperature, nymphs are hatched in 8—30 days and moult 9—11 times before turning into adults. Male chirps. Does not fly very well but spreads easily.

Family: **Mole Crickets**—Gryllotalpidae

5 Common Mole Cricket *Gryllotalpa gryllotalpa.* Locally abundant over whole of Europe. Length 35—50 mm. Forelimbs resemble mole's. Flies clumsily. Adults found from May to September. Lives in earth and digs burrows. Male chirps on warm days. Female lays up to 300 eggs in underground chamber lined with saliva. Nymphs hibernate, mature following spring. Lives on vegetable and flesh diet. Garden pest in some places. Tries to get quickly under ground as it is awkward above it.

Family: **Field Grasshoppers**—Acrididae

6 *Stenobothrus lineatus.* Very common in central Europe. Length 16—23 mm. Lives in dry meadows and steppes. Appears from July to September. Males chirp by drawing teeth on inner aspect of femora over ridges on wing case. Female has ovipositor and lays eggs in ground. Eats plants, but does not do much damage.

5

6

7 *Omocestus viridulus*. Very common in central Europe. Length 13—24 mm. Particularly abundant in uplands. Found in dry places on hillsides and in meadows from July to September. Female greenish, male grey-brown. Lives on parts of plants, but does little damage. Eggs laid in ground.

7

8 *Psophus stridulus*. Abundant local incidence. Length 20—34 mm. Red underwings, seen only when it soars into air. Appears from July to October in dry, sunny, often rocky places, in forest clearings and on hillsides. Male flies with creaking sound. Female lays eggs in piles in ground, wrapping them, like other grasshoppers, in frothy secretion. Eggs hibernate. Larvae, hatched in spring, have huge appetite. Adult form attained after 5 moults. Vegetarian.

9 *Oedipoda coerulescens*. Abundant in places. Length 16—24 mm. Bluish underwings. Seen from July to September.

8

3

4

9

Order: **Bugs**—Heteroptera

Family: **Water-boatmen**—Corixidae

1 Water-boatman *Corixa punctata*. Common all over central Europe. Length about 10 mm. Found in every large pool or pond. Occurs often in winter, below ice. Flies on summer evenings, frequently enters open windows. Produces creaking sounds under water.

Family: **Back-swimmers**—Notonectidae

2 *Notonecta glauca*. Distributed over whole of central Europe. Length about 20 mm, spindle-shaped body. Inhabits stagnant water. Rows with long hindlegs, usually upside down. Predacious. Hunts other insects, stabs them with proboscis and sucks them dry. Its prick can be felt. Flies on summer nights.

Family: **Water-scorpions**—Nepidae

3 Water-scorpion *Nepa cinerea*. Very common in fishpond regions. Length 20—25 mm. Pincer-like forelimbs for catching prey, e.g. insects and fish fry. Long breathing tube at end of body. Lives at bottom of stagnant or slow-flowing water. Sucks prey dry.

4 Water Stick-insect *Ranatra linearis*. Occurs in fishpond regions, at bottom of stagnant water. Long, stick-like body with long legs. Length 30—40 mm. Breathing tube at end of body. Predacious. Catches aquatic insects and larvae with forelimbs and sucks them dry. Stabs painfully.

Family: **Pond Skaters**—Gerridae

5 Common Water-strider *Gerris lacustris*. Common European insect. Length about 20 mm. Found on surface of stagnant water or creeks. End of body and legs covered with non-wetting hairs allowing it to run swiftly over water surface. Predacious, catches insects on surface. Reproduces on land.

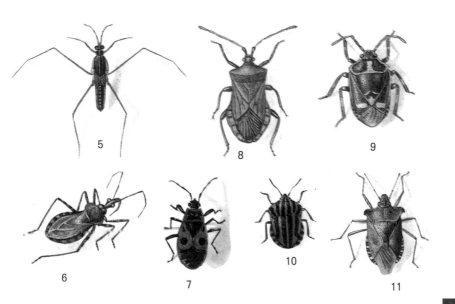

5

8

9

6

7

10

11

Family: **Soldier-bugs**—Reduviidae

6 Red Assassin-bug *Rhynocoris iracundus.* Widespread in central Europe. Length up to 15 mm. Slim body, long legs. Lives on sunny grassy slopes, frequents umbelliferous flowers and other plants. Predacious. Catches insects and sucks their body juices. Lies motionless in wait for prey. Stabs painfully.

Family: **Fire-bugs**—Pyrrhocoridae

7 Common Fire-bug *Pyrrhocoris apterus.* Abundant everywhere in central Europe. Length about 10 mm. Found most often at foot of lime- and chestnut-trees, behind loose bark and on walls. Appears from early spring until late autumn. Occurs in masses, together with nymphs. Lives on juices of dead insects, fruit and seeds.

Family: **Marginated Bugs**—Coreidae

8 Marginated Bug *Coreus marginatus.* Very widely distributed. Length about 15 mm. Has almost square head. Flies on warm days. Lives on bushes and plants. Emits characteristic acrid odour. Vegetarian.

Family: **Stink-bugs**—Pentatomidae

9 Cabbage-bug *Eurydema oleraceum.* Common all over Europe. Length 5.5—7 mm. Metallic lustre, somewhat variable colouring. Occurs on outskirts of fields, etc. Sucks plant juices and in large numbers causes great damage. Mainly attacks brassicaceous plants. Important pest.

10 Striped Bug *Graphosoma lineatum.* Inhabits southern Europe and warm parts of central Europe. Length about 10 mm. Found in gardens on carrot plants, in forests on flowers, raspberry canes, etc. Summer insects. In south does damage to cereals.

11 Red-legged Stink-bug *Pentatoma rufipes.* Very common. Length 13—16 mm. Appears in summer in gardens and woods, especially on oaks and alders. Hunts, stabs and sucks caterpillars, but lives mainly on plant juices. Damages berry-bearing plants, cherry-trees, etc. Nymphs hibernate behind scales of bark.

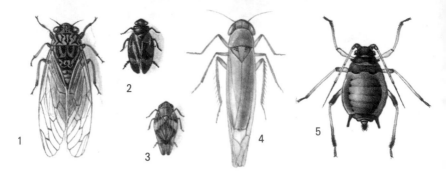

Order: **Plant-bugs**—Homoptera

Sub-order: **Cicadas**—Cicadoidea

1 Mountain Cicada *Cicadetta montana.* Inhabits only warm parts of central Europe, e.g. Danube basin. Length about 25 mm. Males have special chirping apparatus between thorax and abdomen. Punctures bark and twigs. Ground-dwelling larvae suck roots of trees. Development takes several years.

2 Blood-red Spittle-bug *Cercopis sanguinolenta.* Very common in some parts of central Europe. Length about 10 mm. Lives on plants in lowland meadows. Appears from June to August. Female lays eggs in grass. Larvae hatch in spring and suck plant juices. Larvae secrete liquid into which they pump air, turning it into protective froth.

3 Froth-bug *Philaenus spumarius.* Occurs over whole of Europe. Length about 10 mm. Frequents meadows and margins of forests. Female lays eggs chiefly in willow twigs. Hatched larvae suck these twigs. Greenish larva lives in protective froth. Matures after 5 moults. Adult insect can fly and hop well.

4 Green Leaf-hopper *Empoasca decipiens.* Abundant all over Europe. Length about 3 mm. Small and inconspicuous. Appears from June to September in deciduous woods and gardens. In large numbers does damage by sucking trees. Over 200 similar species in Europe, many of which are injurious to cereals and other crops.

Sub-order: **Plant-lice**—Aphidoidea

5 Black Bean Aphid *Aphis fabae.* Very common in Europe. Small and black. Spends winter on spindle-trees, from which winged females fly to poppies, sugar-beet plants, etc. and suck their juices. In large numbers causes plants to wither and die.

6 *Acyrthosiphon onobrychis.* Abundant in central Europe. Summer insect, occurs mainly on peas but also on other plants. Sucks juice in stems. Like other plant-lice, unfertilized females produce live young (parthenogenesis), fertilized females lay autumn eggs. Males, which are smaller than females, hatch from fertilized eggs. Colony is founded by wingless female hatched from fertilized egg.

7 *Megoura vicia.* Common summer insect, forms colonies on vetches, etc. Biology similar to preceding species.

8 Woolly Aphid *Eriosoma lanigerum.* Widespread over most of Europe, but originally from America. Chiefly attacks apple-trees. Lives in colonies which look like white tufts of cotton-wool. Actual body brown, contains blood-red fluid. Larva hibernates behind bark or in ground. During summer reproduces without fertilization. Males and egg-laying females hatch in autumn. One of the most dangerous fruit pests.

9 Yellow Fig Gall-louse *Sacchiphantes abietis.* Widely distributed in Europe. Length about 1.5 mm. Lives permanently on firs. By sucking twigs induces formation of scaly galls. All generations, fertilized and unfertilized, lay only eggs. Fertilized female of last generation lays single egg, larva of which hibernates.

Sub-order: **Scale-insects**—Coccoidea

10 *Eulecanium corni.* Abundant in Europe. Length of female about 5 mm, male 2.5 mm. Lives mainly on plum-trees, ashes, hazels, etc. Wingless female firmly sessile on bark. Lays eggs under its pustulate body. Winged male eats no food. Larvae, after hibernating on roots of trees, suck twigs and females acquire pustulate, sessile form.

10   ♂   ♀

Order: **Wasps, Ants and Bees**—Hymenoptera

Family: **Sawflies**—Tenthredinidae

1 *Pontania viminalis.* Small sawfly, very common round water. Female lays eggs on underside of blade of willow leaves. This induces formation of reddish galls, harmless to trees.

2 Lesser Fir Sawfly *Lygaeonematus abietinus.* Length 4.5—6 mm. Appears at the end of April. Males hatched first. Female lays up to 100 eggs in young fir needles. Greenish larvae, hatched in 4 days, devour needles. In June pupate in mould, in cocoon. Pest.

Family: **Cimbicid Sawflies**—Cimbicidae

3 Cimbicid Sawfly *Cimbex femorata.* Resembles large wasp but has club-tipped antennae. Bright green larva with red-striped back nibbles birch leaves, hibernates on branch in tough, parchment-like brown cocoon and pupates in it following spring. Does no damage.

Family: **Wood Wasps**—Siricidae

4 Horse-tail *Urocerus gigas.* Common, very striking, over 40 mm long, with cylindrical body. Female bores holes up to 1.5 cm deep in healthy fir wood with its long ovipositor. In each hole lays 4 eggs — total up to 350. Appears from June to August. Larvae gnaw tunnels in wood, plug them with debris. Pupate after 2—3 years. Adult insect bites way out, often after wood has been processed. Pest.

Family: **Ichneumon Flies**—Ichneumonidae

5 Giant Ichneumon Fly *Rhyssa persuasoria.* Distributed over large part of Europe and Asia. Length up to over 40 mm. Inhabits large pinewoods. Female looks specifically for wood wasp larvae, pushes ovipositor into tunnel, stabs larva and lays egg in its body. Hatched larva then devours wood wasp larva. Very useful insect.

6 Sickle Wasp *Ophion luteus.* Striking appearance, common in Europe. Length about 30 mm. Curved, flat-sided abdomen. Occurs in clearings, in evening often attracted into houses by light. Parasite of large moth caterpillars. Female stabs caterpillar, lays eggs in its body and larvae devour caterpillar.

Family: **Braconids**—Braconidae

7 Vipionid *Apanteles glomeratus.* Tiny summer insect occurring in woods, gardens and meadows. Female lays eggs en masse in butterfly caterpillars, e.g. whites, fritillaries, etc. Minute larvae first of all live on host's adipose bodies. La-

ter bore way out, immediately spin yellow cocoon and pupate. Caterpillar often surrounded
by cluster of cocoons.

Family: **Aphid Wasps**—Aphidiidae

8 Aphid Wasp *Diaeretus rapae*. Very small and
very common. Female lays egg in abdomen of
plant-louse. Hatched larva devours contents of
host's body and pupates inside it. Adult insect
leaves dead host through hole which can often
be seen on shrivelled plant-lice. Very useful
species.

Family: **Gall-wasps**—Cynipidae

9 Oak Gall-fly *Cynips quercusfolii.* Abundant
everywhere. Adult insect inconspicuous, but
eggs give rise to galls, housing larvae, on underside of oak leaves ('oak-apples'). Larva pupates
in autumn and adults often hatch early in winter.
Females emerging at end of February lay unfertilized eggs in buds and these develop into gall-
wasps of both sexes. Males measure only about
2 mm. Fertilized females lay eggs on leaves and
cycle is repeated.

10 Robin's Pin Cushion or **Bedeguar Gall** *Diplo-
lepis rosae*. Most widely distributed gallwasp.
Length 4—5 mm. Adult insect seldom noticed,
but known from moss-like reddish or greenish
galls containing larvae on rose-bushes and dog-
roses. Only one generation known — females
reproducing by parthenogenesis.

1

2

3

Family: **Beetle-wasps**—Scoliidae

1 Yellow-headed Beetle-wasp *Scolia flavifrons*. Huge wasp living in warm parts of Europe — in central Europe in south-east and south. Length about 50 mm. On sunny days can be seen on flowers. Female lays eggs on larvae of rhinoceros beetle. Hatched larva devours host's body from within and pupates beside its remains.

Family: **Mutillids** or **Velvet Ants**—Mutillidae

2 Velvet Ant *Mutilla europaea*. Common in central Europe. Slight resemblance to ant. Brightly coloured. Female wingless. Male visits flowers, female crawls on ground looking for bumble-bee nests. Lays eggs in body of bumble-bee larvae.

Family: **True Wasps**—Vespidae

3 Hornet *Vespa crabro*. Large wasp, abundant in places. Mainly inhabits old forests. Builds large, yellow-brown, papery nest in tree hollows, nesting-boxes, etc. Fertilized female hibernates in hiding-place. In spring lays foundations of nest by scratching away rotting wood and sticking it together with saliva, and sets up first comb. First larvae develop into workers which continue building nest. Males and females hatch in autumn. After females have been fertilized, whole community except females dies. Hornets are predacious, attack other insects. Their sting is dangerous.

4 Pollistes Wasp *Polistes gallica*. Moderately large wasp, abundant in sunny places. Forms simple papery comb with several cells. Nest attached by stalk to base, usually wall, rock, etc., often also bush. Larvae develop into workers which lay eggs giving rise to males — drones. In the Alps and further north often builds nest in enclosed space, holes, nesting-boxes, etc.

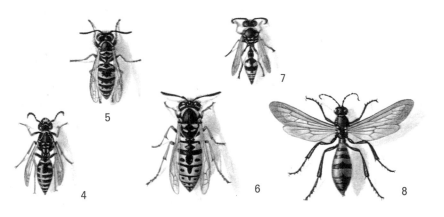

5 Common Wasp *Paravespula vulgaris*. Commonest ground-dwelling wasp. Lives in large colonies founded by female. Builds first cells on stalk in hole in ground and lays eggs. Feeds hatched larvae for 20 days. Workers hatched 20 days after pupating. They extend nest, add storeys separated by stalk-like supports. Carry away grains of sand, etc., to widen hole. Workers can number up to 2,000. Nest has 5—14 combs. Life in community expires in autumn. Females — queens — hibernate in tree hollows, rooms in houses, etc.

6 German Wasp *Paravespula germanica*. Common all over Europe. Builds underground nests in fields. In south huge nests with about 60,000 members. In September nest contains average of 1,600 workers, 1,600 males and 700 females. Likes warmth, does not fly in cold weather. Diurnal insect. Lives on sweet fruit juice, nectar, etc. Offspring fed mainly on insects. Very aggressive if disturbed, attacks all intruders.

Family: **Potter Wasps**—Eumenidae

7 Potter Wasp *Eumenes coarctatus*. Inhabits whole of Europe. Solitary wasp. Length 11 to 15 mm. Builds fat-bellied, short-necked nest of clay and saliva on forest bushes or heather. Feeds larvae on small, hairless caterpillars, especially of geometers. Larvae frequently parasitized by other wasps (fire wasps).

Family: **Digger Wasps**—Psammocharidae

8 Brown Spider Wasp *Psammocharus fuscus*. Common in warm places all over Europe. Length 10—14 mm. Seen early in spring on flowering sallows. In sandy spots digs holes ending in chamber for larva, for which it brings spiders. Paralyzes even large spiders with sting, when helpless drags them to nest. Though paralyzed, spider sometimes lives over a month and larva feeds on its body.

Family: **Ants**—Formicidae

1 Red Wood Ant *Formica rufa.* Abundant in Europe. Several races with different biology. In one, only one female in nest, in another up to 5,000 females and annual production of up to 2 million individuals. Builds large, domed nest of conifer needles, leaves, etc. Winged males and females hold nuptial flight in summer. Omnivorous. Catch any form of life they can. Useful, destroy all insects within distance of 20 m from nest. Length of workers 4—9 mm, females 9—11 mm.

2—4 Black or **Garden Ant** *Lasius niger.* Very widespread. Worker (4) 3—5 mm., male (2) and female (3) much larger. Underground nest with superstructure above ground. Pairing on warm summer days. After nuptial flight return to ground, females shed wings and males mostly die. Female founds new community and as soon as first workers are hatched confines itself only to egg-laying. After a time new males and females are hatched and cycle is repeated. Omnivorous. Partiality for secretions of plant-lice.

Family: **Thread-waisted Wasps**—Sphegidae

5 Red-bearded Fan Wasp *Ammophila sabulosa.* In Europe abundant in dry, sandy places. Length 18—20 mm. Digs burrows about 3 cm long with chamber at end for larva. On leaving covers hole with small stone. Brings paralyzed pine hawk caterpillars for larva. Sits astride caterpillar and tugs it with jaws. Drags it into nest and attaches egg to its body. Firmly fills in entrance to nest and then builds another.

6 Bee-killer Wasp *Philanthus triangulum.* Inhabits warm parts of Europe. Length 12 to 16 mm. Occurs chiefly on sandy slopes, digs nests. Pounces on bees, falls with them to ground, quickly paralyses them and takes them to larvae. In large numbers damaging to honeybee population.

7 Sand Wasp *Bembex rostrata.* In central Europe common in warm, sandy places. Robust body. Prolonged upper lip. Digs tunnels up to 40 cm long in sandy slopes or moors. Usually lives in colonies. Closes entrance with sand but finds nest unerringly. Catches flies, paralyses them with sting and takes them to larva. Also catches large gadflies and hover-flies. Larvae have huge appetite. Although well concealed, nest is found by scorpion-fly which rakes it open and lays egg on sand wasp larva.

Family: **Cuckoo Wasps**—Chrysididae

8 Fire Wasp *Chrysis ignita.* Very common in southern and central Europe. Length about 5 mm. Has concave abdomen and can curl up if in danger. Female has protrusible ovipositor. Frequents sunny walls, fences, etc. Looks for nests of solitary wasps, especially mason wasps of the genus *Odynerus.* Female forces way into nest, places egg on larva and quickly leaves. Fire Wasp larva has large, hard head and jaws and lives on host's body juices. On maturing it pupates and adult insect emerges in spring. Adult Fire Wasp lives on nectar. Flies during summer.

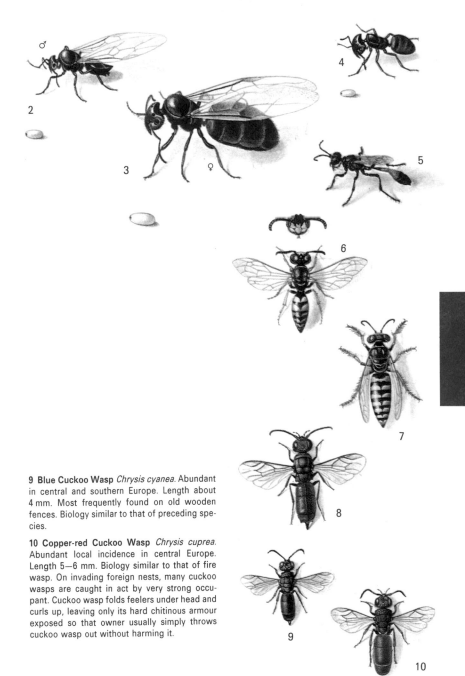

9 **Blue Cuckoo Wasp** *Chrysis cyanea.* Abundant in central and southern Europe. Length about 4 mm. Most frequently found on old wooden fences. Biology similar to that of preceding species.

10 **Copper-red Cuckoo Wasp** *Chrysis cuprea.* Abundant local incidence in central Europe. Length 5—6 mm. Biology similar to that of fire wasp. On invading foreign nests, many cuckoo wasps are caught in act by very strong occupant. Cuckoo wasp folds feelers under head and curls up, leaving only its hard chitinous armour exposed so that owner usually simply throws cuckoo wasp out without harming it.

Family: **Bees**—Apidae

1 Blue Carpenter Bee *Xylocopa violacea*. Inhabits southern Europe and warm parts of central Europe. Resembles large bumble-bee. Has black-brown wings with violet sheen. Female bores vertical shafts up to 30 cm deep in old wood, dividing them into chambers with partitions made of wood debris and saliva. Usually 12 chambers in each of which bee places stock of food and lays one egg.

2 Leaf-cutter Bee *Megachile centuncularis*. Distributed over warm parts of Europe. Length 10—12 mm. Female gnaws tunnels in old wood, lines them with fragments of leaves cut from bushes, chiefly dog-roses and garden roses. Places first cell on floor of tunnel, fills it with pollen, lays egg and closes cell with leaf. 'Cylinder' with 8—10 cells formed in tunnel.

3 Potter Bee *Anthidium manicatum*. Lives in warmer parts of Europe. With partly hairless, yellow-striped abdomen resembles wasp. Male has 'notched' abdomen and is larger than female. Lines nest with plant fluff.

4 Horned Bee *Eucera longicornis*. Lives in southern Europe and warm parts of central Europe. Length 10—12 mm. Locally abundant. Male has extremely long antennae. Appears in spring on sunny slopes and hillsides. Favours plants with composite flowers. Has very long mouth parts and can suck nectar from deep flowers.

5 Black Burrowing Bee *Andrena carbonaria*. Abundant all over Europe except for extreme north. Solitary bee. Length 10—12 mm. Appears early in spring. Likes dandelions. Digs nest in ground, often in colonies. Long, slanting passages branch off into several side-chambers, each containing pollen and one egg.

6 Hairy-legged Mining Bee *Dasypoda hirtipes*. Fairly common in central Europe. Collects so much pollen on long hairs on hindlimbs that appears to be wearing trousers. Builds underground nest like preceding species.

7 Mourner Bee or **Armed Melecta** *Melecta armata*. Abundant in central Europe. Length 10—12 mm. Appears early in spring. Female stays near burrowing bees, enters their nests and lays egg before occupant can close chamber. Hatched larva consumes food stocks and burrowing bee larva starves to death.

1

2

3

8 Digger Bumble-bee *Bombus terrestris.* Very common all over Europe. After hibernating female lays foundations of nest in mouse-holes, etc, up to 1.5 m underground. Lines nest with leaves, moss, etc., found in hole. Builds waxy chambers and fills them with pollen and nectar. Larvae also receive additional food. Up to 150 workers and over 100 young females hatch in 20 days. Workers die in autumn, males, old and young females go into hiding and hibernate.

9 Rock Bumble-bee *Bombus lapidarius.* Widely distributed in central Europe. Black with red-tipped abdomen. Nests underground, in piles of stones, rock crevices, etc. Not more than 300 individuals in nest.

10 Honeybee *Apis mellifica.* Universal insect, probably originally from India. Forms permanent community, always with one female — queen. In summer large number of males (drones) and up to 70,000 workers. Only queen lays eggs, in cells in waxy comb. Three types of cells, for workers, males and females. Queen lays up to 1,000 eggs daily in summer — total for one season up to 80,000. If queen is lost, workers rear new one. Development rapid, for workers 20 days. Queen lives 3—4 years. Swarm once or several times a year, after queen has prepared eggs for new queens. Old queen leaves hive and, accompanied by some workers, forms new community.

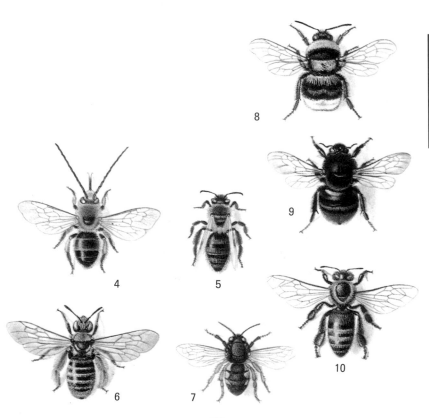

8

9

4

5

6

7

10

Order: **Beetles**—Coleoptera

Family: **Tiger Beetles**—Cicindelidae

1 *Cicindela campestris.* Locally abundant in Europe. Length 12—16 mm. Very large, striking mandibles. Appears from April to June. Frequents sunny, sandy places, paths, deserted quarries, etc. Runs about swiftly looking for prey, spots it reliably at distance of up to 15 cm. Catches mainly insect larvae, spiders and worms. If disturbed, immediately flies away but does not fly in cold weather. Larvae live in burrows up to 2 m deep in clay or sandy soil. Larva has strongly sclerotized head. Waits at entrance to hole for prey (chiefly various insects), seizes it and devours it in burrow. Holds itself fast in passage by means of boss on abdomen. Development of larva takes 2—3 years. Pupates in July, beetles are hatched 4 weeks later and reproduce further following spring.

2 *Cicindela hybrida.* Lives mainly in forested regions. Length 12—14 mm. Beetles found in May and June on sandy forest paths and moors. Biology similar to that of preceding species.

3 *Cicindela silvatica.* Common in places. Length 14—16 mm. Appears in June on forest paths, in clearings, etc., mainly in pine-woods. Biology as for *Cicindela campestris.*

Family: **Ground Beetles**—Carabidae

4 *Carabus hortensis.* Locally abundant in central Europe. Length 24—30 mm. Found in forests and gardens, on bushy slopes, etc. Nocturnal predator. Catches insects, insect larvae, worms and small molluscs. Hides during day behind bark, under stones, etc. Like all ground beetles likes damp environment. In dry, waterless places dies in a few days. Long-bodied, large-jawed larvae also predacious. Catches other insect larvae, worms, etc.

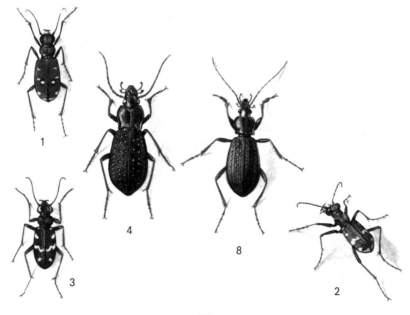

1

4

8

3

2

5 Goldsmith *Carabus auratus.* Abundant in parts of central Europe, particularly Germany, but absent east of Oder. Length 22—26 mm. Seen mainly in May and June, in meadows, fields and gardens. Prefers clayey soil. Also found at higher altitudes. Often hunts in daytime. Eats worms, molluscs and soft parts of insects. Attacks cockchafers when laying eggs. All members of *Carabus* genus spray chewed parts of prey with gastric juice which quickly decomposes connective tissue and organs, making them easy to imbibe. Several beetles may attack a large worm. In spring and summer female lays single eggs in holes in ground — total about 50. Larvae, hatched in 8—10 days, are very predacious. Pupate in chamber in ground. Newly emerged beetles hibernate from end of August, majority of adult beetles die. Development from egg to young beetle takes 78 days.

6 *Carabus coriaceus.* Largest central-European ground beetle. Length up to 40 mm. Occurs in forests mainly in July and August. Nocturnal insect. Hides during day under stones, fallen trees, etc. In rainy weather crawls on to paths. Beetle and larva are both predacious.

7 Violet Ground Beetle *Carabus violaceus.* Very common in central Europe. Length 25—35 mm. Appears mainly in June and July near human dwellings, often found in sheds, cellars, etc. If handled ejects acrid fluid.

8 *Carabus cancellatus.* Very common everywhere in central Europe. Length 17—26 mm. Appears chiefly in May in woods, fields and gardens. Runs very quickly, 1 metre in 5—7 sec. Hides during day under stones, behind bark, etc. Very useful, destroys Colorado Beetles. One specimen devours 9 Colorado Beetle larvae daily, i.e. more than its own weight. Average time of development from egg to beetle takes 71 days under artificial breeding conditions.

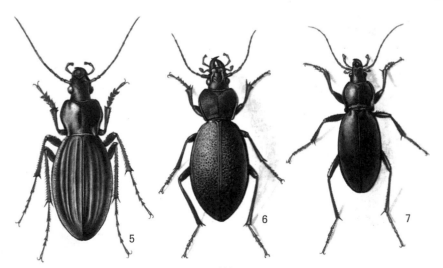

5

6

7

Family: **Ground Beetles**—Carabidae

1 Searcher or **Caterpillar Hunter** *Calosoma sycophanta*. Distributed over practically whole of Europe. Length 24—30 mm. Very handsome beetle. Predacious. Climbs trees in search of prey, chiefly caterpillars. Female after hibernating lays 100—600 eggs. Larvae, hatched in 3—10 days, are likewise highly predacious. In 14 days one beetle (and also one larva) consumes about 40 large caterpillars. In June larva pupates in ground. Adult beetle hatched in September, does not emerge into open until following year in May. Early in July beetles leave trees and again burrow up to depth of 50 cm in ground and hibernate. Beetle lives 2—3 years. Inhabits both deciduous and conifer woods at low and high altitudes.

2 Lesser Searcher *Calosoma inquisitor*. Found everywhere in central Europe. Length 15 to 18 mm. Lives primarily in oak-woods in lowlands. In years with a high incidence of caterpillars appears in great numbers already at end of April or beginning of May. Frequents tree tops, catches mainly caterpillars of geometers and other harmful moths. Retires to burrow in ground at beginning of July and hibernates. Larvae likewise predacious.

3 Bombardier Beetle *Brachynus crepitans*. Common in central Europe. Length 6—9 mm. Several individuals always live in company under stones in warm, sunny spots. When in danger, discharges from anal gland volatile fluid which turns to blue smoke with audible bang. Such 'salvoes' reliably frighten small foes away. The secretion burns and slightly resembles nitric acid.

4 *Pterostichus vulgaris*. Very widely distributed. Length 14—20 mm. Hides during day under flat stones etc. in damp, shady places. Runs quickly. Abundant everywhere, especially in central Europe.

5 *Zabrus gibbus*. Very common everywhere in central Europe. Length 14—16 mm. Adult beetles cling to cereal plants and devour grains. Larvae nibble young spring shoots or grass. In daytime both larvae and beetles hide in holes dug in ground.

Family: **Water Beetles**—Dytiscidae

6 Tiger Water Beetle *Dytiscus marginalis.* Common all over Europe. Length 30—35 mm. Male has widened tarsi. Inhabits ponds and pools etc. with abundant aquatic vegetation. Female makes slits in plant stems and into each pushes one egg. Larva has three-sided head with powerful, hooked mandibles, used for sucking tadpoles, small fish, etc. Beetles also predacious. Larva pupates beside water. Beetles fly in evening.

7 *Acilius sulcatus.* Distributed over whole of Europe. Length about 18 mm. Inhabits stagnant water with at least a little vegetation. Flies at night and sometimes visits man-made pools. Does damage to fish roes. Larvae, likewise predacious, lie in wait for prey among tangled aquatic plants.

Family: **Whirligig Beetles**—Gyrinidae

8 Common Whirligig Beetle *Gyrinus natator.* Common in places. Length 5—7 mm. Small but conspicuous for its gyrating movements on surface of still water. Dives like lightning when in danger. Predacious, catches small insects. Flies well. Larvae have hollow, hooked mandibles. Beetles usually gregarious.

Family: **Water Scavenger Beetles**—Hydrophilidae

9 Great Black Water Beetle *Hydrous piceus.* Locally common in central Europe. Length 35—45 mm. Inhabits stagnant water with plenty of vegetation. Beetle partly vegetarian but eats also fish roes. Female lays eggs in special capsule made of secretory substance and containing about 50 eggs. Larvae, hatched in 16 days, are predacious.

7

8

6   ♂

♀

9

303

Family: **Rover Beetles**—Staphylinidae

1 *Staphylinus caesareus.* Widely distributed all over central Europe. Length 15—20 mm. Summer insect. Adult beetles found on putrefying flesh, rotting matter, etc. Beetles and larvae live on decaying matter but also attack insects, worms and molluscs. Larvae resemble adult beetles but have no wings or wing sheaths.

2 *Oxyporus rufus.* Distributed all over central Europe. Length 7—11 mm. Abounds in different mushrooms starting to decompose. Larvae also live in large numbers in mushrooms. One of the causes of 'wormy' mushrooms.

Family: **Sexton and Carrion Beetles**—Silphidae

3 Common Sexton or **Gravedigger Beetle** *Necrophorus vespillo.* Common European beetle. Length 12—22 mm. In evening and at night beetles look for animal carcass and scrape away earth under body until animal is buried. Female then lays eggs on body and larvae live on putrefying flesh. Larvae pupate in chamber in ground. Beetles often infested by mites of *Gamasus* genus.

4 German Gravedigger Beetle *Necrophorus germanicus.* Locally and sporadically found in Europe. Length 20—30 mm. Found under carcasses of larger animals, e.g. hares, rabbits, etc. Very retiring. Flies only at night. One of the largest but rarest members of this family.

5 Black Carrion Beetle *Phosphuga atrata.* Widespread in central Europe. Length 12 to 16 mm. Wing sheaths have three longitudinal ridges. Found from May under stones, paper,

1

2

3

4

etc., in fields and on paths. Often crawls in open. Lives on dead snails and worms but sometimes attacks even live ones. In danger releases malodorous substance.

6 Four-spot Carrion Beetle *Xylodrepa quadripunctata.* Very common in central Europe. Length 12—14 mm. Inhabits oak-woods. Appears in spring. Lives on trees, attacks and eats caterpillars. Beetles disappear in June and are replaced by flat, predacious, caterpillar-eating larvae. At end of summer larvae pupate in ground. Beetles hatch in autumn, hibernate in ground and emerge following spring.

Family: **Steel** or **Hister Beetles**—Histeridae

7 Steel Beetle *Hister unicolor.* Distributed all over central Europe. Length 7—9 mm. Very hard body. Beetles frequently live in cow dung, horse manure, etc. Catch and eat small insects. Many other species in Europe, some with black, red-spotted wing sheaths.

Family: **Carpet Beetles**—Dermestidae

8 Larder Beetle *Dermestes lardarius.* Carried with furs all over world. Length 6—9 mm. Found in stores, households and open country. Larva's back thickly covered with long hairs. In open larvae live on remnants of skin of dead animals, on feathers, etc. Also found in collections of hides, stuffed birds, etc. Development often takes only 6 weeks. Beetles and larvae frequently found on food remnants, e.g. cheese, meat, etc.

9 Tallow Beetle *Anthrenus museorum.* Distributed all over Europe. Length 2—3 mm. Spherical body. Common pest in natural history collections. Damage done by both beetle and larva. Larvae 5 mm long and hairy. Beetles often seen in flowers.

10 Carpet Beetle *Attagenus pellio.* Occurs everywhere. Length 4—7 mm. Very dangerous to furs, stuffed animals, carpets, upholstery, etc. Often found trying to get out of window. Hairy larva about 5 mm long. Adults often seen also on flowers. In the illustration the rare species *A. punctatus* is shown.

5

6

7

8

9

10

Family: **Stag Beetles**—Lucanidae

1 Common Stag Beetle *Lucanus cervus*. Inhabits whole of central Europe, from south of northern Europe as far west as Portugal. Length of male 37—75 mm, female 30—45 mm. Inhabits oak-woods and mixed forests. Female lays eggs in rotting oak stumps and trunks. Blind larvae develop 3—5 years and attain length of up to 10 cm. Future beetle's sex already discernible in pupa. Beetles hatch in autumn but do not leave hiding place until spring. By day frequent tree trunks with flowing sap. Fly in evening.

2 Balkan Stag Beetle *Dorcus parallelopipedus*. Distributed over large part of Europe. Length 20—32 mm. Abundant in places with sufficient old wood for development of larvae. Beetles rest on branches during day, fly only in late afternoon and evening. Appear at end of April and are still found in September. Larvae develop in rotting wood.

Family: **Chafers**—Scarabaeidae

3 Horned Dung Beetle *Copris lunaris*. Found in warmer parts of central Europe. Length 15—23 mm. Male has pointed horn on head. Mainly frequents cow dung. Makes chamber below dung from which female prepares food stocks for larvae.

4 Dung Beetle *Aphodius fimetarius*. Widely distributed over whole of Europe, Asia and North America. Length 5—8 mm. Female lays eggs in cow or horse dung which provides food for larvae. Some individuals hibernate and can often already be seen on sunny days at beginning of March.

1

5 Great Dor Beetle *Geotrupes stercorosus*. Inhabits whole of Europe. Length 12—19 mm. Exclusively forest-dweller, usually found on carcasses, mushrooms, etc. In May and June digs
vertical shaft up to 60 cm deep, with side-arms,
below excreta. Female fills passages with dung
and lays eggs. Larvae live on dung, hibernate
and do not pupate until following year.

6 Common Cockchafer or **May-bug** *Melolontha
melolontha*. Native of Europe. Length 20 to
30 mm. From May to June female lays 3
clutches of 15—30 eggs in ground. Larvae
(grubs) develop 2—3 years and then pupate.
Hatched beetle spends winter in ground and
emerges following spring. Grubs eat small
roots. Beetles nibble leaves of trees. Fly in evening. Usually swarm in middle of June. Incidence
of cockchafers correlated to whether population development takes 3 or 4 years.

7 June-bug *Rhizotrogus solstitialis*. Distributed
all over Europe. Length 14—18 mm. Very abundant. Flies after dusk, in some years in large numbers. Appears from June to beginning of August. Female lays eggs in July, in soft soil. Larvae, hatched about one month later, eat grass
and cereal roots, etc. Pupate in spring of third
year. Adults eat leaves of fruit trees. Important
pest.

8 Walker *Polyphylla fullo*. Occurs in central Europe and southern England. Length 25 to 36 mm.
Inhabits sandy lowlands. Female lays 25—40
eggs in sandy soil from June to August. Larvae
eat grass roots. Pupate after 3 years. Three
weeks later, in June, adult beetles fly out after
dusk. Larvae sometimes hibernate for fourth
year and beetles do not appear until fifth.
Larvae sometimes do damage to vines.

9 Garden Chafer *Phyllopertha horticola*. Inhabits most of Europe and extends east as far as
Mongolia. Length 8.5—11 mm. Appears from
May to July, often in immense numbers. Frequents gardens, orchards, margins of woods,
etc. Beetles nibble flowers. Female lays eggs in
ground. Larvae, hatched in 2 weeks, gnaw roots.
Development takes 2—3 years.

Family: **Chafers**—Scarabaeidae

1 European Rhinoceros Beetle *Oryctes nasicornis.* Inhabits practically whole of Europe. Length 25—40 mm. Very variable over vast area of distribution. Larvae develop in rotting stumps and trunks of deciduous trees, mainly oaks and beeches, but also in old compost heaps. Larvae very fat, with dilated abdomen, very hard, large head and huge mandibles. Development of larva takes several years according to conditions. Before pupating larva forms cocoon of soil and sawdust in which mature beetle also remains for up to 2 months. Adult beetle appears from June to August. Nocturnal insect.

2 Goldsmith Beetle *Cetonia aurata.* Inhabits most of Europe. Length 14—20 mm. Beetles found from middle of May well into summer on flowering dog-roses, etc. Female lays eggs in rotting tree stumps, etc. and occasionally in ant-hills. Development usually takes one year. Mature larva forms cocoon of sawdust and soil, stuck together with special secretion. Larvae moult twice and attain length of 4—5 cm.

3 Hermit Beetle *Osmoderma eremita.* Inhabits practically all Europe but occurs only locally. Not very abundant. Length 24—30 mm. Beetles appear from end of May to July. Fly well. Female lays eggs in hollows in old deciduous trees, e.g. limes, beeches, oaks. Larvae develop several years (not less than 3) and grow to length of up to 10 cm. Before pupating larva forms sawdust cocoon. Beetle gives off curious odour.

4 *Trichius fasciatus.* Occurs over practically whole of Europe. Length 9—12 mm. Wing case designs very variable. Beetles frequent flowers and flowering bushes on warm, sunny days in summer. Female lays eggs in rotting wood of deciduous trees, especially beeches. Larvae develop 2 years. Particularly abundant in wooded uplands.

Family: **Metallic** or **Flat-headed Wood-borers**—Buprestidae

5 Pine-borer *Chalcophora mariana.* Found in central Europe, only in warm places. Length 25—30 mm. Copper-coloured back, burnished gold underside. Inhabits pine-woods. Fond of warmth like all members of this family. Beetles appear during hottest hours of sunny days. Found on tree trunks. Larvae develop in pine tree stumps and dry trunks. Bore characteristic flat winding tunnels. Flat larva has segmented body and wide head. Does not do serious damage.

6 Lime-borer *Poecilonota rutilans.* Occurs in warm places in central Europe. Abundant in some regions. Length 10—14 mm. Shows jewel-like metallic-blue back when flying. Appears in June and July in lime tree avenues or on limes on outskirts of forests. Female lays eggs in cracks in bark on sunny side of lime trunk. Larvae, which develop 2 years, devour wood. Repeated attacks of lime-borers cause tree to wither. Dangerous pest in large numbers.

7 Common Wood-borer *Buprestis rustica.* Fairly abundant in parts of central Europe. Length 13—18 mm. Tips of wing sheaths straight-edged. Inhabits conifer woods. Larvae live behind bark or in wood of stumps and freshly felled trees, particularly spruces. Development takes 2 years.

8 Metallic Wood-borer *Anthaxia nitidula.* Inhabits warm places in central Europe. Length 5—7 mm. Beetle appears in June and July. Locally abundant, found on roses, dandelions, oxeyes, etc. Larvae live on blackthorns.

9 Two-spot Wood-borer *Agrilus biguttatus.* Widely distributed over central Europe. Length 12 mm. Tip of wing sheaths rounded. Appears on sunny days at end of May on tree stumps and flowers. Larvae live in oak stumps.

1   2   3   4

Family: **Click Beetles**—Elateridae

1 Blood-red Click Beetle *Elater sanguineus.* Occurs over practically whole of Europe. Length 13—18 mm. Inhabits foothill forests. Often appears by end of March. Larvae live behind bark or in pine stumps, often gregariously. Larva measures up to 2 cm.

2 Grey Click Beetle *Adelocera murina.* Distributed all over Europe. Length 11—17 mm. Found at both low and high altitudes. Lives in meadows, fields, clearings and gardens. Larva is field and forest pest, gnaws roots and other parts of all crops and young trees. Also carnivorous. Adult beetle appears from spring to autumn and nibbles beech and oak buds. Often found on ears of corn.

3 Wheat Wire-worm *Agriotes lineatus.* Lives in whole palearctic region. Length 8—9 mm. Found at both low and high altitudes. Beetles appear in meadows in May and June. Larvae eat any plants, do damage to tree nurseries and in south to vineyards, etc. Pupate in soil. Development takes 3—4 years.

Family: **Leather-winged Beetles**—Cantharidae

4 Soldier Beetle *Cantharis fusca.* Widely distributed in Europe. Length 12 mm. Appears from spring to summer on plants, bushes and ground. Catches and eats small insects, occasionally eats also young shoots. Hairy larvae have strong mandibles and are predacious. Live under leaves, etc., look for insects and small molluscs. Larvae hibernate in ground but on sunny days often found in snow. Pupate in early spring after hibernating.

5 *Phausis splendidula.* Very common all over central Europe. Length 9—11 mm. Mainly inhabits outskirts of damp deciduous woods. Nocturnal insect. Males fly in large numbers on warm evenings at end of June and in July. Females wingless, with vestigial wing case, crawl on ground. Has brightly luminescent light organ on underside of abdomen. Females and carnivorous larvae also luminescent. Adult beetle lives only briefly. Light organ probably used to attract partner.

7

8

9

6

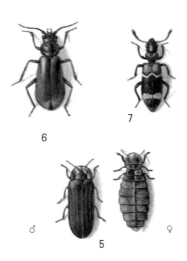

♂   ♀

5

6 *Malachius aeneus.* Very common everywhere in central Europe. Length 7—8 mm. Soft wing case. Appears in spring on almost all flowers. Larva frequents tunnels of bark beetles and other wood beetles.

Family: **Chequered Beetles**—Cleridae

7 Ant Beetle *Thanasimus formicarius.* Abundant all over central Europe. Length 7—10 mm. Female lays up to 30 eggs in groups of 2—4 behind bark scales. Larvae crawl into tunnels of bark beetles and other wood beetles and attack their larvae. Larva seizes prey in first two pairs of legs, turns it on to back, bites through its body at base of abdomen and devours it from within. Larva very active. Both larva and adult beetle can hibernate.

8 Bee-eating Beetle *Trichodes apiarius.* Lives in warm places in central Europe. Length 9—15 mm. Adult beetle frequents flowers and eats other insects. Seen from May to July. Larvae mainly develop in nests of solitary bees and eat their larvae or pupae.

Family: **Death Watch Beetles**—Anobiidae

9 Death Watch *Anobium pertinax.* Common European beetle. Length 5—7 mm. Lives in wood or in houses in old furniture where it bores tunnels. Bangs head on walls of tunnel to attract members of opposite sex. Knocking superstitiously supposed to portend death. Female lays eggs in opening of tunnel. If repeatedly attacked, old furniture may fall to pieces. Beetle 'plays possum' if handled.

3

4

2

1

Family: **Blister** or **Oil Beetles**—Meloidae

3 Oil Beetle or **May-worm** *Meloe proscarabaeus.* Widely distributed. Length 12—35 mm. Female has large abdomen. Wingless with short wing sheaths. Appears in grass early in spring. Female lays eggs in small pits. Hatched larvae grasp different bees, including honeybees, with claw-like legs and are carried to their nests, get into cells and devour host's egg and food stores. After complicated metamorphosis — firstly pseudopupa, then again larva — they pupate.

4 Spanish Fly *Lytta vesicatoria.* Lives in southern Europe and warmer parts of central Europe. Length 11—22 mm. Winged beetles appear en masse in June, mainly on ash trees. Eat leaves. Beetle produces potent poison, cantharidin. Female lays groups of 40—50 eggs in ground. Larvae attach themselves to bodies of solitary bees of *Osmia* genus and develop in similar way as preceding species.

Family: **Snout Beetles** or **Weevils**—Curculionidae

Family: **Darkling** or **Pineate Beetles**—Tenebrionidae

1 Cellar or **Churchyard Beetle** *Blaps mortisaga.* Widely distributed in central Europe. Length 22—28 mm. Appears from April to autumn. Often lives in houses. Hides during day under floor-boards, in cellars, etc., where larvae also live. Does no damage.

2 Meal-worm *Tenebrio molitor.* Today very common everywhere. Bred artificially. Larvae used to feed birds and lizards. Length 14—17 mm. Beetle often lives in houses, refuse, henhouses and dove-cotes. Larvae also eat flesh, e.g. meat left on bones, dead bodies of small birds and mammals etc., otherwise found in meal stores, etc.

5 Pine Weevil *Hylobius abietis.* Abundant on all conifers. Length 8—14 mm. Beetle appears from May to September. Female lays 50—100 eggs in roots, bark of fresh pine, fir and larch stumps. Larvae eat bast and sap-wood. Before pupating form 'cradle'. Beetle lives several years.

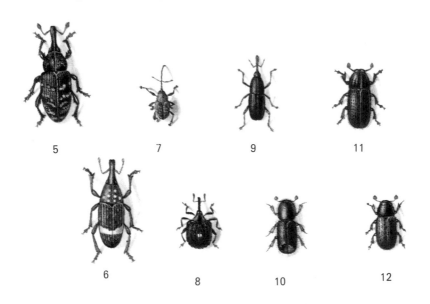

5   7   9   11

6   8   10   12

6 White Pine Beetle *Pissodes piceae.* Locally common in central Europe. Length 7—12 mm. Appears on firs and is very serious pest. Sometimes multiplies to such a degree that tree is attacked from roots to crown. Female lays eggs on bark.

7 Nut Weevil *Curculio nucum.* Common in central Europe. Length 7—8 mm. Characterized by very long 'snout'. Appears from May to July. Female lays eggs in holes she has made with her 'snout' in young nuts. Larvae eat kernels.

8 *Cionus scrophulariae.* Fairly abundant. Length 4—6 mm. Can fold cylindrical 'snout' on underside of thorax. Lives gregariously on fig-wort and mullein. Legless larvae, wrapped in slimy envelope, nibble leaves and perianths. On pupation mucus hardens and protects pupa.

9 Granary Weevil *Calandra granaria.* Original home probably in southern Asia. Carried to all parts of world. Most dreaded grain pest. Length 3—4 mm. Beetle unable to fly and is spread only by carrying. Lives in badly ventilated granaries. Female lays eggs on grains of wheat, rye, etc.

Family: **Bark Beetles**—Scolytidae

10 *Ips typographus.* Inhabits cooler parts of Europe. Length about 4 mm. Dreaded spruce pest. Larvae devour tunnels perpendicular to maternal shaft.

11 *Dendroctonus micans.* Distributed all over central Europe. Length 6—9 mm. Inhabits spruce woods. Larvae form common widening tunnel. Beetles emerge at end of July. Attacks weakened trees.

12 *Myelophilus piniperda.* Widely distributed in Europe. Length 3.5—5 mm. Inhabits large pinewoods. Attacks mainly trunks of felled trees.

Family: **Longicorn Beetles**—Cerambycidae

1 *Prionus coriarius.* Inhabits whole of Europe, extends even to North Africa, Asia Minor and western Siberia. Length 19—45 mm. Male has saw-like antennae with 12 joints, female antennae with smaller teeth and 11 joints. Inhabits old deciduous, mixed and conifer woods. Very abundant in places. Larva develops in rotting trunks and oak, beech, fir, pine stumps, etc., often also in roots. Beetles swarm in July and August, often in daytime.

2 *Ergates faber.* Only locally found in Europe. Length 23—60 mm. Male's antennae longer than body, female's much shorter. Favours old pinewoods. Female lays over 300 single eggs usually on rotting wood which provides firm hold. Larvae often develop in old pine stumps, less often in spruce stumps. Occasionally attacks beams in wooden constructions combined with bricks, which keep wood damp. Also attacks telegraph poles, wooden fences, etc. Larvae measure up to 6.5 cm. Development takes several years. Beetles swarm at night from July to September. Adult beetle lives 3 weeks.

3 *Spondylis buprestoides.* Lives all over Europe and extends as far as Japan. Very plentiful in places. Length 12—22 mm. Larvae develop in old pine and occasionally spruce stumps. Beetles fly after dusk from June to September. Hide during day under logs, etc.

4, 5 *Cerambyx cerdo.* Inhabits Europe. Length 24—53 mm. Male's antennae much longer than body, female's same length as body or slightly shorter. Larvae develop mainly in oaks, occasionally in chestnuts, sycamores, beeches or ash trees. Female lays eggs usually in twos or threes in cracks in bark, preferably in old standing oaks. Larvae, hatched in 12—14 days, start to gnaw bark and hibernate there first year. In spring continue to eat bark and in June—July reach sap-wood and bast where they cause exudation visible as dark patch on trunk. After second hibernation larva bores to depth of 15—50 cm in wood and forms chamber in which it pupates. Adult beetle emerges in same year after 5—6 weeks but does not leave chamber until following year. In living wood beetle's development takes 3 years, in felled trees up to 5 years. Small infestation does no damage but large-scale repeated infestation can cause even large trees to die, while larvae's tunnels depreciate wood. This species has been known to destroy whole oak avenues but is growing steadily rarer because of lack of old oaks. Beetles swarm in June and July, during evening and at night. One of the largest and handsomest European beetles. Can successfully be bred from larvae in captivity.

1

2

314

6 Musk Beetle *Aromia moschata*. Widely distributed in Europe, extends to western Siberia. Length 13—34 mm. Adult beetle found mainly on willows but also on flowers of tall plants. Chiefly attacks old willows and in case of large-scale repeated invasion larvae completely destroy tree in few years. Musk beetle can also develop in poplars or alders. Adult beetle secretes strongly smelling substance. Swarm from June to August. Very beautifully coloured species.

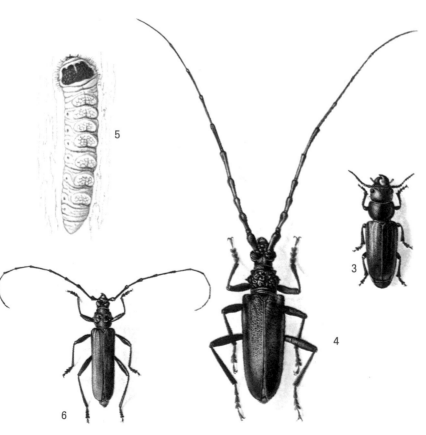

5

3

4

6

Family: **Longicorn Beetles**—Cerambycidae

1 *Necydalis major.* Distributed over Europe, extends up to Siberia. Length 21—32 mm. Incidence localized but abundant, especially in low-lying country. Very short wing sheaths. Larva develops in deciduous trees (e.g. poplars, limes, birches), fruit-trees and conifers (e.g. firs). Beetles fly in June and July and often sit on tree trunks or stacks of logs.

2 *Rosalia alpina.* Inhabits southern and central Europe, extends north up to south of Sweden. Length 15—38 mm. Colouring very variable. Incidence diminishing because of decreasing number of beeches but still quite abundant in places. Larvae develop in old beeches, occasionally in sycamores. Inhabits mountains above altitude of 600 m, found chiefly on warm slopes. Flies in sunny weather from June to beginning

of September. Does practically no damage. Numerous enemies, including woodpeckers, lizards, but especially beetle-collectors attracted by its striking colouring.

3 *Lamia textor.* Abundant in Europe and whole of Asia as far as Japan. Length 15—30 mm. Larvae develop in willows and aspens, mainly in old wood, also in roots. Unimportant pest. In summer adult beetles sit motionless on willow branches and are active only in evening.

4 *Callidium aeneum.* Lives in southern, central and northern Europe, extends east up to Siberia. Length 9—15 mm. Principally mountain-dweller but also often found in lowlands. Very rare in some places. Larvae develop in deciduous trees and conifers, chiefly oaks, beeches and pines. Eat surface of wood. Adult beetles appear from end of May to July.

1

2

3

5 *Callidium violaceum.* Inhabits Europe and whole of Asia as far as Japan. Length 8—16 mm. Abundant everywhere in central Europe, especially in conifer woods both at low and high altitudes. Larva lives in dry conifer woods, rarely in beeches, sycamores and fruit-trees. Eats wood from surface, after pupating bores deeper in wood. Female also lays eggs on felled trees, larvae develop even after wood has been processed and can damage rafters if wood is not divested of bark. Adult beetles appear from May to August.

6 *Leptura rubra.* Widely distributed all over Europe. Length 10—19 mm. Somewhat variable colouring, males usually yellowish, females reddish. Larvae live in spruce and pine stumps or trunks, occasionally found on telegraph poles. Adult beetle appears from June to September on flowering plants and bushes. Occurs at both low and high altitudes.

7 *Rhagium bifasciatum.* Distributed over whole of Europe. Length 12—22 mm. Larva develops in wood of old oaks and conifers. Most abundant on pines, spruces and oaks. Found high up in mountains. Adult beetles sit on flowers and flowering bushes, also on tree trunks. Appear from May to August. Relatively common everywhere in central Europe.

8 *Rhagium inquisitor.* Widely distributed in Europe. Occurs at both high and low altitudes. Length 10—21 mm. Very often seen in dwellings, brought on wood from forest. Larva lives behind bark of pines, spruces and firs. Beetles hatch in autumn but hibernate and appear from following April to beginning of September. Often encountered on stacks of logs, also on flowers and bushes.

6

7

4

5

8

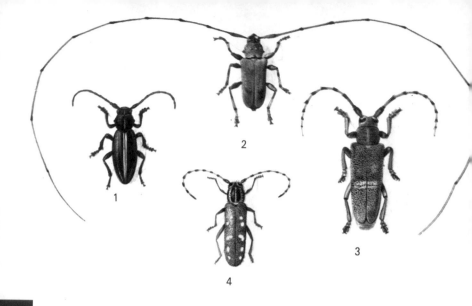

1

2

4

3

Family: **Longicorn Beetles**—Cerambycidae

1 *Dorcadion pedestre.* Occurs in eastern part of central Europe up to Balkans. Mainly inhabits lowlands but occasionally found at higher altitudes. Length 11—17 mm. Very abundant in spring from April to June. Unlike all other longicorn beetles larva develops underground, on grass roots. In steppe country beetles often found in large numbers on grasses.

2 *Acanthocinus aedilis.* Inhabits Europe and Asia. In central Europe common in pine-woods. Length 12—20 mm. Male has extremely long antennae. Larva develops in pines but is most often found in stumps in which it gnaws winding tunnels behind bark. Less frequently found on felled trees or standing trees weakened by other pests. Pupates in bark. Two generations a year — in March and August. Adult beetle appears from March to September. Beetle also sometimes develops in processed wood, e.g. furniture.

3 *Saperda carcharias.* Extends from Europe up to Siberia. Length 20—30 mm. Larvae develop in poplars or aspens and often do considerable damage. Female lays eggs in bark, preferably of young trees. Larvae bore into wood and form oval tunnels. Development takes 2 years. Beetles fly on warm evenings in June and July, nibble leaves or young bark of twigs. Bite rounded holes in leaves. In large numbers do great damage and can destroy young trees.

4 *Saperda populnea.* Inhabits Europe, North America and Africa. Length 9—15 mm. Abundant everywhere in central Europe. Female lays eggs on shoots or in hole bitten in bark, causing swellings on trunk. Larvae develop in aspens, also in poplars and sallows. Larva first of all lives on swelling and then bores into wood. Pupates at end of tunnel about 5 cm long. Beetles fly from end of May to middle of July. In places does serious damage to young cultures.

5 *Oberea oculata.* Very common in Europe at both low and high altitudes. Length 15 to 21 mm. Larvae found in willows and sallows. Female lays eggs singly in holes bitten in twigs. Larva gnaws tunnel up to 30 cm long. Development takes one year. Hatched beetles bite way out through round opening. Swarm in June and July but still encountered at beginning of September. Dozens of beetles often found sitting on willow twigs making grating sounds.

6 *Stenopterus rufus.* Abundant in southern and central Europe. Length 8—16 mm. Found in warm places. Larvae develop in deciduous trees, most frequently oaks. Adult beetles often encountered on flowers from May to August.

7 *Pachyta quadrimaculata.* Distributed over Europe and Asia as far as Mongolia. In central Europe very common in mountainous regions but rare in lowlands. Length 11—20 mm. Strong, robust body. Larvae develop in wood of spruces but often also in other conifers. Adult beetles appear on various flowers from June to August.

8 *Toxotus cursor.* Distributed over Europe and western Asia. In central Europe common in mountains and foothills. Length 25—32 mm. Several races are known, somewhat variable. Larvae develop in spruce, pine and fir stumps. Adult beetles often sit on stacked logs in forest or frequent forest plants in clearings etc. Beetles found from May to August.

5

6

7

8

1

3 Poplar Leaf Beetle *Melasoma populi.* Inhabits whole of Europe. Length 6—12 mm. Frequents mainly poplars but also willows. Adult beetles and larvae nibble leaves often leaving only skeleton. If in danger, larvae emit pungent fluid from special warts.

4 Colorado Potato Beetle *Leptinotarsa decemlineata.* Originally from Mexico, has been carried to all parts of Europe. Female hibernates deep in soil, in spring gnaws germinating potatoes. Lays piles of up to 90 eggs on leaves of potato plants. Larvae gnaw leaves. After 20 days larvae pupate in ground, beetle emerges after 2—3 weeks and in 10 more days can again lay eggs. One female lays up to 700 eggs so that third generation can number 80 million. This prolific beetle has caused great damage in many parts of Europe.

5 Alder Leaf Beetle *Agelastica alni.* Very common in central Europe. Length 5—6 mm. Occurs in large numbers. Fertilized female has large abdomen and lays groups of 50 eggs on underside of alder leaves in May and June — total up to 900. Larvae eat leaves and pupate in ground. Beetles emerge in August, eat leaves and hibernate in foliage.

Family: **Leaf Beetles**—Chrysomelidae

1 *Donacia crassipes.* In central Europe common in places with water-lilies. Length 9—11 mm. Beetles sit on floating water-lily leaves. Female bites holes in leaves and through it lays eggs on underside. Larvae migrate further into depth and make slits in plant's air passages to obtain oxygen. Pupate under water in cocoon, likewise attached to air canal. In summer beetles also sit on other plants.

2 *Clytra quadripunctata.* Very abundant in central Europe. Length 8—11 mm. Adult beetles found in large numbers on willows, alders and limes. Larvae develop in anthills where they form bag-like covering from own excreta in which they hide and later pupate.

6 *Phyllotreta nemorum.* Widely distributed in central Europe. Minute, only 2 mm long. Gnaws holes in leaves of cruciferous plants. Beetles gregarious. If approached, jump in all directions by means of strong last pair of legs. Larvae have developed legs and warty body. Devour inner portions of leaves often leaving only skeleton, so that plant withers. Most abundant in dry summers.

7 *Cassida viridis.* Widespread in central Europe. Length 7—10 mm. Head covered by plate. Occurs chiefly on labiate plants. Larva flattened with spiny sides and abdominal process on which it carries excreta remnants to disguise itself.

Family: **Ladybirds**—Coccinellidae

8 Seven-spot Ladybird *Coccinella septempunctata.* Very common. Length 5—8 mm. Found in most diverse places. Staple diet plant-lice. Female lays total of up to 700 eggs in piles, near plant-lice. Larvae also eat aphids.

9 Two-spot Ladybird *Adalia bipunctata.* Very common in central Europe. Length 4—6 mm. In April and May female lays groups of 6—20 yellowish eggs near plant-lice. Larvae live on plant-lice or scale-insects. One larva consumes 15 aphids daily. Larva pupates after 20—35 days. Most of hatched beetles hibernate. Adult ladybird consumes 10 plant-lice daily.

10 Eyed Ladybird *Anatis ocellata.* Widely distributed in central Europe. Length 8—9 mm. Usually found in large numbers on conifers. In July female lays eggs on underside of needles and on bark. Larvae mainly eat eggs and larvae of Yellow Fig Gall-louse. Very useful insect.

11 Four-spot Ladybird *Exochomus quadripustulatus.* Common all over central Europe. Length 3—5 mm. Occurs mainly on spruces and pines. Eats scale-insects. Pupates in larval skin.

2   3

4   5

6   7

8   9   10   11

1

Order: **Moths and Butterflies**—Lepidoptera

Famili: **Ghost Moths**—Hepialidae

1 White-winged Hop Moth *Hepialus humuli.*
Common in parts of central Europe. Wing span
45—70 mm. Moth appears from May to August.
Flies in evening in low zigzags. Caterpillar yellowish with sparse black hairs. Lives from April
to May on hop roots, also on dandelions, sorrel
and carrots. Pupates in chambers in ground. Female lays eggs on ground. Development takes
2 years. Male white, female brown-yellow.

Family: **Carpenter Moths**—Cossidae

2 Goat Moth *Cossus cossus.* Widely distributed
in Europe. Wing span up to 90 mm. Appears in
June and July. Nocturnal. During day sits on
tree trunks. Female has ovipositor, lays eggs in
cracks of bark. Caterpillar lives in trunks of oaks,
willows, poplars and fruit-trees, gnaws long tunnels in wood. Hibernates twice, pupates in cocoon in May of third year. Perfect moth
emerges 4—6 weeks later. In large numbers caterpillars completely ruin wood.

3 *Zeuzera pyrina.* Occurs in Europe, not very
common. Wing span of males about 50 mm, of
females up to 70 mm. Appears from May to beginning of August. Female lays single eggs on
tree trunks. Caterpillar tunnels in wood. Lives in
deciduous trees, chiefly ashes, elms and horse-
chestnuts, also in many fruit-trees. Development takes 2 years. In large numbers damages
wood. Caterpillar reddish, up to 5 cm long.

Family: **Bear Moths**—Syntomidae

4 *Syntomis phegea.* Common everywhere in
central Europe. Wing span about 40 mm. Appears in June and July. In flight resembles burnet moth. Grey to black hairy caterpillar lives on
various herbaceous plants, chiefly dandelions.
Hibernates and pupates following year in May.

Family: **Burnet Moths** or **Foresters**—Zygaeni-
dae

5 Common Blood-drop Burnet Moth *Zygaena
filipendulae.* Common in Europe. Wing span
about 35 mm. Appears in large numbers in
meadows from beginning of June to end of August. Flies by day, ungainly and clumsily. Sits in
sun on thistles etc. Caterpillar fat and yellowish
with sparse hairs. Found mainly on birdfoot-trefoil but also on other plants. Pupates in brim-
stone-yellow, parchment-like cocoon. Moth releases repellent liquid if caught.

6 *Zygaena carniolica.* Very common in warm
spots in central Europe. Wing span about
30 mm. Flies in June and July, slowly and clumsily. Caterpillar light green with white stripes
and row of black spots. Lives in sainfoin and
birdfoot-trefoil. Pupates in cocoon.

2

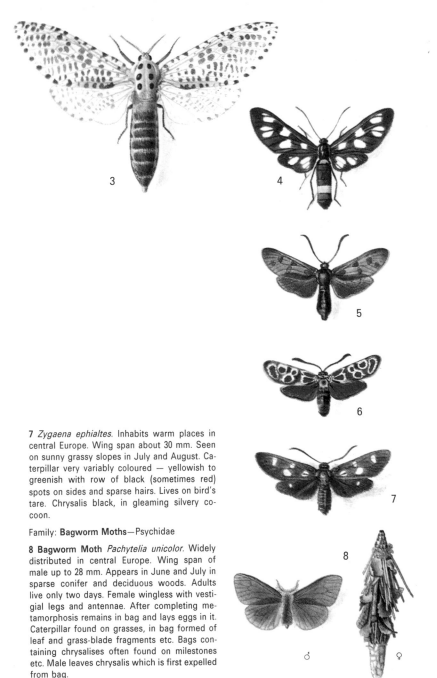

3

4

5

6

7 *Zygaena ephialtes.* Inhabits warm places in central Europe. Wing span about 30 mm. Seen on sunny grassy slopes in July and August. Caterpillar very variably coloured — yellowish to greenish with row of black (sometimes red) spots on sides and sparse hairs. Lives on bird's tare. Chrysalis black, in gleaming silvery cocoon.

7

Family: **Bagworm Moths**—Psychidae

8 Bagworm Moth *Pachytelia unicolor.* Widely distributed in central Europe. Wing span of male up to 28 mm. Appears in June and July in sparse conifer and deciduous woods. Adults live only two days. Female wingless with vestigial legs and antennae. After completing metamorphosis remains in bag and lays eggs in it. Caterpillar found on grasses, in bag formed of leaf and grass-blade fragments etc. Bags containing chrysalises often found on milestones etc. Male leaves chrysalis which is first expelled from bag.

8

♂

♀

1

2

3

4

Family: **Clearwings** — Sesiidae

1 Hornet Clearwing *Sesia apiformis*. Fairly common in central Europe. Wing span about 40 mm. Closely resembles hornet. Wings transparent. Appears from June to end of July. Sits on poplar trunks. Flies swiftly with humming sound. Female lays eggs singly, mainly on poplars, but also on birches, willows and limes (over 1,000 eggs altogether). Caterpillars bore through bark, hibernate, following year tunnel into wood and hibernate again. Pupate in sawdust cocoon. Before moth emerges chrysalis is expelled from opening.

Family: **Puss Moths** — Notodontidae

2 Puss Moth *Cerura vinula*. Widely distributed in Europe. Wing span up to about 70 mm. Flies after dusk from May to beginning of July. Striking, humped caterpillar with typical 'prongs' at tip of abdomen. Found on willows and poplars from July to September. Prongs are claspers converted to tubular appendages from which caterpillar extrudes pink filaments to scare foes. Caterpillar pupates in crack in bark, in cocoon made of wood debris and fragments of bark. Can do serious damage to tree nurseries.

3 Buff Tip Moth *Phalera bucephala*. Very common in Europe. Wing span about 50 mm. Appears in May and June. Flies in evening, prefers lime and poplar avenues. Fine-haired, black-brown, yellow-striped caterpillar found from June to October on willows, limes, poplars and birches. Large number often crowd on single twig. Disperse when older. Pupate in ground. Dark, glossy chrysalis capable of motion.

Family: **Procession Moths** — Thaumetopoeidae

4 Oak Procession Moth *Thaumetopoea processionea*. Very common in central Europe, especially in southern parts. Wing span about 30 mm. Moths frequent only tops of oaks. Fly in August and September. Easily attracted by light. Female lays piles of 200—300 eggs and covers them with hairs from own body. Caterpillars, hatched in May, remain in common nests. Search for food at night crawling in head-to-tail procession. Pupate in July in cocoons, again in common nest.

Family: **Silk Moths** or **Saturnids**—Saturniidae

5 *Saturnia pyri.* Abundant in south of central Europe. Largest European moth. Wing span to over 120 mm. Appears in May, flies on warm evenings in orchards, at margins of woods, etc. Caterpillar found from end of May to August on pear- and other fruit-trees. Has striking light blue tubercles with stiff bristles. Pupates in brown cocoon on bark between branches. Caterpillar makes squeaking sounds.

6 Emperor Moth *Eudia pavonia.* Occurs over large part of Europe. Wing span of male about 60 mm, female up to 75 mm. Flies in May and June. Seen in sparse deciduous woods and at margins of forests. Mature caterpillar bright green with black cross-stripes and yellow tubercles. Found from May to August on deciduous trees or shrubs, e.g. brambles. Chrysalis black-brown in whitish or yellowish-brown, very strong, pear-shaped cocoon.

7 *Aglia tau.* Very common in parts of central Europe. Wing span about 65 mm. Appears in April and May, chiefly in open beech-woods. Male flies in abrupt zigzags, female usually sits on tree trunk close to ground. Caterpillar greenish with white-yellow cross-stripes and one longitudinal stripe on sides. Found mainly on beeches from May to July. Pupates in loose coccon.

6

7

5

1

2

pears in July. Female lays 150—250 large eggs, in piles on pine twigs or needles. Caterpillars, hatched in 3 weeks, eat needles, moult 3 times, descend to ground at end of October and hibernate in loose top-soil. Crawl back to top of trees in spring, grow to 7—10 cm and pupate in June. Some caterpillars hibernate once more. Chrysalis in cocoon attached to nibbled pine shoots or fixed in cracks in bark. Caterpillar brownish and hairy with light stripe on side.

4 Bramble Moth *Macrothylacia rubi.* Widely distributed in Europe. Wing span about 50 mm. Flies on summer evenings, often appears also during day, flies swiftly and jerkily. Female lays eggs mainly on brambles but also on roses and young oaks. Caterpillar velvety black and hairy with narrow orange cross-stripes. Found chiefly in autumn on grassy slopes and in meadows, parks, etc., crawling on ground. Often still seen in November looking for hideout in ground to hibernate. Pupates in spring of following year in soft, greyish cocoon. Many hibernating caterpillars die in ground.

5 Lappet Moth *Gastropacha quercifolia.* Abundant in practically whole of Europe. Wing span up to about 80 mm. Edge of wings indented. Flies from June to August. Caterpillar greyish brown, sparsely haired, with reddish tubercles on sides of back; grows up to 10 cm. Lives on fruit-trees, other deciduous trees and blackthorns. Pupates in soft hairy cocoon. In large numbers damages fruit-tree nurseries.

Family: **Meadow Moths**—Lemoniidae

1 *Lemonia dumi.* Distributed all over central Europe. Wing span up to 20 mm. Flies in evening from September to October, sometimes to November. Caterpillar found from May to July on marsh-marigold, lung-wort, garden lettuce and dandelions. Pupates in ground.

Family: **Birch Moths**—Endromiidae

2 Kentish Glory *Endromis versicolor.* Common in central Europe. Wing span about 50 mm. Moth often appears as soon as end of February, flies until May. Caterpillar lives on birches, sometimes on sycamores, seldom on other trees. Young caterpillars gregarious. Caterpillar green with whitish back and cross-stripes on sides. Chrysalis red, in cocoon.

Family: **Tent Caterpillar Moths**—Lasiocampidae

3 Pine Moth *Dendrolimus pini.* Abundant over whole of central Europe. Wing span of male about 55 mm, female up to 80 mm. Moth ap-

3

6

5

6 Lackey Moth *Malacosoma neustrium.* Widely distributed over practically whole of Europe. Wing span up to 40 mm. Flies from end of June to August. Female lays eggs ring-wise round young fruit-tree, blackthorn, poplar, oak and birch twigs — 200—400 eggs in one ring. Caterpillars not hatched until following May, after eggs have hibernated. Caterpillar thinly haired, with blue head and often blue, white and red stripes down body. Caterpillars gregarious. Weave whitish nests, crawl out in search of food. Disperse after third moult and in second half of June pupate in white or yellowish cocoon on bark or between leaves of trees.

7 *Lasiocampa quercus.* Abundant in temperate zone of Europe. Wing span up to 70 mm. Moth appears in woods and avenues from June to August. Caterpillar mainly brownish yellow with yellowish hairs, grows to 7 cm. Lives on various deciduous trees, also conifers. Hibernates and pupates following May in firm, brown cocoon. In mountains and northerly regions hibernates second time as chrysalis. Does little damage.

4

7

3 Nun or **Black Archer** *Lymantria monacha.* Very common in Europe. Wing span of male up to 45 mm; female up to 55 mm. Colouring very variable, including black aberrations. Appears in July and August. Female lays eggs behind scales of bark on conifers, occasionally also deciduous trees. Caterpillars do not hatch until following year, usually in April. Disperse into tree crowns and eat needles or leaves. Pupate in cracks in bark after about 9 weeks. Very variably coloured. Have few hairs.

4 Gypsy Moth *Lymantria dispar.* Distributed over almost whole of Europe. Wing span of male 35—40 mm, female 55—70 mm. Flies from end of July to September, lives only 7—8 days. Female lays eggs in piles. Caterpillars do not hatch until following April or May; found on deciduous trees, mainly oaks, limes, etc. Caterpillar brownish and hairy, with blue and red tubercles. Pupates in loose cocoon on south side of tree trunks, often in groups.

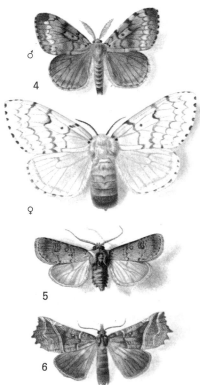

Family: **Tussock Moths**—Lymantriidae

1 Pale Tussock Moth *Dasychira pudibunda.* Abundant in whole of central Europe. Wing span about 45 mm. Appears in May and June, sometimes second generation in October. Inhabits sparse woods, orchards, etc. Caterpillar very variably coloured — yellow, pink or reddish, with hairs of same colour and with yellow or orange bristles on back. Lives on deciduous trees and pupates in yellow, extremely hairy cocoon.

2 Gold-tipped Tussock Moth *Euproctis phaeorrhoea.* Widely distributed in central Europe. Wing span about 35 mm. Flies from end of June to end of July. Female lays piles of eggs on underside of oak leaves and covers them with hairs. Caterpillars hatch in August. Gregarious, hibernate in nests and disperse in spring. Pupate at end of June in cocoon which is hidden in rolled leaf. Do damage in large numbers.

7

8

9

Family: **Owlet Moths**—Phalaenidae

5 *Agrotis segetum*. Common European moth. Wing span about 40 mm. Moth appears in May—June and August—September in fields, meadows and gardens. Caterpillars eat turnips, cereals, grass, etc. Caterpillar smooth and greyish with light lines down back and sides and black spots. Hides during day, comes out to feed at night.

6 *Scoliopteryx libatrix*. Very common in Europe. Wing span about 40 mm. Forewings indented. Moth appears in August and September, hibernates in holes, cellars, etc., and flies again in March and April. Caterpillars found on poplars and willows from May to September. Caterpillar green with yellow band on sides. Chrysalis black.

7 Blue Underwing *Catocala fraxini*. Distributed over all central Europe. Wing span up to about 90 mm. Appears from end of July to September. Sits on tree trunks during day, flies in evening and at night. Caterpillar up to 10 cm long; greyish or greenish, black-speckled, on back with light spot in black band on 8th segment. Found on ashes, poplars and elms.

8 Red Poplar Underwing *Catocala elocata*. Distributed over most of Europe. Wing span about 75 mm. Occurs from July to October. Clings to tree trunks during day. If disturbed, abruptly unfolds forewings, displaying red hindwings to frighten enemy. Caterpillar grey with dark dorsal and lateral stripes. Found mainly on poplars, also on willows, from May to June. Chrysalis reddish brown, dusted with blue.

9 Red Willow Underwing *Catocala electa*. Widely distributed in central Europe. Wing span about 70 mm. Flies in July and August. Caterpillar yellowish grey to brown with small black dots; over 7 cm long. Found on willows in May and June.

Family: **Tiger Moths**—Arctiidae

1 White Tiger Moth *Spilosoma menthastri.* Widely distributed in central Europe. Wing span about 40 mm. Flies in evening in May and June. During day can be seen sitting on plants in forest clearings and in gardens. Caterpillar hairy, dark brown with orange-yellow line down back. Found through summer on various plants, chiefly stinging-nettles and mint. Pupates on ground. Chrysalis black in grey cocoon.

2 *Utetheisa pulchella.* Lives in southern part of central Europe but often strays far north. Wing span about 40 mm. Flies in June and September—October in damp meadows near woods, in clearings, etc. Caterpillar white and soft-haired, with black dots and red spots. Found on forget-me-not, viper's bugloss, rib-wort and other herbaceous plants in May—June and September—October.

3 *Phragmatobia fuliginosa.* Common over practically whole of Europe. Wing span 30—35 mm. Many colour varieties. Moth in April and May, second generation in August. Flies after dark, often enters open windows. Caterpillar grey to reddish brown, with tubercles surmounted by tufts of hairs. Found on forget-me-not, sorrel, bedstraw, wild lettuce, etc. Pupates in greyish white felty cocoon.

4 *Rhyparia purpurata.* Abundant in central Europe. Wing span about 45 mm. Several colour varieties. Flies after dark, in June and July. Caterpillar somewhat variable; usually black with dark red hairs and yellow lateral hairs. Has yellow, red and black spots on sides. Found on milfoil, rib-wort, bedstraw, etc. from autumn to spring.

5 Garden Tiger Moth *Arctia caja.* Distributed over most of Europe. Wing span up to 70 mm. Often very variably coloured. Moth abundant everywhere during summer. In daytime hides under leaves of plants or bushes. Caterpillar long-haired with black and white tubercles; dorsal hairs black, lateral hairs russet. Found on various plants from August to September and, after hibernating, from May to June.

6 *Panaxia quadripunctaria.* Fairly common in central Europe on sunny, and especially limestone, slopes. Wing span about 55 mm. Several colour varieties. Moth appears on grassy slopes in July. Caterpillar found on rib-wort, clover and willowherb, also beeches and oaks in April and May. Grey-brown to black with yellow dorsal and lateral stripes and orange-spotted sides. Pupates in loose cocoon.

7 *Panaxia dominula.* Fairly abundant in central and northern Europe. Wing span about 55 mm. Several colour varieties. Moth seen in June and July among bushes, on outskirts of woods, in avenues, etc. Caterpillar found in autumn and again in spring on stinging-nettle, deadnettle, wild strawberry, forget-me-not and willow, poplar and other trees.

1

2

3

4

5

6

7

Family: **Geometers** or **Emeralds**—Geometridae

8 Emerald *Geometra papilionaria*. Occurs in central and northern Europe. Wing span about 45 mm. Flies from June to August in sparse woods. Sits on tree trunks. Caterpillar green with yellow stripe along sides and five protuberances on back. Found on birch, alder, beech and hazel in May. Chrysalis yellow-green with reddish brown back.

9 Magpie Moth *Abraxas grossulariata*. Distributed over whole of Europe. Wing span up to 40 mm. Moth appears from June to August; common in gardens and in woods with wild gooseberry bushes. Caterpillar whitish with wide black spots on back and orange stripe along sides. Found on gooseberry bushes.

8

9

331

1

Family: **Hawk Moths**—Sphingidae

1 Death's Head Moth *Acherontia atropos*. Inhabits southern Europe, regularly flies to central and northern Europe. Wing span up to about 110 mm. Flies late in evening and at night. Excellent flier; comes in summer from Mediterranean region. In central Europe female usually lays eggs on potato plants, also on henbane. Caterpillars, which by end of summer measure 10 cm, are yellow-green with black, blue and yellow stripes and spots; large spine at tip of abdomen. Pupate in ground in hard clay capsule. In colder parts of central Europe chrysalis dies.

2 Convolvulus or **Morning Glory Hawk** *Herse convolvuli*. Abundant from Atlantic coast as far as Australia. Wing span about 105 mm. Flies after dark in May and June, second generation in August and September. Flies from south to extreme north of Europe. Female lays eggs on bindweed. Mature caterpillar, which measures 9 cm, is usually light brown or greenish with light oblique stripes on sides and dark stripe down back. Caterpillar found mainly on bindweed from June until autumn. Hides during day, often in holes in ground; comes out to feed towards evening. Chrysalis has curved proboscis sheath.

3 Privet Hawk *Sphinx ligustri*. Common in central Europe. Wing span about 90 mm. Appears in May and June, sometimes until August. Flies after dark; often attracted indoors by light. Caterpillar light green with oblique violet stripes, bordered with white on underside, on sides; yellow tip of abdomen. Found on elder, privet and other shrubs from end of June to September. Chrysalis reddish-brown.

4 Pine Hawk *Sphinx pinastri*. Common all over central Europe. Wing span up to about 80 mm. Moth appears in conifer forests from April to September. Sits on tree trunks, blends with surroundings. Female lays eggs on pines and spruces. Caterpillars eat needles. Because of numerous parasites has never multiplied dangerously in central Europe. Caterpillar light green with brownish line on back, narrow white and yellow stripes on sides and red spots. Found on conifers from June to October. Chrysalis hibernates, sometimes twice.

2

5 Willow Hawk *Smerinthus ocellatus.* Common in central Europe. Wing span about 85 mm. Moth appears from May to August, mainly near water with groups of willows or poplars. Caterpillar green with blue cross-stripes on sides, whitish spots and a blue spine. Found from June to September on willow, poplar and young fruit-trees. Moth often attracted indoors by light.

6 Oak Hawk *Marumba quercus.* Inhabits southern Europe, rarely visits central Europe. Wing span up to about 100 mm. Appears in southern Europe from May to August, in central Europe usually in July. Inhabits oak-woods. Caterpillar green with oblique yellow stripes and orange spots on sides. Found from June to October chiefly on young oaks. Chrysalis brown with metallic lustre.

7 Poplar Hawk *Laothoe populi.* Locally abundant in central Europe. Wing span up to about 75 mm. Moth appears in May and June and sometimes in August and early September. Sits on poplar trunks. Caterpillar yellow-green with yellow spots and with oblique yellow stripes on sides. Found from June to September mainly on poplars, but also on willows. Pupates in ground. Chrysalis dark brown.

4

5

7

3

6

Family: **Hawk Moths**—*Sphingidae*

1 Spurge Hawk *Celerio euphorbiae*. Very common in central Europe. Wing span about 70 mm. Moth appears from May to September in clearings and pastures, by rivers and anywhere where spurge grows. Flies after dusk, visits flowers, sucks nectar with long proboscis. Caterpillar found on spurge in July and August. Strikingly coloured; basic colour black, red stripe down back and yellow spots and stripes on sides. Pupates in ground. Moth sometimes does not emerge for several years after several hibernating stages of pupa.

2 Bedstraw Hawk *Celerio gallii*. Common in central Europe. Wing span about 70 mm. Moth appears from May to July, sometimes to September. Flies swiftly after dark. Caterpillar usually dark green with yellow dorsal line and large, yellow, black-ringed spots on sides. Found from July to August on bedstraw, willowherb and spurge. Mainly frequents open sunny places. Chrysalis yellow-brown with dark lines.

3 Elephant Hawk *Deilephila elpenor*. Very common in central Europe. Wing span about 65 mm. Moth appears mostly in May and June, rarely from July to September. Fast flier. Mainly frequents places with willows, e.g. streams, clearings, etc. Caterpillar found from June to end of August on willowherb, bedstraw, vines and other plants. Up to 8 cm long. Three colour types — green, brown and blackish. Brown and white eye-spots on fourth and fifth segment. Chrysalis yellowish-brown with black spots. Moth often attracted indoors by light.

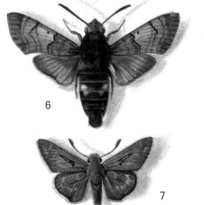

4

5

6

7

4 Oleander Hawk *Daphnis nerii.* Inhabits North Africa and southern Europe. Wing span about 100 mm. In summer visits central Europe where female sometimes lays eggs and caterpillars can be found. Caterpillar up to over 9 cm long; bright green with white lateral stripe from fourth segment and two white, blue-ringed eye-spots on either side of third segment. Found on oleanders and occasionally on winter-green from April to June, second generation in August and September. Chrysalis slim, brown-yellow, marked with black dots.

5 *Proserpinis proserpina.* Distributed over central and southern Europe. Wing span about 40 mm. Ragged-edged wings. Moth appears in May, flies after dusk. Caterpillar green or brownish with black marbling and with yellow, blue-rimmed spots on sides. Found in July and August on willowherb and evening primrose. Chrysalis reddish-brown.

6 *Macroglossum stellatarum.* Common in central Europe. Wing span about 45 mm. Moth flies from June to October, mainly during day, in clearings, forest meadows, etc. Has very long proboscis, sucks nectar from trumpet flowers. Flies very abruptly, hovers like hummingbird when sucking nectar. Caterpillar green with white stripe along sides. First generation of caterpillars appears in June and July, second in August to September. Found on bedstraw and woodruff. Caterpillar hides by day, comes out in search of food at night. Chrysalis grey-brown or blue-green.

Family: **Skipper Butterflies**—Hesperiidae

7 Silver-spotted Skipper *Hesperia comma.* Widely distributed all over Europe. Wing span about 30 mm. Flies very quickly during daytime. Seen from June to August in clearings, on hill-sides and in meadows, also in mountainous regions. Caterpillar dark grey with double black line on sides. Found in autumn on various meadow grasses, hibernates and reappears following spring. Makes itself tube from grass leaves. Chrysalis brownish, dusted with blue.

1

2

3

4

Family: **Meadow Browns** or **Satyrs**—Satyridae

1 Marbled White *Melanargia galathea.* Occurs in central and southern Europe. Wing span about 50 mm. Butterfly abundant from June to August in forest meadows and clearings, on slopes, etc., also at high altitudes. Flies during daytime. Caterpillar yellowish with dark dorsal and reddish lateral line. Hides by day, eats various grasses at night.

2 *Hipparchia circe.* Distributed over whole of central and southern Europe. Wing span up to about 80 mm. Flies from June to August in open woods. Caterpillar has dark brown, white-lined back and yellow-brown sides with russet, white and black lines. Found on different grasses from May to June.

3 *Hipparchia briseis.* Widespread in central Europe. Wing span about 55 mm. Flies from July to September. Frequents sunny rocky slopes, likes to settle on warm rocks or stones. Caterpillar yellowish grey. Dark line on back; one dark and two light lines along sides. Found mainly on sesleria but also on other grasses in autumn and, after hibernating, again until June.

4 *Pararge achine.* Occurs in central and northern Europe. Wing span about 50 mm. Flies in shady woods in June and July. Caterpillar light green with one black and two white lines on back. Found in August and September and, after hibernating, again in May on rye-grass and other grasses, also on wheat. Pupates in May. Chrysalis green with white stripes.

Family: **Fritillaries**—Nymphalidae

5 Peacock Butterfly *Nymphalis io.* Common all over Europe. Wing span up to about 60 mm. Butterfly occurs from March until autumn, sometimes in three generations. Hibernates often inside windows, in cellars and caves, etc. Caterpillar black with white dots and black spines. Caterpillars gregarious, live mainly on stinging-nettle, also on hops and brambles from April to September. Chrysalis light brown with golden spots, hangs head downwards. Butterfly emerges in 1—2 weeks but third generation pupa hibernates.

6 Camberwell Beauty *Nymphalis antiopa.* Common in central Europe. Wing span up to over 70 mm. Flies from June until autumn, hibernates and reappears from end of April. Mainly frequents birch groves. Sits on trunk and sucks sap from injured wood, also drinks nectar. Caterpillar black with striking, red-spotted back and black spines all over body. Gregarious, lives from May to June on birches, also on poplars, willows and elms.

7 Small Tortoiseshell *Aglais urticae.* Common European butterfly. Wing span about 50 mm. Two or three generations of butterflies appear from end of June until October. Hibernating males and females appear early in spring.

Several varieties. Frequents hillsides, clearings, fields and gardens. Often found inside windows, in cellars, etc. Caterpillar black with yellow-green stripes down body and spines. Found from May until autumn on great and small nettle and occasionally on hops.

8 Comma Butterfly *Polygonia c-album.* Abundant in central Europe. Wing span about 50 mm. Several colour varieties. Butterfly in 2—3 generations from May to October, hibernates and reappears in early spring. Flies on outskirts of forests, in glades and in gardens. First third of caterpillar's body russet, remainder white, underside reddish. Armed with spines. Caterpillar found on nettle, gooseberry, hop, elm and hazel leaves. Chrysalis hangs head downwards.

6

7

5

8

Family: **Fritillaries**—Nymphalidae

1 Red Admiral *Vanessa atalanta*. Common in central Europe. Wing span about 60 mm. Butterfly in two generations, from June until autumn. Found almost anywhere in open places. Second generation butterflies hibernate and appear early in spring. Caterpillars variably coloured, most often black with yellow line on sides and with spines. Found in May—June and August—September in rolled leaves, chiefly of stinging-nettle.

2 Painted Lady *Vanessa cardui*. Distributed over practically whole of world. Very common in central Europe. Wing span about 55 mm. Butterfly appears in sunny places from end of May until autumn, in 2—3 generations. Likes to settle on flowers. Caterpillar brownish and spiny, with yellow stripes and dots. Found from May to September on leaves of stinging-nettle, colt's foot, burdock and other plants. Chrysalis grey with golden spots.

3 *Araschnia levana*. Abundant in central Europe. Wing span about 35—40 mm. Butterfly has spring and summer generation. Spring generation (March—April) yellowish-red with black spots, summer generation (July—August) blackish-brown with yellow spots. Caterpillars, gregarious when young, found in June and August—September on stinging-nettle. Resemble peacock butterfly caterpillars but have two long spines on head.

4 Purple Emperor *Apatura iris*. Occurs all over central Europe. Wing span about 60 mm. Upper surface of wings metallic-opalescent. Butterfly from June to August in sparse deciduous woods. Flies low, early in morning, sucks dung, carrion, etc. Caterpillar green with yellow stripes and dots and two long blue horns on head. Found from August on sallow, aspen and willow, hibernates and again eats leaves from April to June.

6

7

then gnaw young violet roots, mainly at night. Pupate at end of June. Caterpillar brownish with yellow dorsal stripe, dark lateral stripes and long yellow spines. Chrysalis found on tree trunks.

5 White Admiral *Limenitis camilla.* Occurs in central, southern and south-western Europe. Wing span about 50—55 mm. Butterfly seen from May to July in open deciduous woods. Favours damp places. Settles on blackberry flowers. Green, red-spined caterpillar found on honeysuckle. Hibernates.

6 Great White Admiral *Limenitis populi.* Locally abundant in central Europe. Wing span up to about 80 mm. Butterfly in July and August. Female has broad white bands on wings. Settles on damp ground, excreta, etc. Gliding flight. Caterpillar green with hairy excrescences. Hibernates in curled leaf and in spring, up to May, eats poplar leaves, mainly that of young trees. Also found on aspens. Butterfly leaves chrysalis in 3—4 weeks.

7 European Sailer *Neptis hylasaceris.* Occurs in warm parts of central Europe. Wing span up to about 55 mm. First generation of butterflies appears in May and June, second in July to August, in open deciduous woods. Local incidence only. Caterpillar yellow-brown with small tubercles. Found on lady's finger.

8 Silver-washed Fritillary *Argynnis paphia.* Very abundant in central Europe. Wing span up to about 70 mm. Butterfly seen from beginning of July to middle of September. Appears mainly in damp forest meadows, clearings, etc. Settles on thistles and sucks nectar. Female lays eggs on violets usually in August. Caterpillars, hatched in 14 days, hibernate until May and

9 Queen of Spain Fritillary *Issoria lathonia.* Very common in central Europe. Wing span 40—45 mm. Butterfly in 2—3 generations from early spring until autumn. Flies in meadows and fields, on hillsides, etc. Caterpillars live on violets and sainfoin and hibernate. Caterpillar brownish with whitish back, brown-yellow lines on sides and short reddish spines.

8

9

339

Family: **Blues, Coppers** or **Hairstreaks** —
Lycaenidae

1 *Lycaena virgaureae*. Abundant in central
Europe. Wing span up to about 35 mm. Male
has golden orange wings, female brown-spotted wings. Frequents clearings, meadows, etc.
in open woods. Caterpillar dark green with yellowish stripes on back and bosses on body.
Lives on sorrel from April to June. Pupates on
stem or in ground.

2 Adonis Blue *Polyommatus bellargus*. Occurs
in central and southern Europe. Wing span
about 33 mm. Butterfly in two generations,
May—June and July—September. Flies in
fields, on hillsides, etc. Sucks nectar from clover
and lucerne flowers etc. Caterpillar blue-green
with dark dorsal stripes and often reddish yellow spots. Found from April to July on clover
and other papilionaceous plants. Usually pupates in the ground. Chrysalis greenish in
colour.

3 Large Blue *Maculinea arion*. Occurs in central
Europe in several forms. Wing span about
25 mm. Butterfly appears from June to August
on sunny slopes and meadows. Likes to settle
on betony flowers. Caterpillar blue-green with
dark dorsal line. Found on betony from autumn.

Hibernates and pupates in anthills. Before pupating lives on ant larvae and pupae. Ants like
its secretion.

Family: **Swallowtails** — Papilionidae

4 Swallowtail *Papilio machaon*. Distributed
over whole of Europe. In central Europe generally two generations, April—May and July—
August, in south up to October. Wing span up to
about 80 mm. Good, enduring flier. Prefers dry
hilly regions. Likes to settle on flowers and
sucks nectar. Female lays eggs singly on umbelliferous plants, e.g. pimpernel, cummin, carrots,
etc. Young caterpillar blackish, mature caterpillar light green with black cross-stripes and
bright red spots. Chrysalis fixed to stems by fibres, head upwards. Some chrysalises hibernate twice.

5 Scarce Swallowtail *Papilio podalirius*. Very
common in central Europe. Wing span up to
about 75 mm. Spring and summer generation.
Occurs mainly on sunny slopes. Female lays
eggs singly on fruit-trees or blackthorn. Caterpillars hatch in 10 days. Caterpillar green with
yellow dorsal stripe branching into oblique yellow cross-bands on sides. Pupates head upwards, held by fibrous loop round chrysalis.
Surface of chrysalis uneven.

6 *Zerynthia hypsipyle*. Inhabits southern Europe and southern parts of central Europe. Wing span about 50 mm. Butterfly appears in April and May, abundant in places. Flies in open sunny spots where birthwort grows. Caterpillar found on birthwort from June to August. Caterpillar russet, reddish or grey with red excrescences. Chrysalis yellow-grey.

7 Black Apollo Butterfly *Parnassius mnemosyne*. Abundant in places in central Europe. Wing span up to about 60 mm. Butterfly appears in June mainly in mountainous regions, but also at lower altitudes. Caterpillar black with rows of red spots. Hides by day, comes out to eat late in evening. Found on fumitory in April and May. Chrysalis fat and yellowish, dusted with white.

8 Red Apollo Butterfly *Parnassius apollo*. Locally common in mountainous regions of central Europe. Wing span up to about 70 mm. Dark form known in the Alps. Butterfly from June to August on sunny slopes. Likes to settle on thistle flowers. Caterpillar black with two rows of large red spots and bluish tubercles. Found in May and June on stone-crop. Pupates in ground in loose cocoon. Chrysalis bluish.

1

2

Family: **Whites**—Pieridae

1 Large White *Pieris brassicae*. Common all over Europe. Wing span about 55 mm. Butterfly occurs from April until autumn in 2—3 generations. Flies practically everywhere. Female lays small piles of yellow eggs on underside of cabbage leaves and similar plants. Caterpillars devour leaves right down to stalk. Found from May to June and from August to September. Caterpillar yellow-green with black dots and yellow stripes on back and sides. Before pupating climbs on to higher object, e.g. wall or tree. Chrysalis yellow-green with black blotches and spots. Important pest. Caterpillars often attacked by ichneumon flies.

2 Small White, Cabbage or **Turnip Butterfly** *Pieris rapae*. Abundant all over Europe. Wing span about 45 mm. First generation of butterflies appear in April—May, second in July, sometimes third in autumn. Appears in fields, meadows and gardens. Caterpillar greenish with yellow stripes on back and sides. Found in June and again in August and September on cruciferous plants, mainly turnip leaves.

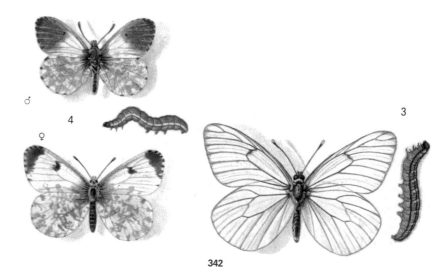

4

3

3 Black-veined White *Aporia crataegi.* Distributed over whole of Europe. Once important pest, now plentiful only in places. Wing span about 60 mm. Butterfly flies in June and July. Female lays eggs on underside of fruit-tree leaves (mainly apple-trees). Caterpillars appear from September, wrap themselves in leaves and hibernate. Early in spring form large nests round buds and eat them. Pupate at end of May on tree trunks etc. Caterpillar blue-grey with black and rusty brown stripes.

4 Orange-tip *Anthocharis cardamines.* Abundant in central Europe. Wing span about 40 mm. Male's forewings tipped with orange. Butterfly appears from beginning of April to June. Male very striking in flight. Flies close to ground in gardens, sunken lanes and forest paths. Caterpillar blue-green with white-striped sides. Found mainly on cress from June to August.

5 Pale Clouded Yellow *Colias hyale.* Very common in central Europe. Wing span about 40 mm. Butterfly appears from May to June and again from August to September. Flies on sunny, grassy slopes and over clover fields, stubble fields, etc. Caterpillar dark green with four yellow stripes down body. Found on vetches and clover in June—July and August—September. Chrysalis grey-green with yellow stripes.

6 Alpine Clouded Yellow *Colias palaenoeuropomene.* Found in central Europe in peat-bogs. Wing span about 50 mm. Butterfly seen from June to July or August over peat-bogs with plenty of crowberry plants on which caterpillars live. Caterpillar green with yellow stripe, edged below with black, along sides. Chrysalis yellow-green.

5

6

7

7 *Colias edusa.* Inhabits practically whole of Europe. Wing span about 50 mm. Basic colouring of male orange to yellowish-red, female whitish to orange and yellow. Two butterfly generations, May—June and July—August. Seen on sunny slopes and in fields and clearings, etc. Caterpillar green with white, yellow-spotted stripe along sides. Found on papilionaceous plants.

8 Brimstone Yellow or **Yellow-bird** *Gonopteryx rhamni.* Common everywhere in central Europe. Wing span about 55 mm. Butterfly seen from July to autumn. Hibernates and reappears on sunny days at end of March. Flies in gardens, fields and meadows, etc. Caterpillar dark green with white stripe on sides. Found from July mainly on buckthorn, in mountainous regions also on bilberries. Chrysalis green with two white stripes on sides.

8

1

2

3

Order: **Two-winged Flies**—Diptera

Family: **Crane-flies**—Tipulidae

1 Crane-fly or **Daddy-longlegs** *Tipula oleracea.*
Plentiful everywhere from April to June. Female
lays up to 500 black eggs in ground. Larvae
hatch in 2—3 weeks. Live on humus, later nibble
roots of crops. Adult insect measures 15—
23 mm. Often attracted indoors by light.

Family: **Gall-gnats**—Cecidomyidae

2 Hessian-fly *Mayetiola destructor.* Common
over whole of Europe. Length 2.5—4 mm. Flies
from April to May and again in September. Female lays eggs singly or in twos on underside of
rye, wheat or barley leaves. Larvae, hatched in 8
days, suck blades. Second larval generation
penetrates to roots of winter seedlings and
causes swellings on plants which usually die.

3 Beech Gall-gnat *Mikiola fagi.* Abundant in
beech-woods. Small and inconspicuous. Female
lays eggs singly on upperside of beech leaves.
Larvae form striking red galls, sometimes several on one leaf. Larvae of related species form
similar galls on leaves of other trees.

Family: **Hair-gnats**—Bibionidae

4 March-fly or **St. Mark's Fly** *Bibio marci.* Very common in woods from March to May. Length 10—13 mm. Black, with extremely long legs. Flies slowly. Larvae found in humus, live on vegetable matter. In large numbers does damage to tree nurseries.

Family: **Gadflies**—Tabanidae

5 Gadfly *Tabanus bovinus.* Distributed over practically whole of Europe, mainly near ponds, lakes and rivers. Length 20—24 mm. Flies during summer. Female attacks warm-blooded animals and man and sucks their blood, needed for development of its eggs. Bite smarts and swells. Female lays eggs on aquatic plants. Larvae crawl down into water and live predaciously in mud. Development slow. After 7—8 moults larva transformed to immobile pupa. Gadflies have numerous enemies, e.g. birds and spiders.

6 Horse-fly or **Cleg** *Haematopoda pluvialis.* Abundant near rivers and ponds. Length 10 mm. Male's eyes hairy; female's are hairless and beautifully green. Flies in summer. Bites viciously, especially before storms. Predacious larvae live in mud.

7 Greenhead *Chrysops caecutiens.* Very common near water. Length 8—9 mm. Female has golden green eyes. Appears from May to September. Female attacks large mammals and man and sucks their blood. Lays glossy black eggs on aquatic plants. Round-bodied, predacious larvae live in mud. Pupate in sand and soil.

Family: **Bee-flies**—Bombyliidae

8 *Hemipenthes morio.* Striking fly frequenting dry clearings. Length 5—12 mm. Found in summer. Female flies over bare ground looking for caterpillars attacked by caterpillar-fly or ichneumon fly larvae. Lays eggs on these and larvae parasitize parasites. Adult insects fly swiftly about in sunny parts of woods, settle on flowers and drink nectar.

Family: **Soldier-flies**—Stratiomyidae

9 Soldier-fly *Stratiomys chamaeleon.* Common, striking fly with flat abdomen. Length 12 to 14 mm. Appears mainly in summer. Flutters on flowers and bushes near water and drinks nectar. Not shy. Female lays eggs on leaves above water surface. Hatched larvae slip into water and live in tangled aquatic plants in shallows. Have long breathing tube. Predacious. Before pupating crawl out of water. Pupate in ground.

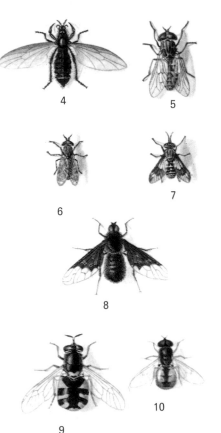

10 Green Soldier-fly *Eulalia viridula.* Abundant on leaves of bushes near water. Length 6—7 mm. On rainy days hides on underside of leaves.

Family: **Hover-flies**—Syrphidae

1 Currant-fly *Syrphus ribesii.* Occurs in central Europe. Length 10—11 mm. In summer and autumn appears on flowers and sucks nectar. Darting flight. In sunny spots often flies in circles. Female lays eggs on leaves. Greenish larvae catch aphids, mainly on currant bushes but also on vegetables. One larva consumes about 300 plant-lice during development.

2 *Eristalis arbustorum.* Common in central Europe. Found mainly in clearings from summer until late autumn. Length 10—12 mm. Larva lives in mud, cesspools and manure. Larva cylindrical and whitish with tail-like breathing tube. Pupates on tree trunks etc.

Family: **Fruit-flies**—Drosophilidae

3 *Drosophila melanogaster.* Abundant in summer and autumn. Length only 3.5—4 mm. Appears in flocks on soft windfall fruit, in houses and on any fermenting material. Develops very quickly. In some places nuisance as carrier of undesirable yeast cells.

Family: **Horse-ticks** or **Forest-flies**—Hippoboscidae

4 Forest-fly *Ornithomyia avicularia.* Very common, especially in woods. Length 5—6 mm. Wings permanent. Parasite of various birds, lives in plumage and sucks blood. Females produce developed larvae which immediately pupate and drop to ground. Perfect insect capable of reproduction in 3 days. Normal life span 4—6 months.

Family: **True Flies**—Muscidae

5 Common House-fly *Musca domestica.* Occurs in human dwellings all over world. Length 7—8 mm. Female lays eggs in dung, manure and rotting refuse. Development takes only 14 days, several generations may occur in a year. Hibernates as larva or as pupa. Since fly alights on excrement and then on food and human skin, can transmit many dangerous infections.

1   2

6 Common Stable-fly *Stomoxys calcitrans.* Very common in cattle country. Length 6 to 7 mm. Female lays eggs in cow dung. Adult insect also flies into homes and bites man. Bites itch. Can transmit different diseases, e.g. anthrax and in south cholera, etc.

Family: **Blow-flies**—Calliphoridae

7 Gold Blow-fly *Lucilia caesar.* Very common everywhere. Settles on tall plants and leaves of bushes. Length 7—10 mm. Brightly gleaming body. Looks for putrefying animal carcasses and human excreta in which female lays eggs and maggots develop.

8 Bluebottle *Calliphora vicina.* Very common in dwellings. Robust body 8—12 mm long. Appears from spring until autumn, betrayed by loud buzz. Female lays eggs in animal carcasses, excrement, cheese and meat. Maggots

3

4

5

6

7

hatch in 24 hours, develop in 4 weeks and pupate in ground.

9 Common Flesh-fly *Sarcophaga carnaria.* Very common everywhere. Length 10—16 mm. Found on flowers, walls, tree trunks and in dwellings. Female lays live, legless maggots on fresh vertebrate carcasses or meat in which maggots develop. Maggots pupate as brown, barrel-shaped pupae. Contaminate food.

Family: **Caterpillar-flies**—Larvaevoridae

10 Caterpillar-fly *Exorista larvarum.* Occurs everywhere in sunny grassy places. Length 6—15 mm. Female lays eggs on caterpillars. Larva penetrates caterpillar's body and devours it from within. Burnet moth caterpillars most frequent hosts but other species also. Mature larvae leave host's body and pupate in ground. Very useful insect as not more than 5 per cent of attacked caterpillars develop into moths.

8

9

10

Cyclostomes, Cartilaginous Fishes and Bony Fishes

Cyclostomes (Cyclostomata) belong to the superclass Agnatha, comprising jawless vertebrates with only a primitive cartilaginous skull and no jaws. Best known of this group are the lampreys (Petromyzoniformes). They do not possess true bone tissue and their skeleton is cartilaginous. The body is long, snake-like and bare, but is bordered by a continuous dorsal fin on the hind part and has a hint of a caudal fin.

Lampreys do not possess paired fins. The circular mouths are without jaws but are furnished with horny teeth. There is only one nostril and that is closed. On either side of the body, behind the eyes there are seven gill slits. The eggs laid by lampreys develop into larvae with eyes covered by skin. The larval stage lasts two to four years. Some species live both in the sea and in fresh water.

Fig. 1. The Salmon (*Salmo salar*) can leap over barriers up to 3 m high.

Fig. 2. The funnel-shaped mouth of the Sea Lamprey (*Petromyzon marinus*) is furnished with horny teeth. The tongue, likewise furnished with teeth, functions like a bore or a piston.

Fig. 3. The Stone Loach (*Noemacheilus barbatulus*) lives on the bed of flowing rivers. It feeds on the larvae of midges (Chironomidae).

Most commonly found in the fresh waters of Europe are two species: the Lampern (*Lampetra fluviatilis*) and the Brook Lamprey (*Lampetra planeri*). However, one might also find the Sea Lamprey (*Petromyzon marinus*), which reaches a length of 100 cm and a weight of 2—3 kg. The Sea Lamprey inhabits the northernmost parts of the Atlantic, off both the North American and European coasts, but in the spring it swims up rivers and larger streams to spawn. It usually breeds on the stony bed in flowing water, where the female lays up to 250,000 eggs. Lampreys that travel to the upper reaches of rivers die after spawning, but those that remain near the sea coast may spawn a number of times. The Sea Lamprey feeds mostly on the blood of fish, but it has also been known to attach itself to a shark or a small invertebrate on the sea floor. The Sea Lamprey is often caught in fish-traps, in Europe mostly off the coast of France, Germany and Britain.

The Lampern also lives in the sea off the coasts of northern Europe. Spring populations swim up rivers and spawn right away; autumn populations overwinter in the river and spawn the following year. Lamperns feed only in the sea. They are of little importance in commerce and are caught mostly in the Gulf of Finland.

Cartilaginous fish are the most primitive stage in the evolution of jawed vertebrates (Gnathostomata) with a skull that has jaws, of which the lower one is free and mobile. They also have paired fins; higher groups have paired limbs.

Cartilaginous fishes (Chondrichthyes) have a cartilaginous skeleton and a typical transverse mouth on the underside of the body. The mouth has jaws furnished with numerous sharp-pointed teeth. When the teeth are worn, they

Fig. 4. The Northern Pike (*Esox lucius*) has a typical dorsal fin, located far back near the tail.

Fig. 5. The predacious pike always seizes its prey crosswise at first, only afterwards turning it lengthwise so that it can swallow it.

bend forward and new teeth grow in behind them. The teeth are of dermal origin. Best known of the cartilaginous fishes are the sharks (Selachiformes) which have an elongated body covered with spiny, placoid scales whose tips are directed backward, making the skin extremely rough to the touch. On each side of the body there are five to seven gill slits.

The skeleton of sharks is still cartilaginous, but calcareous salts are deposited inside it. Their digestive tract is relatively short, leading from the mouth cavity to the pharynx and via a short gullet to the stomach. Sharks have a large liver, containing a large amount of liver fat, for which sharks are often hunted. Shark fins are also considered a delicacy, particularly in China.

Most sharks bear live young. A smaller number lay eggs that are usually square-shaped with long tendrils at each corner, by means of which they attach themselves to various plants.

Many sharks reach a length of only 1 m, but others may be up to 20 m long. Some species will even attack humans. More than 250 species inhabit the seas throughout the world except for the Caspian Sea. Only one species lives in fresh water.

The related rays (Rajiformes) have a dorsally flattened body with greatly broadened pectoral fins. The gill slits, numbering five pairs, are on the underside of the body. The tail is often whip-like.

Bony fishes (Osteichthyes) are a higher evolutionary group of jawed vertebrates. Their skeleton is either cartilaginous or bony, the body usually covered with scales, less often bare. In some species the scales have fused to form armour consisting of bony plates. In practically all instances, the fish have well-developed fins. The paired pectoral and pelvic fins correspond to the fore and hind limbs. The remaining fins are unpaired and consist of one or more dorsal fins, a caudal fin and one or more anal fins. The jaws are armed with teeth or are toothless. Practically all fish have a lateral line along the sides of the body, in which sensory cells are located, enabling them to perceive vibrations produced in the water like a kind of radar apparatus. Fish breathe by means of gills that are protected by a bony covering called the operculum.

Of the soft-boned fishes belonging to the super-order Chondrostei, which have rows of large bony plates down the length of the body and a cartilaginous skeleton, best known are the sturgeons (Acipenseriformes). Sturgeons have a head prolonged into a snout and a toothless mouth in the adult fish. On the underside of the mouth there are tactile appendages (barbels).

True bony fishes of the super-order Teleostei have a bony skeleton. The body is generally covered with dermal scales and the skin contains glands that secrete mucus. The skull is formed of flat, bony plates. Many species occur in shoals numbering millions of fish, for example herrings (Clupeidae). This family includes some 160 species of fish classed in 50 genera. They inhabit tropical and subtropical seas but are also found in the temperate zone, and even in arctic waters. They may also be found in fresh waters. Herrings generally stay far from the coast for most of their lives. During the spawning period they form huge shoals of more than 1 km long and 50 m wide. The annual haul of herrings comprises nearly 40 per cent of all worldwide commercial fishing, which indicates how important these fish are in our diet. Also well known are the salmonids (Salmonidae), which include freshwater as well as marine species, distinguished by having a small rayless adipose fin between the dorsal and caudal fins.

Of the freshwater fish, the best known are the pike (Esocidae) and the commercially important carp and minnow (Cyprinidae) which are bred artificially in ponds. Cyprinids are freshwater fish with toothless jaws but with oesophageal teeth on the last gill arch. Popular game fish are the catfish (Siluridae) which inhabit deeper bodies of fresh water. They have a naked scaleless skin and six long barbels around the mouth. The flesh of eels (Anguillidae) is very tasty. They are distinguished by having an extremely long snake-like body. Perch and their relatives (Perciformes) have hard fin rays in the forward portion of the double dorsal fin. Their number includes both marine and freshwater species. Often fished are mackerel (Scombridae), predacious marine fish with a spindle-shaped body, which occur in huge shoals. Cod and their relatives (Gadiformes) include many commercially important, mostly marine fish, for example Gadidae, which have a single barbel on the lower lip.

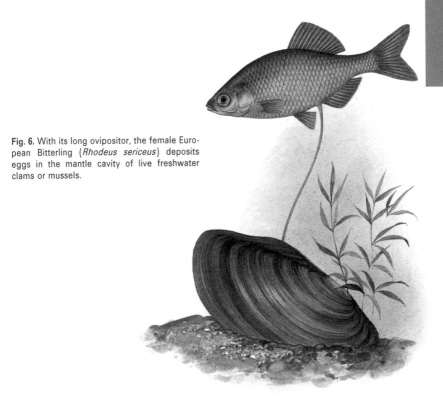

Fig. 6. With its long ovipositor, the female European Bitterling (*Rhodeus sericeus*) deposits eggs in the mantle cavity of live freshwater clams or mussels.

Class: **Lamprey and Hag Fishes**—Cyclostomata

Order: **Lampreys**—Petromyzoniformes

1 Brook Lamprey *Lampetra planeri*. Distributed over whole of Europe. Lives permanently in rivers and streams. Length up to 16 cm. In spring female lays 500—2,000 eggs. Larvae transform to adult individuals after 2—4 years. In spring, after completing metamorphosis, lampreys spawn in upper reaches where larvae also live. Adults die after spawning.

2 River Lamprey *Lampetra fluviatilis*. Lives in sea off coasts of northern Europe. Length up to 50 cm. In autumn migrates up rivers and in April or May spawns near places with sandy bed. Male builds nest — depression up to 50 cm in diameter — in which female lays 5,000—40,000 eggs. Male and female then die of exhaustion. Larvae, hatched in 14—21 days, live on small organisms. Grow to 18 cm, undergo metamorphosis at end of summer of third year. Toothless mouth acquires teeth and eyes emerge onto surface of head. On completing metamorphosis which takes 6—8 weeks, young lampreys migrate to sea where they live predaciously on different fishes. Tear food to pieces with teeth and suck it in. Grow quickly. When adult, return to spawning sites in rivers and streams. Swim 15—25 km daily against current. Lamprey has savoury flesh.

Class: **Cartilaginous Fishes**—Chondrichthyes

Order: **Sharks and Allies**—Selachiformes

3 Lesser Spotted Dog-fish *Scyliorhinus caniculus*. Lives off European coasts, including Mediterranean. Common round England. Length 1 m. Not dangerous to man. Hunts food (molluscs and crustaceans) on sea bed. Nocturnal animal. Female lays up to 20 eggs in hard capsules, with tendrils or corners for attachment to plants. Embryo takes about 6—7 months to develop. Fish's flesh edible but liver supposed to be poisonous.

Order: **Rays and Allies**—Rajiformes

4 Thorn-back Ray *Raja clavata*. Commonest European ray, also found in North Sea. Male attains 70 cm, female up to 125 cm in length. Wide pectoral fins give body rhomboid form. Dorsal skin covered with sharp spines. Ray mainly frequents ooze in shallows. Lives on crabs, shrimps, plaice, etc. Hard egg capsules have process at each of four corners. Eggs laid individually in sand. Embryo takes 4.5—5.5 months to develop. Ray's flesh very tasty.

1

2

3

Class: **Bony Fishes**—Osteichthyes

Subclass: **Ray-finned Fishes**—Actinopterygii

Order: **Sturgeons and Allies** — Acipenseriformes

5 Common Sturgeon *Acipenser sturio*. Abundant off coast of northern parts of Atlantic and in North Sea, Baltic, Mediterranean and Black Sea. Length about 2 m (maximum given as 3 m). Migrates in spring to large rivers to spawn and then returns to sea. Eggs, which resemble frogspawn, are laid on stony bed. One female lays 800,000—2,500,000 eggs. Fry hatch in a few days. Young migrate to sea within 2 years. Sturgeon looks mainly on sea bed for food (molluscs, crustaceans, worms, small fish) using tactile barbels, seizes it in protrusible mouth. Has now practically vanished from European rivers.

6 Sterlet *Acipenser ruthenus*. Lives in rivers emptying into Black and Caspian Seas. In central Europe occasionally appears in Danube as far as Linz. Long snout. Length 50 cm. Spawning season May—June. Catches food in same manner as preceding species. Has excellent flesh. Caviare is eggs or roe of female.

Order: **Herrings and Allies**—Clupeiformes

Family: **Herrings**—Clupeidae

7 European Shad *Alosa alosa*. Inhabits North Sea. Length up to 70 cm. In spring swims upstream to spawn. Female lays up to 200,000 eggs on river bed. Feeds on small animals. Likes clear water.

7

4

6

5

353

Family: **Salmonids**—Salmonidae

1 Salmon *Salmo salar.* Lives in sea off coasts of Europe, Asia and America. In autumn migrates en masse to source of rivers where it spawns in winter. The young (parrs) remain in river 3—5 years and then migrate to sea. Attain adulthood several years later. At spawning site, in cold water about 1 m deep, female makes depression by slapping tail, lays eggs in it and covers them with sand. Unlike other migratory fishes, salmon spawn several times, although many die of exhaustion or are killed by predators. One female lays up to 40,000 eggs. Survivors return to sea in early spring. Adult salmon measures up to 1.5 m and weighs 50 kg. Belongs to disappearing fauna of European rivers, although until fairly recent times hundreds of thousands still migrated inland to spawn every year. In time of migration and spawning does not eat. In sea lives on herrings, sprats, crustaceans, etc. Young salmon eat insect larvae and later small fish.

2 Trout *Salmo trutta.* Several species formerly differentiated, now races. Sea Trout (*S.t. trutta*) lives off coasts from France as far as Baltic. Length 1.3 m. Migrates up rivers only at spawning time. Lake Trout (*S.t. morpha lacustris*) inhabits Alpine and near-Alpine lakes and spawns in their inflowing streams. Female measures up to 80 cm, lays about 30,000 eggs. Most familiar form, Brown Trout (*S.t. morpha fario*) inhabits 'trout zone' of fast mountain streams. Distributed over whole of western, central and northern Europe as far as Finland and south to Italy and Morocco. Length up to 30 cm. Spawns in winter at age of 2—3 years, female lays up to 1,500 eggs. Likes clear water. Lives on insects, molluscs, worms, etc. One of the most popular fishes. Often bred artificially by collecting eggs and separating and cultivating viable ones. Rainbow Trout (*Salmo gairdneri irideus*), originally from North America, also bred in many parts of Europe. Tolerates warmer water, spawns in spring.

1

2

3

3 Huchen *Hucho hucho.* Lives in clean tributaries of Danube. Never migrates to sea. Measures up to 150 cm, weighs 15 kg (occasionally up to 30 kg). Highly predacious, catches fish and other aquatic vertebrates. In March—April swims short distances upstream and spawns on stony beds. Fully grown female lays up to 25,000 eggs. Sometimes bred artificially. Flesh excellent.

4 Alpine Charr *Salvelinus salvelinus.* Resembles trout. Inhabits cold Alpine lakes. Variable colouring and size (in lakes with poor food supply only up to 40 cm). Dark, normal and large form measuring up to 80 cm and weighing up to 10 kg distinguished. First two live on plankton, third on fish. Spawns from November to January near shore or in July on bed, at depth of 20—80 m.

5 Freshwater Houting *Coregonus lavaretus.* Inhabits cold lower reaches of rivers, brackish water and deep lakes in northern part of central and northern Europe. Very variable. Four basic forms, each with own local variability, distinguished. Lives on plankton. Some forms successfully bred in ponds.

6 Grayling *Thymallus thymallus.* Distributed over most of Europe. High dorsal fin. Length up to 48 cm, weight about 1 kg. Inhabits clean rivers and larger streams but likes warmer water than trout. Males larger than females, brightly coloured in spawning season (March—April). Lives on insect larvae, small animals, etc. Valued by anglers for its tasty flesh.

4

5

6

Order: **Pikes and Allies**—Esociformes

Family: **Pikes**—Esocidae

1 Pike *Esox lucius*. Inhabits rivers and stagnant water over whole northern hemisphere. Length up to 1.5 m., weight 40 kg. and more. In Europe spawns in March and April. Female lays up to 1,000,000 eggs in shallow water. Fry sink to bottom. After 2—3 hours attach themselves to aquatic plants or stones by means of special gland at end of head. Mouth and gills do not open for 8 days. Young pike then surface to fill bladder with air. Pike lives on fish, amphibians, etc.

Order: **Carps and Allies**—Cypriniformes

Family: **Carps and Minnows**—Cyprinidae

2 Carp *Cyprinus carpio*. Originally from south-eastern European and Asian rivers (China, Japan), has now been introduced into all European rivers. Bred artificially in ponds. Occasionally can measure up to 1.5 m and weigh 35 kg. River carp (wild form) has low body. Carp have been bred in Europe since 13th century. Many local breeds exist. Fully grown in 3—4 years. Spawning time May—June, at temperature of 15° to 20°C. Female lays 100,000—1,000,000 eggs, fry hatch in 3—6 days. In winter carp retires to deeper, muddy spots and hibernates. Lives on small animals and aquatic plants. Life span up to 50 years.

3 Crucian Carp *Carassius carassius*. Inhabits central and eastern Europe, also distributed in Asia and North America. Lives in stagnant and slow-flowing water. High body, no barbels. Length only 20—30 cm, weight about 1 kg. Spawns in May and June. Female lays up to 300,000 eggs on aquatic plants. Feeds on in-

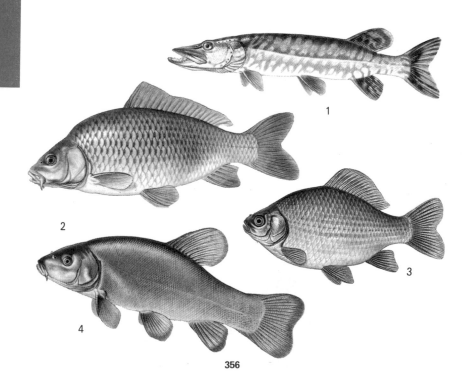

sects, molluscs and small crustaceans. Golden form also distinguished.

4 Tench *Tinca tinca*. Inhabits stagnant and slow-flowing water in Europe and western Siberia. Also occurs in brackish water of Baltic Sea. Length up to 50 cm, weight about 5 kg. Minute scales, slimy skin. Life span 20 years. Large specimens found only in deep lakes. Spawning time May—July. Female lays about 300,000 sticky eggs which adhere to aquatic plants. Nocturnal fish. Tasty flesh.

5 Roach *Rutilus rutilus*. Occurs in all rivers and in stagnant water in central and northern Europe. Also found in brackish water. Abundant everywhere. Length 15—35 cm, weight sometimes over 1 kg. Spawns near bank in April and May. Female lays 100,000 eggs. Important as food for predacious species, e.g. pike. Valueless in fishponds, in rivers popular with anglers.

Lives on river plants, small molluscs, crustaceans and insects.

6 Bream *Abramis brama*. One of largest European freshwater fishes. Length up to 70 cm, weight over 7 kg. High-backed, flat-sided body. Distributed from Urals to west of France and Britain. Inhabits stagnant and slow-flowing water with muddy bed. Spawns in May—July. Female lays 20,000—300,000 eggs at night. Young remain near banks in large shoals. Looks for food (small animals) mainly on bed, surfaces only at night.

7 Silver Bream *Blicca bjoerkna*. High-backed, short, very flat-sided body. Inhabits European rivers and ponds. Usually measures only 30 cm and weighs less than 1 kg. Spawns in May—June. Female lays about 100,000 eggs among aquatic plants. Of no economic importance. Lives on small animals and aquatic plants.

Family: **Carps and Minnows**—Cyprinidae

1 Orfe *Leuciscus idus*. Inhabits rivers and river-fed lakes all over Europe. Length 30—45 cm, occasionally up to 70 cm, weight 1—4 kg. Spawns in large shoals near banks from April to June. Female lays 40,000—100,000 eggs on stones and aquatic plants. Lives on insects, worms, small molluscs and crustaceans. Large specimens also eat small fish but Orfe not counted as predator. Has very tasty flesh but is comparatively rare.

2 Chub *Leuciscus cephalus*. Commonest fish in slow-flowing European rivers and streams. Length 30 cm (occasionally up to 70 cm), weight 0.25—5 kg. Spawning time April and May. Female lays up to 200,000 eggs on aquatic plants. Omnivorous. Eats water plants and small animals, often destructive to young trout populations. Flesh quite tasty.

3 Dace *Leuciscus leuciscus*. Distributed over whole of central and northern Europe. Inhabits fast rivers and streams, also stream-fed ponds. Length 15—20 cm, weight not more than 1 kg. Spawning season March—May. Rival of grayling and trout. Lives on small animals and some plants. Not very popular as food.

4 Asp *Aspius aspius*. Only truly predacious member of carp family. Found near surface of large rivers. Distributed over central and eastern Europe, also found in brackish waters of Baltic Sea. Robust but elongate body. Length 40 to 60 cm, weight 2—4 kg (in rare cases up to 1.2 m and 10 kg). Spawns from March to beginning of June. Female lays 80,000 to 100,000 eggs on sandy bed. Catches fish, amphibians and occasionally young birds, especially of aquatic species. Very retiring. Has tasty flesh so popular with anglers.

5 *Leucaspius delineatus.* Inhabits central and eastern Europe. Occurs in stagnant and slow-flowing water, also in small ponds and pools. Usually found in shoals. Characterized by silvery sheen and shortened lateral line. Length only 5—6 cm, in exceptional cases up to 12 cm. Spawning time April—May. Female lays about 150 eggs in spirals or rings round stems of aquatic plants. Male guards fry and fans oxygenated water towards them with pectoral fins. Young capable of further reproduction in one year. Lives on algae and small organisms. Important as food for predacious species.

6 *Alburnoides bipunctatus.* Inhabits central Europe. Common in southern and western Germany, elsewhere rare. Lives in shoals in fast, clean rivers, but not at altitudes of over 700 m. Length 9—11 cm. Spawns in April—June. Female lays eggs on sandy bed in flowing water. Fish used by anglers as bait.

7 Bleak *Alburnus alburnus.* Distributed over whole of Europe from Alps as far as Volga. Also found in brackish waters of Baltic Sea, but not in Scotland and Ireland. Inhabits lowland rivers or large river-fed lakes and ponds. Stays near surface. Length 10—15 cm. Spawns from March to June in shallow water near bank, to accompaniment of loud splashing. Female lays eggs at roots of trees extending into water, on aquatic plants, etc. Very abundant fish, important component of diet of predacious fishes. Also significant for destruction of large quantities of mosquito larvae. In addition eats plankton on surface of water. Often employed by anglers as bait in catching predatory fish. In places with very high incidence sometimes used for feeding pigs.

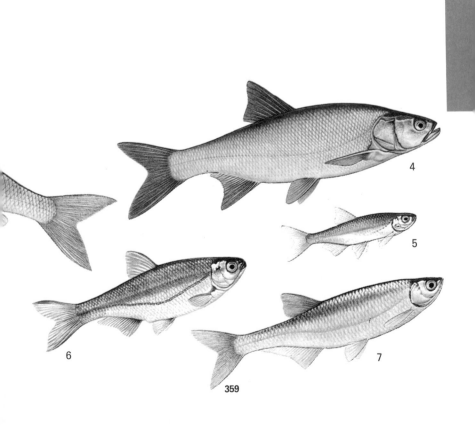

Family: **Carps and Minnows**—Cyprinidae

1 *Pelecus cultratus.* East-European fish. Formerly also inhabited bays of Baltic Sea. Often migrates from Black Sea up Danube. Length up to 60 cm. Lives in shoals. Spawns in May and June in salt and fresh water, some individuals in upper reaches of rivers. Female lays about 100,000 eggs on aquatic plants. Lives mainly on plankton.

2 Minnow *Phoxinus phoxinus.* Inhabits fast-flowing streams all over Europe, including mountains. Length 7—14 cm. Males don bright colours in spring. Spawning season May—July. Spawns in daytime, in shoals, in shallow water with sandy bed. Female lays 100—200 large yellow eggs. Fry grow very quickly. Life span 3—4 years. Lives on insect larvae and worms. Found in shoals near surface.

3 Bitterling *Rhodeus sericeus.* Inhabits central Europe north of Alps. Found in stagnant and slow-flowing water. Length 4—10 cm. Male brightly coloured at spawning time, female grows ovipositor. Fish collect in groups in sandy places with bivalves living on bed. Male releases cloud of milt in immediate vicinity of bivalve, which imbibes it together with water. Female inserts ovipositor into shell and lays egg which is fertilized inside shell. Process repeated until all eggs — usually about 40 — have been 'planted'. Shell protects both eggs and fry, which leave shelter after yolk has been consumed. Bitterling largely vegetarian but also eats small crustaceans and worms. Sometimes bred in aquariums.

4 Nase *Chondrostoma nasus.* Once plentiful in most European rivers, especially Oder and Elbe. Still abundant in Danube, Rhine and tributaries. Head produced to snout. Bottom-dweller. Spawning time March—May. Migrates upstream to stony places and spawns in shoals. Female lays up to 100,000 eggs. Adult fish attains up to 50 cm of length and weighs 2 kg. Lives on water plants and small animals. Flesh not very popular.

5 Barbel *Barbus barbus.* Inhabits whole of central Europe north of Alps, but rare west of Elbe. Lives at bottom of clear flowing water and pools. Length up to 70 cm, weight up to 5 kg. Gathers in shoals. Swims upstream in spawning season (April—June). Female lays 5,000—30,000 golden yellow eggs on sandy bed. Eats small animals, e.g. mayfly larvae and eggs and fry of other fishes. Its own roe is regarded as poisonous.

♀

♂

2

1

6 Rudd *Scardinius erythrophthalmus*. Inhabits stagnant and slow-flowing waters in Europe, in Alps up to altitude of 2,000 m. Adult fish has bright red abdominal, anal and caudal fins. Length up to 30 cm, weight 1 kg. Spawns in April and May. Female lays up to 100,000 reddish eggs on plants. Feeds on greenstuff and small animals. Has tasty flesh.

7 Gudgeon *Gobio gobio*. Distributed from west of France as far east as central Siberia. Absent in Spain and northern Sweden and Norway. Several subspecies. Single barbel on either side of mouth. Strikingly large fins. Lives at bottom of streams and rivers, also in stagnant water with stony and sandy bottoms. Occurs in brackish water in western part of Baltic. Often found in very large numbers in stream-fed ponds. Length 10—20 cm. Spawns from May to June. Female lays 1,000—3,000 eggs in small clumps on stones and aquatic plants. Young hatch in 10—20 days, according to temperature. Lives on small animals and vegetable debris. Gathers in large shoals, often in company of other fishes.

Family: **Carps and Minnows**—Cyprinidae

1 Eastern European Bream *Vimba vimba*. Common in central and eastern Europe. Lives near bed. Protruding upper jaw. Length 20—30 cm, weight up to 2 kg. Back often turns black at spawning time. Spawning season April—June. Thousands of fish frequently throng spawning site. Female lays 100,000—200,000 eggs. Lives on small bottom-dwelling animals. Flesh of no great value as food.

Family: **Loaches**—Cobitidae

2 Weatherfish *Misgurnus fossilis*. Inhabits greater part of Europe, but absent in England, Norway, Spain and Italy. Lives in mud at bottom of stagnant or slow-flowing water. Ten barbels round mouth help it in search for food. Length 20—30 cm. Spawning season April—June. Female lays up to 10,000 eggs on aquatic plants. Weatherfish has accessory intestinal respiration allowing it to live in oxygen-defficient water. Weatherfish has accessory intestinal respiration allowing it to live in oxygen-defficient water. Surfaces, swallows air, forces it down highly vascularized intestine and releases used air through anus. Eats small molluscs and other bottom-dwelling animals, also vegetable debris. Has savoury flesh.

3 Spined Loach *Cobitis taenia*. Inhabits whole of Europe except Norway, Scotland and Ireland. Lives at bottom of clean, slow-flowing or stagnant water with sandy bed. Has 6 short barbels on upper lip and 12—20 round spots on sides. Small, high-set eyes with yellow iris. Length 8—12 cm. Likes to burrow in sand with only head showing. Spawns April—June. Lives on small bottom-dwelling animals. Has accessory intestinal respiration. Below eyes has erectile spine raised when in danger. Hisses if handled.

4 Stone Loach *Noemacheilus barbatulus.* Distributed over whole of Europe except Norway and Sweden. Also abundant in Baltic bays. Lives at bottom of clean, flowing water, less often in lakes and ponds. Smooth snake-like body with scales on sides only. Colouring very variable, but belly always white or bluish. Length 10 to 15 cm. Spawns from April to June. Female lays about 6,000 eggs on aquatic plants. Eats small bottom-dwelling animals. Once regarded as great delicacy.

Family: **Catfishes**—Siluridae

5 European Catfish *Silurus glanis.* Distributed from Rhine as far east as western Asia. Large head with wide snout. Scaleless body. Inhabits deep, slow-flowing rivers, dams and lakes. In deep water may measure up to 3 m and weigh 250 kg. Solitary fish, occurs in pairs only at spawning time. Spawns from May to June near thickly overgrown banks. Female lays up to 200,000 eggs in shallow water at 18° to 20°C. Stays mainly near bottom, but likes to surface at night. Ungainly in appearance, but swift in action. Predacious. Hunts fish, aquatic birds up to size of goose, small mammals. Young specimens eat insects, molluscs and amphibians. Flesh has excellent flavour.

Family: **North American Catfishes**—Ictaluridae

6 Horned Pout *Ictalurus nebulosus.* Originally from USA Introduced into Europe in 1885 and now bred in rivers and ponds. Length up to 45 cm., weight 1 kg. As distinct from European catfish, has 8 barbels (i.e. 2 more) and adipose fin behind dorsal fin. Stays near bottom, active at night. Spawns in early spring, when found in pairs. Female forms nest-pit between roots, male guards eggs and young fry. Lives on small animals, e.g. fish, etc.

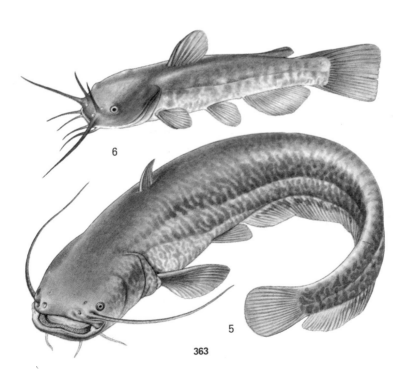

6

5

Order: **Eels and Allies**—Anguilliformes

Family: **Eels**—Anguillidae

1 European Eel *Anguilla anguilla.* Inhabits European coastal waters and rivers. Length over 1 m. (male only 50 cm), weight up to 5 kg. Eels migrate to western part of Atlantic (Sargasso Sea, east of West Indies), spawn in early spring at depth of 400 m and temperature of 17°C and then die. Larvae, formerly described as separate species, travel to European coasts with Gulf Stream. At two years measure about 7.5 cm and reach Europe. At three years acquire typical form and are known as 'elvers'. Invade rivers, develop slowly. Females develop in rivers, males at river mouth. On attaining sexual maturity migrate back to spawning site in sea, taking no food during journey. Male matures at 9, female at 12 years. Predacious fish, lives on different animals. Young bred in ponds.

Order: **Gar Pikes and Allies**—Beloniformes

Family: **Gar Pikes**—Belonidae

2 Gar Pike *Belone belone.* Lives in shoals in north-eastern part of Atlantic, also in Baltic, Mediterranean and Black Seas. Predacious fish. Lives on swimming crabs, fish, insects. Spawns in shallow water. Female lays eggs from May to June, among aquatic plants. Bones turn green when boiled.

Order: **Lophobranchiate Fishes**—Syngnathiformes

Family: **Pipe Fishes**—Syngnathidae

3 Narrow-nosed Fish *Syngnathus typhle.* Common in Baltic and North Sea. Length up to 30 cm. Variable colouring. Inhabits shallow water with dense vegetation. Spawns from April to August. Male carries eggs in special abdominal brood pouch, later deposits fry in sea. Eats small crustaceans and fish fry. Suctorial mouth, imbibes prey together with water.

Order: **Perches and Allies**—Perciformes

Family: **Sea Basses**—Serranidae

4 Sea Bass *Morone labrax.* Inhabits coastal waters of Europe and Africa. Often invades rivers, e.g. Elbe. Length up to 1 m. Spawns at river mouths, also in rivers, from May to July. Sea eggs float, river eggs lie on bed. Fry hatched in 6 days. Predacious fish, pursues pilchard shoals. Has savoury flesh.

Family: **Perches**—Percidae

5 Perch *Perca fluviatilis.* Inhabits rivers, lakes and ponds all over Europe. Common fish. Length up to 40 cm, weight 4 kg. For growth over 30 cm requires 15 years. Consorts in small

1

2

3

4

shoals. Spawning season April to beginning of June. Female lays strings of eggs (total up to 250,000) on aquatic plants etc. Fry hatched in 18 days, take no food up to age of 14 days. Predacious fish, often hunts in shoals. Tasty flesh.

6 Pikeperch *Stizostedion lucioperca.* Distributed over central and north-eastern Europe. Occurs in clean rivers, ponds and brackish water. Length up to 1.3 m, weight 10 kg. Spawns from April to June at depths of 3—5 m. Female lays up to 300,000 eggs in clumps. Predacious fish. When young catches small animals, later different fishes. Flesh has excellent flavour.

7 Pope or **Ruffe** *Acerina cernua.* Inhabits rivers of central and northern Europe. Abundant. Length up to 20 cm. Has preference for deep, clear water and for Baltic bays. Spawning season March—May. Female lays 50,000—100,000 eggs. Predacious fish. Eats insects, worms, crustaceans and eggs and fry of other fishes. Sometimes does serious damage.

8 Streber *Aspro streber.* Occurs only in Danube and tributaries. Lives in flowing water with stony bed. Length only 14—18 cm. Spawns from March to May. Predacious. Lives on worms, insects, small crustaceans and small fish.

5

6

7

8

Family: **Mackerels**—Scombridae

1 Common Mackerel *Scomber scombrus*. Inhabits Atlantic, Baltic, North Sea, Mediterranean and Black Sea. Length up to 50 cm. In summer frequents shallow coastal water, in winter deep water. Forms huge shoals. Spawns from May to August near coast. Female lays up to 400,000 eggs. At 3 years young mackerel measures 30 cm and is capable of reproduction. Lives first of all on small crustaceans, later on small herrings, sprats and molluscs. Has excellent flesh. Popular food all over Europe. Caught with nets while migrating.

Family: **Sculpins**—Cottidae

2 Miller's Thumb *Cottus gobio*. Inhabits practically whole of Europe. Found in swift-flowing rivers and streams, also in lakes. Stays near bottom and often hides under stones. Length 10—18 cm. Spawning season March—April. Female lays piles of eggs (total 100 to 300) in pits. Eggs guarded by male. Lives on small animals, including trout fry.

Order: **Cods and Allies**—Gadiformes

Family: **Cods**—Gadidae

3 Burbot *Lota lota*. Distributed over whole of northern hemisphere. Southern limit in Europe northern Italy. Lives in deep, flowing water or river-fed lakes and ponds. Found at quite high altitudes. Length 40—80 cm, weight up to 3 kg. In spawning season (November to beginning of February) swims short distances upstream and looks for sandy site. Female lays up to 1,000,000 eggs in shallow pits or on aquatic plants. Fry hatched in 4 weeks. Nocturnal fish. Predacious, catches smaller fishes and other animals. Flesh regarded as delicacy.

Order: **Flounders**—Pleuronectiformes

Family: **Soles**—Soleidae

4 Sole *Solea solea*. Found along European coasts of Atlantic, North Sea and part of Baltic. Length up to 50 cm. Colouring adapted to environment. Adults live on sandy bed at depths of not more than 50 m. Active at night. In North Sea spawns from April to August. Young specimens, still symmetrically built, remain near shore up to 2 years and even invade rivers. Eats worms, molluscs, crustaceans and small fishes. Great delicacy. Caught mainly in North Sea.

Order: **Anglers and Allies**—Lophiiformes

Family: **Anglers** or **Fishing Frogs**—Lophiidae

5 Common Angler Fish *Lophius piscatorius.* Occurs in North Sea, off coast of western Europe and in northern part of Mediterranean. Length up to 2 m. Has isolated, free fin rays on head and anterior part of body. Foremost ray carries leaf-like appendage. Several rows of sharp teeth in mouth. Frequents sea bed, usually found in mud. Spawns in March and April at depths of 1—2 km. Eggs rise to surface. Fry very bizarre in shape. Predacious fish. Lies in wait for prey, 'angling' with long dorsal spines. Lives on fishes, including small sharks and rays. Has very good flesh.

Order: **Sticklebacks and Allies**—*Gasterosteiformes*

Family: **Sticklebacks**—*Gasterosteidae*

6 Three-spined Stickleback *Gasterosteus aculeatus.* Distributed all over Europe, but introduced artificially in many places. Also plentiful along coast. Length 4—7 cm. Care of offspring interesting. At spawning time (April—June) brightly coloured male builds spherical nest from plant fragments and defends surrounding area. Female lays 80—100 eggs in nest and male guards eggs and fry. Several females may lay in one nest and one female may lay 5—6 times in one season. At end of spawning season sticklebacks combine in large shoals. Life span 2—3 years. Very predacious fish. Eats eggs and often fry of other fishes and sometimes does considerable damage. Can be kept in large aquariums with cold water.

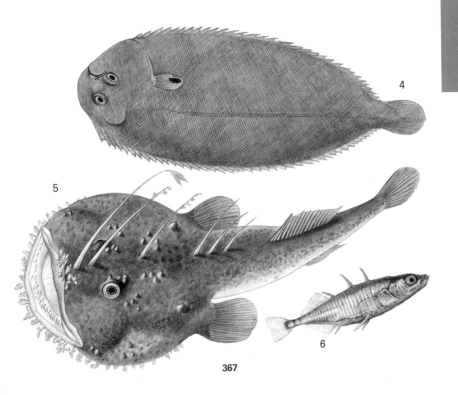

367

Amphibians and Reptiles

Amphibians (Amphibia) are four-footed verte-brates that develop by metamorphosis. The lar-va lives in water and breathes by means of gills, while the adult animal possesses lungs and can live on dry land. Some species, however, are ovoviviparous, that is the female gives birth to live young that have developed and hatched from eggs within her body. The skin of amphib-ians is scaleless and glandulous. It produces se-cretions that are often poisonous.

Tailed amphibians (Caudata) have four limbs that are well developed, although relatively puny, in adults and are used for crawling. The long, flat-sided tail is retained throughout the animal's lifetime and, together with movements of the body, enables it to swim. Tailed amphib-ians have a high regenerative capacity. This means that they are able to grow replacements for lost body parts, including bones. They are very plentiful animals that live on dry land but in rather moist places. In spring they make their way to water, usually to still bodies of water, where the females lay their eggs. During this period the males of many species develop a conspicuous crest on the back and tail. Very occasionally, as in the Alpine Salamander (*Sal-amandra atra*), the female does not bear aquatic larvae but gives birth directly to fully developed young that cast off their gills while still inside the female's body.

The jaws and inside of the mouth cavity are furnished with small simple teeth serving only to seize food. The tongue has little mobility and is usually attached along the whole of the un-derside. The eyes have eyelids. In species living in the dark waters of caves, the eyes are atro-phied; in other species they are large and keen-sighted. The hearing apparatus lacks a middle ear and eardrum, and therefore tailed amphib-ians have imperfect hearing. In the larval stage they breathe by means of gills, in the adult stage by means of lungs and often also through the skin or through the lining of the mouth. It is interesting to note that some species can repro-duce in the larval stage; this is called neoteny. Some species remain in the larval stage their whole life, breathe only by means of gills and never leave the water.

One of the European species that spends its entire life in water as a larva and does not change into a terrestrial form, is *Proteus sangui-nus*, found in the karst region of Yugoslavia, in Dalmatia and Herzegovina and also in neigh-bouring regions of Italy. It lives in the waters of caves in almost constant darkness and has re-duced eyes covered with skin. It will reproduce by means of eggs, but when the temperature reaches 15°C, as is usually the case in these caves, the embryos in the eggs develop inside the female's body and she then bears live young.

Most tailed amphibians live on dry land in the adult stage but still require considerable mois-ture. For this reason they seek places of con-cealment in damp places on warm dry days — in moss, under stones, under fallen tree trunks, or in rock crevices and holes. Most species do not emerge until dusk, when the air is cooler and moister, or during the daytime mainly after a rainfall.

The largest family of this order are the sala-manders and newts (Salamandridae). Best known in Europe is the Fire Salamander (*Salam-andra salamandra*). It is very plentiful in some places, mainly in forests around clear streams. It emerges from its hiding place mostly in the evening or early morning, but also regularly dur-ing the daytime after a rainfall. Its skin secretion is poisonous and may cause an unpleasant burn-ing sensation in the mucous membrane of hu-mans and predators.

Newts (*Triturus*) may be found in almost any still water, including flooded ditches, small pools in sand quarries and the like, primarily in spring. Newts have a very flat-sided tail, which indicates that they spend a great part of the year in water, where they swim primarily with the aid of their tails. During the breeding season the males differ markedly from the females. They develop a tall crest on the back and tail and also become extraordinarily brightly co-loured. At the end of this period the crests and bright coloration disappear and the males again resemble the females.

Frogs and toads (Salientia) are tailless am-phibians, usually with strong, muscular hind legs and webbed feet. Their larvae (tadpoles) have a tail that is absorbed following metamor-phosis, as are the gills. The skin is bare and sli-my. In many species, for example toads (*Bufo*), the fluid secreted through the skin is poisonous. The eardrums are located on the top of the head and are clearly visible. The eggs are laid in clusters or strings, usually in water, although in some tropical, as well as European, species the females lay their eggs on dry land. The tadpoles live in water, breathe by means of gills and undergo metamorphosis. The adult individuals that emerge from the water after metamorphosis breathe with fully developed lungs.

Frogs and toads have a very well-developed sense of territory and direction and this knowledge is, to a certain degree, permanently imprinted. Many species travel several kilometres every year on their return to pools, ponds or other bodies of water where they first developed as tadpoles. Early in spring they may often be seen moving in hordes in the direction of their natal pond. On the way they must overcome numerous obstacles, especially dangerous highways. At regular crossings of this kind, conservationists often erect bands of cloth or plastic alongside the highway, thus forcing the frogs to halt before this insurmountable barrier. They then catch the frogs and carry them to the other side of the road where the frogs can continue, unharmed, on their way across fields and meadows to their goal.

During the breeding season, vocal communication plays an important role and the sounds uttered by the males of many species are very distinctive. Some species remain in water only during the breeding period, for example toads. Others always live near water and still others live in water for most of the year, for example *Bombina*.

Fig. 1. The Moor Frog (*Rana arvalis*) usually inhabits pools on moors, but also occurs in ponds, particularly in spring.

Many frogs and toads have special protective equipment that serves to frighten or ward off attackers, for example the brightly coloured bellies of *Bombina* toads. When danger threatens and the toad cannot escape into water, it lifts its head and places its front legs on its curved back, thereby suddenly showing the warning coloration of its belly. If, in spite of this, a predator seizes the toad in its mouth, it immediately feels the effect of poisonous fluid secreted by the skin, which causes a sharp burning sensation in the mouth. Usually the attacker learns its lesson and the next time it sees the warning coloration it leaves the toad alone.

Fig. 2. Male Crested Newts (*Triturus cristatus*) grow a high, toothed crest down the length of the back during the mating season.

Fig. 3. The Yellow-bellied Toad (*Bombina variegata*) buries itself in mud when danger threatens. When there is not time to do this, it shows the warning coloration of its belly to frighten off the enemy.

Reptiles (Reptilia) are higher vertebrates that no longer require an aquatic environment for their development. The eggs with their embryonic membranes show a marked adaptation to development in a terrestrial environment. The skin of reptiles has a horny epidermis and is covered with horny scales to prevent the body from becoming too dry. Turtles have bony plates fused with certain bones to form a shell.

Reptiles breathe only by means of lungs. They cannot regulate their body temperature; their blood, and thereby their body, gains heat only from the environment around them. When that becomes hotter, they warm up; conversely, their body loses heat as the environment becomes colder. They are then less active or even practically immobile and during the cold season they hibernate. They wait out periods of drought in summer in a similar torpid state, particularly in the case of aquatic reptiles when the body of water they live in dries out.

Sight is a very important sense in many species of reptiles. The eyes are fitted with eyelids that are variously shaped in the different groups, for example fused concentrically in chameleons or completely fused and transparent in snakes (Serpentes) or geckos. The hearing apparatus of reptiles lacks earlobes, the eardrum being protected only by skin or scales. Snakes have no eardrum whatsoever, nor do they have a Eustachian tube, therefore they are deaf to airborne sounds.

The senses of taste and smell are imperfectly developed in most reptiles but in many they are replaced by the so-called Jacobson's organ. Snakes and certain lizards (Sauria) have a broadly forked tongue which they extend, flick from one side to the other, and then retract. With the tip of this tongue they 'collect' molecules of volatile substances from the air, which they then place inside a special paired depression on the upper roof of the mouth for

371

Fig. 4. The poison apparatus of the Common Viper (*Vipera berus*). Venom is produced in a paired gland located in the upperpart of the head far behind the eye. The gland is encircled by constrictors, muscles that contract violently to push the venom, via a small channel, into the fangs.

analysis. This depression contains very sensitive cells, similar to the cells in the human nose. The reptile is thus immediately informed either of prey within reach or of imminent danger. Some reptiles, for example lizards, are also furnished with a sense of smell that is independent of the Jacobson's organ.

Some reptiles are toothed, for example snakes and lizards; others, such as turtles, are toothless and only have jaws that are similar to the beaks of birds of prey. Teeth are usually adapted only for seizing and holding prey. In some species the salivary glands are transformed into poison glands that secrete venom. Venomous reptiles have special grooved or hollow teeth through which the venom can flow into the body of the snake's victim when it is bitten.

Many reptiles have four well-developed limbs; others have variously reduced limbs or none whatsoever.

Reptiles usually reproduce by laying eggs, which have either a hard, calcareous shell or only a leathery or parchment-like cover. Some species are ovoviviparous; that is, the eggs develop within the body of the female. The female then bears live young, or else the young hatch immediately after the eggs are laid.

Turtles (Testudinae) are a distinctive group of reptiles that possess an unusual organ of passive defence—a hard, bony body cover. This is composed of two parts: an upper, dorsal shell called the carapace, and an undershell called the plastron. In some species of turtles, however, the shell is atrophied and sometimes it is covered with a thick, leathery layer. The two pieces are joined at the sides, either firmly or by ligaments, with an opening in front for the head and forelegs and one at the back for the tail and hind legs. The dorsal shell is usually convex, the undershell flat. The surface is covered with horny plates. Some species can conceal the head, tail and legs completely inside the two shells.

The turtle's jaws are toothless and covered by a horny skin, like the beak of a bird. On the edges of the jaws the horny layer is sharp, especially in carnivorous species. The tongue is fleshy and attached along much of its length so that it cannot be extended. Turtles have a good sense of sight; the eye has two eyelids and a nictitating membrane. The legs usually have five digits and are adapted either for burrowing in terrestrial species or for swimming in aquatic species. Some species have fewer than five digits. All turtles reproduce by means of eggs which have a hard, but relatively elastic, shell. The females bury these in sand or loose soil. Turtles can go without food for a long time; some species may fast for over a year.

Fig. 5. Like all snakes, the Grass Snake (*Natrix natrix*) gets its bearings by means of its forked tongue.

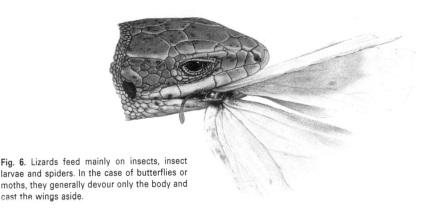

Fig. 6. Lizards feed mainly on insects, insect larvae and spiders. In the case of butterflies or moths, they generally devour only the body and cast the wings aside.

Lizards and snakes together comprise the order Squamata. The distinguishing features they have in common are a body covered with scales and a slit-like cloaca.

Lizards (Sauria) are the largest group of reptiles. They usually have well-developed legs but in some species the legs are atrophied or absent altogether. Their most important sense is sight. The eyes are furnished with eyelids which, in geckos, for example, are fused together and transparent. Many species of lizards have a cartilaginous disc in the tail vertebrae, at which point the tail readily snaps off. This is an important means of defence when danger threatens. The lizard casts off its tail, the enemy generally goes after the moving tail, and the lizard makes its escape. The broken-off tail usually grows in again; the new one can be distinguished by the different shape of the scales. The skeletal parts of the tail do not grow in again, however, and the tail is now stiffened by a band of tough ligaments. This group of lizards includes the European lizards (*Lacerta*) and geckos. Most lizards reproduce by laying eggs, usually enclosed in a membranous cover. Some species are ovoviviparous. Lizards feed on both animals and plants.

Snakes (Serpentes) are a specialized group of reptiles adapted for seizing and swallowing large victims. They are without limbs. The eyelids are fused together and transparent. Snakes shed their skins regularly and every time they do so the skin of the fused eyelids also peels off. Snakes reproduce either by laying eggs which have a soft outer covering, or else they are ovoviviparous. Snakes are carnivores, feeding exclusively on living prey. Some species suffocate their victims first and then swallow them whole, others kill them by injecting venom with their fangs before swallowing their prey.

Fig. 7. The young of the Grass Snake hatch from eggs enclosed in a soft, leathery covering.

Class: **Amphibians**—Amphibia

Order: **Tailed Amphibians**—Caudata

Family: **Salamanders and Newts**—Salamandridae

1 Fire Salamander *Salamandra salamandra.* Inhabits whole of central Europe and extends as far as North Africa. Lives in damp moss, among stones near streams and in small rodent holes. Found at altitudes of over 1,200 m. Hibernates deep underground or in caves, often gregariously. Reappears at end of March. In April—May female deposits up to 70 well developed larvae with gills and 4 limbs and measuring about 3 cm, at source of brook. Metamorphosis (transformation to terrestrial form) takes place after 3—4 months. In rare cases larvae spend winter in water. After completing metamorphosis young leave water. Fully grown after 5 years. Length 20 cm. Lives on spiders, worms, gastropods and insects. Skin secretes poisonous substance lethal for small animals. Life span 18 years. Can sometimes be heard squeaking. Most often encountered on forest paths after rain.

2 Alpine Salamander *Salamandra atra.* Glossy black all over. Inhabits Alpine regions (at altitudes of 700—3,000 m) and certain Balkan ranges. Length about 15 cm. Hides under stones and moss and in bushes. Not dependent on water. Female produces two fully developed young which before birth grow to 5 cm and lose gills. Larvae in female's body live on yolk of eggs which fail to develop. Salamander's diet consists of small insects, spiders, worms and small molluscs. Fully grown after 3—5 years.

3, 4 Crested Newt *Triturus cristatus.* Inhabits whole of central Europe and extends to Urals. Length 14—18 cm. Rarely found at altitudes of over 1,000 m. At pairing time male grows high, doubled crest which starts on forehead and stretches up to tip of tail. Males court females in striking nuptial ceremonies. Crestless female lays over 100 eggs on aquatic plants in stagnant water in April or May. Larvae hatch in 2—3 weeks. Metamorphosis after 3 months when larva measures 4.5—9 cm. Adults remain in water long after egg-laying, often until late summer. Newt fully grown at 4 years. Hibernates under leaves and in holes, occasionally under water in mud. Predacious. Catches small crustaceans, insects and molluscs, also eats frog's eggs and tadpoles and larvae of own species.

1

5 Smooth or **Common Newt** *Triturus vulgaris.* Distributed over whole of Europe. Length 8—11 cm. Very plentiful. Dorsal crest at pairing time less dentated than in Crested Newt and continuous at tail base. Female lays 100—250 eggs singly on aquatic plants, usually from beginning of May until June. Larvae hatch in 2 weeks. Metamorphosis after 3 months. Adults visit water only at pairing time. Lives on insects, worms, gastropods and, in water, on tadpoles, etc.

6 Alpine Newt *Triturus alpestris.* Mainly central-European animal, but also extends further west. Length 8—12 cm. At pairing time male wears low dorsal crest and its orange underside turns red. Found at altitudes of up to 3,000 m. Inhabits clear lakes, mountain pools and slow-flowing water. Female lays eggs from March to June. Larvae, hatched in 2—3 weeks, measure about 7 mm. Metamorphosis after 3—4 months when larvae attain 3 cm of length. Cases of reproduction in larval stage known.

3

4

2

5

6

Order: **Tailless Amphibians**—Salientia

Family: **Discoglossids**—Discoglossidae

1 Red-bellied Toad *Bombina bombina*. Inhabits central and eastern Europe. Occurs mainly in lowlands. Length about 4.5 cm. Lives in ponds, pools, etc. Female lays eggs several times a year but chiefly in May and June. Deposits them in groups on aquatic plants or on bottom. Tadpoles very large. Metamorphosis in September—October. Hibernates in holes, under leaves, etc. Reappears in spring and spends whole of summer in water. Eats small aquatic animals. When in danger, burrows in mud.

2 Yellow-bellied Toad *Bombina variegata*. Inhabits whole of Europe except north and Britain. Eggs laid in June, sometimes later. Tadpoles hatch in 7—9 days. Metamorphosis after 4 months. Hibernates on dry land. From spring, for whole of summer, lives in water. Staple diet mosquito larvae.

3 Midwife Toad *Alytes obstetricans*. Inhabits west of central Europe and south-western Europe. Found in uplands and mountains. Length 5.5 cm. Pairing season early spring to summer. Pairs on dry land. Male winds strings of 20—100 large eggs round legs and carries them until tadpoles are hatched (3—6 weeks). Hatched tadpoles remain in water, undergo metamorphosis in late autumn or following spring. Nocturnal animal. Bell-like call. Lives on insects, worms, spiders, etc.

Family: **Spade-footed Toads**—*Pelobatidae*

4 Spade-footed Toad *Pelobates fuscus*. Distributed over whole of central Europe, extends east to western Siberia. Length up to 8 cm. Nocturnal animal, seldom seen in daytime. From March to May female lays 1,000 eggs in strings 15—50 cm long, in pools etc. Tadpoles black, measure over 10 cm. After metamorphosis toads measure 3 cm. Crawl out on to dry land. Adults also live on land and leave water after eggs are laid. Hibernate in holes up to 2 m. deep. Eat small animals. Toad emits garlicky odour.

Family: **True Toads**—Bufonidae

5 Common Toad *Bufo bufo*. Distributed over whole of Europe and Asia. Length 12 cm, in south up to 20 cm. Abundant everywhere. Occurs in woods, fields, gardens, etc.; often found in cellars. Nocturnal animal. Eats insects, molluscs, worms, occasionally small amphibians. Hibernates in dry holes, etc. Female lays 2 strings of 1,200—6,000 eggs which both parents twine round aquatic plants. Tadpoles, hatched in 12 days, live gregariously. Metamorphosis after 77—91 days; young then leave water. Grow slowly, attain adulthood at 5 years. Life span up to 40 years. Male utters snorting barks.

6 Green Toad *Bufo viridis*. Distributed through western and central Europe as far as Mongolia. Occurs even in dry habitats, in mountains up to altitude of 3,000 m. Digs burrows about 30 cm deep. Nocturnal animal. Lives on insects, spiders, worms, etc. Hibernates on dry land. In spring female lays two strings of 10,000—12,000 eggs, 3—4 m long, on aquatic plants in shallow water. Male's pairing call in spring is pleasant trill. Metamorphosis after 60—91 days. Fully grown at 4 years.

7 Natterjack Toad *Bufo calamita*. Distributed over western and central Europe. Length 6—8 cm. Crawls, does not jump. Good swimmer, climber and burrower (in winter to depth of 3 m). In May female lays 3,000—4,000 eggs on aquatic plants. Metamorphosis after only 42—49 days. Young (1 cm) climb into trees. Nocturnal animal. Loud, croaking call. Eats insects, worms, etc.

5

6

7

1

2 Edible Frog *Rana esculenta*. Inhabits whole of Europe, Asia and North Africa. Occurs at both low and high altitudes. Found only near water. Male attains 7.5 cm of length, female up to 13 cm. In May or June female lays 2,000—3,000 eggs in clumps. Tadpoles hatch in 5—6 days. Metamorphosis after 130 days. Tadpoles sometimes hibernate in water. Lives on insects, worms, spiders and small fish. Adults hibernate at water bed in mud, young on dry land. Fond of taking sun-baths. Males have typical croak (crax-crax).

3 Marsh Frog *Rana ridibunda*. Distributed over central and southern Europe, also occurs in south-eastern England, Holland and on Baltic coast. Found near water in warm places in lowlands. Length 15—17 cm. Pairing time April—May. Female lays 5,000—10,000 eggs. Metamorphosis after 83—125 days. Catches insects, worms, small fish and young of small mammals and birds. Very loud call (cray-cray-cray-cray). Hibernates at water bed. Old individuals often hibernate in slow-flowing water.

Family: **Tree Frogs**—Hylidae

1 Common Tree Frog *Hyla arborea*. Found all over Europe. Length 3.5—4.5 cm. Takes to water at pairing time. In May female lays up to 1,000 eggs in clumps. Metamorphosis after 90 days. Young frogs crawl out on to land. After egg-laying adults return to bushes and trees. Colouring adapted to environment. Lives on insects and spiders. In autumn frogs retire under stones, into holes, etc. Many hibernate in mud. Males have clear tinkling call.

2

3

4 Common Frog *Rana temporaria*. Distributed over most of Europe, extends to eastern Asia. Can be found beyond Arctic Circle. Abundant everywhere. Frequents parks, gardens, woods, etc. In Alps found up to altitude of 3,000 m. Length 10 cm. Often pairs in March, in mountains and north in May and June. Heard only during pairing season. Female lays 1,000—4,000 eggs. Tadpoles hatch in 3—4 weeks. Metamorphosis after 2—3 months but tadpoles sometimes hibernate in water. After egg-laying frog lives on dry land, but in mountains may also remain in water during summer. Nocturnal animal. At end of October returns to water to hibernate but young individuals (up to 3 years) mostly hibernate on land. Eats insects, slugs, spiders and worms.

5 Field Frog *Rana arvalis*. Extends from Belgium across central and northern Europe to Arctic Circle and east to Siberia. Occurs mainly in boggy meadows. Pairs in March and April. Female lays up to 2,000 eggs in 1 or 2 spherical clumps. Spends summer on land, in autumn returns to water to hibernate. Metamorphosis after 2—3

months. Fully grown at 3 years. Nocturnal animal but young also active during day. Lives on insects, molluscs, worms, etc. Deep, muted call. Male turns bluish at pairing time.

6 Dalmatian Frog *Rana dalmatina*. Inhabits central and south-eastern Europe. In north extends to south of Sweden. Lives in damp riverside woods in lowlands. Male attains 6 cm of length, female 9 cm. Very long hind legs (up to 12.5 cm). Jumps 1 m high at distance of 2 m. Pairs at night at end of March and in April. Female lays 600—1,500 eggs in pools, etc. Metamorphosis after 2—3 months. Young frogs crawl out on to dry land. In summer often found far from water. Eats mainly insects. Hibernates chiefly in water. Call barely audible.

6

5

4

Class: **Reptiles**—Reptilia

Order: **Testudinates**—Testudines

Family: **Freshwater** or **Pond Turtles**—Emydidae

1 European Pond Turtle *Emys orbicularis*. Distributed over central and southern Europe, south-western Asia and north-western Africa. Formerly also inhabited England and Rhineland. Length up to 35 cm. Mainly frequents stagnant water, creeks or slow-flowing water with muddy bed and plenty of vegetation. Eats insects, worms, molluscs, small fish and some greenstuffs. Fond of sunning itself beside water. In May or June female lays 3—15 eggs about 3 cm long in small pit in bank and covers them. Young, hatched in 8—10 weeks, measure 2.5 cm. In October turtle retires to mud to hibernate.

Order: **Scaly Reptiles**—Squamata

Suborder: **Lizards**—Sauria

Family: **Skinks**—Scincidae

2 Snake-eyed Skink *Ablepharus kitaibelii*. Distributed over south-eastern Europe, extends to Hungary and Czechoslovakia in central Europe. Length about 10 cm. Inhabits rocky wooded steppes, deserted vineyards and outskirts of dry, open woods. Lives mainly on small insects. Very quick and agile. Female lays 3—8 eggs.

Family: **True Lizards**—Lacertidae

3 Wall Lizard *Lacerta muralis*. Distributed round Mediterranean, extends to western and central Europe. Length up to 20 cm. Expert climber of rocks and trees. Diet consists of insects, spiders and worms. In May or June female lays 2—8 eggs in small pit. Young hatch in 6—8 weeks. Hibernates in holes, crevices, etc. Each animal has own 'preserve'.

4 Sand Lizard *Lacerta agilis*. Very common in Europe north of Alps. Extends west to England and east to central Asia. Length up to 20 cm and over. Male's back predominantly green, female's grey. Frequents warm, sunny slopes, clearings, etc. Found at altitudes of up to 2,000 m. In May or June female lays 3—15 eggs in shallow pit. Young hatch in 7—12 weeks. Hibernates in holes, under piles of leaves, etc. Each animal has own 'preserve'. Eats insects, spiders and centipedes.

5 Green Lizard *Lacerta viridis*. Inhabits southern and central Europe. Length up to 50 cm in south, about 30 cm in central Europe. Frequents warm, rocky places. Expert climber. In spring males fight. In May or June female lays 5—13 (in south up to 21) eggs. Young hatch in 6—8 weeks. Lives on insects, molluscs, small lizards and snakes. Digs burrows up to 1 m deep. Retires to hibernate in October, reappears in April.

1

2

6 **Common** or **Viviparous Lizard** *Lacerta vivipara*. Distributed over central and northern Europe, occasionally found beyond Arctic Circle. Occurs mainly in mountainous regions but also in plains. Female lays 2—12 eggs at short intervals. Young hatched immediately, measure about 3 cm. In north young hatched in female's body but in Pyrenees from laid eggs. Lives on insects, spiders, etc. Young also eat plant-lice.

Family: **Slow-worms**—Anguidae

7 **Slow-worm** or **Blind-worm** *Anguis fragilis*. Distributed from England to south of Sweden and across whole of Europe to Algeria. Length up to about 50 cm. Variable colouring. Very abundant in places. Occurs at altitudes of up to 2,200 m. Found mainly under leaves, stones, etc. in deciduous woods with damp soil. Hibernates in holes from end of October, usually gregariously. Ovoviviparous (young hatched from eggs immmediately); one female produces 5—26 young. Eats molluscs, worms and insects. Tail easily snapped off but grows again.

Suborder: **Snakes**—Serpentes

Family: **Colubrid Snakes**—Colubridae

1 Tessellated Snake *Natrix tessellata*. Extends from south-west of France across Germany to central Asia and to eastern part of North Africa. Length up to 1 m, usually less. Spends greater part of life in water. Found at altitudes of up to 2,700 m. Staple diet small fish, occasionally eats amphibians. In some places wreaks havoc among fish fry. Female lays 4—12 eggs at end of June or in July. Disappears in October, often hibernates in rodent burrows near water.

2 Grass Snake *Natrix natrix*. Common all over Europe, extends east as far as Aral Sea. Found mainly near water. Occurs at altitudes of up to 2,000 m. Has distinctive spots on sides of head. In autumn retires to hibernate in crevices, holes, etc., often gregariously. Eats amphibians, occasionally small fish and mammals. Young also eat insects. In July—August female lays 6—30 (in rare cases up to 70) eggs under leaves, in waterside soil or in moss. Young, hatched in 2 months (in south sooner), measure 11—18 cm.

3 Aesculapian Snake *Elaphe longissima.* Inhabits warm parts of Europe and south-western Asia. Length up to 2 m. Largest European snake. Lives in deciduous woods or areas with plenty of bushes. Found in Alps at altitudes of up to 2,000 m. Climbs trees extremely well, plunders birds' nests and devours young. Main diet, however, small rodents and lizards. At end of June or beginning of July female lays 5–8 tough eggs 5.5 cm long and 3.5 cm wide in holes, hollow trees and stumps. Young hatch in 6–8 weeks. Snake starts to hibernate in autumn. Uses hollow tree stumps, mammals' burrows, rock crevices, etc.

4 Smooth Snake *Coronella austriaca.* Inhabits practically whole of Europe except Ireland and Mediterranean islands. Extends eastwards into western Asia. Length not more than 75 cm. Very abundant in places. Preference for woods and thickets. Found at altitudes of up to 2,200 m. Lives mainly on lizards, occasionally eats small rodents or birds and sometimes other snakes. Young also eat insects. Ovoviviparous. Female lays 2–15 eggs at end of August or beginning of October and young are hatched immediately. Often mistaken for viper.

Family: **Vipers**—Viperidae

5 Common Viper *Vipera berus.* Inhabits central Europe, parts of southern Europe, northern Europe to beyond Arctic Circle and large part of Asia as far as Japan. Length about 80 cm. Variable colouring, typical zigzag line invisible in black specimens. Usually found in mixed forests. Occurs at altitudes of up to 2,700 m. Largely nocturnal, hunts also by day at very high altitudes only. Staple diet small rodents. Potent venom. Does not actively attack man. At end of August or beginning of September female either gives birth to live young or lays 6–20 eggs from which young are hatched immediately. In spring males fight, each attempting to 'flatten' rival but without injuring it. Retires in October. Hibernates gregariously, often together with other snakes, in holes in ground, crevices in rocks, etc.

6 Asp Viper *Vipera aspis.* Distributed over south-western Europe, extends to southern part of Black Forest (Germany). Occurs in rocky places in uplands and on lower slopes of mountains. Nocturnal animal. Lives on small rodents and occasionally small birds. Young catch small lizards. Female gives birth to young in August. Venom very potent, bite fatal in 2–4% of cases. Length not more than 75 cm.

5

6

Birds

Birds (Aves) are higher vertebrates than reptiles, with a constant and relatively high body temperature, ranging from 38—44 °C. Birds have two pairs of limbs, the front pair being in the form of wings, which are normally used for flying. Some species of birds, however, have frail wings that are incapable of flight or are adapted only for swimming. Of the European birds, one such flightless bird was the Great Auk, now extinct. All present-day European birds belong to the group of fliers (Carinata).

The sense organs of birds have developed in different degrees. For instance, birds have little sense of taste because taste buds are usually located quite deep inside an animal's mouth on the soft upper palate and on the mucous membrane underneath the tongue. Also, birds do not

Fig. 1. The Sand Martin or Bank Swallow (*Riparia riparia*) flies swiftly above the surface of rivers, ponds and lakes, capturing insects on the wing.

chew their food but swallow it whole or in chunks and thus are unable to taste it as mammals do. The sense of smell is likewise very poorly developed in birds.

The sense of touch is developed in varying degrees. Birds generally have sensory organs inside the bill and on the tongue, but some also have them at the base of certain feathers and on the legs. Birds that obtain their food from the ground where they cannot see what they are picking up even have these organs at the tip of the bill, for example the woodcock (*Scolopax*). Special organs for perceiving heat are usually located on the unfeathered parts of the body.

A bird's most perfect and important sensory organ is the eye. Birds see far better than other animals. The eye is large and focuses not only by means of muscles squeezing the lens, as in the case of mammals, but also by flattening or bulging. The eyes can be moved independently and thus each can look at a different object at the same time. The eyes are usually located on either side of the head and thus each has its own field of vision. Some birds, however, such as owls, have both eyes facing forward. Colour vision in birds is about the same as in people. In addition to an upper and lower eyelid, birds have another special lid, called a nictitating membrane, which extends from the inner corner and can cover the entire eye. The retina has a greater density of sensory cells than the eye of a human; this is up to five times greater in raptors which can thus spot their prey from a great height.

Fig. 2. The Kingfisher (*Alcedo atthis*) feeds chiefly on small fish, plunging abruptly beneath the water's surface to capture its prey. It then carries this to a branch before swallowing it so that it can savour its meal in peace.

385

Fig. 3. The Eagle Owl (*Bubo bubo*) has large eyes at the front of the head, as do all owls.

Fig. 4. The Barn Owl (*Tyto alba*) has a very keen sense of hearing. The flight of owls is silent. As they fly they can hear even the slightest squeaking of rodents or rustling of leaves on the ground and thus readily capture their prey.

Another important sensory organ is the ear, even though it is less perfect in structure than the eye and still resembles the ear of the reptiles. There is only one earbone, corresponding to the stirrup in the human ear, and the external ear channel is relatively short. Despite this, a bird's hearing is very good and some species, such as the owls, use it to hunt their prey in the dark.

The vocal organs, located at the lower end of the trachea, also play an important role in the life of birds. This organ, called the syrinx, is exceptionally well developed in songbirds. In other groups of birds the vocal organs are simpler and these birds usually have a monotonous call or may only produce raucous sounds. And then there are some birds, such as the White Stork (*Ciconia ciconia*), that have no vocal organs at all and communicate by clapping their beaks.

The bird skeleton is not only strong, it is also light because most of the bones are hollow and filled with air. The long bones, in particular, are tubular. The low weight of the skeleton is an important factor in flight. Birds' feathers are also very light and are arranged to form an impermeable surface that traps pockets of air. The simplest form of flight is passive gliding flight in

Fig. 5. The White Stork (*Ciconia ciconia*) is a mute bird, producing only hissing sounds. Breeding pairs communicate by clapping their beaks. They usually lay their heads along their backs in greeting.

which the bird travels only by means of its outspread wings, supported by the resistance of the air. Another similar form of flight is when the bird takes advantage of rising air currents to soar upward. The chief form of flight, however, is active flight achieved by flapping the wings, which, of course, consumes large amounts of energy. The speed of active flight of various species differs and the wings are adapted accordingly. Birds with long narrow wings are better fliers than birds with short, broad wings.

The bill, covered by a thick and horny sheath, is another important part of the bird's body. The bill shows marked variation in shape in different species of birds, depending on the kind of food they eat. In the bill of raptors, the upper mandible is downcurved and very sharp on the edge, which enables the birds not only to rip and tear the flesh of their victim but also to cut off pieces. Ducks have a flat bill with a serrated edge, which serves to sieve food. Seed-eating birds have a stout, hard, conical bill that enables them to break hard seed coverings. The bill of insectivorous birds is narrow and pointed at the tip to help them to extricate insects from crevices. Herons (Ardidae) have a long, pointed bill which they often use as a spear when hunting. Some birds have an upcurved bill; in others it curves downward, while some specialists, such

Fig. 6. Raptors have a stout, hooked beak that is used to kill and tear prey as well as to pluck it.

Underneath the contour feathers the body is usually covered with fine down feathers with a short, fine quill but without a shaft and with barbules that do not possess hooklets. In many birds, such as ducks, the down feathers play an important role in nesting, for the birds use them to line the edges of their nests. Down feathers provide good heat insulation and prevent the eggs from getting cold during the temporary absence of the female, who covers them before her departure from the nest. Another type of feather is the filament feather which is thin, almost hair-like, with a brush-like tip. These feathers usually grow immediately next to the contour feathers. Growing at the gape of the beak of certain birds are bristle feathers, which serve mainly as tactile organs when catching prey.

Feathers may be variously coloured. Such coloration is of two kinds. One is caused by colouring matter (pigments), the other by the

Fig. 7. The long beak of the Curlew (*Numenius arquata*) is adapted for hunting molluscs and insect larvae in mud, or earthworms in soft soil.

as the crossbills (*Loxia*) have bills with overlapping tips to facilitate the extraction of seeds from the cones of conifers. Other birds have a bill that is adapted for catching fish; some have a bill that is adapted for cracking the hard shells of bivalves.

The body of a bird is covered with feathers. These do not grow over the entire surface, however, but are arranged in definite tracts called the pterylae. The bare spaces between the feathered tracts are called apteria. Because these are masked by the surrounding feathers, they are not apparent at first glance. The feathers that give the body its typical shape are called contour feathers, for example the flight feathers. Such a feather has a long, firm, but flexible, shaft bordered on both sides by a web composed of separate individual barbs which, in turn, carry rows of smaller barbules supplied with hooklets. If the web is damaged in any way, the bird strokes it with its bill or claws, causing the hooklets to catch and restore the web again. The oar feathers, or tail feathers, are also usually long, with strong barbs. In some birds, such as woodpeckers, the tail feathers are remarkably strong and flexible. They serve the bird as a prop while it chisels holes and when climbing. The part of the feather embedded in the skin is called the quill.

refraction of light which gives the feather a metallic sheen. If there is a deficiency in pigment, the feathers will be white; this is known as albinism. On the contrary, when there is an excess of dark pigment and the bird is nearly black, this condition is known as melanism. These deviations may also be partial and then the bird's plumage will be variously streaked.

The feathers of all birds are replaced regularly by the process called moulting. Old feathers are shed, pushed out by the new ones growing in. Some birds moult once a year, but most songbirds and many other groups moult twice a year. The contour feathers are usually shed successively so that the bird does not lose the power of flight. However, in many species of water birds, such as ducks, the flight feathers are shed all at once so that the birds are incapable of flight for a certain period until new feathers grow in. Many species of birds have

Fig. 8. Pigeons have a rather small beak that is soft at the base — only the tip is hard and slightly curved and it is with this that they peck up hard seeds and fruits.

Fig. 9. The Hoopoe (*Upupa epops*) has a slender, pointed beak with which it readily extracts beetle larvae from the soft ground in meadows and pastures as well as from the rotting wood of old stumps.

two differently coloured sets of plumage a year. One is the brightly coloured breeding plumage worn mostly by the male, the other the drabber, non-breeding winter plumage. Some birds acquire different winter plumage following a complete moult in the autumn, and this later changes into the breeding plumage after the partial spring moult. These species include the Brambling (*Fringilla montifringilla*), shorebirds and gulls (Laridae). Sometimes there is a marked difference in the coloration of the male and female; this is known as sexual dimorphism. Good examples are the European Blackbird (*Turdus merula*), Red-backed Shrike (*Lanius collurio*) and the Pheasant (*Phasianus colchicus*). In other species the male and female have the same coloration and cannot be distinguished at first glance, for example the Jackdaw (*Corvus monedula*), Rook (*Corvus frugilegus*) and White Stork (*Ciconia ciconia*).

Birds are not such free souls as some people think. During the breeding season each pair of birds inhabits a given nesting ground or territory. This is a specifically delimited area, with an imaginary boundary, that could be compared to the garden or plot on which a human family builds a house, and its boundaries are generally respected by other birds of the same species.

Some birds, even songbirds, nest in colonies in which the nests cluster close together, sometimes practically on top of each other, as in the case of the House Martin (*Delichon urbica*). Here the nesting ground is so small that it is limited only to the nest and its immediate surroundings. These birds do not quarrel among themselves over territory for they are usually expert fliers and capture food either in the air or fly far from the nest in search of it. Living in colonies has its advantages, primarily that of greater safety.

How can birds tell if a certain territory is already occupied? Songbirds advertise their ownership by song. The male often sings from an elevated spot even before he starts to build the nest, thus notifying other males of the same species that the place is taken. In the case of songbirds, it is usually the males that seek a nesting place, the males of many species arriving from their winter quarters several days ahead of the females. Sometimes the song, especially in young, unpaired males, has another purpose — that of attracting a mate. At the same time it is also intended to serve the purpose of frightening off other males in the vicinity. A strong, healthy bird has a loud, rich song, thus demonstrating its superiority over the weaker individuals of its kind. It is interesting to note that a weaker bird often falls silent as soon as it hears such a loud song nearby.

Fig. 10. Woodpeckers have extraordinarily strong, but flexible, tail feathers, which serve as a prop on tree trunks while they hack holes in the wood or extract wood beetle larvae.

Fig. 11. Stables, barns and passageways are where the Swallow (*Hirundo rustica*) builds its basin-like nest of grass blades and lumps of clay mixed with saliva.

Besides song, most birds also produce other sounds that are typical for the given species. Most important of these is the call note, used by both sexes to communicate among themselves even out of the nesting season, when, as a rule, the males do not sing. In addition to this, other sounds express fright or warning. All of these various sounds are innate to the given species and will be produced even by young birds reared in captivity, which have never heard the voices of their parents. Some birds, such as the Red-backed Shrike (*Lanius collurio*), do not have a song of their own but mimic the various melodies of other songbirds.

Before nesting, birds must build a nest where the eggs will be incubated and the young nestlings reared. Many birds, mostly songbirds, build very solid, complex, truly artistic structures, others make only simple nests and still others simply lay their eggs in a shallow depression in the ground. Special nests are built by birds that nest in cavities, such as woodpeckers (Picidae). These species hollow out cavities in the trunks or thick branches of trees, inside which the eggs are laid freely on the bottom. Other birds seek out ready-made, abandoned cavities or various crevices in which they then build their own nest. Very occasionally, birds do not build a nest at all, but lay their eggs in the nests of other birds; this is done, for example, by the Cuckoo (*Cuculus canorus*). In some species the nest is built by the female, in others both partners share the task of construction, and in still others the nest is built by the male and is then lined by the female.

Some birds build nests that are ingeniously suspended from the branches of a tree; others create a covered nest on the ground. The nest is generally constructed of plant material and lined with feathers and hair. Some birds also use other inorganic material. The Song Thrush (*Turdus philomelos*), for instance, lines the interior of its nest with mud and rotting wood. Other species build the entire nest of mud, for example house martins.

The construction of a nest of a given type is innate to the given species. The nest built by young birds for the first time in spring is identical to that of an older bird that is experienced in this task. The location of the nest is also innate. Most birds build their nests in the same place. For example the Chaffinch (*Fringilla coelebs*) always builds its nest on a branch, the woodpecker in a cavity. Construction of the nest is quite rapid as a rule, usually taking only a few days.

Some birds nest only once a year; others regularly do so twice, and in the case of the

Fig. 12. The Black-throated Diver (*Gavia arctica*) sites its nest right on the water's edge so that it can slip straight in. The reason for this is that its legs are located at the very rear of the body and thus the bird is unable to take to the air from dry land.

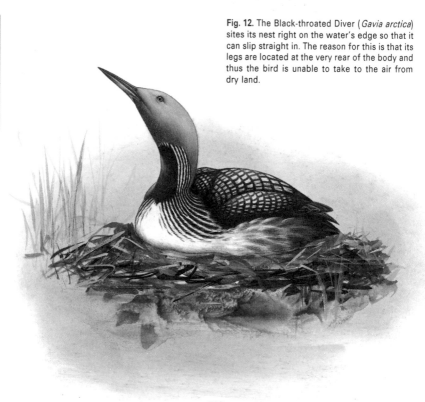

House Sparrow (*Passer domesticus*) even four times a year. Birds that have become associates of, and live in the neighbourhood of, people where feeding opportunities are much more promising, often have more broods a year than woodland birds of the same species.

Fig. 13. A cuckoo nestling has taken over the cup-like nest of the Reed Warbler (*Acrocephalus scirpaceus*), woven around several reed stems.

The colouring of the eggs is likewise characteristic for the given species and the eggs can be identified accordingly. The eggs of some species may show diversity of colour but always within a certain range and certain colour types. As a rule, the coloration of the eggs corresponds to the surroundings of the nest. The eggs of birds that nest in cavities are white because they are well concealed and do not need to have cryptic colours like those of birds that lay their eggs more or less in the open and leave them uncovered, for example, on a sandy shore. The speckled eggs of such birds some-intervals, while in other species the male relieves the female only now and then. In several other species only the male incubates the eggs. The incubation period is characteristic and constant for each individual species. The young peck their way out of the egg with the aid of an 'egg tooth', a special projection on the upper mandible. This is used to cut a small, round opening in the egg shell. This lid then falls off and the way out is open.

Birds are divided into two groups, according to whether they feed their nestlings or whether the young feed themselves: the first are termed nidicolous birds, and the second nidifugous birds. Examples of nidicolous birds are song-

Fig. 14. A Tree Creeper (*Certhia familiaris*) beside its nest, located under a piece of loose bark.

times seem to merge completely with their surroundings. However, some birds, even though they nest in cavities, still have speckled eggs. One such bird is the Kestrel (*Falco tinnunculus*). This species originally nested on rock ledges and it is to this background that the coloration of the eggs still corresponds. Only later did this bird begin to seek out cavities.

Many birds begin incubating after the last egg has been laid and the young then hatch all at the same time. Other birds begin incubating as soon as the first egg is laid and the young then hatch successively. In a clutch of five eggs laid at 48-hour intervals, the difference in age between the first and last nestling is a full ten days. In the case of a larger clutch, the nestlings that hatch last simply cannot compete with their older and larger siblings and they will die.

As a rule, only the female incubates the eggs, while the male brings her food. In some species both parents take turns in incubating at regular

Fig. 15. A Red-backed Shrike (*Lanius collurio*) establishing a larder of spare food against the time when insects remain in hiding because of bad weather. This bird impales its prey on thorns.

birds, woodpeckers and pigeons; examples of nidifugous birds are ducks and gallinaceous birds. In the case of certain species, during the first few days the adult birds bring food to the young in their beaks but the young take it themselves. One such example is the rails (Rallidae) in whom this instinct of bringing food is so innate that even older, independent fledglings of the first brood will bring food to the younger nestlings of the second brood.

The young of many nidicolous birds, particularly songbirds, generally lack feathers on hatching, being covered here and there with patches of thin down. Their eyes are shut tight. In other species of nidicolous birds, however, for instance owls and raptors, the young hatch wearing a thick coat of down. The young of gulls also hatch with a thick coat of down but, in addition, they are able to run about and swim from the very first day.

The young of nidifugous birds are well developed at birth and feed themselves immediately, but the parents still watch over and protect them.

In Australia and certain Pacific islands there lives an unusual family of birds, the Megapodidae, that bury their eggs in mounds of decaying leaves and lava sand. Inside this artificial hatchery heat is produced by the decaying process and the eggs are thus incubated. The newly hatched young are fully independent at birth, needing no parental care whatsoever.

The young of most nidicolous birds are usually cared for by both parents and are also fed by both. In the case of raptors, food is brought by the male, but it is portioned and fed to the young by the female. In many other species, however, larger nestlings are fed directly by the male.

Adult birds usually remain faithful to their nesting site, returning to the same spot every year. Young adult birds establish their own territories during their first year, unless they are colony nesters.

Birds are divided into three basic groups, depending on whether they remain in their breeding grounds or leave for the winter. Resident birds do not leave their breeding grounds even

Fig. 16. A Goldfinch (*Carduelis carduelis*) feeding its offspring.

in winter but remain in the general neighbourhood. Migratory birds leave their nesting grounds every autumn and fly, often for thousands of kilometres, to warmer quarters for the winter. Transient migrants, or dispersive birds, roam far afield, often hundreds of kilometres from their nesting grounds, after the breeding season.

However, there are not always sharp distinctions among these three groups. In some species some members are migratory and others resident. In other species the females are migratory and the males resident. And sometimes among species that were once definitely migratory there occur populations that now remain in the nesting grounds. Blackbirds, for example, were previously migratory, but in the vicinity of people they have become resident and now only some females will depart for the winter.

European birds migrate in roughly three main directions: south-west from northern and north-eastern Europe across western Europe and the Iberian peninsula; straight south from the north across Italy and Sicily; south-east across the Balkan peninsula and Asia Minor. Various populations of the same species may fly in different directions. The migration paths of birds encompass a broad front, although in some places this narrows so that the flock becomes denser, for instance where there is a barrier such as a range of high mountains, when the birds must seek out mountain passes. Many European birds winter no further away than southern or south-western Europe; others journey as far as tropical or even southern Africa.

Such a journey cannot be made non-stop, without a break. Some birds cover 100 km a day, others more. Then they must stop to rest and, more important, obtain food. Some will rest for several days before continuing on their way, and thus the journey to tropical Africa may take as long as several weeks. The birds stay in their winter quarters for only a few weeks, after which they set out again on the return trip to their nesting grounds. The return trip is usually much faster because the birds are urged on by the breeding instinct.

In the vicinity of the nest, birds find their way about mainly by sight, apparently using their memory of the nest's location and various landmarks in the neighbourhood where they normally fly when looking for food. Many birds move in regular circuits, somewhat like the trails of mammals, and these are firmly fixed in their memory.

Some species of birds are declining in number every year, partly due to the lack of nesting sites. Special consideration should be given to birds that nest in cavities. Natural cavities in old trees are few and far between and the birds must often seek alternative sites, nesting, for instance, in a pile of stones on the ground. Here, however, they are exposed to greater danger and become easier prey for their enemies. Such birds can best be helped by people through putting up nest boxes, not only in parks and gardens but in the wild as well. Make sure the boxes cannot be reached by cats.

Fig. 18. The Rook (*Corvus frugilegus*) is not a colourful bird. Its plumage is entirely glossy blue-black and is the same in both sexes, there being no difference between the male and female.

Class: **Birds**—Aves

Superorder: **Carinate Birds**—Carinatae

Order: **Passerine** or **Perching Birds**—Passeriformes

Family: **Crows**—Corvidae

1 Raven *Corvus corax*. Distributed in Europe, Asia and North Africa. In eastern Europe also lives in villages together with jackdaws, on church towers, etc. In central Europe occurs in vast wooded regions. Builds nest on tall trees or on rocks. Uses and adds to it many years. Building done by female, male fetches material (twigs, moss, hairs, etc.). Female lays 5—6 green-spotted and speckled eggs, often at end of February. Young hatched in 21 days, nest-bound about 40 days. Eggs hatched mainly by female with occasional help from male. Diet consists of small vertebrates, insects, debris of animal origin.

2 Carrion Crow *Corvus corone corone*. Distributed over western and central Europe. Completely black. Inhabits wooded areas interspersed with fields and meadows. Often seen looking for food near water. Builds nest in tall trees, usually in March. Nest made of twigs, moss and diverse materials. At end of March or beginning of April female lays 5—6 greenish, dark spotted eggs. Incubates them 17—20 days, fed by male. Young nest-bound for about one month. In winter families combine in large flocks. Both vegetable and animal diet. Collects seeds and berries etc., catches insects and small vertebrates and also eats carrion.

3 Hooded Crow *Corvus corone cornix*. Distributed in eastern and central Europe. Crossing of two subspecies normal along dividing line, which follows Elbe and Vltava to Vienna and crosses Alps into northern Italy. Biology same as for Carrion Crow but often also nests in large town parks. Very suspicious and wary. Frequently plunders partridge and pheasant nests and is consequently shot on sight by gamekeepers and also by farmers.

4 Rook *Corvus frugilegus*. Distributed over practically whole of Europe from middle of France and northern Italy, extends east into Asia north of Himalayas. Forms flocks and nests in colonies (often huge). Likes open country, looks for food in meadows and fields. Sometimes nests in towns, e.g. in cemeteries etc. Builds nests on tall trees; large number of nests on one tree quite common. Female lays 3—5 greenish, dark spotted eggs, usually at beginning of April. Young hatch in 17 days and remain about 5 weeks in nest. In winter migrates southwards in flocks and in central Europe is replaced by more northerly population. Mixed diet. Collects seeds, acorns, etc., also feasts on carrion.

5 Jackdaw *Corvus monedula*. Inhabits whole of Europe, northern Asia and north-western Africa. Lives in colonies. Nests on rocky ledges, in towers, hollow trees, etc. Often found in towns. In March builds nest from twigs, straw, moss, feathers, etc. At end of April female lays 4—6 blue-green, grey-speckled eggs. Eggs incubated 17—18 days, mainly by female. Young remain one month in nest and then roam neighbourhood with parents. In autumn Jackdaws join flocks of rooks. Lives on insects, spiders, molluscs, worms, only occasionally young of small vertebrates; also seeds, berries, etc. Often calls while flying. Easily tamed.

6 Magpie *Pica pica*. Distributed over whole of Europe, large part of Asia, north-western Africa and North America. Characteristic black and white colouring, long tail. Length about 45 cm. Prefers flat country with small copses and shrubs. Builds nest from twigs, turf, blades of grass, leaves, etc. in trees and small bushes. In April female lays 3—10 greenish, thickly speckled eggs. Young hatch in 17—18 days. Fledged after 26 days and remain with parents through winter. Lives on insects, molluscs, small vertebrates, seeds and berries.

Family: **Crows**—Corvidae

1 Nutcracker *Nucifraga caryocatactes*. Distribution area extends from Scandinavia to eastern Asia. In central Europe and Alps inhabits conifer woods, only in mountainous regions. Absent in western Europe. Length over 30 cm. At end of February, in densest branches of tall firs, up to 15 m from ground, builds nest from broken twigs, moss, lichen, hairs, grass, etc. At end of March female lays 3—4 light green, brown- and grey-speckled eggs. Incubates them alone 16 days, fed by male. Young fledged in 21—25 days, but still remain with parents. Eats insects, occasionally young birds, seeds, acorns, nuts, etc.

2 Jay *Garrulus glandarius*. Distributed over whole of Europe, Asia as far as China and north-western Africa. Lives mainly in deciduous or mixed woods. At beginning of April, in tall trees, sometimes only 2 m from ground, builds nest of twigs, grass, moss, etc. At end of April or beginning of May female lays 5—7 grey-green, brown-spotted eggs. Incubated by both parents in turn 16—17 days. Jay is very wary at nesting time. Can imitate call of different forest birds. Jays often fly long distances, not in flocks, but singly, with long intervals. Do not call when flying. Raucously announce approach of humans. Live on mixed diet, make stocks of acorns beside tree stumps, etc.

3 Alpine Chough *Pyrrhocorax graculus*. Distributed mainly in Alps, Pyrenees and some parts of central Asia. Length about 37 cm. Occurs at altitudes of over 2,000 m. Seen in lowlands only in winter. Lives in flocks. Builds nest from twigs, hairs, rootlets, etc. in rock crevices. At end of April female lays only 2 green, brown-spotted eggs. Agile mountaineer. Lives on insects, molluscs, small vertebrates and seeds.

4

5

Family: **Starlings**—Sturnidae

4 European Starling *Sturnus vulgaris.* Distributed over whole of Europe, east into central Asia, also in North Africa. Length 16.5—18.5 cm. Speckled at mating time, otherwise black. In autumn (usually September) migrates to southern Europe and North Africa. Before departing congregates in huge flocks and spends night in sedge. Returns in March. Occasionally resident. Originally nested in hollow trees in deciduous woods, today in orchards, parks and gardens with nesting-boxes. Female builds nest from dry grass, feathers, etc.; male sometimes also fetches material. At end of April female lays 5—6 green-blue eggs, incubated 14 days by both parents. Young fed by parents. After leaving nest form flocks. Lives on insects, worms, cherries and other fruits.

5 Rose-coloured Starling *Sturnus roseus.* Inhabits southern Europe and central Asia. Visits central Europe in flocks and occasionally nests there. Spends winter in northern India. Length about 23 cm. Builds nest in hollows, in piles of stones, in ground or even in open. Lives mainly on locusts, follows them into steppes in huge flocks. Also eats other insects and fruit, in winter rice. Female lays 3—8 pale blue eggs. Young fed by both parents which bring them food at short intervals.

Family: **Orioles**—Oriolidae

6 Golden Oriole *Oriolus oriolus.* Widely distributed in Europe, North Africa and western, central and southern Asia. European population migrates to Africa in winter. Length 21—23 cm. Males have high-pitched, fluting call. Inhabits deciduous woods, large parks and gardens. Nest woven from long grass blades, built by female in fork of branch. Female lays 3—5 whitish eggs with small red-brown and mauve spots. Young hatch in 14—15 days. Lives chiefly on insects and insect larvae, spiders and small molluscs, sometimes fruit, e.g. cherries. Migrates from Europe in August.

6

Family: **Tree-creepers**—Certhiidae

1 Common Tree-creeper *Certhia familiaris*. Distributed over most of Europe, central and eastern Asia and North America. Length 11—15.5 cm. Mainly frequents conifer and mixed forests. Usually builds nest behind peeling bark or in stacked timber. Nest made of twigs, grass, moss and feathers. Female lays 6—7 white, red-spotted eggs in April or May. Incubated by both parents in turn 13—15 days. Sometimes nests twice. Climbs tree spiral-wise. Eats small insects and their eggs.

2 Short-toed Tree-creeper *Certhia brachydactyla*. Distributed in central, western (except England) and southern Europe, also Tunisia. Length about 13 cm. Inhabits old deciduous woods, large parks and gardens. Nesting biology as for preceding species. Tree-creepers are resident, i.e. non-migratory birds.

3 Wall-creeper *Tichodroma muraria*. Distributed in mountains of southern and central Europe, e.g. Alps, Pyrenees, Carpathians, and east across Balkans to Himalayas. Length 16—17.5 cm. Mountain-dweller, occurs in lowlands only in winter. At nesting time in couples, otherwise solitary bird. Skilled at climbing rock faces. Builds nest from grass, moss, etc. in crevices. At end of May female lays 3—5 white eggs with red-brown spots and dots. Incubates them unaided. Eats insects, insect larvae and eggs, spiders, etc.

Family: **Nuthatches**—Sittidae

4 Nuthatch *Sitta europaea*. Distributed over whole of Europe and Asia (except southern Asia). Body length 13—16 cm. Resident bird. Lives in forests, parks, etc., also in towns. Nests in tree hollows, nesting-boxes, etc., to which it brings scales of pine bark or fragments of dry leaves. If opening too large, fills it with mixture of mud and saliva. Female lays 6—8 white, red-speckled eggs in May, incubates them 15—18 days. Both parents feed young. Diet insects, insect larvae, spiders and seeds stored in cracks.

Family: **Finches**—Fringillidae

5 Hawfinch *Coccothraustes coccothraustes*. Distributed over whole of Europe, temperate part of Asia, North Africa. Length 16.5—17.5 cm. Thick beak most characteristic feature. Inhabits deciduous woods, large parks and orchards. Resident bird. Builds nest in April, usually beside trunk, 2—10 m from ground. Nest made of rootlets, grass, hairs, etc., on foundation of thick twigs. At beginning of May female lays 4—6 bluish eggs with grey and mauve spots and streaks. Young hatch in 12—14 days. Eats different seeds and nuts, plus insects at nesting time.

6 Greenfinch *Carduelis chloris.* Distributed over whole of Europe, extends to central Asia and north-western Africa. Length 15—17 cm. Abundant in woods, parks and gardens. In April builds nest from rootlets, dry grass, twigs, etc. in dense branches (chiefly of conifers), 1—20 m from ground. At beginning of May female lays 5—6 whitish eggs with red-brown spots and blotches. Incubates them 12—14 days, fed by male. Both parents feed young. Diet mainly seeds. Some Greenfinches migrate to Italy for winter, others remain behind and live in flocks, together with other birds.

7 Goldfinch *Carduelis carduelis.* Distributed over whole of Europe, Asia Minor, central Asia and North Africa. Length 13—15.5 cm. Inhabits small, open, mixed and deciduous woods, parks, gardens, cemeteries, etc. At end of April builds nest at tip of branch (usually of deciduous tree), 3—10 m from ground. Nest made of moss, lichen, fluff, horsehair, etc. Nests 2—3 times a year. Lays 4—6 white eggs with violet and reddish speckles and dots. Female incubates eggs 12—14 days. Lives mainly on seeds, in summer also eats insects and insect larvae.

4

5

6

7

2 Linnet *Carduelis cannabina.* Distributed over whole of Europe, in east to western part of central Asia, also in North Africa. Length 13—15.5 cm. Inhabits copses, cemeteries, gardens, etc. Partly migratory. In April builds nest 1.5—2.5 m from ground in dense bushes, junipers, etc. Nest made of twigs, grass-blades and rootlets, lined with hairs, plant fluff, etc. In April female lays 4—6 whitish eggs thickly speckled with red. Incubates them 12—14 days. Diet seeds and insects.

3 Redpoll *Carduelis flammea.* Distributed in northern Europe, Asia and America, also England. Occasionally nests in central Europe. Length 12—14.5 cm. Seen in central Europe in winter, in large flocks. Builds nest from thin twigs, grass, moss, etc. in bushes or dwarf trees. Lays 4—6 bluish, brown-spotted eggs, incubates them 10—12 days. Lives on seeds, occasionally insects.

4 Serin *Serinus serinus.* Distributed over most of Europe except England and Scandinavia. Length about 11.5 cm. Lives near human communities, in gardens, parks, etc. Migratory bird. Returns at end of March. Male sings from telegraph wires, tall trees, etc. Nest built by female in branches 2—4 m from ground, from rootlets and grass; lined with feathers, horsehair, etc. Female incubates whitish rusty-speckled eggs 11—13 days. Both parents feed young. After nesting time consort in small groups. Occasionally resident.

Family: **Finches**—Fringillidae

1 Siskin *Carduelis spinus.* Distributed over most of Europe, in east to central Asia. Length 11—13.5 cm. Primarily mountain-dweller but also lives in lowlands. Female builds nest unaided, usually at tip of branch of tall conifer. Nest made of twigs, moss, etc., lined with cocoon silk, hairs, etc. In April female lays 4—6 white eggs with red-brown speckles. Incubates them 12—14 days. Sometimes nests twice. Lives mainly on seeds, in summer also insects. In winter lives in flocks.

5 Bullfinch *Pyrrhula pyrrhula.* Distributed over whole of Europe and temperate parts of Asia. Length 15—19 cm. In central Europe nests mainly in mountains, occasionally in lowlands. Inhabits conifer and mixed forests, also parks and gardens with dense trees and bushes. In April builds nest from twigs, moss, leaves, hairs, etc., relatively close to ground (about 2 m). Female lays 4—6 pale blue eggs with reddish and violet blotches and black dots. Incubates them 13 days. Lives on seeds, shoots, berries, insects and larvae. In winter frequents lowlands in small troupes.

6 Crossbill *Loxia curvirostra.* Distributed over whole of Europe, temperate parts of Asia, North America. Length 17—18.5 cm. Inhabits conifer forests. Nests at different times of year according to supply of pine and fir cones, seeds of which are food for young. Nest built beside trunk or on forked branch. Winter nests have thick walls and deep basin. Female lays 3—4 greyish-white eggs with scattered violet and red-brown spots. Incubates them unaided 14—16 days, fed by male. Newly hatched young have straight mandibles, which begin to acquire typical curved shape after 3 weeks.

7 Chaffinch *Fringilla coelebs.* Distributed over whole of Europe, western Asia, North Africa. Body length 14—18 cm. One of most numerous birds. Lives in woods, gardens and parks. Occurs at altitudes of up to 1,500 m. Many Chaffinches resident, joined by others from north. Nest built in trees and bushes 2—10 m from ground. Rounded woven structure made of rootlets, moss and lichen, thickly lined with hairs, etc. Female lays 6—8 light brown or blue-white eggs marked with red-brown and rusty spots and streaks. Young hatch in 13—14 days. Diet seeds, berries, insects.

7

5

6

Family: **Finches**—Fringillidae

1 Brambling *Fringilla montifringilla*. Inhabits northern Europe and Asia. Length 15 to 18 cm. Nests in birch-woods or mixed woods. Nest usually situated low on tree. Made of birch twigs, moss, feathers, etc. Female lays 5—7 eggs like chaffinch's. Seen in central Europe every year from October in flocks. Often visits feeding troughs.

Family: **Weavers**—Ploceidae

2 House Sparrow *Passer domesticus*. Distributed over whole of Europe, Asia and North Africa, also carried to America and Australia. Body length 14—18 cm. Commonest European bird. Lives near human communities. Builds loose nest from straw, fibres, hairs, feathers, etc. on branches or in hollows. Nests up to 4 times a year. Female lays 3—8 blotched and speckled eggs of somewhat variable colouring. Incubates them 13—14 days. Lives on different seeds, buds and, in summer, insects.

3 Tree Sparrow *Passer montanus*. Distributed over whole of Europe and Asia except India. Length 14—16.5 cm. Lives chiefly in open country, gardens, orchards, outskirts of towns and deciduous woods, etc. Builds nest from straw, wool, feathers, etc. in hollow trees, walls or other birds' nests. Nests up to 3 times a year. Female lays 5—6 grey-green, dark spotted eggs, which are incubated by both parents in turn 13—14 days. Eats insects and different seeds. Young fed mainly on insects. Resident bird.

Family: **Buntings**—Emberizidae

4 Corn Bunting *Emberiza calandra*. Distributed in Europe from southern Scandinavia, south to North Africa, east to Asia Minor. Length 18—20 cm. Usually inhabits large meadows with shrubs. Builds nest in shrubs on ground, or between tufts of grass. Lines it with grass, leaves, wool, hairs, etc. Female lays 3—6 usually reddish-yellow eggs with dark surface spots, deep spots and streaks. Incubates them unaided 12—14 days. Diet seeds, in summer insects.

5 Yellowhammer *Emberiza citrinella*. Distributed over whole of Europe, east to western Siberia. Length 16—20 cm. Abundant in open country or on outskirts of forests. Female builds nest unaided, usually on ground, from blades of grass, horsehairs, etc. At end of April lays 2—5 whitish eggs with numerous dark blotches, spots and streaks. Eggs incubated by both parents 12—14 days. Often nests 3 times. Lives on different seeds, in summer insects, spiders and centipedes. In winter consorts in flocks, often together with other birds.

6 Ortolan Bunting *Emberiza hortulana*. Distributed over whole of Europe and Near East. Length 15—17.5 cm. Inhabits lowlands and uplands, regularly found in orchards. Migratory bird. Winters in southern Europe, returns in middle of April. Ground-nester. Female lays 4—6 whitish-grey eggs with dark brown blotches, spots and scrolls. Incubates them 12—14 days. Some couples nest twice. Eats different seeds and, in summer, insects, spiders, etc.

7 Reed Bunting *Emberiza schoeniclus*. Distributed over whole of Europe and temperate parts of Asia. Length 15—17.5 cm. Found in lowlands near ponds, lakes, etc., thickly overgrown with reeds and willows. Nests on or just above ground in grass or bushes. Female lays 4—6 usually brownish eggs with brown-black spots and streaks. Incubates them 12—14 days. Nests twice. Staple diet different seeds. Winters in southern Europe.

8 Snow Bunting *Plectrophenax nivalis*. Nests in most northerly parts of Europe, Asia and North America. Length 15—19 cm. In winter spreads over whole of Europe. Builds feather- and hair-lined nest between stones. In June lays 5—6 bluish-white eggs with rusty spots and streaks. Incubates them 14 days. In summer lives on insects, in winter on different seeds. Found in central Europe in winter, in company of Bramblings.

Family: **Larks**—Alaudidae

1 Crested Lark *Galerida cristata*. Distributed over practically whole of Europe, temperate and southern Asia, south extends up to tropical Africa. Length 18.5—20.5 cm. Found near towns and villages in open, deserted country, fields, etc. Resident bird. Builds nest from grass blades, rootlets, hairs and feathers in depression in ground. Lays 3—5 whitish, dark-spotted eggs, incubates them 13 days. Young fed on insects. Diet seeds and often horse manure remains.

2 Wood Lark *Lullula arborea*. Distributed over whole of Europe, Near East, North Africa. Length 14.5—17.5 cm. Common in pine-woods, also found near towns. Often sings at night. Migratory bird, winters in Mediterranean region, returns in March. Ground-nester. Nest made of grass blades, moss, etc. Female lays 3—5 usually whitish, finely spotted eggs. Incubation period 13—15 days. Diet mainly insects.

3 Sky Lark *Alauda arvensis*. Distributed over whole of Europe, greater part of Asia, North Africa. Length 15—20.5 cm. Always found in fields. Male flutters high in air, singing. Nest lies in depression in ground; lined with fibres, grass blades, hairs, etc. Female lays 3—5 blotched and speckled eggs of greatly variable colouring, incubates them 12—14 days. Lives on insects, spiders, worms, seeds. In autumn migrates in flocks, returns in February. Occasionally found to be resident.

Family: **Wagtails and Pipits**—Motacillidae

4 Tree Pipit *Anthus trivialis*. Distributed over whole of Europe, in east extends up to Siberia. Winters in central Africa, returns to nesting area in April. Length 15.5—18 cm. Inhabits conifer, mixed and deciduous woods. Common everywhere, often occurs in mountains. Male sits singing on tall trees or telegraph poles. Ground-nester. Nest woven from grass and moss and lined with hairs, hidden in grass. Female lays 5—6 variably coloured eggs marked with spots and streaks. Incubates them 12—13 days. Diet insects and seeds.

5 Meadow Pipit *Anthus pratensis*. Inhabits practically whole of Europe. Winters in southern Europe and North Africa. Length 15—17 cm. Frequents damp meadows and mountain sides, but also found in lowlands. Male sings while flying. Nest built on ground, from moss, sedge, hairs, etc. Female lays 4—5 light-coloured eggs with dark blotches and streaks. Incubates them 13 days. Lives mainly on insects and spiders, in autumn also seeds. In autumn and spring gathers in flocks in fields. Seldom resident.

4

5

6

6 Yellow Wagtail *Motacilla flava*. Distributed over whole of Europe, in Asia north of Himalayas, North Africa. Winters in Africa. Length 16—19 cm. Inhabits damp lowland meadows. Female builds nest on ground, from grass blades, feathers, hairs, etc. Lays 4—6 whitish to reddish eggs thickly marked with grey-brown speckles. Incubation period 13 days. Eats insects, spiders, worms and small molluscs. Migrates in September, after first forming flocks which spend night in rushes.

7 Grey Wagtail *Motacilla cinerea*. Distributed in Europe, large part of Asia, Africa. European birds winter in Africa. Length 17—20 cm. Occurs in both mountains and lowlands. Found near streams and ponds. Usually builds nest in rocky bank, wall, etc. Lays 4—6 yellowish eggs with reddish and brownish spots and streaks. Incubation period 12—14 days. Sometimes nests twice. Main diet aquatic insects and larvae and water-fleas caught in shallows. Migrates in September.

8 White Wagtail *Motacilla alba*. Distributed over whole of Europe, Asia and Africa. Length 18—20.5 cm. Affinity for water, often found in towns. Builds nest from grass blades, rootlets, moss, etc., lined with feathers and hairs, between stones, in hole in wall, etc. In April or May female lays 5—6 whitish eggs thickly marked with dark spots and streaks. Young hatch in 12—14 days. Lives on various insects and larvae, spiders and worms. In autumn gather in flocks, migrate in September—November. Occasionally resident.

7

8

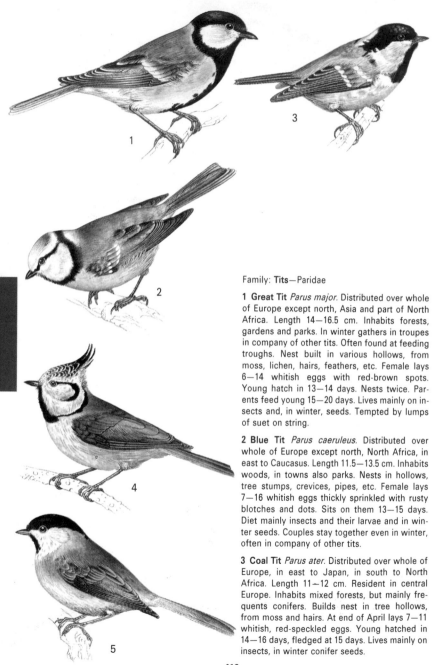

Family: **Tits**—Paridae

1 Great Tit *Parus major*. Distributed over whole of Europe except north, Asia and part of North Africa. Length 14—16.5 cm. Inhabits forests, gardens and parks. In winter gathers in troupes in company of other tits. Often found at feeding troughs. Nest built in various hollows, from moss, lichen, hairs, feathers, etc. Female lays 6—14 whitish eggs with red-brown spots. Young hatch in 13—14 days. Nests twice. Parents feed young 15—20 days. Lives mainly on insects and, in winter, seeds. Tempted by lumps of suet on string.

2 Blue Tit *Parus caeruleus*. Distributed over whole of Europe except north, North Africa, in east to Caucasus. Length 11.5—13.5 cm. Inhabits woods, in towns also parks. Nests in hollows, tree stumps, crevices, pipes, etc. Female lays 7—16 whitish eggs thickly sprinkled with rusty blotches and dots. Sits on them 13—15 days. Diet mainly insects and their larvae and in winter seeds. Couples stay together even in winter, often in company of other tits.

3 Coal Tit *Parus ater*. Distributed over whole of Europe, in east to Japan, in south to North Africa. Length 11—12 cm. Resident in central Europe. Inhabits mixed forests, but mainly frequents conifers. Builds nest in tree hollows, from moss and hairs. At end of April lays 7—11 whitish, red-speckled eggs. Young hatched in 14—16 days, fledged at 15 days. Lives mainly on insects, in winter conifer seeds.

4 Crested Tit *Parus cristatus.* Inhabits whole of Europe, in east to Urals. Length 12—13 cm. Found mainly in conifer forests. Builds nest in holes and cracks. Female lays 5—11 whitish eggs with red-brown spots. Young hatched in 15—17 days, fledged at 20 days. Eat insects in all developmental stages. In winter join and lead flocks of other tits.

5 Marsh Tit *Parus palustris.* Distributed in Europe and south of eastern Asia. Length 12 to 14 cm. Inhabits deciduous and mixed woods, parks and gardens. Hole-nester, builds nest from straw, grass, moss, hairs, etc. Female lays 6—10 whitish, red-spotted eggs. Young hatched in 14—15 days, fed by parents 17—19 days. Couples remain together even in winter, but form small troupes. Lives on insects, spiders, in winter also minute seeds.

Family: Aegithalidae

6 Long-tailed Tit *Aegithalos caudatus.* Distributed over whole of Europe, in east as far as Japan. Length about 15 cm. Very long tail. Inhabits deciduous woods, parks, etc. When not nesting consorts in small flocks. Nests in trees and bushes, preferably on forked branch. Nest ovoid and closed, with side entrance. Made of moss, lichen, cobwebs, etc. Thickly lined with small feathers. Female lays 7—12 whitish eggs with red blotches and dots, incubates them 13 days. Diet insects.

Family: Remizidae

7 Penduline Tit *Remiz pendulinus.* Distributed in southern Europe, south part of central Europe, in east to Japan. Length 10.5—11.5 cm. Found near water, especially ponds. Builds closed spherical nest suspended from tips of terminal willow twigs by fibres made from poplar fluff, etc. Nest has tunnel-like entrance. Female lays 6—8 white eggs, sits on them 12—15 days. Male meanwhile builds new nest. Eats mainly insects and spiders.

Family: **Goldcrests**—Regulidae

8 Goldcrest *Regulus regulus.* Distributed over whole of Europe, Asia, North America. Length 8.5—10.5 cm. Smallest European bird, weighs 5—6 g. Inhabits conifer forests. Builds nest from twigs, grass blades, hairs, cobwebs, etc. on dense fir or pine branches. Female lays 8—11 yellowish eggs marked with dark scrolls. Incubation period 16—17 days. Diet small insects and spiders. In winter moves about in tree-tops in small groups, twittering.

Family: **Shrikes**—Laniidae

1 Great Grey Shrike *Lanius excubitor*. Distributed in Europe, Asia, North America, North Africa. Length 24—27.5 cm. Inhabits open country, especially with thorny shrubs. Sometimes impales prey (insects and small vertebrates) on thorns. Builds nest from dry twigs, straw, moss, etc. on tall bushes. In May female lays 5—7 whitish, grey- and brown-spotted eggs. Young hatched in 15 days, fed by parents 20 days.

2 Red-backed Shrike *Lanius collurio*. Distributed over practically whole of Europe and Asia. Winters in Africa and southern Asia, returns to Europe in middle of May. Length 18—20.5 cm. Frequents areas with thorny shrubs. Nest hidden in thicket, 1—2 m from ground, from twigs, straw, rootlets and moss, lined with hairs. Female lays 3—7 pink, red- and brown-spotted eggs. Young hatch in 14—15 days. Leave nest after 2 weeks but remain in bushes. Lives mainly on insects, also young of small birds and rodents. Impales prey on thorns. Imitates call of other birds.

3 Woodchat Shrike *Lanius senator*. Distributed over whole of Europe except England, in east to Poland, in south to North Africa. Winters in Central Africa. Arrives in Europe at beginning of May, leaves in August. Length 19.5—20 cm. Nests on sunny places. Builds nest in bushes like that of red-backed shrike. Lays 5—6 yellowish or greenish, grey- and olive-spotted eggs. Young hatched in 14—15 days, fed by parents 20 days. Eats mainly insects.

Family: **Waxwings**—Bombycillidae

4 Waxwing *Bombycilla garrulus*. Distributed in most northerly parts of Europe, Asia and North America. Length 19—23 cm. Visits central Europe only in winter, often in large flocks. Most often seen on rowans or berry-bearing bushes, eating berries. In north nests in conifer and mixed forests. Tree-nester, builds nest from twigs or moss. Female lays 4—6 bluish, black- and violet-spotted eggs, incubates them 14 days. Also eats insects.

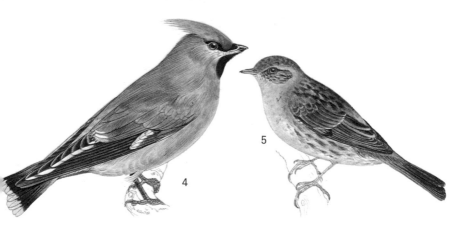

Family: **Accentors**—Prunellidae

5 Dunnock *Prunella modularis.* Distributed over whole of Europe and north-western Asia. Length 14.5—16.5 cm. Common in central Europe, but very retiring. Inhabits dense conifer woods. In dense branches builds relatively large mossy nest lined with hairs. Lays 4—7 plain blue-green eggs in May. Often nests twice. Young hatch in 12—14 days. Eats mainly insects, in autumn small seeds. In October migrates to Mediterranean region.

Family: **Wrens**—Troglodytidae

6 Wren *Troglodytes troglodytes.* Distributed over whole of Europe, temperate parts of Asia, North America, north-eastern Africa. Length 9.5—11.5 cm, weight about 9 g. Resident in central Europe. Solitary bird except at nesting time. Builds spherical nest with side entrance from twigs and moss, lined with hairs and feathers. Lays 5—7 whitish, red-spotted eggs. Young hatch in 14—16 days. Diet insects.

Family: **Dippers**—Cinclidae

7 Dipper *Cinclus cinclus.* Distributed over whole of Europe, extends east to central Asia, Himalayas and north-western Africa. Length 17.5—20 cm. Frequents mountain streams and rivers. Resident bird. Hunts for food (insects and insect larvae) under water, on bed. Also collects material for nest under water. Nests in spaces between stones, often at foot of waterfall. Female lays 4—6 white eggs. Young hatch in 15—17 days, leave nest in 3 weeks.

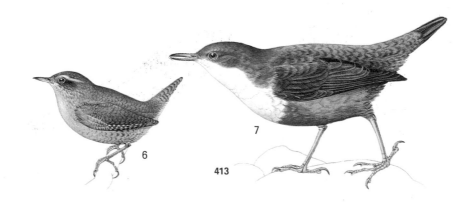

Family: **Flycatchers**—Muscicapidae

1 Spotted Flycatcher *Muscicapa striata*. Distributed over whole of Europe, in east to Mongolia, in south to north-western Africa. Winters in tropical and southern Africa. Leaves in September, returns at beginning of May. Length 14—17 cm. Lives on outskirts of forests or in parks. Builds relatively large nest from grass blades and rootlets, lined with hairs and feathers, usually on horizontal branch or overgrown wall, etc. Lays 4—6 bluish white, grey- and russet-spotted eggs. Eggs incubated 13 days by both parents. Eats insects, catches prey on wing.

2 Pied Flycatcher *Ficedula hypoleuca*. Inhabits whole of Europe, western Asia, north-western Africa. Winters in Africa. Length 12.5—14.5 cm. In some regions abundant. Lives in open deciduous woods and parks. Builds nest from moss, fibres, cobwebs, etc. in hollow trees and stumps. Lays 4—8 bright blue-green eggs. Young hatched in 13 days, fed by parents 18 days. Migrates at end of October. Diet insects.

Family: **Warblers**—Sylviidae

3 Lesser Whitethroat *Sylvia curruca*. Distributed over most of Europe, in east up to Siberia. European birds winter in central Africa. Leave in August or September, return in second half of April. Length 12.5—13.5 cm. Frequents bushes in woods, gardens and parks. Weaves very loose nest from grass blades and rootlets in tall nettles, shrubs, etc. Female lays 4—6 whitish or yellowish eggs with violet-grey and yellow-brown speckles and black streaks. Young hatch in 11—13 days. Eats insects and spiders.

4 Blackcap *Sylvia atricapilla*. Distributed over whole of Europe, in east to river Ob and in north-western Africa. Winters in Central Africa. Leaves in September, returns at end of April. Length 14—15 cm. Inhabits deciduous woods and parks and gardens with plenty of shrubs. Builds nest from grass blades and cobwebs, in brambles, bushes, etc., usually about 75 cm from ground. Female lays 4—6 yellowish or greenish, grey or red-spotted eggs. Young hatch in 13—14 days. Diet chiefly insects, supplemented in autumn by raspberries or bilberries.

5 Garden Warbler *Sylvia borin*. Distributed over most of Europe, in east to western Siberia. Winters in Central Africa. Leaves at end of September, returns in middle of May. Length about 14 cm. Frequents places with shrubs. Weaves nest from stalks among raspberry canes, in brambles, etc., 0.5—3 m. from ground. Lays 4—6 yellowish or greenish eggs with grey and olive spots or marbling. Young hatch in 12 days. Often rears young cuckoos. Eats various insects and their larvae.

1

2

4

5

3

6

7

6 Barred Warbler *Sylvia nisoria*. Distributed in central Europe, in east to western Siberia. Winters in eastern half of Africa. Leaves in August, returns at end of April. Length 16 to 18 cm. Inhabits large parks, overgrown gardens and margins of forests. Builds nest from grasses, blades, horsehair, etc. in dense bushes, 1—2 m from ground. Female lays 4—5 yellowish or greenish, grey-speckled eggs. Young hatched in 14—15 days, fed by parents 16 days. Lives mainly on insects, at end of summer also berries.

7 Icterine Warbler *Hippolais icterina*. Distributed in Europe from central France to upper reaches of Ob river. Winters in Africa. Leaves in August, returns early in May. Length 13—16 cm. Inhabits open deciduous woods and large parks. Builds nest from stalks, leaves, rootlets, etc. in deciduous trees or bushes. Masks it with birch bark. Usually lays 5 pink eggs sprinkled with black dots and blotches. Young hatch in 13 days. Eats mainly different insects.

Family: **Warblers**—Sylviidae

1 Chiffchaff *Phylloscopus collybita*. Distributed over whole of Europe, in east to Lake Baikal, and north-western Africa. Winters in north-eastern Africa. Leaves in October, male's monotonous song heard soon after return at end of March. Length 12—14 cm. Inhabits deciduous or mixed woods and parks. Female builds closed spherical nest from grass blades and moss in clump of grass on ground. Lays 5—6 white eggs with reddish brown dots. Incubates them unaided 13—14 days. Young fed 2 weeks. Eats only small insects.

2 Wood Warbler *Phylloscopus sibilatrix*. Distributed over whole of Europe except north, and in western Asia. Winters in Central Africa. Leaves in September, returns in middle of April. Male chirps. Length 12—14 cm. Inhabits large woods and parks. Ground-nester. Builds closed, hair-lined nest with side entrance. Female lays 6—8 white eggs with dark brown spots and streaks, incubates them 13 days. Young fledged at 12—15 days. Eats mainly insects.

3 Grasshopper Warbler *Locustella naevia*. Distributed over whole of Europe except north and south, in east up to Mongolia. European birds winter in North Africa. Leaves in August, returns at end of April. Length 13—15 cm. Lives hidden

in thick shrubs beside ponds and rivers. Builds deep grass nest on ground under bush. Lays 5—7 pink eggs with rusty blotches and dots. Eggs incubated 13—15 days by both parents in turn. Young leave nest at 10 days, before fully capable of flight. Diet mainly insects.

4 Great Reed Warbler *Acrocephalus arundinaceus*. Distributed over whole of Europe except England and Scandinavia, in east up to Australia, also North Africa. European birds winter in equatorial Africa. Leave in August and September, return in first half of May. Length about 20 cm. High-pitched, screechy song. Inhabits rushes beside ponds, lakes and rivers. Builds basket-like nest between rush stems. Female lays 4—6 bluish eggs with olive green and brown spots. Incubated 14—15 days by both parents in turn. Eats mainly insects.

5 Reed Warbler *Acrocephalus scirpaceus*. Distributed from central Europe to southern England and central Asia. Winters in northern and equatorial Africa. Leaves at end of September, returns in middle of April. Length 15—16 cm. Lives beside water among reeds. Weaves nest from long stalks. Lays 4—5 whitish eggs with olive-coloured surface spots and deep spots. Young hatch in 11—12 days. Male has sweeter song than Great Reed Warbler. Lives on insects and spiders.

4   5

Family: **Thrushes**—Turdidae

6 Fieldfare *Turdus pilaris*. Distributed in central and northern Europe, in east to Lake Baikal. Length 24.5—28 cm. Migratory bird, northern population comes to central Europe in winter. Weaves nest from grass, twigs, moss, etc., usually reinforced with mud. Often nests in colonies (several nests on one tree) in open conifer woods, also in junipers, sometimes quite low down. Female lays 5—7 greenish-white eggs thickly marked with rusty brown spots and streaks. Young hatch in 13—14 days. Eats mainly insects, in winter berries.

7 Mistle Thrush *Turdus viscivorus*. Distributed over whole of Europe, in east to Lake Baikal, in south to north-western Africa. Northern birds migrate south. Length 26—29.5 cm. Prefers conifer woods, occasionally found in large parks. Nest usually situated on pines, about 10 m from ground, woven from rootlets, grass blades and moss, reinforced with mud. Female builds nest, male fetches material. In April female lays 4—5 blue-green eggs with violet, grey and brown spots, incubates them unaided 13—14 days. Eats mainly insects caught on ground. From autumn onwards roams countryside in small troupes.

6   7

Family: **Thrushes**—Turdidae

1 Song Thrush *Turdus philomelos*. Distributed over whole of Europe, Asia Minor, in east to Lake Baikal. Winters in southern Europe and North Africa. Leaves in October, returns in March or early April. Length 22—24.5 cm. Inhabits woods, gardens and parks. Builds nest from stalks, twigs, etc., inner side reinforced and faced with mixture of mud and saliva. Nests on bushes, trees and walls. Female lays 4—6 green-blue eggs sprinkled with black dots, incubates them unaided 12—13 days. Young leave nest before fully fledged. Eats insects, worms, molluscs, and in autumn berries.

2 Ring Ouzel *Turdus torquatus*. Distributed in England, Scandinavia, Alps, Pyrenees, Giant Mountains, Caucasus. Winters in North Africa. Leaves in October, returns in April. Length about 27 cm. Inhabits mountain sides. Nests in dense branches of dwarf pines. Lays 4—5 greenish, thickly marbled and streaked eggs. Incubated 14 days by both parents in turn.

3 Blackbird *Turdus merula*. Distributed in whole of Europe, east over narrow zone to China. Part of population resident, part migrates to Mediterranean region. Length 23.5—28 cm. Inhabits forests, parks and gardens near human dwellings. Makes nest from grass blades, rootlets, etc. on trees, bushes and wooden beams, etc. Female lays 4—6 blue-green eggs thickly marked with grey and brown blotches, dots and streaks, incubates them 13—14 days. Young fed by both parents. Sometimes nests three times a year. Lives on insects, worms, molluscs, berries, fruit, etc.

4 Wheatear *Oenanthe oenanthe*. Distributed over whole of Europe, Asia, North America and Greenland. Winters mainly in tropical Africa. Leaves in August or September, returns in April. Length 15—17 cm. Inhabits stony, unwooded slopes, rocky planes or quarries. Builds nest from grass blades, hairs and feathers among stones, in abandoned holes, etc. In May female lays 5—7 greenish eggs, incubates them 14 days. Young leave nest before fully fledged. Diet mainly insects.

1

2

5 Whinchat *Saxicola rubetra*. Distributed over most of Europe, in east to western Siberia. Winters in equatorial Africa. Leaves in August or September, in small flocks, returns in April. Length 13—15.5 cm. Frequents uplands with large shrub-strewn meadows. Likes to sit on hummocks. Ground-nester. Nest made of grass blades, moss, etc., lined with grass and plant fluff. In June female lays 5—6 bluish-grey eggs, often marked with rusty spots, incubates them 13—14 days. Young leave nest early. Diet mainly insects.

6 Redstart *Phoenicurus phoenicurus*. Distributed over whole of Europe, Asia Minor, in east to western Siberia; also North Africa. Winters mainly in equatorial Africa. Leaves in August or September, returns in first half of April. Length 13.5—17 cm. Lives almost everywhere, in woods, gardens, near human communities. Builds nest from grass blades, rootlets, leaves, hairs, etc. in all sorts of hollows, in walls, between wooden beams, etc. Female lays 5—8 green-blue eggs, incubates them 13—15 days. Nests twice. Eats mainly insects skilfully caught on wing.

7 Black Redstart *Phoenicurus ochruros*. Distributed in central and southern Europe, in west to England, in east up to northern China. European birds winter in North Africa. Leave in October, return at end of March. Length about 15 cm. Originally rock-dweller, now lives in vicinity of man. Builds nest from rootlets, grass blades, hairs, etc. under shed roofs, in barns, on cornices. Female lays 5—6 white eggs, incubates them 14 days. Young leave nest before fully fledged and go into hiding. Diet mainly insects.

Family: **Thrushes**—Turdidae

1 Nightingale *Luscinia megarhynchos*. Distributed in western, central and southern Europe, in east to central Asia, in south to North Africa. Winters chiefly in equatorial Africa. Leaves in August, returns at end of April. Migrates only at night. Length 18—20 cm. Inhabits margins of deciduous or mixed woods, thickets beside rivers and ponds, etc. Male sings during day as well as at night. Song carries long distances. Builds nest from grass blades, rootlets, moss, rush stems, etc., lined with hair, in branches of impenetrable bushes. Female lays 4—6 olive brown, sometimes thickly speckled, eggs, incubates them unaided 13 days. Young leave nest early. Diet mainly insects and worms.

2 Bluethroat *Luscinia svecica*. Distributed over whole of Europe except England and Mediterranean region, in east as far as Mongolia. Winters in North Africa. Length about 15 cm. Seldom nests in central Europe, but often found in large numbers in riverside shrubs during migration. Builds nest from dry grass blades on or near ground, in bushes near stretches of reeds. Female lays 5—6 bluish eggs sprinkled with brown spots. Young hatch in 13 days, leave nest after 2 weeks. Eats small insects and their larvae.

3 Robin *Erithacus rubecula*. Distributed over whole of Europe, Asia Minor, in east to western Siberia. Most birds migrate to North Africa in October, but old males often remain behind. Length 13—16 cm. Frequents thickets in woods, parks and gardens. Ground-nester, hides nest under clump of grass, between stones, in holes, etc. Nest made of moss, rootlets, grass blades, hairs, etc. Female lays 5—7 yellowish eggs marked with red blotches and dots, incubates them unaided 13—14 days. Young fed by both parents. Some birds nest twice. Lives mainly on insects, in autumn and winter supplemented by berries and forest fruits.

Family: **Swallows**—Hirundinidae

4 Swallow *Hirundo rustica*. Distributed over whole of Europe, most of Asia, North America, North Africa. European birds winter in Africa south of Sahara. Leave in September, return in first half of April. Length 18—23 cm. Basin-like nest built by both partners from small lumps of clay mixed with saliva and from grass blades lined with hairs and feathers. Female lays 4—6 whitish, red- and violet-spotted eggs. Incubates them 14—16 days, fed by male. Young fed 3 weeks by both parents. When young are fledged, birds spend night in flocks in sedge beside ponds. Eats mainly insects caught on wing.

5 House Martin *Delichon urbica*. Distributed over whole of Europe, most of Asia, North Africa. European birds winter in Africa south of Sahara. Leave in September, return in second half of April. Length 15—16.5 cm. Builds clay nest on vertical wall, under eaves or cornices. Nest completely closed except for side entrance on top. Birds often form large colonies. Female lays 4—5 pure white eggs. Incubated 12—13 days by both parents in turn. Young fed 20—23 days. Some birds nest again in July. Eats mainly insects caught in air.

6 Sand Martin *Riparia riparia*. Distributed over whole of Europe, large part of Asia, North America, north-western and north-eastern Africa. European birds winter in equatorial and southern Africa. Leave in August, return in second half of April. Length 12.5—14.5 cm. Lives preferably near rivers, lakes and ponds, also in sand-pits with sheer walls, in which it makes burrows 1.5 m long. Nest chamber lined with feathers and grass blades. Nests in colonies. Female lays 5—7 pure white eggs in middle of May. Eggs incubated 15 days by both parents in turn. Young fed in nest 23 days. Lives on insects caught in air.

4

5

6

421

Order: **Woodpeckers and Allies**—Piciformes

Family: **Woodpeckers**—Picidae

1 Green Woodpecker *Picus viridis*. Distributed over whole of Europe except most northerly parts, in east to Ukraine. Length 33—37 cm. Resident, but after nesting season roams long distances. Has predilection for open woods, parks and orchards. Both partners hack hole in rotting tree trunks, finished in 14 days. Line hole only with splinters. Female lays 6—8 white eggs, incubated 15—17 days by both parents in turn. Young leave nest after 17—20 days. Birds live mainly on larvae of different wood-beetles, also rake open anthills and collect pupae and adult ants on their long, sticky, protrusible tongue. Occasionally visit beehives, especially in winter.

2 Great Spotted Woodpecker *Dendrocopos major*. Distributed over whole of Europe, extends east in narrow zone to Japan, in south to North Africa. Length 22.5—26.5 cm. Inhabits woods, parks and large orchards. Resident bird, but in winter roams countryside round birthplace. Hacks hole in deciduous trees and conifers 2—10 m from ground, lines it with small splinters. Female lays 4—8 glossy white eggs in April or May. Young hatch in 13—15 days. Lives on beetle larvae (e.g. on bark beetles), wedges hazelnuts in crevice, cracks shell and eats kernel, also eats seeds of conifers. In winter often consorts with nuthatches or tits.

3 Black Woodpecker *Dryocopus martius*. Distributed over whole of Europe except England and southern parts, in east extends as far as Japan. Length 42—48.5 cm. Mainly inhabits large conifer forests in lowlands and mountains, but also encountered in deciduous woods where it nests in strong beeches or birches. Like other woodpeckers, in spring drums on dry branch stumps. Usually nests over 4 m above ground. Both partners hack hole about 50 cm deep in 2 weeks, making pile of splinters at foot of tree. Female lays 4—5 white eggs. Young hatch in 12—14 days, leave nest after 24—28 days. Eats mainly wood beetle larvae and ants and their nymphs.

4 Wryneck *Jynx torquilla*. Distributed over whole of Europe, in east to Japan. Migratory bird. Winters in northern and eastern Africa. Usually leaves in August, returns in second half of April, immediately utters typical plaintive call. Length 18.5—19.5 cm. Inhabits outskirts of deciduous woods, parks, orchards and large gardens. Does not make own nesting hole, often content with crack in wall. Does not line nest. In May—June female lays 7—10 white eggs. Parents incubate eggs 13—14 days, feed young 24—26 days. Feeds on caterpillars, ant pupae, etc. Wryneck can turn long, flexible neck by up to 180 degrees.

Order: **Swifts and Allies**—Apodiformes

Family: **Swifts**—Apodidae

5 Common Swift *Apus apus*. Distributed over whole of Europe, in east to China, in south to north-western Africa. Migratory bird. Leaves at beginning of August (sometimes end of July), winters in Africa south of Sahara, returns at end of April or beginning of May. Length 18—21 cm. Builds nest under eaves of tall houses, on steples, towers, etc., using pile of plant debris and feathers snapped up during flight and stuck together with saliva. Female lays 2—3 white eggs, incubates them 18 days, fed by male. Young leave nest at 6 weeks, immediately able to fly. Eats insects caught on wing. Swifts like to consort in darting, screeching flocks. Rapid fliers, cover about 900 km a day.

5

4

Order: **Rollers and Allies**—Coraciiformes

Family: **Rollers**—Coraciidae

1 Roller *Coracias garrulus.* Distributed in Europe except England and north, in east to India, in south to north-western Africa. Migratory bird. Leaves at end of August, winters in Africa south of Sahara, returns at beginning of May. Length 30—34 cm. Nests in tree hollows. Female lays 3—5 pure white eggs. Eggs incubated by both parents in turn, young leave nest at 28 days. Keeps look-out for prey, catches it mainly on wing. Lives on insects, small vertebrates, in Africa mainly locusts.

Family: **Bee-eaters**—Meropidae

2 Bee-eater *Merops apiaster.* Distributed in southern Europe, Asia as far as India, north-western Africa. Nests in central Europe in Slovakia, Moravia and Hungary, in recent years also in Sweden, Denmark and Holland. Migratory bird, winters in Africa south of Sahara. Frequents places with sandy or clay banks, in which it makes burrow with beak (in about 3 weeks). Lives in small colonies. Lays 5—6 white eggs, incubated 22 days by both parents in turn. Eats mainly hymenoptera, especially bees and wasps.

Family: **Kingfishers**—Alcedinidae

3 Kingfisher *Alcedo atthis.* Distributed over whole of Europe except north, in east to Asia, and north-western Africa. Resident bird, but northerly population shifts somewhat south. Nomadic during winter. Length 16.5—18.5 cm. Inhabits places with clean water and sheer banks. Makes burrow about 1 m long above waterline, lines nest-chamber with fish scales and bones. Female lays 6—8 white eggs. Young hatch in 21 days. Kingfishers catch prey — small fish — by swooping into water.

Family: **Hoopoes**—Upupidae

4 Hoopoe *Upupa epops.* Distributed over whole of Europe and Asia except northern parts, and practically whole of Africa. Migratory bird. European population leaves in August or September, winters in equatorial Africa, returns in April. Length 28—32.5 cm. Prefers open country with meadows and pastures, also found in old avenues near ponds, or in open deciduous woods. Nests in tree hollows or piles of stones. In May female lays 4—8 greyish or brownish white eggs, incubates them unaided 16 days, fed by male. Eats chiefly beetle larvae. Name describes typical call.

5

4

Order: **Nightjars**—Caprimulgiformes

5 Nightjar or **Goatsucker** *Caprimulgus europaeus*. Distributed over most of Europe, in east to central Siberia, also in north-western Africa. Migratory bird. Leaves in September, winters mainly in Africa south of Sahara, returns in first half of May. Length 26—28 cm. Nests in bare depression in ground. Female lays 2 whitish, grey-speckled eggs indistinguishable from background. Eggs incubated 16—19 days by both parents in turn. Young fed only at night. By day, Nightjar perches lengthwise on branch. Goes hunting after sundown. Lives on insects — mostly moths and beetles — caught on wing.

Order: **Owls**—Strigiformes

6 Snowy Owl *Nyctea scandiaca*. Distributed in European, Asian and North American tundra. Flies south in winter and occasionally appears in central and southern Europe. Length 56—65 cm. Mainly diurnal bird. Likes high perches. Skilful flier. Nests on ground or in cleft rocks. Lays 3—8 white eggs with staggered hatching. Catches mainly rodents, sometimes small birds, occasionally fish.

6

425

2

3

Order: **Owls**—Strigiformes

1 Eagle Owl *Bubo bubo.* Distributed over whole of Europe except England, whole of Asia except southern and northern parts, North Africa. Resident bird, not nomadic during winter. Length 62—72.5 cm, female slightly larger. Inhabits extensive forests, wooded rocks and ravines. Occurs at both low and high altitudes. Nests in tree hollows, in ruins and on ground. Female lays 2—5 white eggs at end of March, incubates them unaided 35 days. Hides during day, flies only at night, fairly close to ground. Hunting radius 15 km. Catches mammals up to size of hare, birds, occasionally fish.

2 Long-eared Owl *Asio otus.* Distributed over most of Europe, in east as far as Japan, North America, North Africa. Resident bird in Europe, sometimes migratory. Length 35—39 cm. Abundant in forests, preserves and parks. Nests in old nests of other birds or squirrels. Female lays 4—6 white eggs, usually in April, incubates them unaided 27—28 days, fed by male. Eats mainly voles, also maybugs and other beetles caught after dark. During day hides in dense branches. In winter often roams countryside in troupes, looking for rodents.

3 Little Owl *Athene noctua.* Distributed over whole of Europe except north, in east as far as Korea, North Africa. Resident bird. Length 23.5—27.5 cm. Inhabits outskirts of woods, ruins, parks, avenues; likes to perch on roofs, behind chimneys. Nocturnal bird, but also hunts in afternoon of dull days. Plaintive call often heard at night near human dwellings. During day hides in holes and hollows. Nests in similar places. Female lays 4—7 white eggs, incubates them 28 days. Catches small rodents, occasionally small birds, especially sparrows, often also insects, chiefly beetles.

4 Tawny Owl *Strix aluco.* Distributed over whole of Europe except north, parts of Asia, North Africa. Resident bird. Length 41—46 cm. Goes hunting after dark. During day hides in dense branches, usually in same place, piles of ejected pellets to be found under tree. Inhabits forests, parks, large gardens and avenues, at both low and high altitudes. Nests in tree hollows, under wooden beams, etc. Female lays 2—5 white eggs, incubates them 28 days. Young fully fledged after 3 months. Catches mainly small rodents, also small birds, amphibians and insects.

1

426

4

5

5 Barn Owl *Tyto alba*. Distributed over whole of Europe, southern Asia, Australia, Africa and America. Resident bird. Length 33—39 cm. Originally rock-dweller, in Europe now lives in vicinity of man. Nests in attics, below eaves, in ruins, towers or dovecots. Female lays 4—6 white eggs on bare base, incubates them 30—34 days, fed by male. Young fledged after 50 days. In years of vole plagues nests several times. In addition to voles and mice catches moles, shrews, sparrows and insects. Young birds often fly far afield.

Order: **Cuckoos and Allies**—Cuculiformes

Family: **Cuckoos**—Cuculidae

6 Common Cuckoo *Cuculus canorus*. Distributed over whole of Europe, most of Asia, Africa. European birds migrate in August or September, winter in Africa south of Sahara, return at end of April when male immediately makes himself heard. Length 31—39 cm. Has preference for open woods with undergrowth. Female lays eggs (average 18) one by one in nests of small birds. Young hatch in only 12 days, after 10 hours throw all other occupants (eggs or young) out of nest. Young cuckoo remains in nest 23 days and is fed by foster-parents 3 more weeks. Eats mainly caterpillars (even hairy ones), spiders, etc.

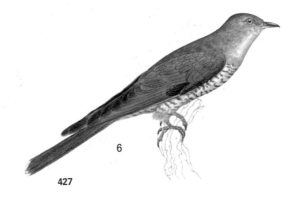

6

Order: **Birds of Prey**—Falconiformes

Family: **Falcons**—Falconidae

1 Peregrine Falcon *Falco peregrinus*. Distributed in Europe, Asia, Africa, North America, Australia. Length 41—50 cm. Wings long and pointed at flight. Nests in cleft rocks, towers, or nests abandoned by other birds of prey. In April lays 3—4 eggs with red-brown spots. Young hatch in 28—29 days. Male hunts for young, female feeds them. Hunts primarily in air. Swoops on prey at velocity of up to 200 km an hour. Catches mainly birds — pigeons, crows, starlings, gulls, etc. Formerly trained for hunting. Young birds migratory, old birds sometimes resident.

2 Hobby *Falco subbuteo*. Distributed over whole of Europe, temperate parts of Asia, North Africa. Migratory bird. Winters in southern Africa, returns to nesting places in April. Length 32—36 cm. Nests in deserted nests of crows or other birds. Frequents small woods. Female lays 2—4 eggs with red-brown spots. Young hatch in 28 days. Male brings prey for young, female feeds them. Catches small birds or insects in air. Can even catch swifts and swallows. Devours prey on tree. Protected.

3 Kestrel *Falco tinnunculus*. Distributed over whole of Europe, Asia and Africa. Length 31—38 cm. Nests on jutting rocks, in abandoned nests of other birds, in towers and hollows. Sometimes nests in colonies. In May female lays 3—8 eggs with red-brown spots. Young hatch in 28 days. Prefers to hunt in open country, fields and meadows. Hovers in air, swoops on prey, mainly small rodents and insects. Migrates in autumn to North Africa, but some birds remain behind.

Family: **Eagles and Allies**—Accipitridae

4 Golden Eagle *Aquila chrysaetos*. Distributed in Europe, Asia, North America, North Africa; in Europe mainly Alps, Pyrenees and Scotland. Length 82—92 cm., wing span about 2 m. Long tail spread during flight. Nuptial flights held in March. Builds nest on rocks, using sticks, clumps of grass, hairs, etc. Female lays 1—3 brown-spotted eggs, incubated 45 days by both parents in turn. Male mostly fetches prey for young, female prepares it for them. Catches mammals and birds up to size of small chamois or goat.

5 Lesser Spotted Eagle *Aquila pomarina*. Distributed in central Europe, in east to southern Asia. Length 61—65 cm., wing span about 150

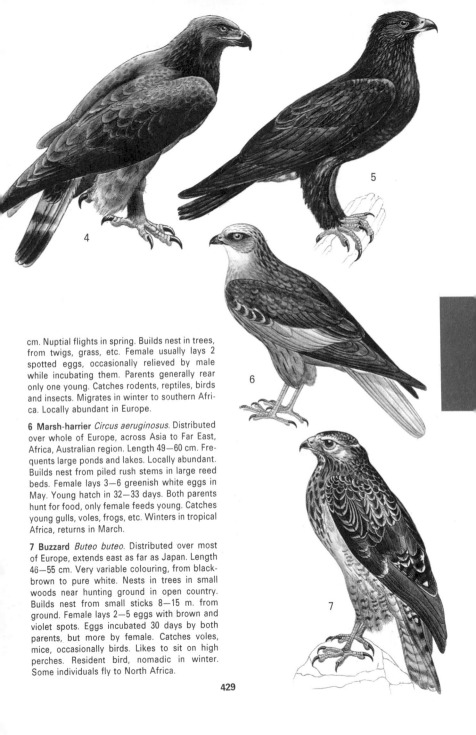

cm. Nuptial flights in spring. Builds nest in trees, from twigs, grass, etc. Female usually lays 2 spotted eggs, occasionally relieved by male while incubating them. Parents generally rear only one young. Catches rodents, reptiles, birds and insects. Migrates in winter to southern Africa. Locally abundant in Europe.

6 Marsh-harrier *Circus aeruginosus*. Distributed over whole of Europe, across Asia to Far East, Africa, Australian region. Length 49—60 cm. Frequents large ponds and lakes. Locally abundant. Builds nest from piled rush stems in large reed beds. Female lays 3—6 greenish white eggs in May. Young hatch in 32—33 days. Both parents hunt for food, only female feeds young. Catches young gulls, voles, frogs, etc. Winters in tropical Africa, returns in March.

7 Buzzard *Buteo buteo*. Distributed over most of Europe, extends east as far as Japan. Length 46—55 cm. Very variable colouring, from black-brown to pure white. Nests in trees in small woods near hunting ground in open country. Builds nest from small sticks 8—15 m. from ground. Female lays 2—5 eggs with brown and violet spots. Eggs incubated 30 days by both parents, but more by female. Catches voles, mice, occasionally birds. Likes to sit on high perches. Resident bird, nomadic in winter. Some individuals fly to North Africa.

Family: **Eagles and Allies**—Accipitridae

1 Rough-legged Hawk *Buteo lagopus*. Distributed in north-European, Asian and American tundra. Always winters in central and southern Europe. Length 53—60.5 cm. Wears feather 'trousers'. Arrives in central Europe in October and remains until March. Often forms large flocks. Catches voles and, in times of shortage, partridges. In native habitat nests in trees, lays 2—7 eggs and lives mainly on lemmings.

2 Black Kite *Milvus migrans*. Distributed in Europe, Asia, Africa and Australia. Length about 56 cm. Inhabits regions with rivers, lakes or ponds. Also frequents human communities in role of scavenger. Builds nest in tree top or uses nests of other birds. Female lays 2—3 eggs, incubates them 30 days, occasionally relieved by male. Lives on small vertebrates, but likes to collect scraps on ground or water surface. Winters in Africa.

3 White-tailed Eagle *Haliaeetus albicilla*. Distributed in central and northern Europe, whole of Asia except southern parts. Also nests in Scotland. Length 75—98 cm, wing span up to 230 cm. Inhabits coast, lakes or large ponds and rivers. Makes nest from branches, usually in tall trees, occasionally on rocks. Uses same nest for years, adds to it. Female lays 2—3 whitish eggs, incubated 6 weeks by both parents in turn. Catches mainly fish, also birds up to size of heron, but chiefly weak individuals.

4 Goshawk *Accipiter gentilis*. Distributed over whole of Europe, Asia except southern parts, and most of North America. Length of male

52—56 cm, female 60—64.5 cm. Colouring often variable. Inhabits small woods, often settles near villages. Radius of nesting area about 5 km. Builds nest from twigs and green sprays on tall trees, adds to it every year. Female lays 3—5 grey-green eggs, often with brown spots, incubates them 38 days, mainly unaided. Catches squirrels, rabbits, birds (mainly jays, pigeons, crows, etc.). Useful bird in falconry.

5 Sparrow-hawk *Accipiter nisus*. Distributed over whole of Europe, most of Asia except north, north-western Africa. Length of male 31—34 cm, female 37—41 cm. Resident and nomadic, some birds migratory. Forest-dweller with preference for conifer woods. Builds nest from dry twigs, preferably in tall spruces, beside trunk. In May female lays 4—6 bluish-green eggs with brown-red spots, incubates them unaided 31—36 days, fed by male. Male fetches food for young, female feeds them. Catches mainly small birds, especially sparrows, but also blackbirds, finches, etc.

6 Honey Buzzard *Pernis apivorus*. Distributed in Europe except north and south, in east as far as Urals. Migratory. Leaves in October, winters in western and central Africa, returns in April. Length 50—57 cm. Prefers deciduous and mixed lowland woods. Frequents chiefly places inhabited by wasps which are its staple diet. Nests in abandoned nests of other birds of prey near clearings or margins of forests. Female usually lays only 2 whitish eggs with red-brown spots. Young hatch in 30—35 days. Digs out wasps' broods, but also eats soft fruits.

2

1

430

Family: Ospreys—Pandionidae

7 Osprey *Pandion haliaetus*. Distributed in central, northern and southern Europe, Asia, Australia and America. Migratory bird. European population leaves in September, winters in Africa, returns in April. Length 56—61.5 cm. Inhabits basins of large rivers, area round ponds and lakes or coastal regions. Builds nest from twigs, clumps of grass, turf, etc. in tall trees, especially pines and oaks. Female lays 2—3 bluish eggs with red-brown spots. Young hatch in 29 days. Lives mainly on fish. Hovers above water, then dives after prey.

Order: **Cursory Birds**—Ciconiiformes

Family: **Herons**—Ardeidae

1 Heron *Ardea cinerea*. Distributed over most of Europe, Asia as far as Japan, Africa. European birds winter in Africa, return at beginning of April. Length about 90 cm. Inhabits regions with ponds and lakes. Builds nest from dry twigs in tall trees. Lives in colonies. Female lays 4—5 blue-green eggs, incubated 25—28 days by both parents in turn. Young hatch in same order as eggs were laid. Catches small fish, amphibians, molluscs, insects, small rodents and birds. Flocks of northern herons often seen in central Europe in winter.

2 Purple Heron *Ardea purpurea*. Distributed in southern, eastern and occasionally central Europe, southern Asia, Africa. European birds winter in Africa, leave at end of September. Length about 80 cm. Inhabits large reed beds round ponds and lakes. Builds nest from grass blades and twigs on flattened rushes. Usually nests in colonies. Female lays 7—8 bluish-green eggs, incubated 24—28 days by both parents in turn. Lives mainly on fish, frogs and insects.

3 Night Heron *Nycticorax nycticorax*. Distributed in southern Europe, southern parts of central Europe, south-eastern Asia, whole of Africa, America. European birds winter in Africa, leave at end of August or in September. Length about 55 cm. Inhabits regions with ponds, swamps, etc. Builds nest from small sticks in trees or bushes. Lives in colonies. Female usually lays 4 green-blue eggs, incubated 21—23 days by both parents in turn. Lives mainly on valueless fishes, hunts over wide area.

4 Little Bittern *Ixobrychus minutus*. Distributed in Europe except England, in east to Siberia, most of Africa, Australia. European birds migrate in August, winter in Africa, return at end of April. Length about 35 cm. Inhabits sedge round ponds, pools, creeks, etc. Builds nest on flattened reeds near water level. Female lays 5—6 whitish eggs, incubated 16—19 days by both parents in turn. Young climb rushes at one week. Eats small fish, frogs and insects.

5 Bittern *Botaurus stellaris*. Distributed over whole of Europe to south of Sweden, in east to Japan, also in Africa. European birds migrate in October to equatorial Africa, return in March.

Occasionally resident. Length about 70 cm. Lives secretively in large reed beds round ponds and lakes. Booming call. Builds nest on flattened rushes. Lays 4—6 green-grey eggs in April or May. Young hatch in 25—26 days. Catches frogs, small fish, insects, etc. Freezes with beak held to sky if disturbed.

Family: **Storks**—Ciconiidae

6 White Stork *Ciconia ciconia*. Distributed in Europe, central and eastern Asia including Japan, North Africa. European birds migrate to Africa at end of August, return in first half of April. Length about 1 m. Builds large nest on tall trees, roofs and chimneys. Female lays 2—6 white eggs, incubated 30—34 days by both parents in turn. Parents fetch food for young, regurgitate it on to nest. Catches insects, amphibians, small mammals and birds. Voiceless, clatters beak.

7 Black Stork *Ciconia nigra*. Distributed in central and eastern Europe, south of Sweden, Iberian peninsula, in east across China to Sakhalin. European birds migrate in September, winter in Africa south of Sahara, return at beginning of April. Length about 1 m. Inhabits wooded regions at both low and high altitudes. Has large nesting area. Builds nest on tall tree close to trunk. Female lays 2—5 bluish-white eggs, incubated by both parents 28—32 days. Lives mainly on fish, but also catches amphibians or small vertebrates and insects. Flies far afield. Does not clatter beak, but utters hoarse hissing sounds.

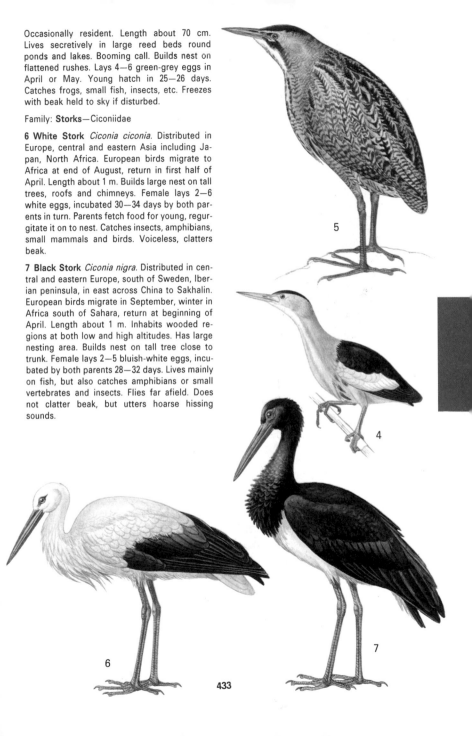

5

4

6

7

Order: **Pelicans and Allies**—Pelecaniformes

Family: **Cormorants**—Phalacrocoracidae

1 Great Cormorant *Phalacrocorax carbo*. Distributed in Europe, Asia, Africa, Australia, North America. Central-European birds migrate in September to Mediterranean region, return at beginning of March. Length 80—90 cm. Nests in colonies. Builds nest in trees, from small sticks. Female lays 3—4 blue-green eggs. Young hatch in 28—30 days, remain 8 weeks in nest. Lives mainly on fish, hunts under water. Often hunts together with pelicans, which do not dive.

Order: **Ducks, Geese and Swans**—Anseriformes

2 Whooper Swan *Cygnus cygnus*. Distributed mainly in northern parts of Europe and Asia. In winter often seen on rivers or ice-free lakes in central and southern Europe. Length 155—170 cm, wing span up to 2.5 m, weight about 10 kg. In native habitat lives beside lakes or bays surrounded by rushes, in which it builds large nest. Female lays 4—6 eggs, incubates them mainly unaided 35—40 days. Lives on small aquatic animals and greenstuff. In severe winters migrates southwards in large flocks.

3 Mute Swan *Cygnus olor*. Distributed in northern Europe and central Asia; in recent years lives in halfwild state on many lakes and ponds in central Europe. Length about 160 cm. Builds nest from twigs, reeds, etc. in reed beds or on ground. Female lays 5—9 white, green-tinged eggs. Incubates them mainly unaided. Male keeps watch but occasionally relieves female. Young hatch in 35 days, on second day take to water with female. Swan with young aggressive. Mainly vegetarian but also eats insects etc.

4 Greylag Goose *Anser anser*. Distributed in Scotland, Scandinavia, in central and eastern Europe, across Asia to Far East. Migrates south at end of October (northern birds winter in England), returns to nesting areas at end of February or beginning of March. Length 78—92 cm. Builds nest using rush stalks and other material, usually in reed beds, but sometimes in small willows. Lines nest with down. Female lays 4—7 whitish eggs, incubates them unaided 28 days. Eats seeds, grass, shoots, etc.

5 Bean Goose *Anser fabalis*. Distributed in northern parts of Europe and Asia, coast of Greenland. Length 73—90 cm. Winters from September in central, western and southern Europe. Frequents ice-free water. In some years appears in huge flocks. Very wary bird. Looks for food in meadows and fields. Returns to nesting area in May. Builds nest from grass blades etc. Female lays 3—6 eggs, incubates them about 26 days. Vegetarian.

6 Brent Goose *Branta bernicla*. Distributed over coasts of northern Asia and North America. Length 58—88 cm. In winter migrates along west coast of Europe to Spain and Morocco. Some flocks stray far inland, into central Europe. Builds nest from grass blades in dry parts of tundra. Female lays 3—6 eggs, incubates them about 25 days. Lives on grass, seeds, lichen.

7 Shelduck *Tadorna tadorna*. Distributed over coasts of northern and western Europe, round Black Sea, in east as far as Mongolia. Length about 65 cm. In winter (sometimes in spring) appears on rivers and ponds in central Europe. Nests in holes and hollows, also uses deserted foxes' earths. Sometimes nests in rocks. Female lays 6—16 plain yellowish eggs, incubates them unaided. Young hatch in 28 days. Lives on greenstuff, insects, worms, small crustaceans, etc.

4

5

7

6

Order: **Ducks, Geese and Swans**—Anseriformes

1 Mallard *Anas platyrhynchos*. Distributed in Europe, Asia and North America, in winter also North Africa and India. Length 49—63 cm. Inhabits overgrown pools, ponds, lakes and rivers. Often nests on small ornamental ponds in town parks. Nest usually built on ground, in clump of grass or under bush, occasionally in tree. Female lays 8—14, generally green-grey eggs, incubates them unaided 26 days. When dry, young follow female to water. Young promptly dive if in danger. Mixed diet. Like all ducks, males have same colouring as females during summer.

2 Widgeon *Anas strepera*. Distributed in southern England, central Europe, in east as far as Amur, and North America. Length about 48 cm. European birds migrate in October to Mediterranean region, return in March. Mainly inhabits overgrown ponds. Nest hidden in reed-grass, nettles, etc. In May or June female lays 8—14 creamy eggs, incubates them unaided 26 days. Mixed diet.

3 European Teal *Anas crecca*. Distributed over whole of Europe except Spain, temperate and northern Asia, large parts of North America. Length 30.5—38 cm, weight about 0.3 kg. European birds migrate in August, winter in southern Europe and North Africa, return in April. Inhabits thickly overgrown ponds. Nests on ground in meadows etc., often far from water. In May female lays 8—10 eggs. Mixed diet. Form flocks in autumn. Swift flier.

4 Garganey *Anas querquedula*. Distributed in Europe, extends east as far as Japan. Length 34—40 cm. In September European birds migrate in flocks to North and Central Africa. Inhabits places with thickly overgrown water. Nests in dense clumps of grass or under bushes. At end of April female lays 8—12 eggs, incubates them about 23 days. Mixed diet.

5 Shoveller *Anas clypeata*. Distributed in western, central and northern Europe, in east across Asia to North America. In September migrates to Mediterranean region, returns in second half of March. Length about 45 cm. Inhabits regions with ponds and meadows. Nests in grass in meadows and fields. Lines nest with dry reedgrass and down. Female incubates 9—12 greyish eggs 23—24 days. Catches mainly small animals in shallows. Wide bill acts as sieve.

6 Red-crested Pochard *Netta rufina*. Distributed in parts of central Europe, western and central Asia. In recent years has spread to many places in central Europe. Migrates in September to southern Europe, returns in April. Length about 60 cm. Nests on small islands or right beside water. Female incubates 7—10 grey-yellow eggs 27 days. Gathers food on surface of open water.

7 Pochard *Aythya ferina*. Distributed mainly in central Europe, in east to western Siberia, North America. Both migratory and resident. Length about 40 cm. Very common. Inhabits large ponds and lakes surrounded by reed beds. Lives mostly on water. Builds nest near water, on clumps of reed-grass or small islands. Female incubates 8—14 relatively large, yellow-green eggs about 24 days. Seeks food — aquatic animals and plant shoots — mainly under water.

8 Tufted Duck *Aythya fuligula*. Inhabited originally northern Europe, Asia and Iceland, but has begun to move south. Today common in England and central Europe. European birds winter on coasts of western Europe and Mediterranean. Leave in October. Length about 38 cm. At end of May builds nest in clump of reed-grass or on ground, close to water. Female incubates 6—9 green-grey eggs 25—26 days. Young completely black. Mixed diet, gathered mainly under water. Excellent diver.

5

6

7

8

Order: **Ducks, Geese and Swans**—Anseriformes

1 Golden-eye *Bucephala clangula*. Distributed in northern parts of Europe, Asia and North America, recently parts of central Europe. Migrates in October to coasts of western and southern Europe, returns to central Europe at end of March. Length about 40 cm. Builds down-lined nest in tree hollows or nesting-boxes, often at great height. Female incubates 8—18 greenish eggs about 30 days. Mixed diet, gathered mainly in water.

2 Eider Duck *Somateria mollissima*. Distributed in most northerly arctic regions of Europe, Iceland, Greenland, North America and north-eastern Siberia. Length about 58 cm. In autumn and winter regularly appears on ice-free rivers in central Europe. Builds nest near sea, in grass, among stones, etc. Female lays 4—5 greenish eggs, packed in finest down, incubates them 24—27 days. Lives mainly on small animals but also eats some plants.

3 Goosander *Mergus merganser*. Distributed in northern parts of Europe, Asia and North America. Regularly appears on ice-free rivers in central Europe, frequently in large flocks, from November to April. Length about 65 cm. Nests inland, often far from water, usually in tree hollows. Female incubates 7—12 dull green eggs 35 days. Young hop out of nest unaided. Lives on small fish, water snails, aquatic insects, etc.

Order: **Divers and Allies**—Gaviiformes

Family: **Divers**—Gaviidae

4 Black-throated Diver *Gavia arctica*. Distributed in northern parts of Europe, Asia and North America. Also nests in Scotland and north of Poland. Occasionally appears on central European rivers from October to April. Length 70—74 cm. Inhabits lakes, mainly in tundra and taiga belt. Nests beside water. Each couple has own nesting 'preserve'. Both parents incubate 1—3 spotted eggs about 25 days. Lives on fish, supplemented by molluscs, large insects, small crustaceans, etc.

Order: **Grebes and Allies**—Podicipediformes

Family: **Grebes**—Podicipedidae

5 Great Crested Grebe *Podiceps cristatus.*
Widely distributed over whole of Europe and
Asia except most northerly parts, whole of Africa and Australia. Winters in western and southern Europe and often on rivers in central
Europe. Migrates by night. Length 54—61 cm.
Inhabits lakes and large ponds thickly overgrown with rushes. Builds nest from aquatic
plants among reeds. Nest sometimes floats. Female usually lays 3—4 dingy greenish eggs, incubated by both parents 25 days. Parents often
carry dark-striped young on back and push food
down their beaks. Catches small fish and insects.

6 Black-necked Grebe *Podiceps nigricollis.* Distributed over whole of Europe except Scandinavia, in east to western Siberia, west to North
America, eastern Africa. Migrates in October or
November to western and southern Europe, returns in April. Length 31—33.5 cm. Inhabits
thickly overgrown ponds and lakes. Often nests
in colonies of up to several hundred couples.
Builds nest in rushes. Female incubates 3—4
(occasionally up to 6) dull white or greenish
eggs 20—21 days. Lives mainly on insects.

7 Little Grebe or **Dabchick** *Podiceps ruficollis.*
Distributed over whole of Europe, southern and
south-eastern Asia, Australia, whole of Africa.
Length about 23 cm. Very common, but shy and
secretive. Inhabits small ponds, pools, creeks,
etc., overgrown with reeds. Arrives in April.
From fragments of aquatic plants builds floating
nest among rushes, close to open water. Female
lays 4—9 white, green-tinged eggs, incubated
20 days by both parents in turn. Eats mainly
aquatic insects. Often resident on ice-free parts
of rivers.

Order: **Doves, Pigeons and Allies**—Columbiformes

Family: **Doves and Pigeons**—Columbidae

1 Wood Pigeon *Columba palumbus.* Distributed over whole of Europe except most northerly part, Asia Minor, north-western Africa, in east to central Asia and Himalayas. European birds migrate in September or October to southern Europe and north-western Africa, return in middle of March. Length about 40 cm. Mostly inhabits conifer and mixed woods, but also encountered in large parks. Builds loose, untidy nest from dry twigs, usually 5—30 m from ground, on spreading branch. Female lays 2 white eggs in April, sometimes second clutch in June. Young hatch in 16—18 days. Lives on seeds of forest plants, but also raids crops.

2 Stock Dove *Columba oenas.* Distributed over whole of Europe except Scandinavia, in east to central Asia, in south to north-western Africa. European birds migrate in September or October to southern Europe and North Africa, return in middle of March. Length about 34 cm. Chiefly inhabits deciduous woods with old beeches and oaks, in hollows of which it builds nest. Also uses nesting-boxes. Female lays 2 white eggs in April and again in June. Young hatch in 17—20 days. Lives mainly on seeds.

3 Turtle Dove *Streptopelia turtur.* Distributed over whole of Europe, in east to central Asia, whole of North Africa. In September—October migrates to Africa north of equator, returns in April. Length about 30 cm. Inhabits young woods and overgrown hillsides with fields and meadows in vicinity. Builds nest in thick undergrowth, in tall, dense bushes, etc., 1—7 m above ground. Female lays 2 white eggs. Young hatch in 14—17 days. Lives on seeds (especially of weeds), small molluscs, etc.

4 Collared Turtle Dove *Streptopelia decaocto.* Inhabited originally southern Asia, Asia Minor and southern part of Balkans. A few decades ago started to spread west, now inhabits whole of Europe and is one of commonest birds. Resident bird. Frequents human communities, lives in town parks, gardens, orchards, etc. and accepts titbits left outside window. Nests several times a year, from early spring to autumn. Winter nesting and laying also known. Builds nest from sticks and grass blades in dense tree tops or tall bushes. Has preference for spruces and ornamental trees in parks. Lays 2 white eggs.

Lives on various seeds, molluscs and insects, in winter will eat scraps and chopped meat. Has loud call.

Order: **Waders and Allies**—Charadriiformes

Family: **Auks, Razorbills and Puffins**—Alcidae

5 Guillemot *Uria aalge.* Distributed over coasts of northern Europe, England, north-eastern Asia, north-western part of North America. Length about 45 cm. In winter frequents coasts of western Europe and Mediterranean countries. Rock-dweller. On ledge of rock female lays single large, spotted egg, incubated 35 days by both parents in turn. Lives on small fish, crustaceans, etc., caught in sea.

6 Puffin *Fratercula arctica.* Distributed mainly over coasts of Scandinavia and northern islands, west coast of England, Iceland, Greenland. Length 30—36 cm. In winter appears along coasts of western Europe and Mediterranean countries. Builds nest in burrow up to 3 m long. Female lays single egg, incubated 35 days by both parents in turn. Catches mainly small fish.

5

6

Family: **Gulls and Terns**—Laridae

1 Black-headed Gull *Larus ridibundus*. Distributed in Europe, extends to Far East. Length 33.5—43 cm. In nesting season has black-brown head, in winter white. European birds winter mainly in western and southern Europe, but many remain behind on ice-free rivers in central Europe. Arrives in nesting area in second half of March. Nests in large colonies on small islands in ponds. Nest made of grass blades, twigs, leaves, etc. Female usually lays 3 spotted eggs of very variable colouring. Young hatch in 22—24 days. Lives on insects, small fish, fruit, e.g. cherries, etc. Follows plough and snaps up grubs and worms.

2 Common Gull *Larus canus*. Distributed in England, northern Europe, northern Asia, north-western part of North America. Winters along coasts of western Europe, often flies inland to rivers of central Europe. Returns to nesting areas in April. Length 38—48 cm. Nests in grass on small islands, etc. Female lays 3 spotted eggs. Young hatch in 25—26 days. Fed by parents 35 days. Eats insects, molluscs, other birds' eggs, fruits and seeds.

3 Herring Gull *Larus argentatus.* Distributed over coasts of northern and southern Europe, northern Asia and North America. Length 55—69 cm. Nests on ground on shore, in Balkans also on roofs of houses. Female lays 2—3 spotted eggs. Young hatch in 26 days, fully fledged after 8—9 weeks. Lives on small animals, scraps, etc. In autumn also roams inlands to rivers, particularly Danube.

4 Great Black-backed Gull *Larus marinus.* Distributed over coasts of Scandinavia, Iceland, England and North America. Length 61—76 cm. In winter lives nomadically along coasts of northern and western Europe. Often accompanies ocean-going liners out to sea, hoping for scraps. Otherwise eats fish, crustaceans and birds' eggs and young. Nests on cliffs. Usually lays 3 spotted eggs. Both parents incubate eggs 29—30 days and then feed young.

5 Arctic Skua *Stercorarius parasiticus.* Inhabits Arctic waters and coasts of northern Europe, Asia and North America. Length about 46 cm. In winter comes to African coast. Common on coast but strays to rivers in central Europe. Nests in colonies. Female lays 2 spotted eggs on bare ground, between clumps of grass. Young hatch in 25—26 days. Lives on different animals caught in sea, also hunts lemmings and eats berries. Chases gulls, forces them to drop food, snaps it up in air.

6 Common Tern *Sterna hirundo.* Distributed over whole of Europe, temperate parts of Asia, North America. Length 34—40 cm. Migrates in August to southern Africa, returns at beginning of May. Nests in colonies. Makes nest on ground, from a few sticks, roots, shells, etc. Female lays 2—4 spotted eggs of somewhat variable colouring. Young hatch in 20—22 days. Diet small fish. Hovers in air looking for prey, dives after it at high speed.

7 Black Tern *Chlidonias niger.* Distributed over large part of Europe, in east to central Asia, part of North America. Length 24—27 cm. European birds migrate at end of July to equatorial Africa, return in May. Lives in small colonies. Builds nest on floating aquatic plants. Female lays 2—3 spotted eggs. Young hatch in 14—17 days. Lives mainly on aquatic insects, small crustaceans and fish, but also often travels several miles to look for insects in fields.

Families: Charadriidae, Scolopacidae

1 Lapwing *Vanellus vanellus*. Distributed over whole of Europe, in east to temperate parts of Asia as far as Korea. Length about 30 cm. Very common. Skilful flier. Winters in western and southern Europe and North Africa, often returns at end of February. Inhabits damp meadows and fields near ponds and lakes. Builds nest on small hummock, lines it with blades of grass. Female lays 4 olive-brown speckled eggs, incubated by both parents 24 days. After 2 days, young disperse and hide in surrounding grass. In autumn forms flocks round ponds. Eats insects, worms, molluscs, seeds.

2 Golden Plover *Pluvialis apricaria*. Inhabits northern Europe, England, Iceland, east coast of Greenland. Winters in west and south-west of Europe and in North Africa. In September to October always migrates across central Europe, can be seen there mainly in fields, usually in small flocks. Length 25—30 cm. Inhabits swampy areas in north. Builds nest like lapwing's on ground. Lays 4 eggs, young hatch in 20 days. Catches insects, worms, etc.

3 Little Ringed Plover *Charadrius dubius*. Distributed over whole of Europe except England and Scandinavia, most of Asia, North Africa. European birds migrate in September—November to equatorial Africa, return in middle of April. Length 16—19 cm. Likes sandy ground beside lakes, ponds and rivers. Nests in small depression in pebbles. Female lays 4 yellowish, dark-spotted eggs, incubated by both parents 22—24 days. Eats insects, insect larvae and worms.

4 Sea Plover *Charadrius alexandrinus*. Distributed along all European coasts except most northerly regions, whole of temperate and southern Asia, whole of Africa, Australia, southern U.S.A. and west of South America. European birds winter on African coast south of equator. Length 16—18.5 cm. Prefers sandy shores beside sea or salt lakes. Female lays 4 spotted eggs in depression in stones, incubates them 24 days. Catches insects, small crustaceans, worms and molluscs. Migrating birds often seen in central Europe.

5 Dunlin *Calidris alpina*. Distributed in England, north coast of Germany, Scandinavia and northern parts of Asia and North America. Winters on coasts of western Europe, Mediterranean region and Africa. Migrating birds seen in large numbers beside ponds from end of August. Length 19—22.5 cm. Nests mainly in tundra belt, builds nest in peat moors. Female lays 4 eggs, incubated by both parents. Lives on insects, worms and molluscs.

6 Ruff (female **Reeve**) *Philomachus pugnax*. Distributed over northern parts of Europe and Asia, but also nests in central Europe, e.g. Poland, Holland and Belgium. Winters in Africa. Appears in flocks beside ponds over whole of central Europe during migration. Length 23—33 cm. Male's colouring very variable. During nesting season males wear 'ruff' and fight duels. Female builds nest lined with grass blades and leaves in small pit. Lays 4 eggs, incubates them unaided 20—21 days. Eats mainly insects, worms and molluscs.

7 Redshank *Tringa totanus*. Distributed over whole of Europe and across temperate belt of Asia to Far East. Migrates in August—October, return at end of March. Length 27—31 cm. Inhabits flat ground beside large ponds and lakes. Builds grass-lined nest in depression in ground. Female lays 4 grey, dark-speckled eggs, incubated 22—25 days by both parents in turn. Young fledged at 25 days. If enemy approaches nest or young, parent birds fly up, screeching. Lives on insects, worms, molluscs, crustaceans and small fish.

Families: Scolopacidae, Recurvirostridae

1 Black-tailed Godwit *Limosa limosa*. Distributed in northern part of western Europe except England, Iceland, northern Germany, central and eastern Europe, across Asia to Far East. European birds migrate in August or September to northern and equatorial Africa, return in first half of April. Length 39.5—49.5 cm; female always much larger. Inhabits water-logged meadows beside ponds and lakes. Makes nest in shallow depression in thick grass or on clod, lines it with a little grass. Female lays 4 dark-spotted eggs, incubated 24 days by both parents in turn. If enemy approaches, flies up into air, uttering piercing, piping cries. Eats insects, insect larvae, worms, small molluscs.

2 Avocet *Recurvirostra avosetta*. Distributed in southern Spain, coast of Germany, occasionally swampy ground round lakes and ponds in central Europe, in east to Mongolia. European birds winter in southern Africa. Length 42—47.5 cm. Builds nest among plants in depression in mud of drained ponds, etc., lines it with a few plants. Female lays 4 olive-green eggs with grey-brown spots. Eggs incubated 24—25 days by both parents in turn. Lives on insects, insect larvae, crustaceans and molluscs found in shallow water and mud.

3 Curlew *Numenius arquata*. Distributed in Europe except south, Iceland, in east to western Siberia. European birds winter in eastern Africa, return at end of March. Length 54—69 cm. Inhabits large, wet meadows or steppe country in vicinity of water. Builds nest in small depression in ground, among grass. Female lays 4 spotted eggs, often strewn with dark dots and streaks. Eggs incubated 26—28 days by both parents in turn. Female responsible for care of young. Lives on insects, insect larvae, seeds of aquatic plants, etc.

4 Woodcock *Scolopax rusticola*. Distributed over whole of Europe except most northerly parts, in east forms belt across Asia to Japan, also found on Azores and Canaries. European birds winter in southern Europe and North Africa, return at end of March. Migrate by night. Length 34—38 cm. Inhabits deciduous or mixed woods where it frequents large, damp, grassy spaces, streams, etc. Nests in a small leaf- or moss-lined depression under a bush. Female lays 4 spotted eggs of somewhat variable colouring, incubates them unaided 22 days. Eats insects, worms and molluscs.

5 Common Snipe *Gallinago gallinago.* Distributed over whole of Europe except south, in east across temperate parts of Asia to Japan. European birds winter mainly in Africa, return in March. Occasionally resident. Length 24.5—31 cm. Inhabits swamps, damp meadows and peat-bogs. Nests in deep depression in dense grass. Female lays 4 eggs with olive and green spots, incubates them unaided 19—21 days. Lives on insects, spiders and worms. In autumn congregates in flocks. At mating time male flies high into air and dives with spread tail feathers, vibrations of which produce bleating sound.

Order: **Cranes, Rails and Allies**—Gruiformes

Family: **Cranes**—Gruidae

6 Crane *Crus grus.* Distributed in northern Europe and Asia. Occasionally nests in north and east of central Europe. European birds winter in North Africa and along Nile, return in April or May. Length 105—120 cm. Inhabits extensive swamps and marshes. Flies in typical V-formation. Couples remain together. Female builds large nest in swamp, from reeds and aquatic plants. Usually lays 2 grey-green, dark-spotted eggs. Young hatch in 29—30 days. Eats mainly greenstuffs, but also insects, molluscs and occasionally small vertebrates.

3

5

4

6

Family: **Rails, Moorhens and Coots**—Rallidae

1 Water Rail *Rallus aquaticus*. Distributed over whole of Europe, in east across temperate Asia to Japan, also North Africa. Winters in southern Europe and North Africa, returns in middle of April. Length about 28.5 cm. Mainly nocturnal bird. Inhabits fishpond regions. Nests on swampy ground under bush etc. Nest made of grass, reed-grass, leaves, etc. Female lays 6—12 yellowish, rusty-spotted eggs, incubated 20 days by both parents. Newly hatched chicks are black. Parents push food into their beaks. Lives on insects, worms and small leaves.

2 Spotted Crake *Porzana porzana*. Distributed over most of Europe, in east to central Asia, north-western Africa. Migrates to southern Europe and North Africa in October, returns in middle of April. Length 21—25 cm. Leads secretive existence. Builds nest from grass and leaves on clump of reed-grass in swamp. Female lays 6—8 spotted eggs. Young hatch in 18—21 days. Eats insects, spiders, molluscs, seeds and parts of aquatic plants.

3 Moorhen *Gallinula chloropus*. Distributed over most of Europe, central and eastern Asia, America, Africa. European birds occasionally resident, but mostly winter in North Africa. Length about 32 cm. Inhabits overgrown lakes, ponds and pools. Makes deep-basined nest from reeds and aquatic plants on surface of water among rushes. Female lays 6—8 yellowish eggs with rusty brown spots. Young hatch in 19—22 days. Lives on insects, worms, seeds and parts of plants.

4 Coot *Fulica atra*. Distributed over whole of Europe, across temperate parts of Asia to Japan, Australia, north-western Africa. European birds winter in western and southern Europe, but often occur in flocks on rivers of central Europe. Return to nesting places in March. Length 38—45 cm. Inhabits any type of overgrown stagnant water. Builds nest on surface of water, at margin of vegetation, from rush stems, sedge, etc., often with a connecting 'bridge'. Female lays 5—15 mauvish, black-spotted eggs. Young, hatched in 22 days, have orange-coloured head. Lives on small aquatic animals, seeds and parts of plants.

Family: **Bustards**—Otididae

5 Great Bustard *Otis tarda*. Distributed in southern and central Europe, in east to China, north-western Africa. Length of male about 100 cm, female about 80 cm. Inhabits steppes and vast fields. Female lays 2—3 brownish spotted eggs in depression in ground, incubates them about 30 days. Large nesting sites near Berlin and in southern Slovakia. Lives on insects, worms, small vertebrates, seeds and parts of plants.

Order: **Game Birds**—Galliformes

Family: **Pheasants, Partridges and Quails**—Phasianidae

6 Partridge *Perdix perdix*. Distributed over most of Europe except northern Scandinavia, in east to central Asia. Length about 26 cm. Inhabits steppes, in Europe mainly fields. Usually at beginning of May female lays about 15 olive-

2   3

brown eggs in pit in ground, incubates them un-aided 23—25 days, but male also cares for young. Eats mainly plants, supplemented in summer by insects, spiders and molluscs. In autumn gathers together in small flocks. Highly prized game bird in Europe.

7 Quail *Coturnix coturnix.* Distributed over most of Europe, temperate parts of Asia as far as Japan, North and South Africa. European birds winter mainly in Africa. Leave in October, return at end of April. Length about 18 cm. Inhabits steppes, meadows and fields. Male polygamous. Female digs small pit, lays 6—18 eggs, usually marked with dark brown blotches and dots, incubates them unaided 18—20 days. Lives on seeds, shoots, small molluscs, worms and insects.

449

Family: **Pheasants, Partridges and Quails**—
Phasianidae

1 Common Pheasant *Phasianus colchicus*. Originally distributed in a few races in central and eastern Asia, but introduced into many parts of Europe and North America. Known in central Europe since 14th century. European races now thoroughly crossed. Length of cock about 80 cm, hen about 60 cm. Inhabits copses, wooded slopes, etc. in lowlands and uplands. Female lines depression in ground with leaves and grass, lays 8—15 plain brownish eggs, incubates them unaided 23—27 days. Cock polygamous. Lives on plants, shoots, seeds and various small animals. Important game bird.

2 Rock Partridge *Alectoris graeca*. Distributed in mountainous regions from southern Europe east to China. Abundant in Balkans and on southern slopes of Alps. Introduction attempted in many places in central Europe. Length about 35 cm. Inhabits rocky slopes. In summer ascends to dwarf timber belt, in winter descends into valleys. In May or June female lays 10—15 light brown, often thickly spotted eggs in depression in rock or in clump of grass. Lives on seeds, grass, insects, etc.

Family: **Grouse and Ptarmigans**—*Tetraonidae*

3 Ptarmigan *Lagopus mutus*. Distributed in tundras in northern Europe, Asia and North America, also England, Spain and Alps. Length about 35 cm. In summer brownish with white wings, in winter completely white except for black tail. White colouring makes it blend with snow. Female usually lays 7—10 russet-speckled eggs in depression among stones or in clump of grass, etc. Eats shoots, buds (e.g. of willows, birches, etc.), seeds and, in summer, insects, spiders and small molluscs. In winter spends night in holes in snow.

4 Black Grouse *Lyrurus tetrix*. Distributed over whole of Europe except south, whole of temperate Asia, but mainly more northerly regions, primarily taiga. Length of cock about 65 cm, hen about 45 cm. Cock weighs about 1.5 kg. Likes deciduous and mixed woods with damp meadows in vicinity. Early in spring birds congregate on special 'parade grounds', in clearing, on moor, in meadow, etc., where cocks fight duels. Cock polygamous. Hen lays 6—10 yellowish, dark-spotted eggs in moss- and grass-lined pit, incubates them unaided about 26 days. Lives on seeds, berries, shoots, insects, worms, etc.

450

4

6

5

5 Capercaillie *Tetrao urogallus.* Distributed in northern England, central and northern Europe, eastwards to Sakhalin. Length of cock about 100 cm, hen 70 cm. Cock can weigh up to 6 kg. Inhabits large forests. Males perform interesting nuptial rites. 'Song' divided into three parts: knocking, trilling and slurring. Hen lays 5—12 yellowish, brown-spotted eggs in shallow depression lined with leaves, conifer needles, etc., incubates them unaided 24—27 days. Lives on shoots, conifer needles, whole tips of conifer branches, insects, molluscs, etc. Most highly prized game bird.

6 Hazel Hen *Tetrastes bonasia.* Distributed over whole of central and northern Europe, extends east to eastern Siberia and south-eastern China. Now scarce in mountains of central Europe, but still abundant in Scandinavia. Length about 38 cm. Inhabits mixed forests, especially with birches and dense undergrowth including bushes, cranberries and bilberries. Female lays 8—12 yellowish, dark-spotted eggs in shallow depression at foot of tree, incubates them 25 days. Lives on seeds, shoots, berries, insects, small molluscs, etc. Flesh very savoury.

Mammals

On the evolutionary scale mammals (Mammalia) are the highest group of vertebrates with a constant body temperature. The only exceptions are certain mammals that hibernate, for example bats, whose temperature drops as low as 0° C in winter.

Mammals' bodies vary in shape and are adapted to the animals' mode of life. The typical body is usually elongated, with two pairs of limbs. In some groups of mammals the limbs have been transformed, for example into wings in bats and fins in cetaceans (the hind limbs of cetaceans are atrophied). The skin is thick and covered with hairs; a few species lack hair, for example dolphins. In other species, such as hedgehogs, the hairs have been converted into spines. Hairs are a product of the skin and are a typical characteristic of mammals.

In some mammals the skin is covered with horny scales, which in scaly anteaters (Pholidota), for example, form a hard armour. Mice and rats have a tail covered with horny scales. Scales are also a product of the skin.

Many mammals have tactile organs on various parts of the body. Beasts of prey have whiskers on the sides of the face. In other mammals tactile hairs are found on the feet or flanks — always on parts that come into contact with the animal's surroundings. The hairs that form the coat or fur of animals are shed regularly and replaced by new ones. This is called moulting and usually takes place in spring when the animals acquire a thinner, shorter coat, and in autumn, when they acquire a long, dense winter coat.

A characteristic feature of mammals is their great number of skin glands. Oil glands keep the skin oily and supple; sweat glands cool the surface of the body through the evaporation of water and also excrete salts and waste substances in the sweat. Some mammals do not have sweat glands, their sweat or oil glands being transformed into scent glands that are located by the anus, on the belly, between the hooves (as in red deer and sheep), on the cheeks, etc. Scent glands in mammals whose activities are governed mainly by the sense of smell are extremely important. Some animals mark out the boundaries of their territories with a secretion from these glands, and scent also plays a vital role in finding a mate. Some mammals, such as skunks (*Mephitis mephitis*) and European polecats (*Mustela putorius*), eject an intensely malodorous secretion when startled,

thus defending themselves against an enemy. Mammary glands have also developed from skin glands. These secrete milk to feed the young. This milk contains 90 per cent water, proteins, fats, sugars and mineral substances. With the exception of monotremes, mammals secrete milk through nipples, of which there are one to fourteen pairs, depending primarily on the usual size of the litter in the given species.

Mammals have characteristic dentition, growing several types of teeth: the incisors are adapted for cutting; the conical, pointed canines are used for holding or killing prey; the premolars and molars are adapted for grinding food. The dentition is adapted to the kind of food the animals eat. The number and shape of the teeth is characteristic for each individual group or species of animal. Very occasionally, some species of mammals lack teeth altogether, for example anteaters (Myrmecophagidae).

Some mammals have developed secondary sex characteristics influenced by the hormones produced by the sex glands. For instance, the male lion has a huge mane, the male roe-deer large antlers, bulls (in cattle) are much larger than cows, male elephants have large tusks, etc. In many species, however, the male and female cannot be distinguished at first glance.

The attainment of sexual maturity differs in the various species and depends, among other things, on the animal's size. A male elephant, for example, attains sexual maturity after eighteen years, the males of small rodents within only a few months.

During the breeding season males come together with females. In some species, however, the partners remain together throughout the year, or even throughout their whole lifetime. Some males are polygamous and have a greater number of female partners. Males usually mate only once a year; some species only once in two to four years, whereas small rodents may have as many as six broods a year. The size of the litter depends on the size of the animal. The largest females generally bear only a single offspring, larger carnivores usually two or three,

Fig. 1. The male Red Deer (*Cervus elaphus*) has huge antlers.

smaller carnivores may bear more than ten. One exception among the small mammals is the bat; the female produces only a single offspring because she must carry it on her nightly flights. The young of some mammals are naked and blind at birth, for example mice. The young of carnivores are also blind at birth, but are covered with hair. Ungulates, on the other hand, give birth to fully developed young that are able to follow their mother within a few hours of birth.

Fig. 2. The Long-eared Bat (*Plecotus auritus*) in flight.

Fig. 3. The young of the House Mouse (*Mus musculus*) are born naked and blind, but become mature at six to seven weeks old.

Mammals are primarily terrestrial animals, but they also include freshwater as well as marine species. They are distributed throughout the whole world. Some 90 species of wild mammals are found in central Europe.

Plentiful in Europe are the insectivores (Insectivora), which hunt invertebrates as well as small vertebrates. Hedgehogs (Erinaceidae) form a large family. European species are distinguished by having the back and sides covered with spines. Underneath their skin hedgehogs have a special muscle by means of which they can curl up into a ball, thereby protecting their vulnerable belly. Hedgehogs are nocturnal creatures and do not set out to hunt until darkness falls. They spend the winter season in hibernation under piles of leaves or in holes. Their body temperature may drop as low as 5 °C at this

Fig. 4. The Common Mole (*Talpa europaea*) is superbly adapted to life underground. It has unusually large, shovel-like forefeet for digging underground tunnels. It often lays in stocks of earthworms, paralyzing them by biting through their nerve centre so that they are unable to move and cannot escape.

time. On awakening from their winter sleep in spring, they begin moving about only after their body temperature has risen to at least 20 °C.

Shrews (Soricidae) are another large family of insectivores. They are small mammals with a mobile, fleshy snout and a short, silky coat. The tail is relatively long. The legs are short and for that reason shrews do not move very fast. They are nocturnal creatures. Some species have become associates of people and roam around in gardens and parks.

Bats (Chiroptera) are a distinctive group of mammals. The members of this order are generally small animals that are covered with silky fur. Unlike other mammals, they are able to fly and capture their prey on the wing. Stretched between the long digits of the forelimbs, trunk and hind limbs is a richly veined membrane which makes flight possible. The digits of the hind limbs are clawed to enable the bat to hang upside down. Extending from the heel is a special projection that serves to stretch the membrane between the hind limbs and the tail. Bats are nocturnal animals, usually setting out in search of prey only after dusk, and passing the day in tree hollows, attics, galleries, etc. Their eyes are small but bats do not really need them when flying at night for they are equipped with a special radar-like system. During flight they emit supersonic sounds, inaudible to the human ear, which rebound from objects and are perceived by the bat's sensitive ear and then analysed. In colder regions bats hibernate, during which time their body temperature drops nearly as low as 0° C.

Hares and rabbits (Lagomorpha) are distinguished by having a second pair of small, narrow incisors behind the upper incisors which grow continuously as they are worn down. When chewing food, the lower jaw moves from

Fig. 5. The colouring of the Red Squirrel (*Sciurus vulgaris*) is extremely diverse. Besides rust-coloured squirrels one may often encounter squirrels that are brown or black. In Britain Red Squirrels are almost extinct, having been usurped by the Grey Squirrel (*S. carolinensis*).

left to right, whereas in rodents it moves from front to back. Hares and rabbits are all plant feeders. Many species live gregariously.

Rodents (Rodentia) have two incisors in both the upper and lower jaws. These are sharp-tipped, chisel-edged cutting teeth that continue to grow as they are worn down. Rodents are the largest group of mammals, not only in terms of number of species but numerically as well. Sometimes they overmultiply, reaching plague proportions and causing much damage. Some rodents yield precious fur, for example, the Beaver (*Castor fiber*) and the Coypu (*Myocastor coypus*), which is bred on a large scale on farms. Rodents live on land, under the ground, on trees and in water.

Beasts of prey (Carnivora) are superbly adapted for seizing and killing live quarry. They are of great importance in the food chain be-

Fig. 6. The Common or European Hare (*Lepus europaeus*) is an important small game animal. What few people know is that it can swim fairly well.

Fig. 7. The Northern Lynx (*Lynx lynx*) — a beast of prey with very keen sight and hearing — is distinguished by having long tufts of hairs on its earlobes.

cause they help to preserve the ecological balance among herbivorous animals, which would otherwise multiply excessively and destroy all the vegetation. Carnivores have powerfully deduveloped teeth which they use as an excellent means of attack or defence. They kill prey with their long, pointed canines. The last premolar on each side of the upper jaw, and the first molar on each side of the lower jaw, called the carnassials, serve to tear meat. Some beasts of prey are exclusively flesh-eaters, others are omnivorous.

The most perfectly adapted beasts of prey are the cats (Felidae), which have powerful, sharp-pointed claws that can be retracted, except in the Cheetah (*Acinonyx jubatus*). Cats have keener eyesight than other carnivores and they also have colour vision.

Dogs (Canidae) are distinguished by their long snouts and long legs. The toes are generally furnished with strong, blunt, non-retractile claws. Dog-like carnivores run swiftly and tirelessly. Their sight is not as keen as that of the cats and they cannot distinguish colours. When dogs are hot and excited, they extend their tongues and pant. This is their way of cooling off, because they do not have sweat glands with openings through which sweat could leave the body. Dogs often roam in packs or troops.

The mustelids (Mustelidae) are a large family of animals that are distinguished by having a long, cylindrical body and short legs. They are very dextrous carnivores. Most species secrete a pungent substance. Some are terrestrial, others arboreal, and still others aquatic, for example the Common Otter (*Lutra lutra*).

Bears (Ursidae) are the largest of the carnivores, with a robust body, wide head, tapering jaws and short tail. The toes are furnished with strong, blunt claws. Bears walk on the whole sole of the foot. Most are omnivorous. Only one species — the Brown Bear (*Ursus arctos*) — lives in central Europe.

Pinnipeds (Pinipedia) are mammals that are adapted to life in water, as evidenced by their torpedo-shaped body. They are relatively large animals. The limbs are paddle-like, the digits webbed and with rudimentary claws. The tail is also rudimentary. The teeth are sharp-pointed and conical. Even the molars are sharp-edged, so that there is little difference between them and the other teeth. The teeth serve only for grasping the slippery bodies of fish.

The European seas are also the home of mammals known as cetaceans (Cetacea), which include the whales, dolphins and porpoises. They are large to huge animals, completely adapted to a marine environment. Their jaws are generally long. Only toothed whales have teeth, all of the same shape.

Of the even-toed ungulates (Artiodactyla), several species are found in central Europe. The weight of the even-toed ungulates is borne on two central toes — the third and fourth toes, which are usually the most developed and are the same shape and size. The other toes are rudimentary or absent. Even-toed ungulates often form herds and are divided into several groups.

Non-ruminants (Nonruminantia) are omnivorous and have complete dentition and one stomach; included in this group are the pigs (Suidae). Ruminants (Ruminantia) have a stomach divided into three, or more often four, compartments. Ruminants have no incisors in the upper jaw and usually have no canines. Deer are ruminants that are characterized by their antlers. In most species only the male deer carry antlers, the exceptions are female reindeer and caribou which also carry antlers, but weaker ones than the males. Musk Deer (*Moschus moschiferus*) lack antlers. Antlers are shed and regrown each year.

Horned ruminants have horns, which are usually carried by both males and females. However, those of the males are usually much larger. Horns are a permanent fixture and grow continually.

Fig. 8. The omnivorous Wild Boar (*Sus scrofa*) is occasionally a pest, particularly in fields which are sometimes visited by whole herds that have come to feed on potatoes and beets, as well as on earthworms and insect larvae.

Class: **Mammals**—Mammalia

Order: **Insectivores**—Insectivora

Family: **Hedgehogs**—*Erinaceidae*

1, 2 European Hedgehog *Erinaceus europaeus.*
Two races — western (*E.e. europaeus*) with
brown underside and dark bands round eyes,
and eastern (*E.e. roumanicus*) with white underside. Dividing line from Oder along upper
reaches of Elbe and Vltava. Hedgehog inhabits
deciduous and mixed woods with dense undergrowth and town parks. Likes dry places. In
Alps up to 2,000 m. Makes nest in hole, under
pile of leaves, etc., usually with two entrances.
Female gives birth to 3—8 (in rare cases up to
10) young with soft white spines. Young open
eyes at 14 days. Nocturnal animal. Hibernates
from end of October to March under pile of
leaves, in burrow, etc. Lives on worms, insects,
small vertebrates, birds' eggs. Also kills venomous snakes without getting bitten and eats
them. Almost immune to snake venom. Length
up to 30 cm, weight over 1 kg. Newborn young
weigh 12—25 g. Life span 8—10 years.

Family: **Moles**—Talpidae

3 Common Mole *Talpa europaea.* Abundant in
whole of central Europe and western Asia. In
Alps up to 2,400 m. Lives underground in damp
places with loose soil. Digs burrows with chambers and passages. Length 13—17 cm, weight
70—120 g. Twice a year female gives birth to
3—9 tiny young which grow very quickly. Open
eyes at 3 weeks, suckled 4—6 weeks, independent at 2 months. Life span 2—3 years. Non-
hibernator.

Family: **Shrews**—Soricidae

4 Common Shrew *Sorex araneus.* Abundant in
whole of Europe except Mediterranean region
and Ireland. Frequents damp places with undergrowth. In Alps up to 2,000 m. Occurs mainly in
damp woods and peat-bogs, also in ditches. Inhabits vole and mole burrows, but sometimes
digs own. In winter found in houses and outbuildings. Length 6.2—8.5 cm, weight 7—15 g.
Newborn young weigh only 0.4—0.5 g. Between
April and September female produces up to
4 litters of 5—7 hairless, blind young. Coat

grows from 6th day, opens eyes at 18—25 days. Active mainly after sundown and before sunrise. Non-hibernator.

5 European Water Shrew *Neomys fodiens.* Inhabits whole of central Europe. In Alps up to 2,500 m. Frequents rivers, streams, ponds and pools. Inhabits rodent burrows and makes own burrow beside water. Likewise found in flooded cellars. Also nests in tree hollows, up to 0.75 m above ground, but always near water. Swims well. Catches insects, worms and small fish. Length 7—11 cm, weight 10—20 g. Female gives birth 2—3 times yearly to 4—10 hairless, blind young, which are suckled 5—6 weeks and reach adulthood at 3—4 months. Nocturnal animal, active mainly in early morning. Life span not more than 1.5 years. Non-hibernator.

6 Common European White-toothed Shrew *Crocidura russula.* Inhabits western, southern and parts of central Europe. Occurs up to altitudes of 1,600 m. Lives in open country, less often on margins of forests, but chiefly in gardens and parks. In winter often frequents human dwellings, cowsheds, cellars, etc. In wild surroundings lives in mouse-holes or digs own burrow. Length 6—8.5 cm, weight 6—7.5 g. Female gives birth to 3—10 young 2—3 times a year. Young open eyes at 13 days, suckled about 20 days, are adult at 4 months. Life span usually about 1.5 years, in rare cases up to 4 years. Non-hibernator. Lives on insects and worms. Nocturnal animal.

3

4

5

6

461

Order: **Bats**—Chiroptera

Family: **Horseshoe Bats**—Rhinolophidae

1 Lesser Horseshoe Bat *Rhinolophus hipposideros.* Inhabits south of central Europe. In Alps up to 2,000 m. During day shelters in attics, steeples, caves, etc. Slow and ungainly in flight. Comes out well after dark and only in warm, calm weather. Hibernates in deep caves, mines, etc. Hangs from roof in groups of up to 100, in long rows. One litter of 1—2 young annually. Young open eyes at one week, are adult at one year. Born in colonies of females. Hibernates from October to April. Life span 14—15 years.

Family: **Typical Bats**—Vespertilionidae

2 Brown Bat *Myotis myotis.* One of commonest European bats. Shelters during day in attics, towers or cellars. Hibernates in caves, mines, etc., often in vast numbers. Goes hunting after dark. Flies slowly and clumsily, at height of 5—8 m, over gardens, parks, etc., at 15 km an hour. Known to migrate distances of over 200 km in spring and autumn. Has one young yearly, in May or June, born in colonies of 100—2,000 females. Young grows quickly, can fly at 5—6 weeks. Hibernates from October to April. Maximum life span 14.5 years.

3 Fringed Bat *Myotis nattereri.* Inhabits most of Europe. Lives in small colonies of up to 30 individuals, males singly. During day shelters in tree hollows, nesting-boxes, etc. Hibernates in mines, caves and cellars. Circles low and slowly round trees. Catches insects sitting on branches. Hunts from dusk to dawn, but not in windy weather. Female gives birth to single young. Long hibernation period. Life span up to 15 years.

4 Noctule Bat *Nyctalus noctula.* Distributed over whole of Europe. During day shelters in small groups in tree hollows. Hunts in woods, parks, over water, etc. Starts early in evening and flies until dawn. In autumn appears in afternoon. Migrates 750—1,500 km south or southwest to hibernate, but sometimes remains in hollows, cowsheds, etc. Female gives birth to 1—2 young, which open eyes at 6—7 days and can fly at 45 days. Flies quickly, 50 km an hour. Hibernates from October to April.

5 Long-eared Bat *Plecotus auritus.* Distributed in Europe, Asia and North Africa. Strikingly large ears. Abundant near human communities. Appears after dark. Flies low, frequently veering. Hunts on outskirts of forests, in parks and also within woods. In June female gives birth to 1—2 young which are independent at 6 weeks. Hibernates in caves, cellars, etc. from October to end of March, alone or in groups of 2—3 individuals.

4

5

Order: **Hares and Rabbits**—*Lagomorpha*

6 Snow Hare *Lepus timidus*. Inhabits Ireland, Scotland, northern Europe, Asia, North America. One subspecies also in Alps. In summer ascends to 3,400 m, in winter comes down below 600 m. In winter shelters in snow, marmot burrows, etc. Weighs up to 3.5 kg. In summer grey-brown, in winter pure white. Between May and August female gives birth to 2—5 young with open eyes, suckles them about 3 weeks. Life span 8—13 years. In Europe protected.

7 Common or **European Hare** *Lepus europaeus*. In Europe distributed over cultivated grasslands, other races inhabit large areas of Asia and Africa. In Alps up to 3,000 m. Also lives in forests. Weighs up to 8 kg. Between February or March and September female produces 3—5 litters of 2—7 young with open eyes. Suckles them only 2—3 weeks. Active after dusk and at night. Hides in bushes during day. Herbivorous. In some regions important as game.

6

7

Order: **Hares and Rabbits**—Lagomorpha

1 European Wild Rabbit *Oryctolagus cuniculus*. Originally from west of Mediterranean region. Since Middle Ages introduced into other parts of Europe; now relatively abundant everywhere. In mountains seldom found above 600 m. Inhabits open woods, parks, etc. Weighs up to 2 kg. (rarely 3 kg). Digs burrows. Between March and September female produces 3—6 litters of 5—12 or even 15 blind young which open eyes at 10 days, are suckled 4 weeks and attain adulthood at 6—8 months. Life span 10 years. Forms colonies (warrens). Hunted for flesh. Can become pest. Ancestor of domestic rabbits.

Order: **Rodents**—Rodentia

Family: **Squirrels**—Sciuridae

2 Red Squirrel *Sciurus vulgaris*. Distributed over whole of Europe, extends across Asia as far as Japan. Forest-dweller, occurs in mountains up to limit of tree belt. Builds large spherical nest from twigs, leaves, moss and hairs, in trees; also uses deserted birds' nests and tree hollows. From January to August female produces 2—5 litters of 3—7 blind young. Lives on tree seeds, fruits, mushrooms, insects, birds' eggs and young; also gnaws shoots. In August lays in stocks of food under moss. It does not hibernate.

3 European Ground Squirrel *Citellus citellus.* Inhabits eastern part of central Europe as far as China. Does not live in western Europe. Steppe-dweller. Occurs on grassy slopes up to altitude of 700 m. Digs burrow 1—4 m deep and up to 7 m long. Female gives birth to 6—11 young which open eyes at about 4 weeks. Lives on grass, fruit and insects. Hibernates in burrow from October to April. Does not lay in food stocks.

4 European Alpine Marmot *Marmota marmota.* Inhabits Alps, Carpathians and mountains in Asia. Frequents rocky slopes at 800—3,000 m. Digs burrows 1.5—3 m deep and up to 10 m long, with several entrances. Lives in colonies. For winter digs special burrow and blocks entrances. Hibernates from end of September until April. Builds up body fat deposits in autumn. Female gives birth to 2—6 blind young which open eyes at 20 days. Active both during day and at night. Very cautious, utters warning whistles. Lives on grass, seeds, berries, insects. Does not store food. Life span up to 18 years.

Family: **Dormice** —*Gliridae*

5 Fat Dormouse *Glis glis.* Distributed from north of Spain across central Europe to Asia Minor. Inhabits deciduous woods at altitudes of up to 1,500 m. Common in orchards and parks, frequents also buildings. Length up to 19 cm. Between June and August female gives birth to 2—9 blind young which open eyes at 20 days. Nocturnal animal, lives on buds, shoots, seeds, fruit, insects and occasionally young birds. Hibernates from end of August until May. Makes moss-lined nest in hollows or nesting-boxes.

6 Garden Dormouse *Eliomys quercinus.* Distributed from Portugal across central Europe to Urals, in south to North Africa. Mainly inhabits conifer woods with undergrowth, but also parks. Builds spherical nest in rock crevices, tree hollows, etc. Litter comprises 2—8 young which open eyes at 18 days. Nocturnal animal, excellent climber. Lives on shoots, berries, fruit and insects. In autumn enters human dwellings. Hibernates in hollows, nesting-boxes, squirrels' nests and attics, from September to April.

7 Common Dormouse *Muscardinus avellanarius.* Distributed in Europe as far as central Sweden, part of England, in south to Italy. Absent in Spain. In mountains up to 2,000 m. Inhabits dense thickets, especially young undergrowth. Sometimes found in gardens. In summer builds spherical nest up to 12 cm across with side entrance, usually 1—1.5 m, but sometimes 20 m, above ground. Lives on seeds, berries, buds and insects. Hibernates from October to end of March in tree hollows, cleft rocks or under pile of leaves. Body temperature drops to 1°C. Litter comprises 3—9 young which open eyes at 16 days.

6

7

5

465

Family: **Old World Rats and Mice**—Muridae

1 House Mouse *Mus musculus.* Distributed over whole of Europe, originally from Asian, North-African and Mediterranean steppes. In Alps at up to 2,700 m. Lives in dwellings, outbuildings, woodpiles, etc. Good climber. Makes nest in holes, skirting-boards, walls, etc. Female produces litters of 4—8 (occasionally up to 12) blind, hairless young several times a year. Young open eyes at 12—14 days, become mature at 6—7 weeks. Life span about 1.5 years, in captivity up to 4 years. Does not hibernate. Lives on waste matter, seeds, etc. In large numbers does damage to food stocks.

2 Harvest Mouse *Micromys minutus.* Distributed in Europe, in east to south-eastern Asia, but not very abundant. Lives on margins of forests, in reed beds beside ponds, in oat- and other fields. Builds spherical nest with side entrance between stalks, 40—80 cm above ground. Female produces 2—3 litters of 3—12 blind young a year. Young open eyes at 7 days. Also builds sleeping nest with two entrances. In winter visits barns, outbuildings, etc. Climbs and swims very well. Active mainly at night. Lives on seeds and insects. Non-hibernator. Life span 4 years.

3 Long-tailed Field Mouse *Apodemus sylvaticus.* Distributed over whole of Europe, in north to Iceland, in south to Crete. Very abundant. In Alps up to 2,500 m. Inhabits dry conifer and mixed woods, thickets and fields, in winter appears in houses, but only on ground floor. Nesting burrow has 2—3 entrances. Female produces up to 4 litters of 2—9 young a year. Young open eyes at 12 days. Climbs well and can jump distances of up to 80 cm. Can also swim. Nocturnal animal. Non-hibernator. Lives on seeds, roots, shoots, insects. Maximum life span 6 years, average 1.5 years.

4 Black Rat *Rattus rattus.* Originally from tropical belt of Old World, spread by ships all over globe. European incidence now localized (usually near large rivers, in harbours and towns). Frequents attics and storehouses. Climbs and jumps well. Female produces up to 6 litters of 4—15 (rarely 20) naked and blind young a year. Grow coat in 7 days, open eyes at 13—16 days. Lives mainly on vegetable matter and household scraps. Non-hibernator. Life span up to 7 years.

5 Brown or **Norway Rat** *Rattus norvegicus.* Originally from north-eastern Asia, has been carried all over globe. Very common in whole of Europe. Important pest, carrier of many diseases. In mountains up to 1,600 m. Frequents places with water, canals, sewers, rubbish dumps, etc. Via waste pipes enters cowsheds, cellars and buildings, mainly in winter. Lives in groups. Builds nest in burrows. Digs well and can swim and dive. Female produces 2—7 litters of 6—9 (or even 22) young a year. Young open eyes at 13—17 days. Non-hibernator. Omnivorous. Also attacks small vertebrates. Life span 4 years.

3

4

5

6

Family: **Hamsters**—Cricetidae

6 Common Hamster *Cricetus cricetus*. Distributed from France across central Europe as far as Yenisei river. Inhabits cultivated lowland steppes. Digs burrows (30—60 cm deep in summer, over 2 m in winter) with several exits, nest chamber and storeroom. Female produces 2—3 litters of 6—18 young a year. Young open eyes at 14 days. Nocturnal animal. Hibernates from October to March, body temperature falls to 4° C. Wakes every 5 days and eats from stocks, which can weigh up to 15 kg. Omnivorous. Eats plants, seeds, invertebrates and small vertebrates. Carries food to burrow in facial pouches.

Family: Voles—Microtidae

1 Musk Rat *Ondatra zibethica.* Originally from North America. Introduced into Europe near Prague in 1905, has spread over whole of Europe, advancing 25 km a year. Lives in lakes, ponds, pools and rivers, in mountains up to 1,000 m. Digs burrow about 1 m deep in bank with one or more entrances. In large numbers can do considerable damage to earthworks. Builds winter structures 1 m high and 2 m in diameter over water, from rushes and sedge. Female produces up to 4 litters of 5—14 young a year. Young open eyes at 11 days and leave nest at 3 weeks. Good swimmer and diver. Active mainly at night and in morning. Non-hibernator. Lives on aquatic plants, molluscs, occasionally fish. Life span about 5 years.

2 Bank Vole *Clethrionomys glareolus.* Distributed over whole of Europe except south, Asia as far as Yenisei river. Similar form in North America. In Alps up to 2,200 m. Abundant. Lives on outskirts of forests, in bushes, etc. Ground-dweller. Builds spherical nest from grass, moss, etc. in bushes, up to 1 m above ground, otherwise underground. Female produces 3—4 litters of 3—8 young a year. Young open eyes at 9 days. Climbs well and can jump. Non-hibernator. Lays in food stocks, e.g. seeds, covers them with leaves. Lives mainly on vegetable matter, occasionally insects. Life span 1.5—2.5 years.

3 Common Vole *Microtus arvalis.* Distributed in Europe except England and Scandinavia, in east as far as China. Inhabits cultivated steppes, fields, dry meadows and open woods. Often occurs in large colonies. Digs branching passages in surface soil and nest chamber at depth of about 0.5 m. In winter tunnels under snow. Female produces up to 12 litters of 3—13 young a year. Young open eyes at 8—10 days. Active mainly at night. Non-hibernator. Lives on grass, shoots and field crops. Life span 1.5—4 years. Important pest.

Family: Beavers—Castoridae

4 European Beaver *Castor fiber.* Once inhabited whole of Europe, now almost completely exterminated. Today found in only a few parts of Europe, mainly in north and east. Extends east as far as Mongolia. Lives beside stagnant and slow-flowing water. Digs burrows in bank, with shaft leading below water level. Also builds 'lodges' 2—3 m high on water. Lodges are made of branches and small trunks which beaver fells by gnawing and drags to building site. Builds dams across flowing water, from branches, grass, etc. Couples live in colonies. Very good swimmer and diver. At end of April female gives birth to 2—7 fur-coated young with open eyes, suckles them about 8 weeks. Nocturnal animal. Not true hibernator. Lives on plants and tree shoots. Lays in winter stocks, e.g. willow branches, etc., under water. Life span up to over 30 years. Very valuable fur.

Family: **Nutrias**—Myocastoridae

5 Nutria or **Swamp Beaver** *Myocastor coypus.* Comes from South America. Bred in Europe on farms. Now also found wild there (descendants of escapees). Weighs up to 8 kg, sometimes more. Spends much time in water. Digs burrows in bank, 6 m long and 3 m deep. Also builds nest in waterside shrubs. Excellent swimmer but poor diver. Female produces 2—3 litters of 4—7 open-eyed young a year, suckles them 8 weeks, but young start to take solids after only 10 days. Lives on grass and aquatic plants. Active after dusk and during day. Non-hibernator.

4

5

Order: **Beasts of Prey**—Carnivora

Family: **Cats**—Felidae

1 Common Wild Cat *Felis silvestris*. Distributed in Europe, Near East, central Asia, North Africa. Lives only in deep forests, chiefly in mountains. Shelters in tree hollows, old badger sets, etc. Female gives birth in shelter to 3—7 blind young, which open eyes at 9—11 days. Suckles them 4 months, but at 6 weeks young can already take hunted food. Cat has clearly demarcated 'preserve', but in mating season or times of food-shortage roams up to 100 km. afield. Except for mating season lives singly. Does not hibernate. Active at night. Catches small vertebrates and insects. One of its subspecies may be ancestor of domestic tabby cat.

2 Northern Lynx *Lynx lynx*. Distributed over eastern and northern Europe and Balkan mountains. In central Europe still abundant in Czechoslovakia. Also occurs in French Alps. Inhabits wooded, mountainous country up to 2,500 m. Solitary animal except at mating time. Nocturnal. Hides during day in cleft rocks, hollows, etc. Weighs up to 30 kg, occasionally 45 kg. Excellent vision and hearing. Climbs well, runs swiftly. In May female gives birth to 2—3 (rarely up to 5) spotted young which open eyes at 16 days and are suckled 2 months. Life span up to 17 years. At night catches mammals up to size of roe deer and birds (chiefly game birds). Lies in wait for prey and pounces on it.

Family: **Dog Tribe**—Canidae

3 Wolf *Canis lupus*. Once inhabited whole of Europe, but was practically exterminated. Still to be seen in north-eastern Europe. In central Europe quite common in Czechoslovakia and Poland. Occurs at altitudes of up to 2,500 m. Lives in large forests and shrub-grown steppes. In spring and summer lives in families, in autumn forms large packs. Weighs up to 50 kg (in rare cases 70 kg). Gestation period 60—65 days. In April or May female gives birth to 4—8 blind young which open eyes at 10 days. Nocturnal animal. Travels long distances (up to 70 km) in search of prey, catches it by 'round-up' system.

1

2

3

Can run up to 160 km during night. Pack takes on large domestic animals, but gives man wide berth. Eats different vertebrates, insects, molluscs and even fruit. Perhaps only ancestor of domesticated dogs.

4 Red Fox *Vulpes vulpes*. Commonest European member of this family, also occurs in Asia and North America. In Alps up to 3,000 m. Inhabits forests, game preserves, large parks, etc. 'Snoops' round human communities and steals small livestock. Digs 'earth' with several exits. Sometimes occupies it together with badger. Gestation period 51—54 days. Between February and May female gives birth to 4—12 blind young which open eyes at 12—15 days. Eats voles, other small mammals, birds, insects and molluscs, but also forest fruits. Life span 10—12 years. Useful animal rather than nuisance, unless too numerous.

Family: **Mustelids**—Mustelidae

5 Common Otter *Lutra lutra*. Originally common in whole of Europe, Asia and North Africa, but exterminated in many parts of central Europe. Inhabits stagnant and flowing water with unregulated banks. Adapted for aquatic existence. Excavates lair in banks, or uses various types of hollows. Lair has entrance 50 cm below surface and 1 or 2 ventilation shafts. Swims and dives extremely well, can stay under water 6—8 minutes. Gestation period 61—63 days. Female gives birth to 2—6 young which do not open eyes for 4 weeks. Eats mainly fish, also crustaceans, amphibians, etc. Life span 10—18 years. Valuable for fur. In central Europe protected.

4

5

Family: **Mustelids**—Mustelidae

1 Pine Marten *Martes martes*. Distributed over practically whole of Europe, in east as far as Asia Minor. Forest-dweller. Climbs trees extremely well and leaps from tree to tree over distances of up to 3.5 m. Makes lair in tree hollows, deserted birds' and squirrels' nests and sometimes owls' nests. Female gives birth to 2—7 young which do not open eyes for 34 days. Catches small mammals (especially squirrels), birds and insects; in autumn also eats fruits and berries. Life span 8—14 years.

2 Stone or **Beech Marten** *Martes foina*. Distributed over whole of Europe except British Isles and Scandinavia, in east across Asia to Himalayas and Mongolia. In Alps up to 2,000 m. Fairly common. Frequents vicinity of human dwellings and often settles in attics, even in towns. Makes grass lair under roofs, in ruins, in cleft rocks and often in hole in ground. In spring female gives birth to 3—7 young which open eyes at 34 days. Suckles them 3 months, but young can already take solids at 6 weeks. Active at night. Catches birds, steals poultry and eggs, also likes fruit, e.g. plums.

3 Common Stoat or **Ermine** *Mustela erminea*. Distributed in Europe; southern limits Pyrenees, Alps and Carpathians. In Alps up to 3,000 m. Found in both dry and damp environments, in steppes and woods or in gardens near dwellings. Mostly red-brown in summer, white with black-tipped tail in winter. Makes lair in holes in ground, in walls, under outbuilding floors, etc. In April or May female gives birth to 3—7 young which do not open eyes for 40 days. Climbs well and can swim. Lives on small rodents and birds, occasionally eats invertebrates and fruit. Life span 5—10 years.

4 Weasel *Mustela nivalis*. Distributed over whole of Europe except Ireland, North Africa, northern and temperate parts of Asia. In Alps up to 2,700 m. Commonest member of this family. Very slim, can slip through narrow holes, e.g. of ground squirrels and rats, etc. Inhabits forests, hedges, parks and gardens. In winter approaches dwellings and shelters in cowsheds, barns, haystacks, cellars, etc. Female gives birth to 3—7 (rarely up to 12) young which open eyes at 21—25 days. Suckles them 6—7 weeks. Very useful animal; catches mice, voles, young rats and ground squirrels. Occasionally also eats invertebrates. Life span 4—7 years.

5 European Polecat *Mustela putorius*. Distributed over practically whole of Europe, temperate parts of Asia, Morocco. Lives in woods and fields, but also frequents dwellings. In winter shelters in barns, sheds, etc. Makes lair in rabbit burrows, tree hollows or pipes. Locally abundant. Mainly terrestrial; does not like climbing, but swims well and can dive. In April or May female gives birth to 3—11 white-coated young which open eyes at 30—37 days. Nocturnal animal. Eats small mammals, birds and their eggs, invades chicken-roosts, steals eggs and bites hens.

6 Ferret *Mustela furo*. Domesticated form of polecat, used for catching wild rabbits. Can be crossed with polecat. Has similar colouring, from pure white to dark. When ferret is placed in rabbit burrow, rabbits rush out and are snared in nets. Easily tamed if caught young.

7 Common Badger *Meles meles*. Distributed in Europe and temperate parts of Asia. In Alps up to 2,000 m. Mainly inhabits woods, also shrub-strewn hillsides and sometimes town parks. Digs 'set' composed of chamber, several passages and ventilating shafts. Likes warm, dry places. Female gives birth to 2—6 blind young which open eyes at 3—4 weeks. Nocturnal animal. Not genuine hibernator, wakes up every few days. Omnivorous, eats anything from insects to small vertebrates and forest fruits. Life span 10—15 years.

2

Family: **Bears**—Ursidae

1 Brown Bear *Ursus arctos.* Several races, from Europe to Asia and North America. Rare in central Europe. In recent years has multiplied in Czechoslovakia and neighbouring Poland. Inhabits wooded, mountainous regions. Found at altitudes of up to 2,600 m. Makes lair in hole in ground, under uprooted tree or in cave. Males larger than females; in Europe weigh up to 350 kg. Female gives birth to 2—5 very small, blind young which open eyes at 4—5 weeks. Littering period December to February. During this time female lies in den, not eating, and warms young by holding them close to body with paws. In spring, at 4 months, young follow mother and remain with her 2 years. Long winter sleep (November to March), but not true hibernation as body temperature does not fall. Life span 35—60 years. Omnivorous, eats practically anything — insects, worms, reptiles, birds, mammals up to size of deer. In times of shortage attacks sheep or even cows. Catches fish and has weakness for honey. In autumn eats forest fruits, berries, etc.

Order: **Pinnipeds**—Pinnipedia

2 Harbour or **Hair Seal** *Phoca vitulina.* Distributed in coastal waters of North Atlantic and North Pacific. Strays up rivers, e.g. up to 700 km inland up Elbe. Occasionally seen in western Baltic. Gregarious, lives in herds. Diurnal animal. Males weigh up to 150 kg. Gestation period about 340 days. At beginning of June or in July female gives birth to 1—2 young weighing 10—15 kg and measuring 90 cm. Suckles them 4—6 weeks. When weaned, young live 6 weeks on shrimps. Can dive as soon as they are born. Adult at 3—4 years. Can stay under water 5—6 minutes, in exceptional cases up to 15 minutes. Sleeps under water, floats up to surface with closed eyes for air. Swims at about 17 km an hour (at 35 km when hunting). Lives mainly on fish. Life span up to 30 years.

Order: **Whales**—Cetacea

3 Common Porpoise *Phocaena phocaena.* Distributed in North Sea, Baltic, Mediterranean, Black Sea, Atlantic and North Pacific. Still fairly common off coasts of Europe, especially Germany. Often swims inland up rivers, e.g. Rhine, Elbe, Thames, etc. Consorts in small groups. Gestation period 10—11 months. Female gives birth to one young weighing 6—8 kg. Adult weighs up to 80 kg. Huge appetite. Lives on fish such as herrings, mackerels and salmon. Unpopular with fishermen as often tears nets when caught in them. Its flesh is edible.

3

4 Bottlenose Dolphin *Tursiops truncatus.* Distributed in Baltic, North Sea, Mediterranean, Black Sea and Atlantic. Length 2.5—3 m. Has long jaws. Gregarious, communities often large. Female gives birth to single young late in summer, suckles it very long. Swims extremely well, up to 35 km an hour. Predacious animal. Both jaws armed with strong teeth. Lives mainly on fish frequenting upper layers of sea. Also eats octopus, squid, sea snails and other marine animals. In places where there are few fish often does great damage and is mercilessly destroyed by fishermen. Males fight each other at mating time. Bottlenose likes to leap out of water while swimming.

1

Order: **Even-toed Ungulates**—Artiodactyla

Family: **Pigs**—Suidae

1 Wild Boar *Sus scrofa.* Widespread in Europe, Asia and North Africa. Inhabits forests with undergrowth. Lives in families and herds, but old boars are solitary. Hides in thickets during day, comes out to feed at night. Gestation period 16—20 weeks. Sow gives birth to 3—12 striped young in bed of moss and grass. Young attain adulthood at 5—6 years. Life span 10—12 years. Omnivorous, but prefers berries, fruit, roots, grass, etc. Roots in soil for worms, insects and small vertebrates. In large numbers can severely damage potato and sugar beet crops, etc. Boar weighs up to over 200 kg. Game animal. Excellent flesh. Ancestor of domesticated pigs.

Family: **Deer**—Cervidae

2 Common Fallow Deer *Dama dama.* Originally inhabited Mediterranean region and Asia Minor. Brought to Europe in 10th and 11th century and bred for hunting. Later escaped from preserves and today, in some parts of Europe, is found in large forests. Lives in small herds or singly. Occurs chiefly in lowlands, but also in uplands. Males have palmated antlers. Weight of male up to 125 kg, female 50 kg. Rutting (mating) season from middle of October to November. Gestation period about 230 days. In June or July doe gives birth to one (occasionally 2—3) young. Nocturnal animal. Lives on grass, field crops, acorns, bark, shoots, etc. Game animal. Life span 20—25 years.

3 Red Deer *Cervus elaphus.* Several subspecies distributed in Europe, Asia, North Africa and North America. Inhabits both plains and mountains. Found in Alps at altitudes of up to 2,000 m. Forms herds of about 6—12 animals (rarely up to 80) led by old female (hind). These herds contain hinds and calves. Except at rutting time, old males (harts) live alone or combine in small herds led by strongest. Hide during day, come out at night to feed in clearings, at forest margins, in meadows and fields. Keep within fixed limits and use regular tracks. In rutting season (September—October) males separate and strongest wage battles for herd of hinds. Gestation period 231—238 days. Hind gives birth to one (occasionally 2) young which joins herd with mother on 8th day. Hart weighs up to 225 kg, hind 120 kg. Game animal. Antlers are prized trophy.

4 Sika Deer *Cervus nippon.* Originally native of nothern China and Japan. Imported and bred in Europe in preserves, now found there even wild. European animals mostly outcome of crossing of several races. Lives in plains and hills. Spotted during summer. Male weighs up to 55 kg, female 45 kg. Few tines on antlers. Rutting season October—November. One or two young born in June. Life span about 20 years. Same diet as other deer; grass, field crops, shoots, acorns, bark, twigs, etc.

5 Roe Deer *Capreolus capreolus.* Distributed over most of Europe and large part of Asia. In Alps up to 2,400 m. Inhabits forests with undergrowth, copses, meadows with bushes, etc. Lives within specific limits. In summer occurs singly or in small groups, in winter in large herds led by old dams. Except for rutting time, males lead solitary existence, however. Weight 15—30 kg. Primary rutting season July to beginning of September, secondary season November and December. Longer gestation period after summer fertilization. Female gives birth to 1—3 young in May or June. Lives on grass, shoots, forest fruits, etc. Life span 10—17 years. Important game animal.

3

4

5

Family: **Deer**—Cervidae

1 Elk *Alces alces*. Distributed in northern Europe, Asia and North America. Not resident in central Europe, but seen there many times in recent years (from Poland). Lives in large, dank forests, swampy scrublands, beside lakes and pools, etc. In summer lives alone or in families. In winter forms herds of 10—15 animals, but without old males. One of largest European animals. Weighs up to 600 kg. Male has huge, palmated antlers. Rutting season end August to October. Gestation period 35—38 weeks. At end of April or beginning of May female gives birth to 1—2 (seldom 3) young which accompany her after 3—4 days. Grazes towards evening and early in morning. Lives on shoots, aquatic plants (gathered standing in water), twigs, etc. Life span 20—25 years. Game animal, but protected in central Europe.

Family: **Hollow-horned Ruminants**—Bovidae

2 Chamois *Rupicapra rupicapra*. Inhabits high European mountains, extends east to Caucasus. In some places brought down to lower altitudes. Found in Alps up to 3,000 m. In summer ascends to snowline, in winter comes down to lower altitudes. Lives on steep, rocky slopes with little vegetation. Climbs nimbly and can leap 8 m. Except for old males lives in herds, usually led by female. If startled, utters warning whistle. Male weighs up to 60 kg, female 40 kg. Horns curved at tip, thicker in males than in females. In rutting season (October—December) males wage fierce duels. In April or June female gives birth to one (rarely 2 or 3) young which remains with mother 2 years. Diurnal animal. Grazes on grass, leaves, shoots, etc. Life span 15—20 years.

3 Ibex *Capra ibex*. Distributed in high parts of Pyrenees, Alps, Caucasus and central Asia. In Alps above forest belt. Even in winter usually remains at altitude of 2,300—3,200 m. Herd consists of females, young and young males. Except at rutting time, adult males live in separate communities of up to 30 animals, old males singly. Males weigh up to 110 kg, females 50 kg. Rutting season from middle of December to beginning of January. Gestation period 22—23 weeks. At end of May or beginning of June female gives birth to one (rarely 2) young which follows her only a few hours after birth. Ibex leaps and climbs extremely well. Lives on mountain plants, leaves, lichen, etc. Life span up to 30 years.

4 Mouflon *Ovis musimon*. Originally native of Sardinia, Corsica and Cyprus. Introduced into many parts of central Europe. Inhabits dry, rocky places in wooded uplands and hills. Lives in herds of usually 10—20 animals, in winter over 30. Found mainly in deciduous and mixed woods. Old rams in separate troupes, very old rams solitary. Male weighs up to 50 kg. Rutting season October—December. Gestation period 21—22 weeks. Between end of March and beginning of May ewe gives birth to one (seldom 2) young. Primarily nocturnal animal, rarely ac-

1

tive in daytime. Lives on various grass, leaves, shoots, etc. Life span 20 years.

5 European Bison or **Wisent** *Bison bonasus.* Wild European stock exterminated at end of 18th century. Now bred in a few national parks and zoos. Caucasian race completely extinct. Frequents mixed forests with dense undergrowth. In summer prefers damp localities, forest meadows and peat-bogs, in winter drier places. Lives in herds of 6—40 animals led by old cows. Only very old bulls are solitary. Male weighs up to 1,800 kg. Rutting season August and September. Gestation period 40—41 weeks. In May or June cow gives birth to usually one calf (occasionally 2). Both diurnal and nocturnal animal. Grazes mainly in evening and morning. Lives on leaves of bushes and trees, twigs, grass, bark, etc. Life span 30—40 years.

2

3

4

5

INDEX OF ILLUSTRATED SPECIES

Plants

Animals

495